Henry Hilliard Earl

A Centennial History of Fall River, Massachusetts

Henry Hilliard Earl

A Centennial History of Fall River, Massachusetts

ISBN/EAN: 9783337366827

Printed in Europe, USA, Canada, Australia, Japan

Cover: Foto ©ninafisch / pixelio.de

More available books at **www.hansebooks.com**

A

CENTENNIAL HISTORY

OF

FALL RIVER, MASS:

COMPRISING A

RECORD OF ITS CORPORATE PROGRESS FROM 1656 TO 1876,

WITH SKETCHES OF ITS

MANUFACTURING INDUSTRIES,

LOCAL AND GENERAL CHARACTERISTICS,

VALUABLE STATISTICAL TABLES, ETC.

PREPARED UNDER THE DIRECTION OF A COMMITTEE
OF THE CITY GOVERNMENT, BY

HENRY H. EARL, A.M.

NEW YORK:
ATLANTIC PUBLISHING AND ENGRAVING COMPANY.
1877.

S. W. GREEN,
PRINTER AND ELECTROTYPER
16 and 18 Jacob Street,
NEW YORK.

PRESIDENT'S PROCLAMATION.

BY THE PRESIDENT OF THE UNITED STATES.

A PROCLAMATION.

Whereas, A joint resolution of the Senate and House of Representatives of the United States was duly approved on the 13th of March last, which resolution is as follows:

"*Be it Resolved*, By the Senate and House of Representatives of the United States of America, in Congress assembled, that it be and is hereby recommended by the Senate and the House of Representatives to the people of the several States, that they assemble in their several counties or towns on the approaching Centennial Anniversary of our National Independence, and that they cause to have delivered on such day, an historical sketch of said county or town from its formation, and that a copy of said sketch may be filed, in print or manuscript, in the Clerk's office of said county, and an additional copy, in print or manuscript, be filed in the office of the Librarian of Congress, to the intent that a complete record may thus be obtained of the progress of our institutions during the first centennial of their existence;" and

Whereas, It is deemed proper that such recommendation be brought to the notice and knowledge of the people of the United States;

Now, therefore, I, Ulysses S. Grant, President of the United States, do hereby declare and make known the same, in the hope that the object of such resolution may meet the approval of the people of the United States, and that proper steps may be taken to carry the same into effect.

Given under my hand, at the City of Washington, the 25th day of May, in the year of our Lord 1876, and of the Independence of the United States the one hundredth.

By the President,   U. S. GRANT.

HAMILTON FISH, *Secretary of State*.

PUBLIC RESOLUTION No. 1.

IN XLIVTH CONGRESS.—FIRST SESSION, A.D. 1876.

Joint Resolution on the Celebration of the Centennial in the several Counties or Towns.

Be it Resolved, By the Senate and House of Representatives of the United States of America, in Congress assembled, that it be and is hereby recommended by the Senate and the House of Representatives to the people of the several States, that they assemble in their several counties or towns on the approaching Centennial Anniversary of our National Independence, and that they cause to have delivered on such day, an historical sketch of said county or town from its formation, and that a copy of said sketch may be filed, in print or manuscript, in the Clerk's office of said county, and an additional copy, in print or manuscript, be filed in the office of the Librarian of Congress, to the intent that a complete record may thus be obtained of the progress of our institutions during the first centennial of their existence.

Approved, March 13, 1876.

COMMONWEALTH OF MASSACHUSETTS.

SECRETARY'S DEPARTMENT,
BOSTON, June 13, 1876.

TO THE CITY CLERK:

SIR: I have the honor to transmit herewith an order of the Legislature of Massachusetts, which has this day been received in this department, and a copy of the Resolution of Congress therein referred to.

Very respectfully your obedient servant,

HENRY B. PEIRCE, *Secretary*.

COMMONWEALTH OF MASSACHUSETTS.

EXECUTIVE DEPARTMENT,
BOSTON, April 24, 1876.

TO THE HONORABLE SENATE:

I have the honor, herewith, to inclose for the disposition of the General Court, a Joint Resolution of the Senate and House of Representatives of the United States, transmitted to me by the Secretary of State.

ALEXANDER H. RICE.

COMMONWEALTH OF MASSACHUSETTS.

HOUSE OF REPRESENTATIVES, April 27, 1876.

Ordered, That the Secretary of the Commonwealth transmit to the Clerks of the several cities and towns in the Commonwealth, a copy of the Joint Resolution of Congress on the celebration of the Centennial in the several counties or towns, transmitted to the Senate by His Excellency the Governor, April 24th, 1876.
Adopted, Sent up for concurrence.
GEO. A. MARDEN, *Clerk*.

SENATE, April 28, 1876.

Concurred.

S. N. GIFFORD, *Clerk*.

CITY OF FALL RIVER,
MAYOR'S OFFICE, June 4, 1877.

GENTLEMEN OF THE CITY COUNCIL:

I am pleased to call your attention to a matter which, I have no doubt, will be of interest to you as well as to the citizens generally, if it can be accomplished,—one that failed to be carried out last year, owing to the limited time given to undertake the work. I refer to "The Centennial Volume," or "History of Fall River."

The President of the United States and the Governor of the Commonwealth have recommended the preparation of such volumes by every city and town, and that such volumes should be preserved in the Congressional and Public Libraries, and the Historical Collections of every community. I am informed that a considerable portion of this work has already been accomplished by private enterprise, particularly the manufacturing industries of our city. Availing ourselves of what has already been done, I am of the opinion that, at a moderate cost, a complete history of our city can be obtained. I would recommend this matter be referred to a committee with authority to co-operate with the parties interested in the work, and the expense attending the same be charged to Contingent Account.

Very respectfully,
JAS. F. DAVENPORT, *Mayor*.

IN BOARD OF ALDERMEN, June 4, 1877.

Referred to Committee on Accounts, and sent for concurrence.

GEO. A. BALLARD, *City Clerk*.

IN COMMON COUNCIL, June 4, 1877

Laid on the Table.

A. H. LEONARD, *Clerk*.

IN COMMON COUNCIL, June 18, 1877.

Taken from the Table and concurred in.

A. H. LEONARD, *Clerk*.

FALL RIVER, September 5, 1877.

At a meeting of the Committee of Accounts, held this day, to whom was referred the communication of His Honor the Mayor, respecting a "Centennial Volume," or "History of Fall River," present Aldermen Durfee and Davol, and Councilmen Webster and Greene ; Councilman Greene having been elected Clerk, it was

Voted, That Henry H. Earl, Esq., be invited to co-operate with the Committee, and to supervise the preparation of a "Centennial History of Fall River."

WM. S. GREENE, *Clerk*.

CENTENNIAL HISTORY OF FALL RIVER.

TABLE OF CONTENTS.

	PAGE
FALL RIVER: SKETCH OF ITS ORIGIN AND CORPORATE EPOCHS,	1–6
Its Natural Advantages,	6–8
Cotton Manufactures from 1810–1820,	9–22
" " " 1820–1830,	22–35
" " " 1830–1845,	35–56
" " " 1845–1860,	56–62
" " " 1860–1876,	62–70
GROWTH OF THE COTTON INDUSTRY IN AMERICA,	71–97
MACHINES AND PROCESSES OF MANUFACTURE,	98–111
STATISTICS OF COTTON MANUFACTURE IN FALL RIVER,	112
ORGANIZATION OF CORPORATIONS,	113–118
SKETCH OF EACH CORPORATION,	118–150
EDUCATIONAL, RELIGIOUS, MUNICIPAL, AND FINANCIAL FEATURES OF FALL RIVER:	
Public Library, Churches, Cemeteries, Parks, Drives, Local Nomenclature, Water Works, Fire Department, Banks and Savings Institutions, Custom-House and Post-Office, and City Hall,	151–184
NEWSPAPERS AND STEAM MARINE:	
History of Press of Fall River, Steam Marine of Mount Hope Bay,	185–197
HISTORICAL, POLITICAL, AND SOCIAL PHASES:	
Reminiscences of Col. Joseph Durfee; Fall River in the Civil War; Fall River's "West End;" Settlement of State Boundaries, 1862; Great Fire of July 2, 1843; Population of Fall River from 1810–1875; Valuations, etc., from 1854–1875,	198–219
CELEBRATION OF THE ONE HUNDREDTH ANNIVERSARY OF AMERICAN INDEPENDENCE AT FALL RIVER, JULY 4, 1876,	220–222
CORPORATE ANNALS OF FALL RIVER:	
Sketches of Mayors; Act of Incorporation of Fall River in 1803; Change of Corporate Name; Town Officers from 1803 to 1854; Members of Congress; Mayors; State Senators and Representatives; Formation of a City Government; List of City Officers for 1877,	223–248

ILLUSTRATIONS.

		PAGE
CITY HALL,	View,	Frontispiece
AMERICAN PRINT WORKS, .	" .	. 37
ANTHONY, DAVID,	Portrait, .	11
BORDEN, JEFFERSON,	"	41
BORDEN, RICHARD, .	"	47
BORDER CITY MILLS,	View, .	143
"BRISTOL" STEAMER,	"	189
BUFFINTON, JAMES,	Portrait,	. 225
CHACE, OLIVER,	"	15
CITY PARK, . .	View, .	158
CUSTOM-HOUSE AND POST-OFFICE, .	"	182
DAVOL MILLS,	"	58
DAVOL, STEPHEN,	Portrait, .	56
DAVOL, WM. C , .	"	61
DURFEE, NATHAN,	"	53
EDDY, JESSE,	"	34
ENGINE-HOUSE,	View,	167
FALL RIVER BLEACHERY.	"	147
FALL RIVER IN 1812, MAP OF,		4
FALL RIVER SAVINGS BANK,		170
MECHANICS' MILLS, .	View,	129
MERCHANTS' MILLS,	"	127
SLADE SCHOOL-HOUSE, .	"	151

FALL RIVER

AND ITS  INDUSTRIES.

SKETCH OF ITS ORIGIN AND CORPORATE EPOCHS.

NEAR the head of Mount Hope Bay, at the date of the landing of the Pilgrims, a small stream, stealing its waters from a succession of long, narrow and deep lakes that lay in an elevated plateau a short league distant from the shore line, made its way westward to the sea. The stream was insignificant both in volume and expanse, its broadest part hardly exceeding a rod, yet it ran down a constantly descending, often abrupt, channel with such vehement rapidity that its daily contribution to the beautiful estuary was far from inconsiderable. Its course from the start was over a hard granite formation, and its last half mile of life a constant struggle to hold its own with the air and rock, and save as much as possible of itself for the outstretched palm of Narragansett. The Indian vocabulary found a fitting expression for the little stream in the word Quequechan, " Falling Water," while the lakes were named Watuppa, or place of boats.

It is doubtful if Quequechan, though in the midst of the hunting grounds of populous tribes, and paying its tribute to the Bay at a point nearly opposite the rocky mount upon which the Wampanoags and Pocassets under King Philip had erected their strongest fortress, was any thing more than a babbling rivulet in the savage estimation, and the name was but an ordinary and natural application of Indian sentiment. Time, however, has preserved the sense if not the letter of aboriginal nomenclature; Watuppa remains the name of the lakes, and Falling Water is still suggested in the less poetical Fall River of our own day.

The first settlement of the region comprising and immediately adjacent to the city of Fall River was in the regular course of expansion of the Plymouth Colony, and about the year 1656. In this year, on the 3d of July, the General Court of Plymouth granted to a number of Freemen of the jurisdiction a tract of land east of Taunton River, four miles in width, and from six to seven in length, bounded on the south by Quequechan, and on the north by Assonet Neck. Three years subsequently this grant was confirmed by a warrantee deed signed by the local sachems, the consideration being "twenty coats, two rugs, two iron pots, two kettles and one little kettle, eight pairs of shoes, six pairs of stockings, one dozen hoes, one dozen hatchets, two yards of broadcloth and a debt satisfied to John Barnes, which was due from Wamsitta to John Barnes." This grant was termed the Freemen's Purchase, and after incorporation in 1683, Freetown. "The first settlers," says that industrious and correct student of local history, the late Rev. Orin Fowler, in a series of papers published in 1841, " were principally from Plymouth, Marshfield, and Scituate. Some were from Taunton, and a few from Rhode Island. The early names were Cudworth, Winslow, Morton, Read, Hathaway, Durfee, Terry, Borden, Brightman, Chase, and Davis. The Purchase was divided into twenty-six shares, and the shares were set off—whether by lot or otherwise does not appear—to the several purchasers. After the division into shares was made, there was a piece of land between the first lot or share and Tiverton bounds, which in 1702 it was voted by the proprietors be sold 'to procure a piece of land near the centre of the town for a burying place, a training field, or any other public use the town shall see cause to improve it for.' Accordingly this piece of land was sold to John Borden, of Portsmouth, R. I., the highest bidder, for nine pounds and eight shillings, and was the territory on which that part of the village south of Bedford street, and north of the stream, now stands. This John Borden is believed to be the ancestor of all who sustain his name in this vicinity."

The occupation of the region north of Quequechan by settlers attracted attention to the locality, and a legitimate result was a second grant by the Governor, Treasurer and Assistants in 1680, to eight persons—Edward Gray, of Plymouth; Nathaniel Thomas, of Marshfield; Benjamin Church, Daniel Wilcox and Thomas Manchester, of Puncatest; and Christopher and John Almy and Thomas Waite, of Portsmouth, R. I.—of a tract extending southward along the Bay, from the stream Quequechan to the town of Dartmouth and Seaconnet, and inland from four to six miles. This grant was likewise of territory bought from the Indian sachems for the sum of £1100, and was termed the Pocasset Purchase, its township name being after incorporation Tiverton.

Of the Pocasset Purchase Mr. Fowler records a division into shares, following the precedent of its neighboring grant; we quote his words in full, as having a double interest in awarding due credit for the first practical realization of the value of Quequechan, and identifying the original entire control of the water-power with a name that has ever since been so worthily associated with the growth of Fall River. The Benjamin Church referred to was the great captain in the King Philip wars, a man verily for the time, before whose intrepid courage and wise command the great chief of the Wampanoags fell a victim, and his successor Annawan yielded himself captive. "The Pocasset Purchase (after reserving thirty rods wide adjacent to the Freemen's Purchase and the river, and some other small tracts) was divided into thirty shares and distributed among the proprietors,—the lot nearest the river being numbered one. This piece of land, including the water-power on the south side of the river to (the present) Main street, and on both sides east of said street to Watuppa Pond, containing sixty-six acres of land, was also divided into thirty shares and sold to the original purchasers. Colonel Church and his brother Caleb, of Watertown (who was a millwright), bought twenty-six and a half of the thirty shares, and thereby became the chief owners of the water-power. On the 8th of August, 1691, Caleb Church sold his right in this property (13½ shares) to his brother Benjamin, who then became the owner of twenty-six and a half shares. Probably John Borden purchased the other three and a half shares. In 1703, Colonel Church had moved to Fall River and improved the water-power, by erecting a saw-mill, grist-mill and fulling-mill. His dwelling-house stood between the present residence of Colonel Richard Borden and that of his brother Jefferson, and remained till within forty years. He continued at Fall River but a few years; and Sept. 18th, 1714, sold the above named twenty-six and a half shares to Richard Borden of Tiverton, and Joseph Borden of Freetown, sons of John; and thus the lands on both sides of the river, with all the water-power, came into the possession of the Borden family, John Borden having previously purchased that on the north side west of Main street."

The writer adds in a foot-note that Caleb Church sold his interest for £100. "At this rate the whole sixty-six acres was valued in 1691 at about $740. The piece on the north side cost John Borden about $31.34; total, $771.34. This included the whole of the water-power and most of the land where the village now stands, together with a strip east to Watuppa Pond. Twenty-six and a half shares of the above sixty-six acres were sold by Colonel Church in 1714 for £1000."

The neighborhood annals do not indicate an extraordinary increase in the population or other relative importance of the two towns create out of the Plymouth grants, during the century succeeding their original settlement. From *data* that still remain, it is evident that the settlers were generally engaged in agriculture, with the usual proportion that prosecute the small mechanical and other industries patronized by a rural community, and possibly a larger component attracted by local associations to seafaring pursuits. For some years the original centre of population of the Freemen's Purchase, or Freetown, was at a point a little south of the small tributary of the Taunton known as Mother's Brook, not far from the extreme northern bound of the proprietary. At the southern boundary a colony was gathered, where Colonel Church's mills were located on the stream (which began to be called Fall River—the Indian name giving place to the more prosaic term of the whites), and with the progress of time exhibited a gradual accretion, mostly from newcomers. This growth was, however, very small for several decades, and appears to have almost ceased at the commencement of the present century, notwithstanding the excellent harbor and the natural advantages of the water-power. "In the year 1803," observes the reliable authority before quoted, "there were only eighteen dwelling-houses and about one hundred inhabitants where the village now is. In North Main street there were six houses, occupied by Charles Durfee, Daniel Buffinton, John Luther, Abner Davol, John Cook, and Mary Borden. In East Central street there were four, occupied by Nathan Bowen, Perry Borden, Seth Borden, and Elihu Cook. In West Central street there were two, occupied by Nathan Borden and Daniel Borden. In South Main street there were five, occupied by Simeon Borden, Richard Borden, Thomas Borden, Benjamin Brayton, and Francis Brayton. Near the shore there was one occupied by Thomas Borden. Of these eighteen families nine were Bordens."

By Act of Legislature of Feb. 26th, 1803, a considerable part of the ancient proprietary of Freetown was detached and erected into a township named Fall River (changed to Troy in 1804, and again to its present name in 1834), the first corporate existence of the place now known all over the globe as, with one exception, the largest cloth-producing community on its surface.

Before, however, the embryo municipality should find itself permanently bounded or even an undivided whole under a single state or township government, a question long at issue between first the provinces and subsequently the federal States of Massachusetts and Rhode Island was to be settled. This question, due to an original conflict of royal patents granted to the two provinces, finally resolved itself into a dispute as to boundaries,

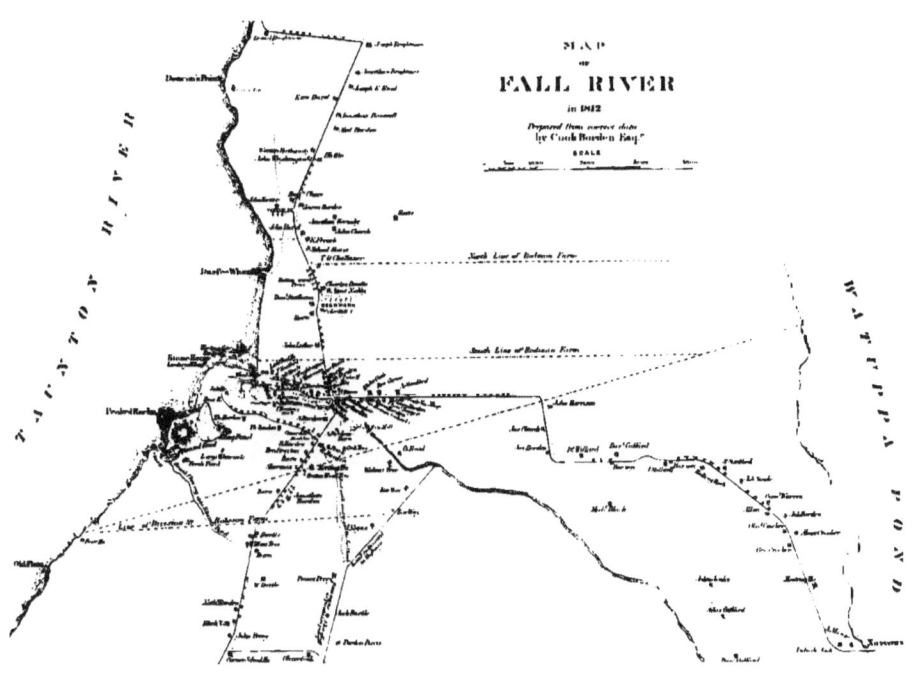

a royal confirmation of a commission's report in 1746 having set over to Rhode Island several towns previously within the sovereignty of Massachusetts. One of these towns was Tiverton, the old Pocasset proprietary. For many years, so far as the territorial transfer was concerned, it was conceded by Massachusetts; but an uncertainty existed as to the correct execution of the King's orders defining the line of boundary. Even after the colonial independence was established, this indefiniteness of the survey remained, succeeding commissions in 1791 and 1844 being unable to determine the matter. The difficulty grew with consecutive years and with a greater ratio as the manufacturing enterprise of Fall River developed, annually adding, both to the population and capital absorbed in its special industries; the assumed and conceded northern line of Tiverton, though quite a remove south of the purchase boundary upon the stream itself, under the *status quo* exercising jurisdiction over and claiming taxes from a very considerable part of its people and property. In 1854, the thriving town having attained the conventional dignity of population, was made a city, and the vexatious complication became yet more serious. But yet seven years were still to elapse before a solution of the difficulty was reached and the boundary correctly adjusted. In 1861 this object was finally accomplished, and Fall River, no longer obliged to acknowledge two jurisdictions, found herself richer in territory by nine square miles, in population by 3593, and in taxable property by $1,948,378.

The foregoing very brief chapter of history simply sketches the origin and corporate epochs of Fall River. Its annals during the Revolutionary War and the later contest with the mother country are so like those of other localities on the coast, exposed to invasion by their convenient access and secure harborage, that it is not needful to embody them in a purely industrial work. The little community, suffice it here to say, during both struggles bore its part loyally and bravely in support of the Declaration, repelling important assaults of British troops as well as crushing a dangerous demonstration of Toryism within its own limits; and those who read the record of the early period will find prominently associated with the organization and conduct of the patriot cause, conspicuous in counsel and action, the same names, the Bordens, Durfees, and others, that are identified with every stage of the material progress of Fall River.

From a very interesting little local publication, designed as a convenient medium of information, and admirably combining *in petto* the departments of history and directory, we extract the following general view of Fall River and its industries, as a preliminary to a more detailed account of their united development:

"The busy, bustling city of Fall River is the embodiment of the sagacity, energy, and successful industry of her own people. No city or town engaged in similar pursuits has greater cause for satisfaction, or can refer to stronger reasons for the exercise of a just pride in the achievements of her own citizens. Most of the large manufacturing towns of New England are the representation of the surplus capital of the older commercial cities. Fall River is the outgrowth of home industry and good management, which, under the blessings of a benign Providence, have given her a foremost rank in manufacturing cities, and a continued success rarely enjoyed by those engaged in manufacturing or commercial pursuits. Her citizens have at various times met with reverses, in the way of conflagrations and strikes, but upon recovering from them, increased prosperity has been the result; and whether in manufacturing or other business, the immense capital which is wielded here is strictly within the hands of her own citizens.

"The words or motto of her corporate seal, 'We'll Try,' have thus received a most significant and practical exposition, and, to-day, the swiftly developing interests of Fall River represent a productive force at least double that of any other New England city engaged in the same class of pursuits. Business is managed with a thrift and exactness seldom attained; but thrift and exactness are not allowed to degenerate into littleness, nor are preconceived opinions held with a tenacity which amounts to stubbornness. Her manufacturers are conscious that the world advances, and desire to advance with it, adopting those suggestions which are reasonable, keeping fully up to the demands of educated labor, desirous of promoting the interests of their employés in wages, hours of labor, and mental and physical requisites, and making them feel that the interests of employer and employed are one and inseparable.

"Fall River is a city and port of entry of Bristol county, Mass., and is pleasantly situated on a rather abrupt elevation of land, rising at the head of Mount Hope Bay, an arm of Narragansett Bay. It comprises an area of about thirty-six and a half square miles, and about 23,330 acres, including both land and water. It is eminently a manufacturing place, but is specially noted for its cotton manufactories; while its favorable position as regards railway and steamboat communications, its improvements in commercial and mechanical industry, and its recent almost unparalleled increase in population and wealth, have given it a name and importance second to none in the commonwealth.

"In the union of hydraulic power and navigable waters, it is perhaps without a parallel upon the American continent. Its hydraulic power is derived from a small stream—Fall River—whence the name of the city which has its source, or is in reality the outflow of a chain of ponds lying two miles east of the bay, covering an area of some 3500 acres, and having a length of about eight miles, and an average breadth of three quarters of a mile. They are mostly supplied by perennial springs, though receiving the outlets of several other sheets of water. The extent of country drained is comparatively small—not over 20,000 acres, and the quantity of power therefore is to be attributed to the springs alluded to, and to the great and rapid fall of the river, which in less than half a mile is more than 132 feet. Within this distance there are no less than eight falls, each occupied by mills—the height of fall at each mill being as follows:

Dam to Troy	2 feet	6 inches.
Troy C. & W. Manufactory	15 "	5½ "
Pocasset Mill	21 "	8 "
Quequechan Mill	21 "	0 "
Watuppa Mill	15 "	4½ "
F. R. Print Works	10 "	0 "
F. R. Manufactory	11 "	5½ "
Annawan Manufacturing Company	14 "	8½ "
F. R. Iron Works Company	13 "	11 "
	129 feet	1½ inches.

The whole of this fall occurs in a distance of 2300 feet. In one case the falls are only 136 feet apart, and this distance occurs between the two greater falls. The flow of the river is one hundred and twenty-one and a half cubic feet per second, or 9,841,500,000 imperial gallons in a year of three hundred days, of ten hours each. The remarkable advantages of this river as a mill stream have been increased by building a dam at the outlet of the ponds, which gives the water an additional fall of two feet; and its lower banks are entirely built up with large manufacturing establishments, which so rapidly succeed each other as scarcely to leave space between some of the buildings sufficient for light and air. The river for almost its entire length runs upon a granite bed, and for much of the distance is confined between high banks, also of granite. Differing therefore from most other water-powers, this one allows the entire space between the banks to be occupied, and most of the water-wheels connected with the older factories are placed directly in the bed of the river. Moreover, while the river affords an almost uniform and constant supply of water, it is never subject to excess, and an injury in consequence of a freshet has never yet been known. The river is perfectly controllable, and thus it is that the mills were built directly across the river, the wheels placed in the bed of the river, and yet from an excess of water no damage was to be apprehended. In later years, however, most of the breast wheels employed in these older mills have been supplanted by the modern appliances of turbine wheels and steam power.

"With the increase of wealth and skill in manufacture, and the entrance upon the stage of action of younger men of enterprise and ambition, new projects were formed, and as the older mills occupied all available space upon the river banks, new situations were sought out and appropriated, and the 'New Mills,' so called, were first erected on the margin of the ponds to the south and east of the city, and of which the stream is the outlet, and afterwards in the northerly and southerly sections of the city, on the banks of Taunton River and Laurel Lake. The growth of the city in this respect was almost marvellous, no less than *eleven* large mills, of from 30,000 to 40,000 spindles each, having been erected in one year (1872), involving an outlay of capital to the extent of $10,000,000, employing 5000 hands, and adding an immediate population of some 15,000 persons. Villages rapidly sprung up and clustered around each mill, while much of the intermediate space was divided into house lots, and appropriated for dwellings and stores. This sudden occupation of outlying sections, and the necessary throwing out of streets and lanes, progressed with unexceptional rapidity, especially for a place of seventy years' settlement. In fact, so rapid was the change in appearance, that what were once familiar scenes remained so no longer, varying from day to day, as though viewed through a kaleidoscope.

"The number of incorporated companies for the manufacture of cotton goods is now (1876) thirty-three, owning forty mills, or forty-three, counting those having two mills under one roof, with an incorporated capital of $14,735,000, but a probable investment of $30,000,000, containing 1,269,048 spindles and 30,144 looms.

"The latest statistics report the total number of mills in the United States as 847, containing 186,975 looms and 9,415,383 spindles, manufacturing 588,000,000 yards of print cloths per annum. Of these, New England has 489 mills, containing 148,189 looms and 7,538,369 spindles, manufacturing 481,000,000 yards of print cloths. Fall River has thus over one eighth of all the spindles in the country, or one sixth of those in New England, and manufactures over a half of all the print cloths.

"The following table will show the number of spindles in the mills of Fall River at the close of each year respectively:

1865	265,328	1871	780,138
1866	403,624	1872	1,094,702
1867	470,360	1873	1,212,694
1868	537,416	1874	1,258,508
1869	540,614	1875	1,269,048 "
1870	544,606		

Notwithstanding the great natural advantages of the locality and their appreciation by the colonial grantors, who had expressly reserved the water and adjacent land on both sides as being of superior available value, except the grain mill of Church, and subsequent small ventures by other persons in the same general direction, no permanent foundation of Fall River manufacture was made till after the war of 1812.

In 1811, however, at Globe village, as it has since been known, within the then town of Tiverton, but the present southern wards of the city of Fall River, Colonel Joseph Durfee, in company with a few other persons, erected a small wooden building, which was, chronologically speaking, the first cotton factory in the neighborhood. The little mill stood on ground which is now the northeast corner of Globe and South Main streets. Its operations continued till 1829, when it was turned into a print works, and so occupied till its destruction by fire in 1838.

In soliciting subscriptions to the capital of this initial enterprise, tradition has it that the most effective argument put to the local magnates was that "cotton cloth would darn much easier than linen." It seems difficult to realize that the period is so short a remove from our own era when such persuasion was necessary. We must remember, however, that even in England, until the decade from 1780 to 1790, which saw the full development of Hargreaves' and Arkwright's inventions, it was thought necessary to make the warp of linen, using cotton simply for the weft of cloth. This was due to two reasons: that the fibre of flax was so much longer and capable of a greater tenuity than that of cotton, enabling it to be spun much more successfully on the domestic spinning-wheels or the mill-jennys, and that the raw material of the former was much cheaper than that of the latter. Nearly all the cloth worn by New England people at this period was home-spun and woven, the wheel and hand loom being essential properties of every household.

How much of the work of yarn-making in Colonel Durfee's mill was done by machine process does not admit of positive assertion. The raw cotton was given out to the farmers' families of the neighborhood and hand-picked. The yarn likewise was distributed among the diligent housewives to be woven into cloth, then collected, put in merchantable shape, and thrown upon the market. We may presume that the machine appointments of the mill included a few of the Arkwright spinning-frames, carders, and probably a calender.

The success of Colonel Durfee's enterprise was not great at any time, and generally its operation seems to have been disastrous to its promoters. They exhibited great energy and considerable nerve, but with hardly commensurate judgment, due probably to want of practical knowledge. One of their experiments is still remembered as illustrative of their operative ability. Having heard that a "tub-wheel" would run better and easier than a breast-wheel, they put one into the mill. A short trial, however, soon dissipated their sanguine anticipation, the new affair not working at all well, but running without steadiness, being difficult of control, and consequently breaking the ends of the thread in the spinning processes.

Occasional reference will be made to the original Durfee mill, and its subsequent fortunes detailed as we proceed. Colonel Durfee was a citizen of considerable local prominence. During the Revolutionary war and the British occupation of Newport and Rhode Island, he was a zealous patriot, and received his grade of lieutenant-colonel, with the command of a regiment recruited from the neighboring region, in merited recognition of his gallant service.

From such contemporary memoranda as are accessible, and the use of a very valuable MS. record, written nearly half a century subsequently by a gentleman now deceased, who was one of the originators of cotton manufacturing, we are able to sketch the village as it was in size and population about the year 1813.

The resident community of Fall River, or Troy, as it was then called, was located about what is now the centre of the city, the main street following the line of the present principal thoroughfare northward, and another considerable street trending eastward to the lake. The greater part of the residences were in these two avenues. Within a territory approximating to one and a half miles square, which would be designated at that day the village, were about thirty dwelling-houses, three saw-mills, four grist-mills, one fulling-mill, a blacksmithy with trip-hammer, and several small stores. The population was estimated at three hundred.

One small, three-masted vessel, which had been engaged in foreign trade, but was, for a short period after the war, hauled up in the creek where the "Old Depot" was afterwards located, and a few small sloops, carrying cord-wood to Newport and Bristol, constituted the local shipping interest. There was no regular conveyance to Providence, and what freight was transferred between the two places went by craft plying between Providence and Taunton, which, in default of wharfage convenience at the Falls, stopped at the ferry two miles up the river, where all the cotton and merchandise was landed for some years. The first craft regularly sailing to Providence was a small schooner, or two-masted lighter, large enough to load ten bales of cotton and a small additional cargo of flour and miscellaneous goods. This was succeeded by the sloop Fall River, of thirty or forty tons capacity, and that again by the sloop Argonaut, and another craft whose name is forgotten, which sustained the communication till the steamer Hancock was put on.

The religious and educational structures of the village were far from suggestive of their present number, convenience, or architectural beauty. "In 1813," says our chronicle, "there was one poor old dilapidated wooden meeting-house, neither plastered nor lathed, which stood upon the line dividing the States, occupied occasionally. The regular place of worship on the Sabbath was at the Narrows, about two miles east. There was one, and only one, good schoolhouse in the village, which stood on the corner of Annawan and South Main streets." The residences were of the usual simple and plain construction adopted in early New England communities, the most pretentious one being erected by Charles Durfee in 1811, and standing until 1857, when it was burned down. The richest resident from 1813 to 1824 was estimated worth $40,000, "and there were but a small number of this class." The entire valuation for some years did not exceed $500,000, and the total taxation in 1813 was $1500.

SMTI LIBRARY

The year 1813 is memorable as inaugurating the first regular cloth-manufacturing enterprise, on a substantial basis, in Fall River, this twelve-month witnessing the organization of two companies and the erection of two considerable factories. The corporate names were the Troy Cotton and Woolen Manufactory and the Fall River Manufactory, the former having a capital of $50,000 and the latter of $40,000. About fifty per cent of the subscriptions for the foundation of enterprises so considerable for the period were secured in neighboring towns, notably Tiverton, Newport, Warren, Rehoboth, Swansea, and Somerset. The companies were both formed in the month of March, the prominent promoters of the Fall River being David Anthony, Dexter Wheeler, and Abraham Bowen; and of the Troy, Oliver Chace, Nathaniel Wheeler, and Eber Slade. Mr. Anthony was chosen treasurer and agent of the former company, and Mr. Chace agent of the latter, with Mr. Slade as treasurer.

David Anthony, to whose previous experience of mill-work was due the construction of one of the two original cotton mills of Fall River, and through whose far-sighted and enlarged appreciation of the future of cloth manufacturing was subsequently wrought what may be termed "a departure," to which Fall River industry is believed by many persons to owe a large degree of its present advancement, was born in Somerset, Mass., January 9th, 1786. At the age of fourteen he left the home farm to enter the service of the rich man of the neighborhood, a large real-estate owner and country merchant, John Bowers, who resided near by on Somerset shore. Young Anthony's occupation was various for the first two years in Mr. Bowers' service. But he was faithful and intelligent, and soon rose from the duties of "chore-boy" to the more responsible office of grain and salt measurer at the store, varied by an occasional rent-collecting expedition, or a trip to Providence or Taunton, on his master's business. In order to educate him in book-keeping he was shortly taken into the counting-room, and not long after charged with the superintendence of the retail department of the store.

In 1804, to the amazement and great disturbance of the neighboring region, Mr. Bowers' affairs became so embarrassed as to force his suspension. By the concurrent action of all parties, the youthful manager, then in his nineteenth year, was employed in closing out the stock of goods and settling up the bankrupt estate.

Young Anthony's educational advantages had not been of a large nature, but he was one to realize the best possible result of whatever opportunities were offered him, so that his intelligence was of a thorough and correct standard. In the winter following his conduct of Mr. Bowers' affairs, the local authorities engaged him to teach a small school. He accepted, and of his experience was accustomed to say that he found himself so poorly prepared for imparting knowledge as to necessitate his own constant application to the various studies pursued, in order to avoid a failure. Though urged to remain the teacher a second season, he declined, satisfied that the discipline of tuition had been of more profit to himself than to his pupils.

Leaving the pursuit of teaching, he made a four months' engagement with John P. Hellen, a crockery dealer of Providence, travelling from Somerset on horseback with his little pack of personal effects, and with a boy mounted behind him to return the horse. Not choosing to take the horse all the way, he finished the last half of his journey on foot. Mr. Hellen was so well satisfied with his services that he continued him in the same situation for two years.

Mr. Anthony's connection with manufacturing commenced in 1808, when he moved to Pawtucket, where Samuel Slater had been operating a cotton-spinning mill for some years successfully, and obtained employment in the factory of that extraordinary man, of whom he often afterwards spoke as the "father of the cotton-manufacturing business in this country." In Mr. Slater's service, and that of the brothers Wilkinson, who at that day were also large yarn producers, Anthony acquired all that experience and contemporary knowledge could impart of the infant pursuit. His industry, honest determination, and intelligent aptness made him both valued and kindly regarded by Mr. Slater, himself a prodigious worker and persistent projector of work, while his own natural inclination for mechanical business was developed, and the course of his future life shaped out.

Having to his satisfaction acquired a thorough practical knowledge of manufacturing, Mr. Anthony in April, 1812, not finding the occupation suited to his ambition in Pawtucket, went to Rehoboth, Mass., where Dexter Wheeler, with other persons, was operating a small factory. His connection there does not seem to have been permanent, as he left Rehoboth in March, 1813, and moved to Fall River, where he spent the remainder of his life.

Mr. Anthony's immediate purpose in moving to Fall River was probably to organize a cotton-manufacturing company. Dexter Wheeler, associated with him, had run a small yarn mill by horse-power at Rehoboth as early as 1807, and possessed experience both as manufacturer and machinist.

The Fall River mill, which was the result of the efforts of these two men, both yet in early manhood, was finished in October, 1813. It was erected at the head of the third fall from tide-water, a structure sixty by forty feet in dimensions, three stories high, and intended for fifteen hundred spindles. The lower story was of stone and the upper two of wood, an alleged reason for using the latter material in completing the factory being that " there was not enough stone in Fall River to finish it with." A better explanation may have been the general ignorance of the use of derricks for some years throughout this region, an exemplification of which will be observed in the account of the erection of the Annawan mill farther on. Though it is matter of tradition that stone was not regularly quarried in Fall River till 1823, the suggestion of its insufficient supply for any conceivable scheme of erection, even though it contemplated building all the Pyramids along the shores of Watuppa, seems absurd enough in view of the fact that the city is full of immense granite structures constructed of material taken out of ledges on the premises.

Mr. Anthony's subsequent life was identified with the progress of Fall River. He retired from active business about 1839, having won the success which his vast resources of judgment and energy were sure to achieve. Of his return to his old pursuit of manufacturing twenty years after, in the seventy-fourth year of his age, the subsequent record will include the proper mention. When seventy years old, in a brief review of his own career, he wrote the following words of counsel to young men: "Happiness and success in a business life are promoted by correct habits, systematic living in all matters, and great promptness in fulfilling engagements."

David Anthony was the first, in point of time, of the strong, energetic and sagacious natures that have built up a community of substantial and progressive industries. No better analysis of his own sterling character could be made than is indicated in his sententious counsel to a youthful friend quoted above, each of the qualities therein mentioned as requisites to happiness and success being distinctly and conspicuously his own.

Mr. Anthony was socially known as Deacon Anthony, he holding that office in the First Congregational Church from 1834 till his decease. He was President of the Fall River Bank from its organization in 1825 for forty years. He was three times married, his last wife, whom he survived but four years, being the daughter of Thomas Borden. Of his seven children, two sons are still resident in Fall River, and another, John B. Anthony, of Providence, worthily known as for some years the executive officer and head of the Providence Tool Company, is the President of the Union Mill Company.

David Anthony died in Fall River on the 6th of July, 1867, closing a long, useful, and honored career, as one to whom the "well done, good and faithful servant" is spoken through all the centuries.

As above stated, the structure of the Fall River mill was completed, and the machinery, made for it by Dexter Wheeler, in operation in October, 1813, seven months from the initial movement of the enterprise. With all the resources of the great machine shops of the United States and Great Britain, such expedition as this would be extraordinary did we not remember that the processes available in 1813 were hardly a third of those now necessary to the equipment of a cotton factory. But even with this consideration, this possibility suggests itself, that a part of the machinery set up in the new mill may have been transferred from the Rehoboth factory. However the case may be, it is certain that this mill, started by David Anthony and Dexter Wheeler, was the first cotton-spinning organization in the village known as Fall River.

Coincident with the starting of the Fall River manufactory was that of the Troy Manufacturing Company. The articles of association upon which this enterprise was inaugurated are dated, as approved, March 8th, 1813: " Articles of agreement for the regulation and well-ordering the concerns and proceedings of the subscribers associated for the purpose of building a manufactory of cotton or other goods in the town of Troy, county of Bristol and Commonwealth of Massachusetts, with a capital stock of $50,000, divided into one hundred shares, to be paid by instalments. Article First: The company shall be known and called by the name of the Troy Manufacturing Company, etc." The articles, eleven in number, were signed by the followingnamed persons, together subscribing for all the shares, namely: Amey Borden, Clark Chase, Oliver Chace, James Maxwell, Jonathan Brown William Slade, N. M. Wheaton, Oliver Earl, Eber Slade, Joseph G. Luther, Sheffel Weaver, John Stackford for Charles Wheaton and self, Nathaniel Wheeler, James Driscol, Benjamin Slade, Moses Buffinton, Nathan Slade, Daniel Buffinton, Hezekiah Wilson, Benjamin E. Bennet, Joseph Buffinton, Walter Durfee, William Read, Robinson Buffinton, John Martin, and Benjamin Buffinton. Article Second providing for an annual meeting, at which were to be chosen a moderator, clerk, and standing committee, consisting of five persons, " whose duty it shall be to transact and do all the business of the company during the year;" this annual meeting of the stockholders was holden on the 7th of June, and James Maxwell, Sheffei Weaver, Nathan Wheeler, Benjamin Slade, and Jonathan Brown were chosen Standing Committee for the ensuing twelvemonth. At this meeting it was voted to petition the Legislature for a charter of incorporation. This charter having been issued, February 22, 1814, a meeting was holden, July 25th, 1814, to organize under the Act, and the name of the company was changed to the Troy Cotton and Woolen Manufactory. There is also a record of a meeting on the 7th of the same month, at which it was voted to increase the amount of capital $16,000, assessing each share $40, payable quarterly during the ensuing year.

The Troy Company's mill was built of stone gathered from the neighboring fields, and designed to run 2000 spindles. The building was one

hundred and eight feet long, thirty-seven feet wide, four stories, and had a low hip roof. It was located at the foot of the fall, near to or directly on the site of an old saw-mill. The date of its commencing operation was about the middle of March, 1814, the building having been finished in the previous September.

At the first meeting on March 9th, 1813 (after the capital had been subscribed), of the Standing Committee chosen by the stockholders the previous day to superintend the affairs of the company till the annual meeting, it seems the Committee effected an arrangement with Oliver Chace as agent. The following extracts from the minutes of this meeting are interesting:

"Agreed with Oliver Chace to superintend the company's business, as agent for and on behalf of the Committee until the annual meeting in the 6th month next, at two dollars and fifty cents per day, he to find himself horse and to do the company's riding; said company to pay his board and expenses and find the horse provender, etc., when in their service.

"Agreed to build the factory of stone, one hundred feet by thirty-six feet, two stories above the main sill; the windows in the body thereof to be seven by nine glass, and for the loft six by eight.

"Agreed to have an iron shaft for the water-wheel seven inches square in the middle and six at each end, fourteen feet long; said wheel to be fourteen feet diameter and twelve feet float.

"Agreed to build a machine shop, twenty-five feet by thirty-six, two stories high, and a blacksmith's shop, sixteen by twenty-five feet, with two forges; the two shops to be rented to John Borden, Junior, at one hundred and fifty dollars per year."

John Borden, Jr., above named, and his brothers Isaac, Asa, and Levi, were born on the island of Rhode Island. Their father pursued the trade of a blacksmith, and after learning it in his shop, they went to Waltham and worked in the machine shop there. John, who had probably acquired a knowledge of cotton machinery at Waltham, where Mr. Lowell's manufacturing enterprise was then developing, came to Fall River in 1813, and by him, in association with his brother Isaac, probably, the machinery for the Troy Manufactory was constructed. He finally moved to Indiana, where he died many years since.

Oliver Chace, the originator and agent of the Troy mill, had been brought up as a carpenter and wheelwright, and could often be seen in his early days with his broad-axe on his shoulder, around among the farmers repairing their carts and farming utensils, an active, restless nature with a keen eye for business, and not disposed to settle down in one place or occupation. He was progressive, energetic, and always ready to look into and entertain new projects. When, therefore, attention was invited to the comparatively new enterprise of cotton-yarn spinning by power, he was at once an interested observer, and soon was induced to embark personally in the business at Dighton. With the experience of manufacturing thus acquired, he came to Fall River, and of the entire list of stockholders in the Troy was the only one having a practical acquaintance with the industry.

The spinning enterprise in Fall River was started at a period when the stimulus of a market closed to foreign production was giving an inflated encouragement to domestic enterprise. The mills were hardly finished and ready to operate before peace was declared and a revulsion came, cotton cloth going down fifty per cent in price, and a general depression ruling the country, so that factory stock was not worth more than half the original investment. The depression was, however, but temporary; yet, what with the effect of the panic and the difficulties attending a new business, the Troy does not seem to have made a profit during its first few years. The following memorandum of a new contract with the agent, passed by the Committee Dec. 30, 1816, indicates an economizing disposition: "Agreed with Oliver Chace to transact the business of the company in behalf of the Directors, and to give him two dollars per day and find him sufficient house room for his family (and garden), and he, the said Oliver, to board the Directors at these meetings, as heretofore, without making any charge to the company; this until further agreement."

The matter of salary must have been a frequent and annoying subject of settlement between the Board and its agent. The original contract with him for three years from December 3, 1813, gave him "one thousand dollars a year and a convenient house for his family to live in, unless he shall build one sooner, in which case he is to live in his own house." Whatever may be thought of the smallness of the agent's remuneration, however, it seems really munificent in comparison with that awarded the treasurer, Eber Slade, who was annually voted "ten shillings per day, he to board himself."

Power-weaving was first done in the Fall River Manufactory, early in 1817, Sarah Winters starting the first loom, Mary Healy the second, and Hannah Borden the third. The last named (Mrs. William Cook), who was then fourteen years of age, possesses a thorough recollection of the then new feature of factory work. The looms used were the invention of Dexter Wheeler. They were very heavy and clumsy and constantly getting out of order, weaving one yard of good cloth and ruining the next through the want of control of the shuttle. The dressing was very poor, and at times the yarn would mildew and rot on the beam, causing large quantities to be thrown away, and a consequent great waste of material.

In the interesting MS. previously quoted, the statement is made that "looms were first built in Fall River by John Orswell and Wheaton Bailey, for the two above-named companies, perhaps about the year 1817, each company putting in operation twelve to fifteen." This is probably an error as to time, and the machines constructed by Orswell and Bailey were doubtless on the model of the Cartwright or Scotch loom, introduced into the country in 1816, by Gilmore. In the records of the Troy Company is found the following memorandum of action taken at a meeting, June 5th, 1820: "Voted that the agent build and put in operation ten pair of water-looms, with preparations, besides the present ten now building, if he shall deem it expedient." And again at the quarterly meeting the succeeding September, the agent was instructed to put in "a new flume where the old saw-mill stood, and cut down the raceway as low as that of the main stream, and remove the machine-shop up to the said new flume, for the purpose of putting in a new water-wheel, to carry machinery for spinning or weaving as he shall think most expedient." Both of the above memoranda may be accepted as indications that water or power looms were not set up in the Troy mill prior to the last quarter of the year 1820.

The first weavers in the Fall River Manufactory were hired by the week, at the rate of $2.50 per week; but, when the looms were made to operate more regularly and the weavers had acquired some experience, so that one could run two looms and produce thirty yards of cloth from the pair, the system of paying by the yard was adopted, and one cent per yard or thirty cents per day became the average wages. Cloth was woven one yard wide, and sold at twenty-five cents per yard, the production of water-looms at first being plain cloth only.

As a suggestion of the number of employés in an early cotton factory of the average size, the following statement, also embodying Mrs. Cook's recollections, is interesting. The Fall River Manufactory employed in the weaving-room fifteen persons to tend thirty looms, in the dressing-room three, the spinning-room ten, and the carding-room three; so that, including overseers, the total number directly engaged in cloth production in 1819 probably did not exceed thirty-five.

When the Troy commenced the production of stripes (1821), the company colored its yarn in a small dye-house belonging to the mill.

The spinning frames set up in the two mills were of seventy-two spindles each, and the best spinners could tend a pair of frames, producing two and a half skeins per spindle in a day's work.

Previously to 1820 stripes were woven in hand looms, and termed 1 and

3, or 2 and 2, as there was one white thread and three blue threads, or two white and two blue, etc.

The two companies found it necessary not only to conduct the details of manufacturing, but, it is evident, to exercise all the enterprise and shrewdness of merchants in disposing of their production. The Fall River mill sold a fair portion of its yarn in Philadelphia, and through commission houses. The Troy sought a market in Massachusetts and New Hampshire, and especially in Maine. This adding merchandising to producing rendered the business much more like drudgery than our own times afford any instance of. With the Providence mill-owners weekly sending their yarn into every nook of the country to be woven, it was hard enough finding a farm-house whose women-folk had not already been employed by those earlier birds from Rhode Island ; but it was harder yet to sell the goods in those days when the voice of the broker was not heard in the land—at least not as much as it is now. The following resolution of the Troy Directors, October 18th, 1819, touches this matter : " Voted and agreed to establish a store at Hallowell, in the District of Maine, for the purpose of vending cotton and other goods, for and on account of the Troy Cotton and Woollen Manufactory, and that Harvey Chace was chosen agent to conduct the business there, to be paid for his services at and after the rate of $300 per year, his board to be paid by the company. The company's agent was also authorized to make a shipment of cotton and other goods to the State of Georgia this fall (if he shall think it expedient), for the purpose of purchasing cotton and other kinds of Southern produce on account of the company."

The Harvey Chace above named, now proprietor of the Albion Mills at Valley Falls, R. I., was a son of the agent. Succeeding minutes of record from time to time indicate the continued support of his mission Down East by the directors of the Troy, and also their approval of the Georgia shipments. In this connection we refer again to the interesting *Memorabilia* previously quoted : " In the cotton business of that day there was a great amount of book-keeping and clerical work, of which very few manufacturers now have any idea. Every bale of cotton put out to be picked was booked, as was also every web given out to be woven. A mill of seven thousand to ten thousand spindles required more labor to take care of the yarn after its leaving the reel and prepare it for or get it into the market, than all the spindles in Fall River now (1859) demand.

" The price paid by the mills for picking the cotton given out was four cents per pound, and five or six pounds was considered a fair day's work. The Fall River mill secured Blair's Picking Machine, the first one in the place, and it was in fact just introduced in the country. This acquisition in 1814 was calculated to save three quarters of the cost of picking. The improvement encountered a violent opposition in the ignorant prejudice of consumers both of yarn and cloth, who believed its operation was detrimental to the staple and consequently to the cloth itself.

"The dressing of the yarn for the looms was at first attended with much difficulty and vexation. The first dresser used by the Fall River Company warped the beam by sections, say, one eighth of a yard at a time, the beam which received the yarn having as many sections as there were quarters of a yard to the web. This process of dressing was so trying and troublesome that an altogether different machine was devised, an improvement upon the Waltham dresser, which received the yarn of section warps from beams revolving over a small round roll. It was some years before this device gave place to the dresser now in use.

"Until about the years 1820 to 1825, the roping was made in cans, with open tops, or with tops which required to be wound upon the bobbin, by hand, for use. The want of a better roving machine was a serious evil in early manufacturing, greater speed of process being sadly wanted. Speeders, so called, were used of various designs: Hinds', Arnold's, Simmons', Orswell's (a kind known only in Fall River), and the Waltham, which, with all the other Waltham inventions, for a time enjoyed the precedence.

"The yarn spun was reeled from the bobbin upon reels, 18 inches over, into skeins of 7 knots, 80 threads to the knot. Twenty skeins was termed a doff, for which some three or four cents were paid; the yarn was next *sorted*, and every skein weighed separately, thus determining how many skeins weighed a pound.

"The yarn so sorted was put up into five-pound bundles, ready for market.

"In the early stages of cotton spinning, only a small proportion of yarn was spun over No. 16, for simple want of a demand. Yarn designed for plain cloth, sheetings, or shirtings, was bleached upon the grass, no chemicals being used, and a good whitening required from four to six weeks. Most of the yarn produced was woven into blue and white stripes, chambrays, tickings, etc. The several prices were, for stripes 38 cents, shirtings 11 cents, sheetings 50 cents, and tickings occasionally as high as $1 per yard.

"The wearing apparel of male operatives was generally cotton velvet, five eighths wide, costing about $1 per yard. Females wore stripes, 1 and 3, 2 and 2, 4 and 2, etc., for their dresses, the making up costing from 50 cents to 75 cents.

"The imperfect development of the weaving machinery of the loom, particularly through the unreliable motion of the shuttle, made a great deal of poor cloth during those opening years of our manufacture. The best weaving was at the rate of 85 to 100 picks per minute, turning out from 17 to 20 yards a day as an excellent result. Power-loom production was also regarded at first suspiciously, some still clinging to hand-wove fabrics, while others insisted upon the threads being all warp, on account of its having more twist than the weft spun for filling. A popular use for the warps then made, the coarser yarns, among the country people, was to weave them into flannels for sheets and underclothing; but for the finer article of production, really fit for good shirtings, we were still dependent on the foreign manufacturers.

"During the years 1813-14 both the Troy and Fall River companies erected several tenement houses, at a cost of $1500 each, for their work-people, in which the agents also lived. The capacity of these first tenement structures in the place was large enough for four families.

"The operatives, with the rare exception of an occasional Englishman, were all natives. Very many of them, and nearly all the overseers, were persons whose previous occupation had been seafaring, the suspension of commerce during the war obliging them to seek a new industry. Capable and good men could be hired as overseers at from 4s. 6d. to 7s. 6d. per day, payable mostly from the factory stores. Female operatives received from $2.75 to $3.25 per week, having to pay $1.75 for their board. Groceries were exceedingly high—tea 10s. 6d. per pound, sugar 25 cents, coffee 33 cents, molasses from $1 to $1.25 per gallon, and flour $17 per barrel. Fuel (wood exclusively) and house rent were of course very much lower than they are at the present time (1859), however, so that families were able to live quite comfortably."

The first dividend paid to the stockholders of the Troy was in 1820: "At a meeting of the directors the fifth day of sixth month, at nine o'clock A.M., it was voted and resolved that the treasurer be authorized and directed to pay out to the stockholders a dividend of twenty-five ($25) dollars on a share at the expiration of three months from this time, and another dividend of the same amount at the expiration of six months from this date."

Succeeding dividends are recorded, but one of which seems to have a present interest, however: "At a regular meeting of the directors at Troy, fifth month, twenty-fifth day, 1824, voted that a dividend of twenty-five dollars on a share be paid to the stockholders in goods on demand, at the following prices, namely:

3/4 Brown shirtings	at	10	cents.		3/4 Gingham shirtings	at	14½	cents.
7/8 " "	at	11	"		3/4 Check "	"	14	"
4/4 " "	"	13½	"		7/8 " "	"	16	"
9/8 " "	"	15	"		4/4 " "	"	18	"
3/4 Stripes "	"	14	"					

Fair quality.

At the quarterly meeting, September 5, 1820, it was voted "to run the mill evenings from the fifth day of tenth month to the first day of third month, 1821, and keep a watch all night for the same term of time."

"Also, to stop the practice of making fires in the vicinity of the mill for the purpose of boiling clothes."

The two provisions against conflagration above recorded seem almost prophetic, for the mill was burned down so completely that only a portion of the walls were left standing, in the succeeding October. Immediate preparations were made for rebuilding, and machinery ordered of Harris, Hawes & Co.; but there must have been some delay, as the agent was authorized by resolution, September 3d, 1822, to dispose of half of the contract. It was also voted "that the agent be authorized to have what money he may find necessary for the company, if it does not exceed two thousand and five hundred dollars, before our next quarterly meeting."

In December, 1821, we find that negotiation was pending to lease for a term of five years the Globe Manufactory, real estate and machinery, and "also the Union factory in said Tiverton for one year." It does not appear certain that the company secured the control of the Globe—Colonel Durfee's original enterprise, in which he had met with disaster only, and which was operated by various parties for some years preceding its occupation as a print works in 1829. At any rate its own new mill was completed and in condition to run in the fall of 1823.

In 1821, the Troy Company had erected a small building where the old saw-mill, previously referred to, stood, which was called the "Little Mill." This addition was nearly ready for occupation when the main building was burned, and was immediately equipped with the few carders and looms rescued from the fire, and a small supplement of machinery from the Globe, and put in operation.

In 1843, an addition, of stone, three stories high, and 75 by 47 feet in proportions on the ground, was made to the original Troy Mill. Ten years later this new part was raised two stories and the building extended 80 feet on the south, all the old wooden erections being removed. In 1860 the original mill of 1823 was removed, and the part known as the New Mill erected, on the north, reaching to Bedford street, 296 feet long, 70 feet wide, and five stories high.

Oliver Chace remained agent of the Troy until 1822, when he accepted a similar position with the Pocasset Company. He was succeeded by his son Harvey, who filled the place till 1842. The agents of the Troy since 1842 have been: Stephen Davol, 1842–1860; Thomas J. Borden, 1860–1876; and the superintendents since 1827 (when the office of agent was divided into the two now termed treasurer and superintendent), William C. Davol to 1843; Abel Borden, 1843–1849; Joseph D. Brown, 1849–1872; John C. Bartlett, 1872–1873; Chas. Green, 1873–1874; and William E. Sharples, 1875 to the present time.

During the reconstruction of the Troy Company's factory, other manufacturing enterprises being in contemplation, the control and preservation of the water-power seem to have been subjects of consideration, and instructions were voted to the agent "to use his best endeavors to prevent the water being turned, or any part of it, from any of the ponds that empty themselves into the one from which we draw our water, and for him to pay our proportion of all expenses that may arise from legal or other means that shall be deemed proper to prevent the course of said waters being turned, either by digging, building, or otherwise."

At a meeting, held June 13th, 1822, it was voted that James Driscoll, on the part of the Troy Company, should be empowered to settle with the Pocasset Company upon "a permanent mark for the height of flowage of the pond."

From the mass of record and reminiscence accumulated in the foregoing pages, it is hoped the reader will be able not only to compose for himself a picture of Fall River as it was during the period from 1813 to 1820, but also to form a correct appreciation of domestic cotton manufacturing in its inchoate stage. If the illustrations and authorities furnished are wanting in detail, or have been discursively and incoherently presented, a generous consideration for such defaults of construction is asked, in view of the fact that the generation which witnessed the origin of Fall River industry has passed away, the oldest now living, to whose memory appeal has been made, having been but children at the period narrated; and thus, with the exception of oral testimony on a few isolated points, the writer has been obliged to depend upon minutes of record, which certainly were not made in anticipation of future historic treatment, and upon memoranda, provokingly suggestive of what their author could have done, jotted down nearly half a century after the events and circumstances they indicate.

The ten years from 1820 to 1830 beheld a decided advance of the local industry, not only in its cotton manufacture, but in other directions of effort as well. During the period there were organized the Pocasset Manufacturing Company, the Annawan and Massasoit, Robeson's, or the Fall River Print Works, the Satinet Factory, the Fall River Iron Works Company, and the Watuppa Reservoir Company, besides several minor establishments, and additions were also made to the older mills.

The Fall River Manufactory was enlarged in 1827, a small brick mill, three stories high, being erected on the north. This mill, called the "Nankeen Mill," was run by Azariah and Jarvis Shove, for the manufacture of nankeen cloth, until it was torn down, together with the old "Yellow Mill," as the first mill of the Fall River Manufactory was called, to make way for the "White Mill," put up by the same company in 1839.

In 1821, the land, including the falls just west of Main street, came into the possession, largely, of the Rodmans of New Bedford, who organized the

Pocasset Manufacturing Company with the original paid-in capital of $100,000, with Samuel Rodman as President and principal owner.

Mr. Rodman was a gentleman of the "old school," and wore short clothes, with long, fine silk stockings, knee-buckles, and buckled shoes; a coat, broad-skirted, wide-cuffed, and of a drab color; and a long waistcoat, with broad flaps over the pockets. His appearance in town was always a great source of attraction to the boys, who admired his tall, straight figure, set off by his old-time costume.

The company proceeded at once to develop their property, voting at first to erect a grist-mill, but subsequently changed their plans, and having engaged Oliver Chace, of the Troy Mill, as agent, began the erection of the old " Bridge Mill," as it was known. This mill, standing just north of the stream, and in front of the present Granite Block, Main street, was built of stone, about 100 by 40 feet, three stories high, with a long ell on the south end, parallel with, and extending over, the stream. The company's first purchase of machinery for this mill was a thousand spindles, which were placed in the south half, the north half being leased to D. & D. Buffington, for the manufacture of warp and batting. The old grist-mill, which formerly stood on this spot, was torn down to make room for the new structure, but the old fulling-mill still remained just to the south. The latter was the only mill of the kind in this region. It was run by Major Brayton, and in it was cleansed and fulled all the cloth woven by the farmers for heavy winter clothing. Both of these mills were destroyed in the " Great Fire of '43."

The Pocasset Company seemed to have made it a point to encourage smaller manufacturers, and to this end erected buildings successively for some ten or fifteen years, which were leased to other parties. A small building, to the west of the ell of the old " Bridge Mill," was occupied by Job Eddy, of New Bedford, and subsequently by Edward and Oliver S. Hawes and others for printing calicoes in a small way; but this was of short continuance.

In the fall of 1824, Andrew Robeson, of New Bedford, came to Fall River to establish a calico-printing business, and made arrangements with the Pocasset Company to occupy a part of the building erected in 1825, and known as the Satinet Factory. The capital ($50,000) for this enterprise was generally subscribed in New Bedford. The south half of this building was occupied by J. & J. Eddy for the manufacture of woollen goods (whence the name " Satinet "), and continued to be so used by them till the erection of the Wamsutta Steam Woolen Mill, on " Mosquito Island," in 1849. In 1826 a stone building, on the site of the present Quequechan Mill, known in those days as the " New Pocasset," was erected and leased to A. & J. Shove, who sub-leased the north half to Chase & Luther, both firms engaging in the manufacture of cotton into yarn and cloth. The succeeding year still another stone building was put up, which was afterwards known as the "Massasoit," and now as the "Watuppa Mill." It was a building so large that it was considered no one firm would want to occupy the whole of it, hence a partition wall was run from the foundation to the roof, and two wheel-pits put in.

But a man had now come on to the stage of action whose ideas were somewhat larger than those of his predecessors; young in years, but confident in his own powers and capacities, and with a training which specially fitted him for the sphere in which henceforth he was to move and to occupy a commanding position, Holder Borden stepped forward and leased the whole mill for fifteen years, from Jan. 1, 1831. Doubtless the uncertainty of the business, already exhibited in its ups and downs as affected by high tariffs or low tariffs, by the defects of machinery as yet unperfected, or the irregularities of a business not yet systematized, may have had their influence in deterring others from attempting too much in this direction; but the time had now arrived when it was to assume a more solid basis, and call into service men of broad scope, far-sighted, comprehensive, and self-confident, to take hold and advance the industry as it had never before been, at least in this country. Such a man was Holder Borden; and while old men shook their heads and had their doubts and made their timid suggestions, he proceeded with a firm hand and clear head to develop one scheme after another, till he gave to Fall River an' impulse and a direction, a force and example, which she has not outgrown to the present day.

Holder Borden, then but thirty-one years of age, assumed the management of the Massasoit Mill. Making openings in the partition between the two parts of the mill, he immediately filled it with machinery, and commenced the manufacture of sheetings, shirtings, Marseilles vesting, stuff for corded skirts, and other fabrics. Discarding the old method of distributing power by heavy gearing, he was the first in this vicinity to introduce belting, by which much of the noise and racket of machinery was done away with, and a steady and more uniform motion secured to the different processes, to say nothing of the reduction of friction and gain in power.

The mill at once acquired a reputation abroad, and in Providence, for example, young men were advised "to go into business in Fall River," where Holder Borden's great mill had just been started. This mill, which seems so small in our day, had 9000 spindles, and *was* large, *very* large, when compared with the 2500 or 3000 spindles heretofore considered sufficient for one mill.

In a work published in Edinburgh in 1840, James Montgomery, who visited America in 1836, and was, for a short time, Superintendent of the York Mills at Saco, discussing the relative merits of shafting or belting, says: "There are two mills at Fall River, in the State of Rhode Island, which seem to decide the question in favor of the belts. These factories have equal water-power, as the one takes exactly what passes through the other. The one is geared with belts, the other with shafts, etc., and it is found that the former can put in motion a considerably greater quantity of machinery than the latter." The mill first referred to was probably the Massasoit.

The enterprise was successful from the first, and did much to give character and tone to a business which heretofore had met with only partial success. From this period the main industry of Fall River was fully and definitely determined, and, though the steps were sometimes slow and far between, they have ever been forward. New hands and thoughtful minds have from time to time turned their attention to the industry, and, as new exigencies have arisen, have applied the skill of inventive genius, or the wisdom of experience, to advance its interests, until to-day Fall River stands foremost as the centre of Cotton Manufacture in America.

With the establishment of the Pocasset Company and the various manufacturing enterprises, growing out of that new and pushing organization, all of which were located upon and using the fall, it became necessary to establish a general and responsible control of the water-power furnished by the stream and the parent lake. Soon after the commencement of the Pocasset Company's actual operation, the Troy Company, as appears from a minute of its action on the 13th of June, 1822, instructed James Driscoll, one of its Directors, to confer with the Directors of the Pocasset upon a permanent mark for the height of flowage of the pond.

The Troy Company acquired its ownership of the upper fall upon which its mill was located, and a relative control of the whole water-power, through the concession of its first-named stockholder, Amey Borden, who received eleven of the one hundred shares of stock constituting the original capital of the company, in consideration of her grant of the land and water privilege. Mrs. Borden was the widow of Simeon Borden, a great-grandson of Richard, one of the two sons of the original John Borden, who in 1714, by purchase from Colonel Church of the twenty-six and a half shares belonging to him, became possessed of the land on both sides of the river, and consequent owners of the entire fall. Probably during the century which elapsed between this original acquisition and the organization of cotton manufacturing in 1813, a considerable part of this property had passed out of the hands of the descendants of the two brothers Richard and Joseph. It is evident, however, that the Troy Company, as a representative of Mrs. Amey Borden, in a certain degree controlled the general privilege, and its records indicate that any violation or invasion of its rights was jealously watched and guarded against.

In 1825, after a general conference of the parties interested, the question of permanent preservation and control of the water-power was settled. The Watuppa Reservoir Company was formed "to build a new dam above the dam belonging to the Troy Company, for the purpose of raising the water two feet above the present dam, and to pay the expense of flowage occasioned thereby." The Troy Company gave the Reservoir Company the privilege of building the new dam upon their property. Acts of Incorporation were secured from the Legislatures of Rhode Island and Massachusetts, the latter of which bears date June 20th, 1826, and a code of by-laws was adopted. The corporators were David Anthony, Nathaniel B. Borden, Oliver Chace, and Bradford Durfee, they being representatives of the several manufacturing establishments on the Fall River stream, namely, the Troy Cotton and Woollen Manufactory, the Pocasset Manufacturing Company, the establishment of Andrew Robeson, the Fall River Manufactory, the Annawan Manufactory, and the Fall River Iron Works Company.

The company proceeded immediately to accomplish the object of the organization, building the dam, in 1832, south of the present line of Pleasant street, and paying the damage occasioned by the flowage of the land along the banks of the river. The dam was constructed of quarried stone, under the superintendence of Major Durfee, and attracted universal attention in the village because it was the first stone laid in cement, and obviated a difficulty never before entirely overcome, namely, the leaching of the water through the crevices.

The building of factories and filling them with machinery naturally led to an early demand for skilled machinists, and as early as 1821, the firm of Harris, Hawes & Co. was formed and occupied two floors of a building put up for their use by the Pocasset Company; the lower floor or basement was used by Miller Chase as a grist-mill, and near by was a water-wheel, in constant demand for the washing of clothes by the wives and daughters of the leading men of the place, whose residences were then mostly on Central street, and the vicinity of the Four Corners.

Much of the machinery of the Bridge Mill and the improvements made in that of the Troy and Fall River was made by this firm. They subsequently moved into the north end of the Satinet Factory, continuing the business under the name of O. S. Hawes & Co. After Job Eddy removed his printing machinery to New Bedford, the building was occupied by different parties as a bleachery and in 1829 by the Fall River Bleaching and Calendering Company.

Just east of the present Watuppa Mill was a small building which had been used several years by Edward Bennett & Brother as a carding factory. It had but one set of machines, and employed some three or four hands.

Thus had the Pocasset Company fostered the manufacturing enterprise of those days by providing a place to make beginnings.

While these changes were taking place near the head of the stream, still others were going on below. In 1825, the Annawan Manufactory was organized with a nominal capital of $160,000, in 30 shares, and the brick building, still standing, was erected near the junction of Annawan and Pocasset streets. The Annawan ran from 5000 to 7000 spindles. The brick for the construction of this mill were burnt at Bowenville, from clay brought from Long Island. Major Bradford Durfee was the Agent of the mill and superintended its construction. Thirteen persons took all the stock, as follows: Abraham and Isaac Wilkinson, 4 shares; Bradford Durfee, 2; William Valentine, 2; Joseph Butler, 2; Richard Borden, 2; Holder Borden, 4; Benjamin Rodman, 8; Francis Rotch, 1; William B. Rotch, 1; Thomas Swain, 1; William Swain, 1; Charles W. Morgan, 2. Of this capital $100,000 was paid in.

Major Durfee, then thirty-nine years of age, was an active, stirring man, seeming to be in his element when engaged in some out-of-doors occupation; with the exception of a year or two spent as a ship-carpenter near New Bedford, most of his life was passed in Fall River, where he was always a leader among the independent, self-confident men of his time. He was one of the original eight owners of the Fall River Iron Works Co., formed in 1821, and was conspicuously active in the improvement of what is known as "below the hill." In building operations, in the construction of wharves, in the getting out of stone, in devising means to accomplish certain ends, in readiness of comprehension and clearness in imparting ideas, in all the various ways in which one man gains and retains an influence over others, perhaps Major Durfee has never had a superior in the city.

During the seven years succeeding the commencement of the cotton business, the growth of the village was extremely gradual, its census in 1820 showing but fifty dwelling houses and about five hundred inhabitants. From this date may be reckoned the more rapid and steady advance of population and enterprise, the next ten years witnessing especially many and important changes. There was no regular communication with the neighboring towns till 1827. In that year the Steamer Hancock commenced running daily between Fall River and Providence. Other steamers had previously attempted to establish communication with neighboring places, but with only partial success. Sailing vessels had also been employed, but of course were subject to wind and tide. Kinsley's baggage-wagon went once or twice a week to Boston, carrying down cotton yarn and bringing back two or three bales of cotton, with other goods or merchandise. Fall River was one side from the post-roads, and letters had to be sent or carried to Taunton. The goods manufactured were sheetings, shirtings, twills, ginghams, blue and white stripe, etc., and were sold in Boston, New York, and Philadelphia, through commission houses.

The hours of labor began at 5 A.M., or as soon as light, and work continued till 8 A.M., when half an hour was allowed for breakfast. Another half-hour was given at 12 M., for dinner; and work then resumed till dark or till half-past 7 P. M., in winter. Supper came after that. The male help were treated to New England rum at 11 A.M., and considerable excitement was created in 1827, when one of the mill foremen, recently deceased, refused to carry it around among his help, saying " he was hired to oversee the carding-room, not to distribute liquor."

The superintendent of a mill in 1830 received $2 per day, which was thought to be an enormous price. Five shillings (83 cents) and a dollar per day were considered good wages. Doffer-boys had 25 cents a day, and overseers of rooms $1.25 per day. Very much the same machines were used then as now, though of course vastly improved in these later days. There was the picker, by which the cotton was opened from the bale; the first carding-machine, called breaker; the second carding, called finisher; the set of speeders, by which the roving was made (more carding being done in those days than at present, resulting in fine, smooth threads, free from lumps); then hand mules for filling; throstle spinning for warp; spooling; warping; and finally dressing; the latter operating eight beams at once—four on each end, and making one web for drawing in and weaving.

The first print cloths were made in the Bridge Mill, seven eighths to a yard wide, and were bought and printed by Andrew Robeson. They were considerably coarser than the 28 inch 64 by 64 of the present day, being only 44 picks to the square inch, and of No. 20 or No. 25 yarn.

In the construction of the mills no derricks were used, but the stones for the upper stories were carried up on hand-barrows or rolled up long inclines, and it was thought quite wonderful when Major Durfee used oxen to draw up the stone, brick, timber, etc., on the Annawan and White Mills.

At first only Americans worked in the mills, as there were very few foreigners in the place. The establishment of Print Works effected an immigration of English and Scotch, and after the "Great Fire," the Irish came in considerable numbers to work in the Mills and Iron Works, and as day laborers. Several of the mills had corporation stores, from which the help were supplied with their groceries, dry goods, and other necessaries.

Thus there were on Main street the Pocasset and Troy Stores, while the wholesale store was Burr's, afterward Lindsey's, at the shore. Most of the supplies were brought in sloops from New York. A hundred-ton sloop was called large, and return freights of cloth, etc., were often divided as too valuable to risk on one vessel. There were also a number of vessels engaged in the West India trade, taking out cargoes of New England rum and cloths, and returning with a freightage of indigo, drugs, and other articles.

By reason of the inconsiderable size of the place, Fall River was little affected by the changes of national policy on the tariff question, and hence suffered little in the business depressions of 1817 and 1825, though more in that of 1829. The early tariff acts, while intended to be fully protective of our infant manufactures, were, in fact, only partially so. Nearly all the duties were 15 per cent or less, and the disparity between our people and those of Europe in capital, skill, and other resources was too great to be overcome by so slight a barrier. When the war of 1812 began, it was seen that a more radical protective policy was necessary, and all duties were doubled with the twofold purpose of increasing the revenue and of stimulating manufactures. The effect of this legislation was instantaneous. Every existing enterprise in the country was quickened into new life, and many new industries were created. In 1816, shortly after the close of the war, duties were again lowered, and as a result, British manufacturers held almost complete possession of our markets from that time till the enactment of the tariff of 1824. The tariff of 1824 was the first thoroughly protective tariff act passed by Congress in time of peace. In 1828 the duties were still farther increased, and a wonderful impetus given to the industry of the whole country. The marked result of this policy was to advance the textile fabrics in number and finish, laying the foundation of cloth printing, and as a consequence, greatly extending the domestic market for raw cotton. The stimulating effects of these measures, so far as they affected Fall River, are seen in the number and variety of enterprises started during those ten years, from 1820 to 1830. Before the introduction of calico printing, the industry in the United States was considered to be in such a precarious condition, that no one would venture on the production of the finer fabrics, and not until the making of dress and other colored goods was the manufacture of cotton placed upon a permanent basis.

Andrew Robeson, of New Bedford, was the pioneer of calico printing in Fall River. Related by marriage to the Rodmans, when they came to organize the Pocasset Company, he soon after made his advent in the place. His father had several large flour mills at Germantown, Penn., which were operated under the son's direction before he came North, and hence he was often designated as the "old millwright." He was a tall, robust man, with a large, powerful frame, black hair, quick movement, and withal an ardent lover of the horse. Retaining his domicile in New Bedford, it was his daily custom to drive over to his business avocations, making the journey of fourteen miles upon a notoriously heavy road, frequently in a fraction over an hour. Upon one occasion, hearing that his factory was on fire, he forced the speed of his favorite roadster to its extreme achievement, and reached the scene of conflagration in an hour, but the good horse fell dead in his tracks at the end of his route. Mr. Robeson's extraordinary physical power likewise found occasional illustrations, his best display of it, the piling of three barrels of flour perpendicularly one upon the other, being still a remembered feat.

Without previous experience, Mr. Robeson entered upon the business of calico printing, then in its infancy in this country, with all the interest, pluck, and enterprise of an ardent temperament. His first efforts, with the assistance of imported help, English and Scotch, was in the direction of simple colors, as blue and white; afterwards block printing came into vogue, and the number of colors was increased to four, six, and seven. His progressive spirit manifested itself in numerous experiments in his works, and naturally any improvements or new results acquired would quickly be subjected to a trial in his establishment. He thus kept abreast with the spirit of the age in which he lived, and his business rapidly enlarged and became very remunerative—in no long time outgrowing the limits of his first shop in the north end of the old Satinet Mill. In 1826 he purchased the land and water-power now occupied by the Fall River Print Works, and proceeded immediately to the erection of the necessary buildings. These in turn were increased in number as from time to time the business required, and in 1836 the last and largest of all was built. The factories of Mr. Robeson always attracted attention from their clean, neat appearance, occasioned by the peculiar finish of the exterior walls—a rough coat of blue mortar. Mr. Robeson hired the workmen from Pennsylvania to construct his first mill in this style, and it proved a great novelty in this section of the country.

Probably the first printing machine in the United States was constructed in Mr. Robeson's works. It was the joint production of Mr. Ezra Marble, who came to Fall River, from Somerset, in 1824, and, at the age of seventeen, went to work in the blacksmith shop of the printery, and a Frenchman also employed in the shop. The latter having seen a printing machine in France, imparted the idea to Marble, and, combining their efforts, the two were successful in putting together a machine which was set up in

1827 in the printery, and, after a few alterations and a continued practice in running it, was operated successfully for many years.

The works were known as the Fall River Print Works, and later two sons of the founder, William R. and Andrew, Jr., were associated in the firm of Andrew Robeson & Sons, which operated them. Copper rollers were introduced in 1832, and yard-wide rollers in 1837, seven eighths having been in use previously. The services of Alvin Clark, subsequently distinguished as an optician and the manufacturer of the largest and finest astronomical instruments in America, were secured, and by him acids were first introduced in the preparation of the colors. Block printing continued till 1841, the works containing some one hundred tables at that date, when, in consequence of a strike, machine printing was adopted and pursued so long as the works were run as a printery. During the panic of 1837, a large stock of goods accumulated, which were sold to great advantage when the market again opened. One of the greatest obstacles to be overcome in the early days of print works was to get the cloth properly dried. The process of machine drying had not then been commenced, and large dry-sheds were erected in which the cloth could be exposed to atmospheric influences. A succession of damp days would make a short supply of cloth, and the works would occasionally have to shut down in consequence. The great and continued success attending this business gave the firm of Andrew Robeson & Sons a name and reputation abroad which insured an unlimited credit, and they were induced to engage in kindred enterprises in a number of other cities.

The depression of 1848 found them with a business very extended and with a large stock of goods on hand, and as a result, the impossibility of gathering up the scattered ends quickly enough caused their suspension. In this calamity the firm had the sympathy of the whole community. They immediately made over their whole property to their assignees and creditors; the help in the mills were paid in full, and such a division of the balance made as realized in many cases even more than the original debt. Mr. Robeson had ever the full confidence of those associated with or under him. In the interests of his operatives, he established a school at his own expense, and constantly had their best welfare at heart. Quick to see opportunities for improvement, he made a number of important suggestions which largely contributed to the development of the place, and the advancement of its special industry. The fear of bringing greater disaster and loss upon the community was one of the main causes which led to the suspension of the firm, and as business subsequently turned, if they had continued a while longer they would have successfully overcome their difficulties and have gone on to even greater prosperity.

The Fall River Print Works was soon organized as a corporation, and the printing continued with two modern machines, and one (the first ever built in America) as a reserve; a specialty was made of Indigo Blues, and but little attempted in other styles. In 1858-64 cotton machinery was introduced, the printing machines from time to time removed, and finally the works converted into a cotton factory for the manufacture of print cloths.

The old Satinet Factory, which was demolished soon after the "Great Fire," occupied a portion of the site of the present Pocasset Mill, the south end abutting on Pocasset street, and the north end extending about half-way between the stream and Central street. It was built of heavy granite blocks, and was three stories high on the east side, and four or five on the west, according to the formation of the land.

The manufacture of woollen cloth into a fabric known as Satinet, made with a cotton warp and wool filling, was commenced in this mill in 1825. The business was carried on by Samuel Shove and John and Jesse Eddy, under the firm name of Samuel Shove & Co. The firm was dissolved in 1834 by the withdrawal of Samuel Shove, and the business passed into the hands of the remaining partners under the firm name of J. & J. Eddy.

About two thirds of the mill was occupied as the Satinet Factory and the remainder by Hawes & Marvel, the lower story as a machine shop, and the upper in the manufacture of cotton warp for J. & J. Eddy. It was in a portion of this building that Andrew Robeson first commenced the manufacture of calicoes, removing to his own mill about the year 1827.

The looms were in the third story, the lathes swinging laterally, and the vibration or oscillation of the building in the upper story was some four inches or more, alarming the help at one time so that all left the building in a panic. They soon returned, however, and after that very little attention was paid to the matter, though at times barrels of water in the attic would spill over, if the water was within six or eight inches of the top.

In the management of the business John Eddy was the manufacturer, and Jesse the buyer and seller. The last-named member of the firm was obliged to travel all over New England and some portions of the West for the purchase of the necessary supply of wool; his business also demanding a weekly trip to Boston, which was accomplished in his own private carriage, there being no public conveyance. It was his custom to go the whole distance of fifty miles on one day, returning the next, and on several occasions when dispatch was required, the trip both ways occupied but a single day,—of course a relay of horses being previously provided for.

In the times referred to (1825-35), the younger operatives in the several manufacturing establishments were divided into three classes. The first, and the largest numerically, was popularly denominated "Cotton Bugs," from the particles of that staple adhering to them, and the second "Blue Niggers," from the peculiar blue tint given to their unwashed faces by an admixture of dye-stuffs and oil incident to their employment. The employés in the calico works, comprising the third class, were without any distinguishing title, though perhaps occasionally called "Calico Boys," when a particular term was needed. The relation to each other of these distinct classes was not widely dissimilar to that existing between different tribes of Indians, amicable at times, and at others directly the opposite, according to circumstances, which were dependent upon the seasons of the year and the presence or absence of snow. The principal antagonism was between the "Cotton Bugs" and "Blue Niggers," the "Calico Boys" occupying a neutral position, ready to take sides with either party, as occasion might dictate.

The winter campaign generally opened with the first snow-fall of sufficient depth to allow of making a snow-ball, commencing with a sort of desultory warfare or skirmishing, and finally developing into regular pitched battles. At first only the boys engaged in these contests; but as the season drew towards the close, armies of adults, the card-strippers, mule-spinners, jack-spinners, ropers, and even overseers, became interested and took a hand. These scenes were re-enacted with variations winter after winter, until the friendly rains of spring melted the snow and the animosities of the belligerents at the same time.

The proprietors of the Satinet Factory were remarkable for their affiliation with their help, with whom they were ever on terms of easy intimacy, always seeming to regard them as their equals in the social scale.

In the long Saturday evenings of the winter months many were the gatherings around the old stove in the finishing-room, when the Messrs. Eddy were present and joined with their work-people in discussing the topics of the day. To this encouragement and kind companionship on the part of the principals is attributable, perhaps, the fact that so many of the employés have risen in subsequent years to honorable positions in life.

The production of Eddy's satinets was largely increased from year to year, and they became well known in all the principal markets as the best goods of that style of fabric. In 1843, however, the satinet manufacture was discontinued, and a fabric of all wool, called "Cassimere," was commenced. It was made in various shades of mixtures, and in stripe and plaid effects, and almost entirely superseded the use of satinets for the best trade. Two years later, in consequence of the demolition of the old Satinet Factory, to make way for the larger Pocasset Mill for the manufacture of cotton goods, the business was removed to a place known as "Eagle Mill," situated about three and a half miles south of Fall River, in the town of Tiverton, R. I.

Shortly after, the firm of J. & J. Eddy was dissolved, but the business continued in the above locality for a few years, until the property was destroyed by fire.

In the mean time Jesse Eddy, in connection with Joseph Durfee, bought and located a mill on a tract of land just above the dam, and near the outlet of the pond known as "Mosquito Island," designing to manufacture the same kind of goods produced by J. & J. Eddy. But, as they were about ready to commence operations, Joseph Durfee died, and it was not until January, 1849, that manufacturing was begun in the new mill. Jesse Eddy became the proprietor, and shortly after took his son, Thomas F., into partnership, under the firm name of Jesse Eddy & Son, by whom the business was conducted for twenty-one years.

In 1873, upon the decease of the father, the business passed into the hands of his two sons, Thomas F. and James C., who still continue the manufacture under the name of Jesse Eddy's Sons.

Jesse Eddy was born in Northbridge, in 1801. While yet a young man he engaged in manufacturing at Woonsocket, R. I. Remaining but a brief period at Woonsocket, however, he moved to Fall River, where he permanently established himself in the business pursuits detailed in the foregoing pages.

Mr. Eddy, though singularly unpretentious in his personal nature, was one of the best known citizens of Fall River. A man of generous sympathies, his kindly, genial bearing won the friendship of all who came in contact with him. His sterling character as a citizen and thorough integrity in his relations to the public were recognized by several positions of large responsibility. As early as 1828, he was chosen one of the original Trustees of the Fall River Savings Bank, and for many years was vice-president of that institution and chairman of its Board of Investment. At a later period his sound judgment in financial matters was distinguished by his election as President of the National Union Bank.

Mr. Eddy's exceptional kindliness of nature, as developed in a constant regard for the welfare of his employés, has been remarked in its proper connection. He was a consistent, practical Christian in his action—one of the too rare exemplifications of the truth that

"He prayeth best who loveth best
All things, both great and small;"

and the highest tribute of society at his decease was a universal regret for the ending of a life, unobtrusive and unselfish, full of good and gentle deeds.

The manufacture of cotton goods having been brought to some degree of perfection, the larger manufacturers began to look about them for a market for their production, and finding a growing demand for calico prints, many of them started small works of their own, which subsequently grew into concerns with a national reputation. Thus the Spragues, Allens, Dunnells and others had their own printeries, and the success of these establishments doubtless suggested to the Fall River manufacturers that something of the kind might be attempted here. Such an enterprise was just suited to the temperament of Holder Borden, who had by this time got his Massasoit Mill into perfect running order, and whose restless disposition could not brook inactivity while other avenues of business were opening before him. Accordingly, a joint-stock company was formed in 1834, and the American Print Works started under the agency and principal management of Mr. Borden.

Holder Borden was born June 17, 1799, and at the age of eighteen or nineteen entered the service of David Anthony, who was then running the Fall River Manufactory. He remained with him perhaps a couple of years, when he removed to Pawtucket, and was at first clerk for the Wilkinsons, large cotton manufacturers, but soon after was made agent of the Blackstone Company, owned by Brown & Ives. Here his independent, self-reliant character speedily manifested itself, for having been instructed to invest, as he saw fit, quite a large sum of money belonging to the company, but then lying idle, he proceeded at once to buy up all the cotton he could find for sale, and the amount was so large that he shortly found the whole market in his own hands,—in fact, that he had made a "corner in cotton." The company was at first astonished, then frightened ; it was wholly unprecedented that an agent should buy and sell of his own motion without consultation with his principals. Holder Borden, however, was equal to the emergency ; he offered to make the purchase his own, which was accepted, and in the end actually sold a portion of it back to the company at an advance, realizing a very handsome percentage on the whole transaction. The boldness of the operation, requiring, as it did, great nerve and confidence, as well sagacity, illustrated perfectly the character of the man as it manifested itself throughout his brief but brilliant career. He was a thorough business man, a merchant as well as a manufacturer, knew how to buy and how to sell, varied his productions to suit the market, gave up old methods when new ones were better, and so kept fully up to, if not a little ahead of the spirit of his time.

In 1827, the Massasoit Mill was erected on the stream and leased for fifteen years by Brown, Ives & Borden, and filled with machinery for the manufacture of cotton goods at a probable investment of $100,000. When, some years later, on account of trouble with low water, Brown & Ives wished to move out the machinery to Lonsdale, Holder Borden, being too much of a Fall River man to permit such a change, bought out their interest and operated the mill on his own account. He subsequently became interested as an owner in the Troy Cotton and Woolen Manufacturing Company, the Annawan Mill, the Fall River Manufactory, Fall River Iron Works, etc., and later became agent of the print works at the Globe. This, however, continued but a year, when he became the prime mover and active manager in the organization of the American Print Works.

This enterprise he pushed forward with characteristic energy. Having matured his plans, he proceeded one morning below the hill, took all the teams and men he could find, staked out the foundation alongshore, set the men to work, and drove off to Providence to attend to his other duties as agent of the Blackstone Company. Such was the style of the man, constantly scheming and planning something new, keeping his counsels to himself until ready for action, then pushing on vigorously to the completion of his project. Not much of a talker, rather slow and deliberate in his speech, he had little patience with discursive remark in others, especially at board or committee meetings, and always demanded close attention to the subject in hand. In person he was tall and slim, in complexion dark, and, contrary to the usual custom, allowed his beard to grow for the protection of his throat. In his dress and personal appointments he was extremely careful: he walked with his head inclined slightly forward. He was a great smoker, and a lover of a good horse—a necessity to him in his frequent journeys to and from Providence. Although so full of business, he was as attentive to details as to larger matters, and being somewhat of a nervous disposition, any inattention or inaccuracy in little things was sure to excite his comments, and call forth his displeasure. He possessed the happy faculty of impressing others with his own views and aims, and in consequence was naturally a leader among leaders. Rarely has one so young in years as Holder Borden attained such prominence in a community and held it so securely during his entire career. Rarely has so successful and so brilliant a business life been compassed by fifteen years, especially when those are the first and early years of manhood. Rarely does one from the start combine those three elements of assured success, "bold energy," "untiring industry," and "unbending integrity."

The throat difficulty with which he had been troubled several years developed finally into that insidious New England disease—consumption. It ran its course rapidly, causing his death September 12, 1837, at the comparatively early age of thirty-eight years.

The American Print Works, which is perhaps the most prominent legacy of Holder Borden to the business world, was started up in January, 1835, running four machines, with an average production of 2000 to 2500 pieces of prints per week. One half to two thirds of this quantity had a portion of the colors blocked in. The Works continued under the management of Holder Borden till February, 1837, when, in consequence of ill-health, he resigned, and Jefferson Borden was elected agent and principal manager. This management continued till February, 1876, a period of thirty-nine years, when Thomas J. Borden was elected to the position.

This company stands pre-eminent among all the calico-printing establishments of the country for the persistent energy of its management, the skilful adaptation of means to ends, its indomitable perseverance in the face of the heaviest misfortunes and losses, and the appreciation of its efforts by the public in the patronage received. Starting out, mainly as an experiment, adjunct to the manufacture of print cloths, this corporation has gone directly ahead on its own judgment, and won a place among the permanent institutions of the city and country.

In 1840, the Works were enlarged, a new machine building, dye-house, etc., being added, and the production of prints about doubled. In 1857, the company obtained a charter of incorporation, when Colonel Richard Borden was elected President, and so continued till his death, in February, 1874. In 1858, the Bay State Print Works, then under the management of Thomas J. Borden, was purchased by the American Print Works, and became a part of the same corporation. By this arrangement, both establishments were continued under the management of Jefferson Borden, and the capacity for production largely increased.

In 1867, a portion of the buildings of the American Print Works were taken off, and a new structure of Fall River granite was commenced, but on the 15th day of December of the same year, when the new building was just about completed, and in appearance much like the present magnificent structure, a fire broke out in one of the old buildings, which, notwithstanding the untiring efforts of the firemen, destroyed the whole new part of the establishment, with about half of the old, and their contents. This fire was preceded, on the 6th of the same month, by a fire at the Bay State Works, which laid in ashes the boiler-house and machine-room buildings of that establishment, with most of the machinery and a small portion of the goods.

It was a terrible blow, involving, in the destruction of property and the disruption of business interests, an estimated loss of two million dollars, half of which went down with the buildings. Great sympathy was expressed in all business circles with the sufferers, and capitalists abroad proffered their aid in loans to the company.

But the old heroic spirit that had controlled and organized the former concern, did not quail before this unlooked-for disaster, and courteously thanking their friends for their proffered aid, the company proceeded to reconstruct the whole affair on a broader foundation. Notwithstanding the total unexpectedness of the disaster, coming as it did on the very day before occupancy, three hundred workmen were on the premises, clearing away the rubbish and preparing the ground for rebuilding, by ten o'clock the next morning. Few instances of similar energy are on record. In one year and four months from the date of the conflagration, the remains of the old buildings were removed, a new foundation laid, and the present building erected and filled with machinery. The amount of labor performed in this interval can hardly be over-estimated, and the energy shown by the agent, Jefferson Borden, in accomplishing so great a work in so short a time, has been rarely, if ever, paralleled in the history of manufactures.

The main building is a handsome, massive granite structure, upon Water street, near the wharf of the Old Colony Steamboat Company, and, including basement and Mansard roof, is five stories high. It is 60 feet in depth, and presents a front of 406 feet on Water street, broken only by a finely proportioned tower, some 110 feet in height, furnished with a large bell, and one of Howard & Co.'s celebrated tower clocks, with four eight-feet dials. In this tower is the main entrance. The front is principally built of beautiful ashlar work. The first story has a succession of large arched windows, separated by a single hammered granite pillar, with cap and base, and attracting the eye by their graceful proportions.

Within the main room on the lower floor is space for twenty printing machines. These machines are of a capacity to print about eighty million yards of calico per annum, and to keep them in operation requires the united skill of a whole corps of draftsmen and color mixers. Reckoning all the force employed about the establishment, in all departments, the number is nearly or quite a thousand persons, with a monthly pay-roll of about $30,000. To drive the machinery for this work are used one thirty-four-inch engine, four and one half feet stroke; one thirty-inch, six feet stroke; one sixteen-inch, four feet stroke; two nine-inch and two six-inch engines, and one brass turbine water-wheel. To furnish steam for their impulsion, fifty-eight boilers are constantly available.

The main building is flanked on the west by four Ls, all built of granite, with substantial finish, and each separated from the main building by division walls extending above the roof. The north wing and shed is 310 feet by 80 feet, five stories; the second, 68 by 40 feet, three stories; the third, 195 by 57 feet, three stories; the fourth, 173 by 41 feet, and five stories high. The length of these added to that of the main building is 1152 feet, the whole appearing as solid and substantial as a fortress. In addition, there is one boiler-house, 100 by 50 feet, three stories, and another 195 by 55 feet, two stories; one engine-house, 50 by 30 feet, and two stories; one dye-house, 100 by 50 feet, two stories; a carpenter-shop and blue-dye house, 267 by 43 feet, and two stories; a shell-house, 90 by 34 feet, and two stories; a chemical shop, 63 by 45 feet, one story; and a pump room, 38 by 16 feet, and two stories high. The total length of these subordinate structures, 903 feet, added to the aggregate of the main printery, with its Ls, gives the enormous extent of 2055 feet of solid stone masonry, and probably no similar establishment in America can show so extended a frontage.

The different floors of the main building are fitted up for the various operations in printing and dyeing. Four elevators are in constant use. The arrangements for guarding against fire are as complete as they can be made, consisting of two Worthington's duplex steam pumps of the largest size, two rotary fire pumps, also the largest size, and one force pump attached to the water-wheel. Sixty-eight hydrants are distributed about the premises, so that in case of a fire as many as one hundred and thirty-nine streams of water can be made to play upon the buildings at once. Bracket balconies (double width), or fire-escapes, are attached to each story, two sets being on the main building and one on each of the Ls, while all communications between the buildings of the new part have double doors, one of which is iron. The area of the works is 816¼ square rods of land. Two additional buildings, on the opposite side of the street, will be soon connected with the main structure by means of a tunnelled way under the thoroughfare. They are substantial brick erections, one 156 feet by 50, and three stories in elevation; the other 156 by 92, and two stories. The former will be occupied for offices, designing-rooms and storage, the latter for shearing, folding and packing rooms.

The building of the American Print Works is one of the finest devoted to the printing business in the country, if not in the world, and attracts the attention of all strangers as they enter the city by steamboat or railway. It requires no less than *six* large mills to supply its printing machines with cloth. Its ample rooms are furnished with modern appliances of science and skill in each department, and the productions of this company are to be found in all sections of the country from the Atlantic to the Pacific.

The great improvements made during the last few years in the texture, style, and coloring of calicoes, or, as they are now better known in the dry-goods market, "American Prints," are due to the enterprise, and in some measure to the business competition, of leading manufacturers, who have brought to bear upon their production every appliance which the progress of art and science has placed within their reach. The best designers in the Old as well as in the New World have been sought out and kept constantly employed in producing new and pleasing effects. The most skilful dyers and printers have also been pressed into the service, while the substitution of aniline and alizarine colors for the old madder process of dyeing has given a variety of delicate shades and a perfection and finish to the work never before attained. At the same time, the cost of these goods has been kept down to a point which places them within the reach of all classes. The result of this enterprise and improvement is seen in an enormous and steadily increasing consumption, and, especially in days of popular economy, in a large substitution of prints for the more costly descriptions of dress goods. But there is no class of goods in which the caprices of fashion are so arbitrary and exacting.

The skill and resources of the manufacturers are continually taxed for the production of novelties in coloring and design, and such is the demand of this nature, that no printing company can now hope to be successful unless it is prepared to observe these caprices of popular taste, by changing its styles at least twice a year, and to bring out just so many fresh and attractive lines of fancies every spring and fall at the opening of the season. The magnitude of the work involved in this continual change can be imagined when it is stated that a single printing company has put on the market two thousand different patterns (each with several combinations of coloring) during one year. This constant versatility of production is an absolute law of trade, which must be obeyed.

But there are cycles in these fashions, and a style of print which goes out one year comes in again as new after the lapse of three, four, or perhaps half a dozen years. Some styles run out in a single season, while others last through several. Hence the necessity of great caution in not producing any surplus to be carried over, since goods that are a little out of style have to be forced off, generally at a sacrifice. No specialty, unless of rare merit, can be made to run over two seasons, while any striking innovation, such as the Dolly Varden and Centennial prints, has usually but a very brief existence. Bright colors are the rage for a season, then only the subdued or dead shades are wanted. The styles have also to be adapted to the different sections of the country where they are sold, as, for instance, the production of "Quaker" prints for the Pennsylvania market, which is quite an important specialty. Of necessity, therefore, the productions of a printery have to be of an almost infinite variety, from the most tasty *percale* to the indigo print, which still holds its place in domestic use.

The Bay State Print Works, the smaller of the two belonging to the American Print Works Company, is situated at Globe Village, upon a stream which issues from Laurel Lake and empties into Mount Hope Bay, and which has been utilized for manufacturing purposes for more than sixty years. It is really the outgrowth of the first cotton-mill built in this vicinity, which, after passing through several hands subsequent to Colonel Jos. Durfee's control, was purchased by Potter & Chatburn in 1829, and converted into a print works. Its first goods were printed in September, 1830. Since that date it has been enlarged from time to time, and with varying degrees of success been run in 1833-34 by Holder Borden, in 1835-39 as Tiverton Print Works, 1839-42 by Walter C. Durfee, agent, 1843-44 by Prentiss & Marvel, 1845-53 by W. & G. Chapin, 1853-58 as Bay State Print Works, until finally purchased by the American Print Works Company, and run in connection with their larger establishment at Fall River. It employs 250 hands, has five printing machines, and turns out twenty million yards of printed calico annually. Its engine is a thirty-inch cylinder, six feet stroke, and requires thirteen boilers for the generation of sufficient steam for the works. On the 6th of that same December, 1867, which witnessed the entire destruction by fire of the main works at Fall River, a terrible explosion occurred in the boiler-room of the Bay State Print Works. The boiler-house, containing several boilers, was burst into fragments; the side and roof of the dye-house were completely destroyed, and the building immediately enveloped in flames. Much damage was done to the other buildings in the vicinity, but, as few of the workmen had arrived, no serious injuries were inflicted upon the help. This calamity threw one hundred and fifty persons out of employment, and caused a loss of $100,000, partially covered by insurance. The energy of the company was conspicuous, also, in recovering from this disaster. In three months from the date of the explosion the works were entirely repaired, the machinery refitted, and the whole in successful operation.

Mr. Jefferson Borden,—through whose great energy and intensely hopeful spirit the devastating effects of the fire were so speedily removed, even from the vision of the neighborhood, and the Print Works again set in operation, the oldest living person of the residents of Fall River who have been identified with the inception, growth, and the present established supremacy of its distinctive industry,—was born on the 28th of February, 1801, in the then village of Freetown. He was one of thirteen children of Thomas Borden, in the fourth generation from John Borden the founder of the family in Fall River. His father's farm was situated in the east part of the village, comprising a tract upon which have since been erected the Richard Borden, Chace, and other mills. Jefferson worked on the farm, going to school regularly as the local season commenced, until September, 1816, when, in his sixteenth year, he left home for the first time, and obtained a position as clerk in the provision store of William Valentine, in Providence. In 1819 he returned to Fall River, thoroughly educated in the routine details of a business of trade and barter, but already entertaining the ambitious vision of a commercial career that would recognize no limits of its operations. His brother Richard, six years his senior, was running the craft Irene and Betsey in trading trips, in connection with his grist-mill, located on the lower stream. For the ensuing year Jefferson, when not absolutely needed on the farm, joined Richard in the sloop expeditions to Conanicut and Prudence. In 1820 the two brothers bought out the small store of Holder Borden, and Jefferson was put in to conduct the business. In 1821, upon the organization of the Iron Works enterprise, he was chosen clerk of the establishment. He retained this position till September of the following year, when the company opening a warehouse and salesroom in Providence, the business experience and proclivities he had already demonstrated pointed him out as the most eligible representative of the growing industry. Mr. Borden was a few months over his majority when he undertook the office of agent of the company at Providence; but the shrewd, sagacious promoters of the Iron Works knew they had chosen the right man for the place. The event amply proved the correctness of their judgment, the agent's wise, systematic control really directing the home production of the company, while his keen perception and clever manipulation of the market constantly extended the field of its operations throughout the Union.

For fifteen years Jefferson Borden remained at his place in Providence. In 1837 the ill health of his cousin Holder made a vacancy in the management of the American Print Works, and he was recalled to Fall River.

For thirty-nine years Mr. Borden was the executive officer and managing agent of the Print Works, retiring from active control only during the spring of the present year. He assumed the position at a period which will not be forgotten in our financial annals as the extreme test of industrial and commercial endurance. No panic has been more severe and no depression of business more general than that of 1837, and its distressing stringency upon all elements of recuperative life was greater than it could ever again be, in the degree that all industry and enterprise was comparatively immature, the country itself lacking the great elasticity it now possesses in the wonderful development of its natural and productive resources. To undertake the work of carrying a great establishment successfully through such a period of embarrassment on every hand, was a terrible trial of a business man's best powers; and it is undoubtedly safe to say, that when an all-wise Providence removed Holder Borden, the projector and worker, from the control and direction of the enterprise, the only person thoroughly fitted for the exigency by experience and managing power, and probably superior to Holder in his approved financial ability and estimation among capitalists, was wisely and fortunately chosen.

Upon the destruction of the American Print Works by fire in 1867, Mr. Borden's extraordinary capacity for recuperation and support through a most trying period, was again in forced requisition. The rapid restoration of the establishment in all its operative powers has already been remarked. The eyes of all were able to observe with startled wonder the immediate re-erection of the great structure, the spacious rectangle of solid granite going up almost like the Khan's palace in Coleridge's phantasy, and the huge engines and machines reassuming their old places with a concurrent promptness; yet few appreciated or even guessed that greater difficulties than these mere material matters, difficulties calling for rare credit and unquestioned responsibility, had been met and overcome.

Since his return to Fall River, Jefferson Borden has been largely concerned in the various enterprises that have marked the progress of the city. A partner of the deceased Colonel Richard in the important special undertakings of his later years, he was with him interested in the old Bay State Steamboat Company (of which he at one time owned three fifths of the stock), the Fall River Railroad Company, the Borden Mining Company, and other extensive operations.

Mr. Borden's retirement from immediate connection with active business has not severed his close relation to the earnest life and progress of his native city. He is still President of the American Print Works; the Fall River Iron Works Company; the Fall River Bleachery; the American Linen Company; the Troy Cotton and Woollen Company, and the Borden Mining Company; Director of the Annawan Manufacturing Company; President of the Metacomet National Bank, and officially concerned in other business organizations. His long life, full from the start of honest purpose, intense application, and constantly hopeful energy, claims for him at last exemption from the cares of business routine, and Providence has yielded to its declining years the blessings such careers worthily demand, competence, the serene joy of a beautiful home, and the affectionate esteem of the community.

Another of the great establishments of the city is the Fall River Iron Works, established in 1821. After Major Durfee had learned the shipbuilder's trade, in his sojourn at New Bedford, he returned to Fall River, and, in conjunction with Colonel Richard Borden, then a young man running a grist-mill near the foot of the stream, engaged in the construction of a number of small vessels at the mouth of the creek. After completing the labors of the day, the two would spend a good part of the night in a blacksmith's shop near by, executing the necessary iron work, or the Colonel with his brother John would be up betimes in the morning, and over to Copicut or down to Hellburn Woods to get out timber, knees, braces, etc., which the Major and his assistants would work up during the day. Working along in this way for a few years, the field and facilities for a larger business soon developed themselves, especially in the working up of iron into spikes, bars, rods, and other articles of constructive use.

The result of this exceedingly small and adventitious beginning, while quite in the nature of Fall River successes, is also thoroughly characteristic of the men whose correct perception, rich suggestiveness, and indomitable energy builded the substantial prosperity of the city. The Fall River Iron Works Company, as one of the most remunerative properties of the kind in the United States, is an existing and perfectly logical and reasonable fact, representing a moderately appraised value in stock and property of $1,500,000; but the original premises of this practical argument were a miller and a ship carpenter, and a business of sloop-building.

The financial basis upon which the Fall River Iron Works was started,— Richard Borden and Bradford Durfee being the two promoters, but associating with themselves Holder Borden, David Anthony, and William Valentine, Joseph Butler and Abram and Isaac Wilkinson, of Providence,—was $24,000. Soon after its commencement of operations, the two Wilkinsons desiring to draw out their contribution, $6000 was returned them, reducing the working amount to $18,000. In 1825 the association became a corporation under the law of Massachusetts. Its capital at this time was $200,000, which in 1845 was increased to $960,000; but all of this last aggregate, with over $500,000 more employed in the works of the company and other constantly remunerative enterprises, has accumulated from the earnings, not one dollar having been added by subscription or otherwise to the net $18,000 originally invested.

Farther on may be discovered occasional suggestions of the circumstances that have aided a success so exceptional; yet it is safe here to say, that with a projection less energetic and sagacious, a control less wise and determined, and in a community less industrious and provident, no such success could ever have been achieved.

The first works of the Iron Company were erected on the ground now occupied by the Metacomet Mill, and the production, hoop-iron, sold to New Bedford trade for binding oil casks. Various sizes of bar-iron were also made, and the manufacture of nails commenced, for which two machines were set up. In those days, the heading of the best nails was done by hand, and was necessarily a rather slow process. When a sufficient quantity had been made, Colonel Borden would load up a sloop and sail to New York and up the Hudson until he effected a sale. The company's nails always ranked well in the market, and when, on one occasion, a few had been shipped as a venture to Mobile, their superiority to the Pittsburg nail, made of soft iron, was so marked, that a whole cargo was at once ordered, anticipating the product of some days' operation.

The business proving very profitable, the works were enlarged from time to time, other branches of production being added, until in 1840 the plant and business were moved to their present location near High Hill, so called, where, with the advantage of better organized buildings and more space, the possession of wharves and a water front is also secured.

The company has suffered twice by fire. On June 2d, 1843, the rolling-mill was entirely destroyed. The fire broke out at half-past one o'clock in the morning, and the whole establishment was in ruins in a very short time, but *before sunrise* lumber was being hauled from various yards and preparations were going on to rebuild it. The owners did not even wait for the fire to cool before the plan of reconstruction was adopted and measures taken to replace their losses. In six weeks from the date of the fire the mill was again in full operation. Such cool persistency always wins, and there is no occasion to wonder that success of the most pronounced type has followed the efforts of the company.

Again on the 11th of November, 1859, the rolling-mill was discovered to be on fire, and the flames obtained the mastery for a second time, completely destroying the building; but the same indomitable spirit met the misfortune as calmly as before; the mill was immediately rebuilt, and in a short time in active work.

The works are operated wholly by steam, employ 600 hands, and consume 40 tons of scrap and pig iron per day. The operations are carried on in three separate buildings—a rolling-mill, nail-mill, and foundry. Thirty-two thousand tons of iron are used annually in the production of nails, hoops, rods, castings, etc. There are 105 nail machines, the product of which is about 115,000 kegs of nails per annum. The monthly pay-roll averages $25,000.

When the Iron Works Company was first formed, it purchased for $10,000 the whole section of land lying along the shore to the south and west of the Creek, as far as Annawan street on the south, and east to Canal street, and the land south to Ferry street was also secured afterward. In the development of this property, Major Bradford Durfee took a prominent and leading part. Born in 1788, the earlier years of his manhood were spent in ship-building and kindred work. Up to 1821, about one vessel a year of from 20 to 75 tons burden was constructed, and the sloops Fall River, Golden Age, Reindeer, the schooners High Flyer, the Irene and Betsey, and others were launched and engaged in the coasting or West India trade. The superior abilities of Major Durfee as a manager and constructor in all mechanical departments here manifested themselves, and when the Iron Works Company was formed with its eight owners, Colonel Borden was chosen agent, and Major Durfee superintendent. The latter, then thirty-three years of age, entered upon the work with all the ardor of a young man in his prime, and was never so much in his element as when putting up mill buildings, arranging machinery, constructing wharves, or forwarding some kind of outdoor work. Thus the Iron Works wharves, the hammered stonework in the basement of the Annawan Mill, and the superstructure itself, the canal to the Print Works Pond, the dam, the new buildings and additions of the Iron Works, were all under his direction. When the steamboat line between Fall River and Providence was established, he took charge of that also, and regularly, without fail, was on the wharf at the arrival and departure of the boats. When the rolling-mill was destroyed by fire, Major Durfee was in the midst of the ruins while they were yet hot, and with men and oxen hauled out the lumber and material for rebuilding.

In 1838, in company with William C. Davol, he visited Europe, to examine the improved machinery in various departments of industry, more especially in cotton and iron manufacture, and as a result, brought out the Sharp & Roberts self-acting Mule, the first one of which was set up in the Annawan Mill, and lettered "Tippecanoe." It was the wonder of the town, and was visited and examined by the whole community. The good judgment of Major Durfee brought together the members of the firm of Hawes, Marvel & Davol —Mr. Hawes the shrewd financier, Mr. Marvel sagacious and practical, and Mr. Davol the skilful designer and inventor, an association of peculiar faculties, which has had no inconsiderable share in advancing the manufacturing interests of Fall River. They entered immediately upon the construction of the English mules, securing the castings from the Iron Works foundry, and finishing them in their own shops, and thus introduced a machine which largely reduced the cost of manufacturing, and increased the production manifold.

But this was not the only result of that visit. The travellers secured measurements and drawings for the "egg-shaped" furnace and boiler, by which steam for motive power is generated without the cost of extra fuel, and some of the original furnaces, constructed in this style, are in use to the present day. Other information was acquired, and applied practically, upon their return home, so that Fall River could hardly have sent forth two men to better

purpose, in securing practical results, than Major Durfee and William C. Davol.

Major Durfee was a large, finely-formed man, tall, with black hair, a face full, and generally considerably flushed—a peculiarity of the family—free, genial, and companionable in company, and affectionate and considerate at home. Being so much of an "outside man," he was well known by the whole village, and when, shortly after the "Great Fire" in 1843, he was suddenly prostrated by disease, brought on, as is supposed, by his great exertions in that terrible calamity, the sympathy of the whole community went out for him, and at his death, after only twenty-four hours of sickness, it was felt almost as if his place could not be filled.

But he who had so long been associated with Major Durfee in the management and development of the varied interests of the Iron Works Company, was ready to assume the double burden, and it fell to Colonel Richard Borden to carry forward, single and alone, the growing business of that large concern.

Colonel Borden, as he was always called, was born on the 12th of April, 1795. What is now Fall River was then a portion of the town of Freetown, and he was in his eighth year when Fall River was incorporated, in 1803. After the period of boyhood, his early years were spent as a farmer, and to the end of life he continued his interest in that honorable pursuit. But, step by step, he became identified with all the different leading business interests of the rapidly growing town, village, and city. He was early identified with the maritime interests of the place, and gave fresh impulse to the local shipping pursuit, when as yet it was but a rural village. While still a young man, he ran a grist-mill (1812–20), which stood just west of the present Annawan Mill, where the corn of the whole region was ground. In company with his brother Jefferson, it was his custom to go down to Prudence and Conanicut Islands, in the sloop Irene and Betsey, which carried about 250 bushels of corn, and having secured a load, to return to Fall River and tie up at a little wharf within the creek, and discharge directly into the mill. The Irene and Betsey was also a sort of packet between Fall River and the neighboring places, and the surplus meal was sold in Warren, Bristol, or Providence, and a return freight secured, of provisions, groceries, cotton, etc. Another mill was placed on the north bank of the creek, at the next fall above, where the Annawan Mill is now, and a tramway had been constructed from this mill (known as the Davenport Mill, but owned by Richard Borden, the uncle of Colonel Richard) to the shore, and a car run up and down this incline, drawn by a rope. This rope was wound on a drum, which connected by gearing with the water-wheel, and thus the water-power was made to do double service. The great strength of the Colonel was always a marvel to the small boys, sent on horseback with a grist to grind, it being his ordinary feat, after putting two or three two-bushel bags of meal on the horse with the greatest ease, to take the boy and lift him to his place on top of all. It was about this period he joined Major Durfee in the construction of several small vessels, the lumber for which was prepared in a saw-mill adjoining the gristmill. Here, too, the strength of the Colonel found development, as, singlehanded, he would roll into position great white oak or mahogany butts, two feet through, and twenty feet long.

In the organization of the Fall River Iron Works Company in 1821, that "earliest germ of the wealth of the city," Colonel Borden took an active part, and was appointed treasurer and agent, a position which he filled ably and satisfactorily up to the day of his final withdrawal from business, a period of over fifty years. The Iron Works Company meeting with assured success almost from the start, soon turned its attention to the improvement of its landed estate, water-power, etc., and as part owners became largely interested in enterprises somewhat foreign to its own legitimate sphere of work. The agent of the company as its representative thus became an active participant in all these schemes, and the business tact and skill of Colonel Borden were brought into fullest exercise. In this way, the Iron Works Company became owner in the Watuppa Reservoir Company, organized in 1826; in the Troy Cotton and Woollen Manufactory; in the Fall River Manufactory; in the Annawan Mill, built by it in 1825; in the American Print Works, whose buildings were all erected by the Iron Works Company in 1834, and leased to the Print Works Company; in the Metacomet Mill, built in 1846; in the Fall River Railroad, opened in 1846, in the Bay State Steamboat Line, established in 1847; in the Fall River Gas Works, built in 1847; as well as in the erection at various times of buildings which were leased to individuals for the establishment of business or private manufacturing enterprises.

The care and development of the interests of these corporations brought into exercise those qualities which mark the highest order of business talent, and which in him were combined to a remarkable degree, namely, clearness of perception, excellent judgment and great energy, together with the highest and purest moral integrity. Colonel Borden was a thorough business man, and devoted himself untiringly to the trusts imposed upon him. These were enough to crush any common man, but he possessed that happy faculty of dropping one subject completely and taking up another as occasion required; and when he left his office he left his business there, too, putting it off as an outer garment, so that in his home and in his family he was untrammelled and free from care, the loving father and grandparent, the genial host, the centre of the heart's warmest affections and highest esteem. It is not surprising, therefore, that he filled a most uncommon list of offices of trust in the community and in the State. In the cotton-manufacturing industries of the city he was conspicuously interested, being identified with several companies either as originator, or director. He was President and Director of the American Print Works, the American Linen Company, the Troy Cotton and Woollen Manufactory, the Richard Borden Mill Company and the Mount Hope Mill Company, and Director of the Annawan and the Metacomet Mill Companies. He was President and Director of the Fall River National Bank, Director and Treasurer of the Fall River Iron Works, President of the Watuppa Reservoir Company, Agent of the Fall River Furnace Company, and Director of the Fall River Gas Company. In corporations operating outside his own home, his interests were also large, and his administrative ability recognized. He was President of the Bay State Steamboat Company, Providence Tool Company, Cape Cod Railroad Company, the Borden Mining Company of Frostburg, Md., and Director in the Old Colony Railroad Company. One of those men whom office has to seek, though his patriotism and conspicuous public service in an individual capacity might easily have secured him any position his ambition could have aspired to in his native commonwealth, the legislative terms he filled both in the Senate and House of Representatives were probably the most ungrateful duties of a long life of duty, and yet while the highest political position possessed no exaltation to attract him, his genuine appreciation of a citizen's duty would not allow him to refuse the humble town or village dignity of assessor or highway surveyor, when his service seemed obviously needed. If there was one only public recognition of his patriotism and public worthiness, those who knew him can fancy he took pleasure in, it was doubtless the honor accorded to him by the people of casting one of the electoral votes of Massachusetts for the second time for Abraham Lincoln.

Colonel Borden's shipbuilding and boating experiences fitted him for further enterprise in the same line, and under the auspices of the Iron Works Company, a regular line of steamers was established between Fall River and Providence, commencing in 1827 with the steamer Hancock. Other steamers had previously attempted to establish communication between Fall River and the neighboring places, but with only partial success. The Hancock was succeeded in 1832 by the steamer King Philip, the King Philip succeeded in 1845 by the steamer Bradford Durfee, and in 1874 the steamer Richard Borden was also placed upon the route. The popular excursion steamer Canonicus is used as a spare boat, and to run during the summer months to Newport, Block Island, and Rocky Point.

One of the largest debts of gratitude which Fall River owes to Colonel Borden (and in this connection his brother, Jefferson Borden, still living and honored in his native city, will not be forgotten) is for the present admirable system of communication with New York and Boston. Up to 1846 there was no communication direct by steam with either city, though the traveller could, by going to Providence or Stonington, catch a train or a boat. At this time Colonel Borden projected, and mainly by his own effort constructed, a railroad from Fall River to Myrick's, to connect with the New Bedford and Taunton Railroad, and using the latter to join the Providence Railroad and complete the route by rail to Boston. This was an eccentric way of reaching the State capital, and the next advance was consequently made to South Braintree, striking the Old Colony Railroad of that day. A satisfactory through route was thus secured; but Colonel Borden, not satisfied yet, was ambitious not only to have the communication opened for his favorite city, but to make it self-sustaining. With this view he organized the Cape Cod Railroad Company, of which he was president, and constructed a line from Middleborough down to the Cape, as a feeder for his Fall River route. The care, administrative and executive ability, and the financial involvement—for he was not only the designer but the banker of the enterprise—were excessive demands to be made upon one man in that comparatively early day; but Colonel Borden's resources in all respects were equal to the exigency. It was his good fortune soon to see his railroad enterprise at least relatively a success. His purpose in freeing Fall River from its isolation was at any rate accomplished, and in a year or two he was relieved of his new responsibility by a consolidation of the roads he had constructed with the Old Colony.

In the mean time, being the second year (1847) of the Fall River Railroad, observing the success of the two steamboat lines running between Stonington and Norwich (Conn.) and New York, Colonel Borden determined to inaugurate a similar water communication for Fall River. His sole associate in this enterprise was his brother Jefferson. The capital appropriated was $300,000, and the line was started in 1847 with the Bay State, a fine craft for that day, built for the company, and the old Massachusetts chartered as an alternate boat. The following year the Empire State was launched and put on the route, and in 1854 the mammoth Metropolis, the most superb boat of her period on Eastern waters. Both of these boats were paid for out of the earnings of the line, which was indeed such a success as in 1850 to pay six per cent monthly dividends for ten successive months.

In 1864, dissatisfied with his connection with Boston *via* the Old Colony Railroad, Colonel Borden[*] obtained an act of organization and set about a second through route to Boston, starting from the west side of Mount Hope

[*] Jefferson also was prominent in this scheme at the start.

Bay, opposite Fall River. It was a great scheme, with a warranty of profitable result, through its control of the New York boat connection, but entailing great effort and care upon a man, however energetic and indefatigable, who was far advanced in life. Unquestionably the road would have been constructed, but the Old Colony corporation could not permit a competing route to either terminus, and its policy, as it could not prevent the action of the new company, was to control it by a purchase. The proposition was accordingly made to Colonel Borden to transfer his charter to the Old Colony Company, upon terms of a very favorable character to himself and his stockholders. Had he been in middle life, retaining the physical as he still did the mental vigor of maturity, it is doubtful if he would have entertained any proposition, however favorable. In his consideration of the business he determined to make it a condition of his acceptance that the Old Colony Railroad Company should purchase the steamboat line to New York. With this proviso, he made known his acquiescence in the proposition, and, after a short deliberation, the Old Colony became possessed of the most profitable water route to New York, and at the same time secured relief from the certainty of a very dangerous competition.

It is hardly necessary to add, that, with the exception of a short interval, during which the line was operated by the late James Fisk, the Old Colony Railroad Company has sustained it in a manner acceptable to the public and largely profitable to the region for which it furnishes an outlet and communication with the metropolis. The two immense steamers, Providence and Bristol, originally built to equip a projected route, whose eastern terminus was to be Bristol, R. I., but through a default in that enterprise, falling into the control of Fisk's company, have for some years been the summer boats of the Old Colony route, attracting by their extraordinary size and magnificent appointments altogether the greater part of the travel between New York and New England. The sister craft, the Old Colony and Newport, designed for winter navigation, are smaller boats, of exceptional strength and staunchness, but equally rich in all the appliances of comfort and luxury.

During the war of 1812, the young Richard Borden joined the local militia company as a private, and was promoted while yet in his minority. From this first promotion he rose, step by step, till he attained the rank of colonel, when he withdrew from the service that others might gain for themselves as noble or higher honors. His patriotism during our internecine war developed in a most active interest on behalf of the Union and an earnest care for the well-being of its defenders, will not be forgotten, while the beautiful monument and grounds of the soldiers' burial-place, given by him, at the entrance of Oak Grove Cemetery and the Richard Borden Post of the

Grand Army of the Republic, named in honor of his benevolence to the soldiers and their families in the trying days of the rebellion, remain to perpetuate his memory.

Personally, Richard Borden represented the best type of that pure, straightforward, stalwart Saxon virtue which has proven New England's best inheritance from the mother country. His sympathies were given to all good things; he was a man broad in his views, true and steadfast in his convictions and feelings. A sincere, outspoken Christian in early life, identifying himself with those observant of the Sabbath, the public services of the sanctuary and the requirements of the gospel, he became, in 1826, a member of the First Congregational Church of the city, and afterwards one of the leaders of the Central Congregational Church, which, to his energy, liberality, piety, and judicious counsel, is largely indebted for the success that has marked its subsequent history. In the mission Sabbath-school work he engaged with his characteristic energy, for a long time going seven miles out of the village for this purpose. His interest in this department of work continued so long as he lived. The benevolence of his nature flowed out as a deep and silent stream. He gave as to him had been given. None sought aid from him in vain, when they presented a worthy cause. He was always willing to listen to the appeal of the needy, and sent none such empty away. "Home and foreign charities alike found him ready, yea, often waiting to attend on their calls, and among our institutions of learning not a few are ready to rise up and call him blessed for the timely aid rendered in the hour of their greatest need. Thus he came to be looked upon as the foremost citizen of the place, and his death left a void in the community which no *one man* will probably ever fill again. Generous, noble-hearted, sagacious, enterprising, of untiring energy and spotless integrity, far-seeing, judicious, ever throwing his influence and his means on the right side, he presents a character for admiration and example, which is fragrant with all the best qualities of our New England life."

The cursory sketch of his business career which space has permitted will suggest the conspicuous qualities of Colonel Borden's mind and temperament, as the world saw them and events caused them to develop. It is doubtful, however, if any qualities of his can be termed more conspicuous than others, among those who really knew him, so well rounded was his nature. His achievements were many and great, a few of them extraordinary in view of his resources and experience, yet he did not possess one spark of the so-called genius, to which exceptional successes are generally ascribed. His brain was like his body, robust and full of forces; his mental process direct and simple; his faculties of perception and deduction more than the

average in quickness and correctness of action; his scope of observation and consideration general and yet effective. He had, moreover, a thorough self-reliance and self-assertion, yet was not over-sanguine. The possession of such a mental structure always assures excellence of judgment and consequent success, if combined with a suitable temperament, and such was the fact in the present instance. Colonel Borden's nerve was strong and undisturbed by sudden or severe trials. Exceedingly honest of purpose, he was wonderfully persistent when his judgment supported his efforts, never giving up when legitimate means and thorough industry could compass an end he had started for. His industry was his conspicuous quality—if he had one. He was an indefatigable worker while the day lasted.

Fall River, in every development of its thrifty daily life, its marvellous, yet substantial, progress; its financial stability in the storm that has shaken older communities; its constant advancement in the industrial arts; its conservation and harmony of industrial forces; its industrious, law-observing population, bears the impress of the Bordens, Durfees, Anthonys, and Davols, the sterling mark of honest artisans upon pure coin. As Samuel Smiles says of Josiah Wedgwood: "Men such as these are fairly entitled to take rank as the Industrial Heroes of the civilized world. Their patient self-reliance amidst trials and difficulties; their courage and perseverance in the pursuit of worthy objects are not less heroic of their kind than the bravery and devotion of the soldier and the sailor, whose duty and pride it is to heroically defend what these valiant leaders of industry have so heroically achieved."

From the panic of 1837, which affected every business centre in the country, Fall River seems to have speedily recovered, since within a few years from that date nearly every mill in the place was enlarged, though only one new one built. The lease of the old Massasoit Mill, started by Holder Borden, having nearly expired, a new mill, called also the Massasoit, was built in 1843 near the shore, and the machinery transferred thereto. This mill was better known locally as "the Doctor's Mill," because in later years it was largely owned and run by Dr. Nathan Durfee.

Dr. Durfee married the eldest sister of Holder Borden, whose widowed mother, a sister of Colonel Richard and Jefferson Borden, had previously married his cousin, Major Bradford Durfee. After the death of Holder Borden, Dr. Durfee became identified with the manufacturing interests of the town, which Holder Borden, Major Durfee, and Colonel Borden had so successfully started, though his personal attention was not much given to the details of management.

Dr. Durfee was born in Fall River, then Freetown, in 1799. He was a graduate (with his brother Thomas R.) of Brown University in 1824, they being the first college graduates from this town. He studied medicine and received the degree of M.D. at Harvard University, but the practice of the profession was not suited to his tastes, and he continued in it but a brief period of time. He opened a drug-store on what is now Central street, a little distance west of Main, erecting for this purpose the first brick building in the township. It was very small, but was then remarkable for its neatness and beauty, and its adaptedness to the use for which it was constructed. This he occupied until the erection of his brick dwelling-house on the corner of Bank and North Main streets, where the Mount Hope House now stands. The first story of this house he occupied for his store until he gave up the business, after a brief experience in it.

He soon discovered an interest in the growing industries of the place, and though not entering directly upon the management of any one business, was associated with others in the general direction of many new enterprises coincident with the progress of Fall River. In this way he became a director in the Fall River Iron Works, American Print Works, the old Fall River Railroad, and the Cape Cod Railroad; was one of the proprietors of the Bay State Steamboat Line; was largely interested in several of the banks, and, in later years, entered heartily into the new manufacturing projects of the city, and at his death was director in at least seven of the corporations and president of three. In earlier times, as a mercantile venture, he embarked in the whaling business, fitting out, in company with other persons, at this port, several vessels for the whale fishery, and establishing oil works. The venture did not prove very successful, however, and was finally abandoned. A more successful enterprise was a flour-mill, which did an extensive business for many years. As before stated, he was principal owner of the Massasoit Steam Mills, for the manufacture of print cloths, which were destroyed by fire in 1875.

Besides filling various municipal offices, Dr. Durfee was a Representative to the General Court for several years, and was always one of the most public-spirited of citizens. After the "Great Fire" he erected the Mount Hope Block for a public house, not as a profitable investment, but to give character and respectability to the then growing town. At the time of that great calamity, his mansion house, which had been erected that year, was thrown wide open for the reception and shelter of the suffering community, its spacious halls and drawing-rooms affording sleeping accommodations for eighty persons, whose homes had been destroyed.

Dr. Durfee was a large land proprietor, owning nearly one thousand acres, a portion of it valuable for real-estate purposes, in and about the city.

He was always more fond of agricultural pursuits than of the details of business. He took great pleasure in reclaiming swamp land, and bringing into a high state of cultivation, and consequent utility, rocky and almost valueless pastures. This taste closely identified him with the agricultural interests of the commonwealth. Besides being for some years the president of the Bristol County Agricultural Society, he was the originator and president for a long period of the Bristol County Central Society, and contributed liberally both of money and zeal to its advancement. He was a trustee of the State Agricultural College, and its treasurer until declining health necessitated his resignation. Kind-hearted and genial in his disposition, he was ever ready to help and encourage the unfortunate and despondent, the frequent losses sustained by him in his readiness to aid those seeking his assistance never chilling his sympathy or preventing his efficient action when again sought by any who needed a helping hand. His large charity of nature forgave and forgot hasty expressions of feeling, so frequent in active life, and closed his heart against harsh or bitter recollections of differences with his fellow-men. Dr. Durfee was always largely interested in the education of youth, and aided many institutions by his contributions. He was a strong advocate of the cause of temperance, and, during the active period of his life, was a public and efficient worker in it. His public spirit was conspicuously illustrated by his liberality to the city in opening streets and avenues through his property without charge, and ornamenting them with shade trees transplanted from his own grounds, under his personal supervision. His spacious lawns and greenhouses, which were kept in a high state of cultivation, were always open to the community, and in the season of fruits and flowers especially, affording gratification and delight to multitudes of people; and this gratification of others always gave him the greatest pleasure.

The moral and spiritual welfare of his native town and city was ever prominent in the mind of Dr. Durfee, who was one of the earliest projectors of the Sunday-school work, and instrumental in establishing several suburban mission schools. He was closely identified with the Central Congregational Church, being an original member and contributor of one quarter of the lot upon which the society's first house of worship was erected. Always one of its most active and efficient members, he took an especially deep interest in its development, and, with the late Colonel Richard Borden, furnished a large portion of the funds used in the construction of the new and elegant edifice erected in 1875, and considered one of the most perfect ecclesiastical structures in the country.

Dr. Durfee was made up on a large plan, not with a calm and even temperament; he was not destined to the treadmill of life, but rather to larger conceptions of things; to deal with wholes, and not with parts. While he received much by nature, and added to it by culture, he was not scholarly in minutiæ, but scholarly in general. His opinions were to be regarded as not open to question, but to be accepted as facts; such was the impression made by him upon instructors, preachers, and public men. His life was closely interwoven with all the life of the city, and while circumstances often mould life, it was his part to mould circumstances, not to float on the tide, but rather to seize opportunities and to use them to advantage. His talents were not hid in a napkin, they were put at usury; and in developing and advancing the interests of others he was blessed in his own. He died April 6th, 1876.

Up to 1846, the mills for cotton manufacture were all small, about 100 by 40 or 50 feet, and two or three stories high; but at that time the experience acquired by thirty years' practice led some of the manufacturers to believe that a larger mill could be worked more economically and to better advantage. The improvements in machinery also demanded a different arrangement from that heretofore adopted.

The Pocasset Company was the first to put this theory into practice by building the present Pocasset Mill, 219 feet by 75 feet, and five stories high. There were not wanting those who predicted a failure as the result of this innovation, but the man who had planned the mill was not one to lose heart because of adverse criticism. The mill rose story by story, and in the end fully justified the anticipations of its builders. To Stephen Davol, then superintendent of the Pocasset Company's mills, belongs the credit of first venturing on this improvement. From childhood he had been connected with cotton-mills, beginning with the Troy, where he rose through all the grades from doffer boy to agent (1842 to 1860), and whence he was called, when only twenty-six years of age, to the superintendency of the Pocasset Mill in 1833. By him were drawn all the plans for the erection and alteration of the mills of the company. Up to the building of this mill it had been customary to arrange the machinery floor by floor, introducing the belts or gearing, often at a disadvantage or at great expense, wherever required; but in this construction the plan of the whole interior was determined upon in advance, the sectional drawings made, and the best connections provided for. This fact becoming known, manufacturers from abroad came to inspect the drawings and satisfy themselves that what had before been regarded as an impossibility had really been accomplished. The skill and experience of Mr. Davol as a cotton manufacturer have been largely called upon in later years, as indicated by the fact of his election on no less than ten different boards of directors.

Stephen Davol is now one of the oldest, if not the very oldest, cotton manufacturers in New England, if we consider the number of years devoted exclusively to that pursuit. Born in November, 1807, he entered

the Troy Mill in 1818, standing at the foot of the ladder of which for years he has kept the highest round. His elder brothers were already doffer boys, and he cried because he could not likewise be earning money in the carding-room instead of going to school. His urgency finally prevailed with his father, who apprenticed him for three years, after a first trial of the cotton-mill, in the print works of Duncan, Wright & Co. The work there being irregular, one week on and two off, he was not satisfied with it, and returned, after a few months' trial of the printing business, to the Troy Manufactory, of which, as has been stated, he was eventually to be the chief executive officer.

In 1846, also, the Metacomet Mill was erected by the Iron Works Company, and filled with machinery. The plans of this mill were brought from England by Major Durfee and William C. Davol, and varied in a number of particulars from any in this country. The original mill, in Bolton, was the "model mill" of England at that time, and its production was the standard to determine the rating of all the cloth produced in the cotton-manufacturing districts. It was a wide mill, 75 feet, and had iron posts and girders. In all the old mills, timber alone had been used, and where these were exposed to moisture, they became soft, and the floors settled slightly, producing friction and a consequent loss of power. The new arrangement obviated this difficulty, and was seen to be an improvement at once. The mill started up smoothly from the first, turned out a good production, and made money for its owners. The death of Major Durfee left Mr. Davol as the only one conversant with the plans, and the machinery was made, put in, and arranged wholly under his supervision, and the success of the enterprise is largely due to his skill, judgment, and experience.

William C. Davol was born January 5, 1806, in Fall River, and while yet a lad entered the Troy Mill, then just commencing operations. He was made overseer of the spinning in 1819, and superintendent in 1827, a position which he occupied until 1841, when he became partner in the firm of Hawes, Marvel & Davol, and engaged in the manufacture of cotton machinery. He was an intimate friend of Holder Borden and Major Durfee, and, when the latter went to Europe in 1838 to investigate the improvements in cotton and iron machinery, accompanied him. Increased consumption necessitated increased production, and foreign competition demanded a large reduction in the cost. For instance, skeins or hanks of yarn cost 11 cents here, but only $3\frac{1}{2}$ cents in England; and Mr. Davol, being a practical manufacturer, made it a point to ascertain the kinds of machinery used, and the methods of working the raw cotton into the finished cloth. By letters of introduction, a little Yankee ingenuity and persistence, he accomplished his purpose so far as to effect an arrangement with the owners of the Sharp

& Roberts self-acting Mule, to secure patents for their manufacture in the United States, and the manufacture of cotton and other kinds of machinery from the most approved patterns was entered upon at once by the new firm of Hawes, Marvel & Davol. Mr. Davol soon projected improvements to beautify and perfect the operation and durability of the self-acting mule, and from these patterns built 180,000 spindles. In 1847, a new set of patterns were made, which superseded the old, and from which 100,000 spindles were soon constructed. In 1852 and in 1854 other new mules were perfected with a combination of improved principles for spinning fine yarn. At the same time Mr. Davol's inventive genius was at work upon other parts of cotton machinery, resulting in patent carders, speeders and drawing-frames, by which the productive power was quadrupled. The advantage to any manufacturing community to have among its number one such man, cannot well be estimated, and the high opinion of Mr. Davol's practical worth may be gathered from the opinion of a well-known cotton manufacturer, as expressed in the statement that "William C. Davol was worth more to Fall River, for the twenty years succeeding the building of the Metacomet Mill, than all others put together, because of his improvements in cotton machinery." This is high praise, but is in some respects justified by the statement of another noted manufacturer, who said, "There's more in the man than in the mill."

The Davol Mills for the manufacture of sheetings, shirtings, silesias, etc., were named after Mr. Davol, who was elected and still holds the position of president of the corporation.

In securing for the benefit of American cotton manufacturers the self-acting mule of Sharp, Roberts & Co., Mr. Davol, by his clever persistency, repeated the act of Samuel Slater in bringing over in his brain the spinning machinery of Arkwright. Great Britain, while preaching free-trade to every other industrial nation on the globe, and even spending largely of her gold to undermine the protective policy in whatever country her manufactures have sought a market, has never lost an opportunity to protect her own industries. Shrewdly appreciating the fact that there is more than one mode of protection, and realizing the inconsistency of doing the work by imposts, while she was advocating the abolition of imposts by competing countries, she has availed herself of many ways to effect her purpose: in one case encouraging her exports by a drawback in the shape of a remission of tax on particular production; in another, fostering a foreign trade by granting handsome subsidies to a shipping line; and in a third, securing all the economical advantages of invention and improvement to her own production, by a rigid Parliamentary prohibition of the exportation of labor-saving machinery. From the very dawn of her own industry, no people has been so intolerant of for-

eign competition in its own markets as the English, and no government answered so fully and quickly the appeal of its subjects for protection, in one shape or another, as that of England.

In our colonial days, if a guild of London artisans found a small lot of hats, made in the lean-tos of Massachusetts, or Pennsylvania farm-houses, underselling their own manufacture, whether in England or any spot of its domain, their immediate recourse was a petition to the lords in council, praying that Americans be forbidden sending their fabrics for sale out of their own provinces, and a favorable response was certain, without much tying or untying of red-tape. When a fancy grew among the Manchester and London weavers, during the first quarter of this century, that their American and Continental brethren were interfering with their interests, by weaving English-spun yarn, they beset Parliament for an act prohibiting the spinners exporting yarn at all, and probably would have gained their wish, if they had not assailed a more solid power in capital and influence than they possessed in numbers,

As England was foremost for half a century in the machining of cotton, a favorite policy of the government was to monopolize and retain every mechanical improvement or invention in that department of industry. Baines, in his "History of the Cotton Manufacture," published in 1835, in a very serious consideration of the dangers of foreign competition to the supremacy of the English production, lays this same flattering unction to his soul: "English manufactures can be sold cheaper than those of other countries, especially owing to the extensive employment of machinery. This country excels every other in the making of machines, and in the means of making them advantageously; and besides this, for the reason just mentioned, our manufacturers are interested in having their goods produced as much as possible by machinery." It is curious that neither he, nor any English writer on this theme, has even suggested the well-known fact, that government always forbade the exportation even of drawings of a new machine, at once its decided economical value became recognized.

When the water-frame spinning system of Arkwright was introduced in England, its appreciation by government was so high, that a prohibition was immediately enforced against its exportation, and so rigid restrictions instituted, that every passenger for America was searched at the customhouses, with the view of preventing the departure from the country of that great improvement, even in the shape of patterns or drawings. To the correct eye, retentive brain, and constructive mechanical ability of Samuel Slater, who had operated the machines for a considerable period, in one of the inventor's own mills, was alone due the possession of the improvement in the United States, for some years.

The story of Davol's securing the Roberts self-acting mule, a much more elaborate machine in its action, is interesting, and develops, at a much later day, the same monopolizing policy of the government. Mr. Davol spent some weeks in Manchester, while Major Durfee had gone with other friends to make a tour on the Continent, for the express purpose of studying the various improvements in English machinery, and especially the new mule, which had been patented by Mr. Roberts in 1830 and 1835, the most perfect development of Compton's original idea. Major Durfee had hardly reached the Continent before he wrote Mr. Davol that the Roberts machine must be secured for Fall River. Ere his return to England, an arrangement had been made with the inventor for the patenting of the improvement in America, and its manufacture under royalty, and a machine purchased, to be shipped, as Mr. Davol supposed, at once. Upon applying, shortly before his own time to take passage, for information as to his freight, he was apprised that *the mule would be delivered in the yard of the works.* Surprised by such an unaccommodating mode of business, his inquiry elicited the fact, of which he was heretofore utterly ignorant, that the sending or permitting the invention to go abroad, in any shape, was not only disallowed by the authorities, but a severe penalty prescribed against any attempt to evade the law. In this position of affairs, no longer amazed by the non-action of Sharp, Roberts & Co., but still determined to possess the machine, an answer was made in response to his anxious query how the freight could be placed on board ship at Liverpool, that a certain person in King street was accustomed to attend to such business. Mr. Davol at once approached this mysterious agent, and after a few words of mutual assurance, a verbal agreement — a written contract being refused — was made, that the contraband freight should be shipped as soon as possible, the reward to be seventy per cent of its cost, payable on its arrival at New York. Satisfied at last that the machine would be sent at an early moment, Major Durfee and Mr. Davol sailed for America. With all due allowance for custom-house *espionage* and the consequent difficulties, they looked for the arrival of their important freight a few weeks after their own return. Some months elapsing, and still no receipt, they wrote. More than a year passed, an unsatisfactory correspondence being the only result, the English side obviously fearing to compromise itself by letters at all matter of fact. Finally, the organization of a new mill necessitating a considerable machine equipment, it was decided to send out an order for £10,000 in English machinery, with the stipulation that the long-expected self-acting mule should be shipped at once. About two years from the date of Mr. Davol's original

purchase in Manchester, an invoice of small metal-ware, packed in the broad, thin cases peculiar to plate-glass shipments, was entered through the New York custom-house, for Fall River order. It came in a vessel from Havre, suggesting the probability that the English authorities had been advised of the presence of American manufacturers' agents in Manchester, and were consequently on the watch for shipments to this country. The cases were in due time received in Fall River. Upon opening them the machine was discovered, its framework and every considerable piece, of iron or wood, with the greatest neatness, sawn into bits a few inches in length. The assembling of these bits together into the complete mule was, though a matter of difficulty, and requiring a degree of patience, soon achieved by Mr. Davol, and the Roberts invention at last entirely at his disposition.

In previous pages Mr. Davol's success in introducing the new spinning machine, and his own improvements upon the English invention, have been narrated. Any account of the full results of his enterprise, however, would be imperfect without a supplementary relation, involving an episode which seems to be inseparable from the careers of almost all who originate or improve the details of production.

As already indicated, no sooner had the merits of the self-acting mule and its production in Fall River become known, than an instant demand for it sprang up in all directions. Manufacturers of cotton machinery resorted to every possible device to possess themselves of the patterns, many of them sending their draftsmen to inspect and furtively carry away working sketches of them; while one builder, bolder than the rest, declared openly that he had come with his designer to secure drawings of the whole machine. He was told he could have the patterns and a right to manufacture by paying a royalty, but warned at his peril not to infringe the patent.

This default of success was succeeded by attempts to break down the patent through claims of previous invention, similarity to other machines, and various kindred subterfuges, until finally, discovering that they could not accomplish their purpose covertly, the cotton manufacturers and machine builders combined openly to wrest the advantages, profits, and control of the new machine from the patentees. For a single small firm to oppose such a combination seemed almost an absurdity. But Mr. Davol was not a man to surrender to difficulties easily, and securing the best legal talent the country could produce, fought the case to a successful issue. The cause attracted universal attention, as it was one of the first patent suits brought prominently into the courts, and was regarded as in some measure determining the rights of inventors and the boundaries of inventions.

In the prosecution of his rights, Mr. Davol received much encouragement and personal assistance from Micah H. Ruggles, agent of the Pocasset Manufacturing Company. Mr. Ruggles had come to Fall River in 1826, and seems to have made an impression upon the community almost at once; for on the organization of the Fall River Savings Bank in 1828 he was made its president, and continued in the position until the year of his death, in 1857. In 1837 he was appointed agent of the Pocasset Company, and for twenty years conducted its increasing business with a skill and success which manifested executive talent of the first order. From the ease with which he grasped alike minute detail and general principles, and his knowledge of the leading principles of law, it was obvious that if he had turned his attention to that profession he would have taken rank with the foremost among its great leaders. A prudent counsellor, far-seeing and sagacious; an excellent observer, clear, quick, accurate; executing with ability whatever he undertook, and having a mind stored by experience with a large and unusually varied knowledge of men and things, he was invaluable as a friend and helper in a case which assumed such proportions and involved such interests as did that of Mr. Davol's. It was, as it were, Fall River against the country, and *Fall River won.*

Mr. Ruggles always occupied a prominent position in the Fall River community. He was its representative to the General Court from 1833 to 1838 inclusive. He took a leading part in politics, and was conspicuous in the great Anti-Masonic movement of 1831. His sympathies were strongly on the side of freedom, caring but little for the trivial details of conventional life; he manifested a degree of independence in the formation and expression of his opinions but seldom met with. Rising above mere party views upon the great questions of the day, it was sometimes his fortune to stand alone in his policy and action. Believing that what was worth doing, was worth doing well, he carried this sentiment into practice, and, when the great fire swept away the old "Bridge Mill" and contiguous buildings on Main street, as agent of the Pocasset Company he projected and carried to completion the erection of the Granite Block, and a year or two later the present Pocasset Mill. The former has ever since been one of the principal features of the centre of the city, an enduring monument in its massive proportions and substantial construction of the liberal forecast and sterling honesty that reared its walls. While, therefore, Mr. Ruggles was not so prominent as a manufacturer, in other and important particulars he exerted a marked influence in the community up to the time of his death, in 1857.

In 1852, a new enterprise was established in the formation of the American Linen Company for the purpose of manufacturing the finer linen fabrics on a large scale. As it was the first enterprise of the kind in the country, considerable interest was manifested, both at home and abroad, concerning the success of the undertaking. The buildings of the company, of stone, were erected on an extensive scale and in a very substantial manner. These consisted of a factory, 300 feet by 63, four stories high, with store and heckling-house, 150 feet by 48; a bleach house, 176 feet by 75, and a finishing building, 176 feet by 45, three stories high, with 10,500 spindles and 300 looms. An agent was sent to Europe to select and import the necessary operatives, and to meet their immediate wants it was necessary also to import several hundred tons of flax fibre. In the spring of 1853, the first productions were sent into the market. These consisted of blay linens, coating and pantaloon linen, sheeting, pillow and table linen, huckaback, and damask towelling, crash and diaper, which were received with such favor by the trade that at first it was impossible to supply the demand. But before the mill was in full operation, the demand for such goods as the company proposed to manufacture almost entirely ceased, for the reason that cotton and thin woollen fabrics were very generally substituted for linen goods. On this account it was determined, in the year 1858, to remove the machinery from the main mill into the outer buildings, and substitute machinery for the manufacture of cotton print cloths, and in this department the company has continued to the present time.

Up to the year 1859, what may be termed a sort of centralization characterized and directed the progress of industry in Fall River. One business organization, the Iron Works Company, exercised over the enterprise and advancement of the place a recognized power and influence. Prosperous in its own legitimate pursuits, successful in all its outlying projects, numbering among its stockholders the large land-owners and leading capitalists, and thus representing, if not itself owning, interests in every productive institution; through its riparian property commanding that part of the shore-line most eligible for wharfage, and thereby controlling both water and land communication, this corporate Briareus, with the brain of Mercury, for nearly four decades, seemed to hold the growing town and city, with all its industries and enterprises, in its hundred arms. That this embrace had been a kindly and fostering one, our previous record abundantly witnesses. In the nature of things, however, it could not last forever; the day must come when the child would leap forth from his guardian's and mentor's lap,—when the very material strength and wisdom that guardian had imparted would prove the essential features of his charge's independence.

While the Iron Works had enjoyed for so many years the direction and control of the interests of the place, introducing, promoting, and fostering new industries, and more firmly establishing in its own prosperity the fortunes of the community, the individual wealth was year by year increasing, and the business men of the city gradually acquiring the means which, when the inspiration should come, would be available for a new departure. But the suggestion was needed, and in 1859 it was given by a citizen supposed to be outside the circle of industrial pursuits.

Hale Remington, to whose instrumentality was mainly due the last stage of Fall River manufacturing development, came to the city in 1833, entering the drug-store of Dr. Nathan Durfee. In a short time he purchased the entire interest from his principal, and extended the business by adding to the stock dye-stuffs and chemicals consumed in manufacturing. Subsequently, his restless and ambitious temperament requiring occupation more active, he engaged in the coal business, adding to it in time a general insurance agency. For the latter, his genial and affable bearing, combined with a nature full of energy, gave him especial fitness, and he became popularly and worthily known throughout New England as a leader in the business.

Mr. Remington's general acquaintance with the individual resources of Fall River, and his observation of the success of combined movement in other places, led him to propose the organization of a cotton-manufacturing company, based upon the general contributions of men of small capital. Fortunately he found a counsellor and active coöperator in David Anthony, who, though in his seventy-fourth year, was still earnestly interested in local progress, and the man of all, from his thorough experience in manufacturing and the general esteem he possessed as a practical business operator, to assure the success of a new enterprise. Indeed, it is very doubtful if, without Mr. Anthony's active association, Mr. Remington would have attained any substantial success, his own identity with the cotton industry having been limited to a brief agency of the Globe Print Works.

The result of the combined efforts of Mr. Remington and Mr. Anthony was the formation of the Union Mill Company. The latter subscribed very largely to the capital and was chosen treasurer, Mr. Remington being one of the original directors. The president of the company to-day is John B. Anthony, of Providence, a son of the man so largely instrumental in the industrial progress of Fall River.

A fortunate hit as to the time of starting, and the excellent management of the veteran treasurer, made the Union Mill a splendid and immediate success. Recognizing no antagonism between the new departure and the old controlling influence of local industry, the example of combining a multitude of small resources became speedily a topic of consideration and discussion, and the successful precedent gave such a stimulus to popular enterprise, that the formation of similar companies was an almost immediate result. Within fifteen years succeeding the development of Mr. Remington's original suggestion, twenty-five distinct manufacturing corporations have been organized, adding an immense number of spindles, and a corresponding increase of capital, business, and population, and raising the city to its permanent supremacy among the cloth-producing centres of America.

The way once opened, and the first experiment proving that the idea was not only among the possibilities, but capable of a realization even beyond the hopes of its most sanguine projectors, others were not slow to pursue the lead, and the Union Mill Company was followed in 1863 by the formation of the Granite Mills, in 1866 by the Durfee and Tecumseh Mills, in 1867 by the Davol, Merchant's, and Robeson Mills, and in 1868 by the Mechanic's Mills.

But it was the two years 1871-2 that witnessed the most surprising developments in this direction. For a city of its size, wealth, and population, it would seem that two or three new companies were sufficient to absorb its surplus capital, energy, and ambition; but company succeeded company, until *fifteen* new corporations had been formed, the land purchased, laid out into mill sites and tenement lots, the foundations put in, and the massive walls reared story by story, the machinery contracted for, received and set in place, and the busy hum of more than a million spindles added to the pervading anthem of labor and production.

So surely does enterprise beget enterprise, that scarcely had one company been organized and located, before a second, a third, and even a fourth would purchase the neighboring property; and what had before barely given a farmer's family its moderate subsistence, became the home of hundreds, and furnished a product in manufactured goods to the value of thousands of dollars. The price of land took an immense leap upward, that in the centre of the city doubling and trebling in value, while in the outskirts a foot was held almost at the former rate per rod. Masons, carpenters, and mechanics were in excessive demand; wages were increased, and work was abundant. The machine shops at home not having the capacity to supply the immediate demand, cotton machinery was imported in large quantities from abroad, special agents being sent out in some cases to hasten it forward. Everywhere was hurry and bustle. Shares in the new corporations were at a premium before even the foundation was in. The news spread abroad, and capital flowed in from the neighboring cities. Old conservative manufacturers, traders, and bankers at first stood aghast, then yielded to the subtle influence, and finally rivalled the most venturesome in their investments and in the formation of still other companies.

Young and old partook of the spirit of the times and made their subscriptions, and while some of the companies had less than fifty stockholders, others had from three to four hundred. By a wise provision of State law, under which the various companies were incorporated, the shares (whatever was the capital stock in total) were made one hundred dollars each, thus giving an opportunity to all, to rich and poor alike, as well to the man of moderate means as to the man of wealth, to become owners in these various enterprises; and it not unfrequently happened that the operatives of a mill became joint owners with the larger capitalists, and sharers in the proceeds of their own productive industry. The subscriptions were made payable in instalments of about ten per cent per month and spread over a year, so that there was no sudden draft to bear onerously upon the stockholders, and the principle of partial payments enabled many to make small investments of from one to five or ten shares each.

When at length the summer of 1872 drew to a close, and a little space was given to review the proceedings of the past two years, to gather up the scattered threads of enterprise here and there, to comprehend as a whole what had been done, and to devise plans for the future, it was found that the fifteen companies just organized, involved an outlay of capital to the extent of $13,000,000, had added over half a million spindles to the number already running, required 6000 more hands, and had brought into the city an immediate population of some 20,000 persons.

In full running time (averaging ten hours per day), the mills now incorporated will employ 14,000 hands, using 135,000 bales of cotton yearly, in the manufacture of 340,000,000 yards of cloth. The monthly pay-rolls amount to over $400,000, which are paid as follows: one fourth of the mills paying the first week, another fourth the second week, and so on consecutively through the month.

From statistical reports for the year 1872 (the era of "new mills"), and a comparison of the relative wealth of the cities of the commonwealth, it appears that Fall River ranked fourth in valuation of personal, and sixth in real estate valuation; that the aggregate gain in one year (1872) was $8,701,300, or forty-one per cent—with one exception the *largest* gain, either in amount or percentage, in the whole State. In the scale of tax rates, the city stood third on the list, but two having a lower rate, and in point of population advanced from the eighth to the fifth.

It is especially noteworthy, that notwithstanding the extraordinary growth of the industries of the place during the last decade, but a small proportion of foreign capital is invested, or has been sought for, in so remarkable developments of enterprise. This statement, while particularly true of the later growth, will, moreover, apply to the history of thirty years back with almost equal justice. The wealth of Fall River is its own earnings, and to the studious economist there is no more interesting example of an accretion of resources through the provident care of small beginnings, an unpretentious and silent, but unremitting energy, and a singularly wise and tenacious grasp of opportunities, than this true history, stranger than any fiction, more exciting than any romance, affords.

Some small suggestion of the original contributions to the industrial capital of the place has been given in the foregoing pages. About half the original investment in the year 1813, for instance, was furnished in the adjacent towns of Massachusetts and Rhode Island. The advent of the Robeson family brought in $50,000 of New Bedford money. The larger part of the $100,000 upon which the Massasoit was started was furnished by Brown & Ives, of Providence; and from one third to one half of the Annawan's original capital was raised out of town. But in six or seven years Holder Borden's management of the Massasoit had made so much profit for the firm, that he was able, out of his own share, to purchase the interests of his Rhode Island backers; and this is but one instance.

In the case of the Linen Mill Company, $200,000 of its whole capital of $500,000 was invested by outside parties, and when the original amount required an additional $200,000 to rearrange the factory for a production of cotton, the aggregate was reached by an assessment of stockholders.

A very cautious and conservative citizen, whose means of information were exceptionally good, writing of the resources of Fall River about 1858, before the extraordinary development of the place had commenced, remarks: "My impressions are, that several years after the commencement of business in Fall River the valuation of all the property in the whole town reached only $500,000. It is now over $9,000,000." His estimate of the aggregate of original investments in manufactures up to that time, "owned by the residents, brought into the place, and earned," is $650,000. "The valuation of property by the assessors is about ten millions of dollars—about as much of real as of personal estate. The items may be set down as follows:

"Cotton Mills (150,000 spindles), water-power and land	$2,000,000
Print Works	200,000
Woollen Mill	50,000
Iron Works	1,000,000
Furnaces	20,000
Steamboats	700,000
Bank Capital and Deposits	2,000,000
1500 Dwellings	1,500,000
Real Estate, including Wharves	1,000,000
Miscellaneous Stocks	250,000
Invested in Trade and Merchandise	150,000
Invested in Vessels	100,000
Market and Cemetery	100,000
Religious Edifices	150,000
Educational Edifices	70,000
	$9,290,000

".At the present time there are ten or possibly more residents worth $100,000 and over; one may be estimated at half a million. Probably there are from twelve to fifteen worth $50,000. In the year 1831, two of our citizens reckoned up a list of ten persons worth $10,000 and upwards, and in 1837 were able to add to it seven others."

Such plain and simple figures as the foregoing introduce with almost dramatic effect the statistical exhibit of Fall River in 1876, which we extract from Mr. Sanborn's interesting paper read before the Social Science Association, at its meeting in Saratoga, in September.

"The population of Fall River fifty years ago was less than 3000; in 1840 it was 6738; in 1850, 11,524; in 1855, 12,680; in 1860, 14,026; in 1865, 17,481. Up to that time, which was the close of the civil war, its increase had been no greater than that of other thriving towns in Massachusetts. Exclusive of the 3300 inhabitants gained from Rhode Island by annexation in 1862, it had neither increased nor diminished its population during the civil war; while some Massachusetts cities, Worcester and Springfield, for example, had gained from twenty to forty per centum during the war; and others, Lowell and New Bedford, for example, had lost from six to fifteen per centum of their population. But immediately upon the close of the war Fall River began to gain in population and wealth with remarkable rapidity. In 1870 it contained 26,766 inhabitants, or almost twice as many as in 1860; in 1875 it contained 45,340, or more than three times the population in 1860. The only other Massachusetts city that has trebled its population in these fifteen years is Holyoke, which from 5000 in 1860 grew to 16,260 in 1875.

"But Holyoke shows no such gain in wealth as Fall River made during the same period. The assessed valuation of Fall River, which in 1861 was but $11,261,065, and which so late as 1869 was but $21,400,000, had risen in 1873 to $47,416,000, and in 1875 to $51,401,000. Holyoke, which in 1861 had a valuation of $2,270,439, and in 1869 of $5,370,000, had only risen to $8,578,000 in 1873, and to $9,681,000 in 1875. Thus the taxable and actually taxed wealth of Fall River increased nearly 400 per centum in the fifteen years from 1860 to 1875, and it more than doubled (an increase of 121 per centum) in the four years preceding the panic of 1873.

"The growth of a single industry in Fall River since the civil war is even more extraordinary. In 1865 the city reported fifteen cotton-mills, with only 241,218 spindles; in 1875 there were thirty-eight mills, with 1,280,000 spindles. In 1865 the annual product of these mills was reported at less than 30,000,000, while in 1873 it was more than 330,000,000 yards, or eleven times as much. The reported capital in 1865 was but $3,126,500; in 1875 it was $20,368,000, or more than six times as much. Between 1870 and 1874 the number of cotton-manufacturing corporations was increased from eighteen to thirty-four. In 1865 the reported number of cotton factory operatives, in a population of 17,481, was 2654, of whom 1037 were males and 1617 females. In 1875 the number of cotton factory operatives, in a population of 45,260, was 11,514, of whom 5467 were males and 6047 were females. Within ten years, therefore, this portion of the population had increased from fifteen per centum of the whole to more than twenty-five per centum of the whole. In fact, the persons of suitable age and capacity to labor, who are directly or indirectly at work upon the cotton industries of Fall River, are no doubt more than half, and may reach two thirds, of the whole industrious population. The capital employed in cotton manufactures bore even a larger ratio to the whole capital of the city in 1875, and so did the value of the manufactured product to the whole product of the city industries. Thus the whole capital reported in 'manufactures and related occupations' being $23,078,000, that employed in cotton manufactures was $20,484,000, or almost 90 per centum; while of the manufactured product ($23,027,000) $20,228,000, or about the same percentage, were of cotton goods. In 1870 the whole manufactured product of cotton goods in the United States was valued at less than $180,000,000, so that Fall River manufactures more than a tenth part of all that are produced in the country. There is no single city in the United States that manufactures so much cotton as Fall River, and it has even been asserted that there is no city in the world which has a larger cotton manufacture. This is a mistake for Manchester in England, in 1871, employed 20,346 persons in its one hundred and eleven cotton factories. But when we consider that Manchester has ten times the population of Fall River (476,000 in 1871), while Fall River employs more than half as many cotton spinners as Manchester, it is easy to see that our American city may soon surpass its English prototype in this special industry. Ten years more like the last ten would see this accomplished.

"It is proper to mention in conclusion, that the wealth of Fall River is owned almost wholly by residents, and that its business interests are controlled by its own people, rather than by persons living at a distance. This is one of the causes of its prosperity; for all its citizens have a direct interest in making it prosperous, and work industriously to that end. It is also, perhaps, the chief reason why the cotton manufacture there has not given way during the depression of prices for two years past. 'If you want your work well done,' says the proverb, 'you must do it yourself.' The Fall River manufacturers have attended to their own investments, and their operatives, being citizens of the town, and having a deep interest in its success, have submitted to restrictions and reductions of wages which might not have been available in cities like Lowell. In the recent conflicts between capital and labor at Fall River there have been faults on both sides, but the result seems to show that on neither side was serious injustice done. The future is uncertain, but there is a fair prospect that the overgrowth of a single industry there will prove to have been but a slight excess, which was, perhaps, unavoidable in firmly establishing a manufacture that may prove itself able to compete in the markets of the world with the same industry in countries where it has been long established."

The forty cotton mill structures of Fall River are located in groups, and may be distinguished as those on the stream, those at Mechanicsville at the north, those at Globe Village (originally Tiverton) at the south, and a small number on the shores of Mount Hope Bay. Ascending the stream are situated the Metacomet, Annawan, Fall River Manufactory, Fall River Print Works, Watuppa, Quequechan, Pocasset, and Troy. These are the oldest mills in the place, and all of them are below the dam.

On the stream above the dam, following nearly to its head along its east side, are the Union Nos. 1 and 2, Durfee Nos. 1 and 2, Granite Nos. 1 and 2, Crescent, Merchants, Barnard, Wampanoag, Stafford, Flint, and Merino, the last five, with their tenements, forming a community by themselves known as Flint's Village.

On the west bank of the stream, above the dam, are the Tecumseh No. 1, Robeson, Davol, Richard Borden, Tecumseh No. 2, and Chace Mills.

Some two miles north of the stream, at Mechanicsville, are located the Mechanics, Weetamoe, Narragansett, Sagamore, and Border City Nos. 1 and 2.

At the extreme south, some four miles from the Mechanicsville group, taking their water from Laurel Lake, are the Slade, Montaup, Osborn, King Philip, and Shove Mills.

The American Print Works, the Fall River Iron Works, the American Linen Company's Mills, Nos. 1 and 2, and the Mount Hope Mill are located successively on the Bay southward from the stream.

THE GROWTH

OF THE

COTTON INDUSTRY IN AMERICA.

THE first culture of cotton in the United States for the purpose of raising a material to be worked up into a fabric was pursued on the peninsula between the Chesapeake and Delaware Bays as early as 1736, it having been before that time chiefly regarded as an ornamental plant, and reared only in gardens on the eastern shore of Maryland, the lower counties of Delaware and occasional localities in the Middle States. Previously to this date—about 1733—its culture seems to have been experimentally undertaken in South Carolina, where it was to be met with in gardens. An exportation of seven bags from Charleston, in 1747-8, is recorded; but doubt is thrown upon its growth in the colony. A few years later it was a recognized production of the Carolinas, in a very small way, as also of French Louisiana. But cotton was not to any appreciable extent a production of the Southern States anterior to the Revolutionary War, and its use as a material to be spun and woven, with its relative value as an article of national wealth, was hardly thought of in comparison with hemp and flax. Whatever was raised was consumed at home, and in 1770 the total entries of American cotton at Liverpool amounted to three bales from New York, four from Virginia and Maryland, and three barrels from North Carolina.

In 1784 an importation of eight bags of cotton at Liverpool was seized, on the assumption that so large a quantity could not have been of American production. The next year, however, the exportation from Charleston regularly commenced, one bag being shipped to England from that city. During the same twelvemonth twelve bags were entered at Liverpool from Philadelphia, and one from New York. The increase thenceforward was marked. The bag averaged 150 lbs., and from 1786 to 1790 the following quantities were exported: 1786, 6 bags; 1787, 109 bags; 1788, 389 bags; 1789, 842 bags; 1790, 81 bags—aggregating 1441 bags, or 216,150 lbs.

In 1786 the culture of cotton had become so successful that Mr. Madison, in a convention at Annapolis, Md., called to consider the depressed condition of the country, remarked, in his address, that "there was no reason to doubt the United States would one day become a great cotton-growing country."

The invention of the cotton-gin by Eli Whitney in 1793-4, by which the labor of one man could clean for market a thousand pounds of cotton instead of the five or six pounds by the usual hand process, at once gave an impulse to the culture of the plant. In 1795 South Carolina exported $1,109,653 in value of production, and the growth of the whole country reached 8,000,000 lbs., of which three quarters were shipped abroad. In 1801 the product aggregated 40,000,000 lbs., of which half was exported, South Carolina alone yielding 8,000,000 lbs.

The following table, carefully prepared by B. F. Nourse, Esq., of Boston, and perfected to the present time, shows the total annual production of cotton in the United States from 1825 to the present year, inclusive:

Years ending August 31.	Production. Bales.	Consumption. Bales.	Exports. Bales.	Average Net Weight per Bale.	Average Price per lb. N.Y. Cents.
1825-'26	720,027	....	....	...	12.19
1826-'27	957,281	149,516	854,000	331	9.29
1827-'28	720,593	120,593	600,000	335	10.32
1828-'29	870,415	118,853	740,000	341	9.88
1829-'30	976,845	126,512	839,000	339	10.04
1830-'31	1,038,847	182,142	773,000	341	9.71
1831-'32	987,477	173,800	892,000	360	9.38
1832-'33	1,070,438	194,412	867,000	350	12.32
1833-'34	1,205,394	196,413	1,028,000	363	12.90
1834-'35	1,254,328	216,888	1,023,500	367	17.45
1835-'36	1,360,725	236,733	1,116,000	373	16.50
1836-'37	1,423,930	222,540	1,169,000	379	13.25
1837-'38	1,801,497	246,063	1,575,000	379	10.14
1838-'39	1,360,532	276,018	1,074,000	384	13.36
1839-'40	2,177,835	295,193	1,876,000	383	8.92
1840-'41	1,634,954	267,850	1,313,500	394	9.50
1841-'42	1,683,574	267,850	1,465,500	397	7.85
1842-'43	2,378,875	325,129	2,010,000	409	7.25
1843-'44	2,030,409	346,750	1,629,500	412	7.73
1844-'45	2,394,503	389,000	2,083,700	415	5.63
1845-'46	2,100,537	422,600	1,666,700	411	7.87
1846-'47	1,778,651	428,000	1,241,200	431	11.21
1847-'48	2,439,786	616,044	1,858,000	417	8.03
1848-'49	2,866,938	642,485	2,228,000	436	7.55
1849-'50	2,233,718	613,498	1,590,200	429	12.34
1850-'51	2,454,442	485,614	1,958,710	416	12.14
1851-'52	3,126,310	689,603	2,443,646	428	9.50
1852-'53	3,416,214	803,725	2,528,400	428	11.02
1853-'54	3,074,979	737,236	2,319,148	430	10.97
1854-'55	2,982,634	706,417	2,244,209	434	10.39
1855-'56	3,665,557	770,739	2,954,606	420	10.30
1856-'57	3,093,737	819,936	2,252,657	444	13.51
1857-'58	3,257,339	595,562	2,500,455	442	12.23
1858-'59	4,018,914	927,651	3,021,403	447	12.08
1859-'60	4,861,292	978,043	3,774,173	461	11.00

Years ending August 31.	Production. Bales.	Consumption. Bales.	Exports. Bales.	Average Net Weight per Bale.	Average Price per lb. N. Y. Cents.
1860-'61	3,849,469	843,740	3,127,568	477	13.01
1861-'62	....	....	....	....	31.29
1862-'63	....	....	....	..	67.21
1863-'64	....	....	....	....	101.50
1864-'65	....	....	....	...	83.38
1865-'66	2,269,310	666,100	1,554,654	441	43.20
1866-'67	2,097,254	770,630	1,557,054	444	31.59
1867-'68	2,519,554	906,636	1,655,816	445	24.85
1868-'69	2,366,467	926,374	1,465,880	444	29.01
1869-'70	3,122,557	865,160	2,206,480	440	23.98
1870-'71	4,362,317	1,110,196	3,166,742	442	16.95
1871-'72	3,014,357	1,237,330	1,957,314	443	20.98
1872-'73	3,930,508	1,201,127	2,679,986	464	18.15
1873-'74	4,170,388	1,305,943	2,840,981	466	19.30
1874-'75	3,832,991	1,207,601	2,684,410	463	15.
1875-'76	4,669,288	1,356,598	3,252,994	471	13.

The history of cotton manufacture in the United States commences with the organization of a factory at Beverly, Mass., in 1787. Previously whatever cotton had been made into cloth had been spun on the ordinary spinning-wheel, which was a property of nearly every household, and woven on the hand-loom. The first spinning-jenny seen in America was exhibited in Philadelphia, in 1775, constructed by a Mr. Christopher Tully after the plan of Hargreaves. This machine, spinning twenty-four threads, was secured by an association of persons desirous to establish domestic enterprise, who formed themselves into a company, termed "The United Company of Philadelphia for Promoting American Manufactures." This Company, besides operating Tully's machine, employed four hundred women in hand-spinning and weaving. The Company was speedily a success, the stock rising from its par value of £10 to £17 6s. 6d. in two years. The business, however, was not long carried on by the Company, but in a few years was controlled by one of the directors, Samuel Wetherill, who during the Revolution had contracts for woollen fabrics for the army.

Though some years before the close of the war the spinning-frames of Arkwright had been operated in England, it was next to impossible to procure patterns, or even drawings, of them for the United States. Not only did parliamentary legislation prohibit the exportation of new inventions, but the statutes were rigidly enforced, to the degree even of searching private effects and preventing the emigration of skilled artificers from the country. Thus in 1786 a complete set of brass models of Arkwright's machines, packed for Philadelphia, was seized on the eve of shipment; and in 1784 a German was fined £500 for attempting to form a colony of English workmen for one of the Low Countries.

In 1786, the Hon. Hugh Orr, of Bridgewater, Mass., employed two brothers, Robert and Alexander Barr, recently come from Scotland, to construct for him, at his machine-shops, three carding, roving, and spinning machines. It is probable Col. Orr did not contemplate himself inaugurating a manufacturing enterprise, but was actuated by a desire to promote a new industry. At any rate he succeeded in securing a favorable report from a Legislative committee appointed to examine the machines, and a grant of £200 to the machinists, supplemented by the gift of six tickets in the State Land Lottery, in which there were no blanks, "as a reward for their ingenuity in forming those machines, and for their public spirit in making them known to this Commonwealth."

The cost of the machines was £187, and they included probably the first stock card in the country.

The approval of the Commonwealth was next given to a model of an early and imperfect form of Arkwright's water-frame, brought from England by Thomas Somers. Col. Orr, still the medium of the State's liberality, was commissioned to advance £20 to the artisan, who had visited England at his own risk and expense, for the purpose of perfecting his construction, which was exhibited with the machines of the Barr Brothers, and called the "State's Model." A water-frame, built from drawings made after this model by Daniel Anthony, of Providence, who had engaged with Andrew Dexter and Lewis Peck to establish a manufacture of jeans and other "homespun cloth" of linen warp and cotton filling, was subsequently set up and operated in Providence.

The factory at Beverly, previously alluded to as the first establishment in the United States actually producing cloth by machinery, was equipped with one or more spinning-jennies and a carding-machine, the latter imported at a cost of $1100. The Legislature appropriated £500 as a public aid to the enterprise. The factory was visited by General Washington during his New England tour in 1789, and his diary refers to the processes pursued as follows: "In this manufactory they have the new invented carding and spinning machines. One of the first supplies the work, and four of the latter, one of which spins 84 threads at a time by one person. The cotton is prepared for these machines by being first (lightly) drawn to a thread on the common wheel. There is also another machine for doubling and twisting the threads for particular cloths; this also does many at a time. For winding the cotton from the spindles and preparing it for the warp, there is a reel which expedites the work greatly. A number of looms (fifteen or sixteen) were at work with spring shuttles, which do more than double work. In short, the whole seemed perfect, and the cotton stuffs which they turn out excellent of their kind; warp and filling both cotton."

The Beverly factory was a brick structure run by horse-power, a pair of large bay horses, driven by a boy, giving motion to the wheels. The establishment, under the management of John Cabot and Joshua Fisher, was continued for some years. The raw cotton was obtained from the West Indies in exchange for fish, "the most valuable export in possession of the State." In 1790, in answer to a petition for State aid, another grant of £1000, to be raised in a lottery, was made conditionally upon the proceeds being used "in such a way as will most effectually promote the manufacturing of cotton piece goods in this Commonwealth."

Up to this time (1790), it is believed—notwithstanding the efforts of Somers and the Barrs to construct Arkwright's machinery—that spinning was done at Beverly and in Rhode Island by the jenny alone. The Bridgewater essays, probably imperfect realizations of a very crude original knowledge of the English invention, had served but to stimulate the public mind to patronize domestic enterprise.

In such a situation of the industry, the *deus ex machina* appeared in the person of Samuel Slater.

Samuel Slater, a native of Derbyshire, born in 1768, when fourteen years of age was apprenticed to Jedediah Strutt, at Milford, a cotton manufacturer and partner with Sir Richard Arkwright in the spinning business. He served Mr. Strutt the full time of his engagement (six years and a half), and continued still longer with him superintending the construction of new works, his design in so doing being to perfect his knowledge of the business in every department. Previous to the termination of his apprenticeship, Slater had read a newspaper account of the interest awakened in America, and the bounties offered for the production of suitable machinery for cotton manufacture, and had quietly determined, after thoroughly familiarizing himself with the improved machine processes, to try his fortune in the New World.

Aware of the impossibility of taking away models or drawings, as the custom-house officers scrupulously searched every passenger, Slater pursued his study of the minutiæ of the business with the most diligent and thoughtful exactness of observation, and—thanks to a rare retentiveness of memory controlled by a very clear and positive brain power—made himself an absolute master of the industry in all its details.

On the 17th of November, 1789, he landed at New York. The following January, dissatisfied with the opportunities offered by the New York Manufacturing Company, with which he had corresponded, for developing his ideas, he came to Providence and contracted with Brown & Almy to produce a "perpetual card and spinning" system for them. This firm, at the head of which was the then venerable Moses Brown, had already operated a sort of hybrid spinning device constructed after the Bridgewater designs, which turned out "too imperfect to afford much encouragement," and was predisposed to patronize the thorough acquirements of one who claimed to have worked under both Strutt and Arkwright. On the 18th of January, Mr. Brown took Slater out to Pawtucket, and, providing him with the needed facilities, set him at once at the production of the improved machines. Laboring almost entirely by himself, Slater succeeded on the 20th of December in starting three cards, drawing and roving, with seventy-two spindles, entirely upon the Arkwright principle. They were run by the water-wheel of an old fulling-mill for the period of twenty months.

In April, 1793, Almy, Brown & Slater erected a small mill, known to this day in Pawtucket as the Old Factory, running at first seventy-two spindles, and gradually increasing machinery and space as the business warranted.

In 1798 Slater, associating himself with Oziel and William Wilkinson and Timothy Green, under the firm name of Samuel Slater & Co., started a new factory in Pawtucket. In 1806, in connection with his brother John, who came from England bringing a knowledge of the most recent improvements and processes, he organized a new establishment in Smithfield, R. I., which developed into the present large village of Slatersville.

David Anthony, one of the founders of cotton manufacturing in Fall River, who died in 1867, from 1806 to 1812 was in the employ of Samuel Slater, and of the brothers Wilkinson. For the former he entertained a most exalted esteem, often speaking of him as "the father of the cotton manufacturing business in this country." "He was not only a manufacturer of cotton and the first in the business, as machinist and mathematician, but he was a rare business man. He was always attired in his business suit of velvets" (the dress worn in the cotton mills of the period), "and looked like an overseer so far as outward appearance indicated his position. His pay for taking the agency of two mills was $1.50 per day from each. He was, of course, by no means an educated man, but he was a constant worker, saying of himself that sixteen hours' labor a day, Sundays excepted, for twenty years, had been no more than fair exercise."

The introduction of the Arkwright "perpetual spinning" system by Samuel Slater gave an almost immediate impulse to cotton manufacturing throughout the country. Several persons, learning the processes under him, left his employment and started individual enterprises. The celebrated

"New York Mills" at Utica originated in a small factory put up in 1807-8, by B. S. Wolcott, Jr., who worked in Pawtucket. The first factory in New Hampshire was put in operation in 1804, by one Robbins, another of Slater's graduates. At Cumberland, R. I., a mill was started in 1801; and at Rehoboth, Mass., opposite to Pawtucket, R. I., a second factory (the first being Slater's "White Mill") was erected in 1805.

The Secretary of the Treasury, Mr. Gallatin, in his report on domestic industry, April 17, 1810, made the following statement: "During the three succeeding years, ten mills were erected or commenced in Rhode Island, and one in Connecticut, making altogether fifteen mills erected before the year 1808, working at that time 8000 spindles. Returns have been received of 87 mills, which were erected at the end of the year 1809, 62 of which were in operation, and worked 31,000 spindles, and the other 25 will be in operation in the course of the year 1810."

According to Benedict's *History of Rhode Island*, in 1809 "there were 17 cotton mills in operation within the *town* of Providence and its vicinity, working 14,296 spindles; and in 1812 there were said to be, within thirty miles of Providence, in the State of Rhode Island, 33 factories, of 30,660 spindles; and in Massachusetts 20 factories, of 17,370 spindles, making 53 factories, running 48,030 spindles.

Cotton factories were started at Watertown, Mass., in 1807; at Fitchburg in 1807; at Dedham in 1808; in Dorchester in 1811, and in Waltham in 1813. In 1808 the companies at Peterborough and Exeter, N. H., were organized; in 1809, one at Chesterfield; in 1810, one at Milford, Swanzey, Cornish, and Amoskeag Falls; in 1811, one at Walpole, Hillsborough, and Meredith; there being at the commencement of the second war probably fifteen cotton mills in New Hampshire, operating from six to seven thousand spindles.

The first cotton factory in Maine, then a district of Massachusetts, was built at Brunswick in 1809.

The Census of 1810 furnishes the following classification of the industry by States:

Massachusetts	54	Pennsylvania	64
New Hampshire	12	Delaware	3
Vermont	1	Maryland	11
Rhode Island	28	Ohio	2
Connecticut	14	Kentucky	15
New York	26	Tennessee	4
New Jersey	4	(None in any other State.)	

The war of 1812, of necessity raising the price of cloth extraordinarily (articles, previously imported from England, and sold at 17 to 20 cents per yard, bringing 75 cents by the package), stimulated the infant industry in such a degree, that at its close there were reported, within a short radius of Providence, 96 mills, aggregating 65,264 spindles. The average number of spindles in mills of the period was 500; the largest in the country, that of Almy, Brown & Slater, ran 5170.

In 1815 was compiled for a committee of manufacturers a statement of the number of mills and spindles in Rhode Island, Massachusetts, and Connecticut. This statement, made for the purpose of providing a just basis for assessment to pay the expenses of an agent to represent the manufacturing interest before Congress, furnishes the subjoined items:

	Mills.	Spindles.
Rhode Island	99	68,142
Massachusetts	52	39,468
Connecticut	14	11,700
	165	119,310

The Committee on Manufactures of the United States House of Representatives the same year, in a report to Congress, tabulated the condition of the cotton-manufacturing industry, as follows:

Capital	$40,000,000
Males employed, of the age of 17	10,000
" " under 17	24,000
Females, including children	66,000
Wages of 100,000, averaging $1.50 per week (sic)	15,000,000
Cotton manufactured, 90,000 bales	27,000,000
Number of yards	81,000,000
Cost, averaging 30 cents per yard	24,300,000

Succeeding the close of the war of 1812, and prior to the effective operation of the tariff of 1816, a severe and general depression fell upon the industry, many companies suspending, and the strongest struggling on with difficulty.

From 1815 to 1820, a second revolution in the business, hardly less important in its results than the introduction of the water spinning-frames had been, was to be experienced in the addition of the power-loom to the series of mill processes. Previously to this application of power, the work of manufacture in the factory had been limited to the carding, drawing, and spinning stages. The product of yarn was sent out to be woven into cloth on hand-looms, and, as will be seen in subsequent pages, more than half the drudgery and detail of the mill agent was to conduct the manifold and complex system of outside production. The mills in the neighborhood of Providence kept wagons running constantly into the rural districts, invading both Massachusetts and Connecticut, bearing out yarn to be woven and returning with the product of the hand-looms, worked by the farmers' wives and daughters of the country side. In the period anterior to the introduction of jennies and water-frames, and the assembling of the different stages of preparation under organized systems of factory labor, all the details of cloth-making had been the legitimate pursuits of the domestic circle. Thomas Jefferson—who was himself a household manufacturer of this early type, having two spinning-wheels, a carding-machine, and a loom in his dwelling, by which his home folk made more than two thousand yards of cloth annually—though finally an advocate and even a partisan of organized factory industry, was in 1786 an eloquent writer in behalf of the time-honored custom of production in the family. It was not, indeed, without at least a show of resistance, that the old style gave way to the new, the former subsidizing the same art of invention to its support, through which the latter has won its eventual triumph. In 1812, when the water-frame with its seventy-two or more spindles was building up the industry in constantly increasing mills, portable spinning-frames capable of spinning from six to twenty-four threads, made expressly for family use, were sold about the country, meeting particular welcome in districts remote from the manufacturing centres. The construction of these domestic jennies and billies—as they were termed—was pursued on quite a large scale. The twelve-spindle billy sold for $48; the carding-machine, suitable for a large household, $60; the spinning-machine, for cotton, of twelve spindles, $25; and the loom, with flying shuttle, weaving twenty yards a day, $65. At the great Industrial Exhibition of this first Centennial of the Nation, in the American department, were to be seen instances not only of the old foot-worked spinning-wheel, but likewise of these later more pretentious devices, by which the lingering spirit of old time housewifery sought to assert itself against the progressive future.

The power-loom, though invented by Cartwright and put in operation at Doncaster, in 1785, was not recognized as a success, or even as a practicable suggestion, when Samuel Slater left the old country. Improved by various succeeding inventors, and finally made practical through the warp-dressing appliance of Radcliffe and Ross, and the modifications of its working details by Horrocks in 1813, it had by that year become an object of favorable consideration with the English manufacturers, and, despite the riotous antagonism of the hand weavers, two thousand four hundred were in use in Great Britain. Some years prior to this, rumors of the invention had reached the United States, and (though as in the case of the water-frames the impossibility of securing models or drawings of the invention was well enough known) stimulated the leaders of domestic cotton manufacture to efforts in the same direction. As early as 1806, according to Mr. Samuel Batchelder, whose brief record of the "Cotton Manufacture in the United States" is our authority for many statements in these pages, T. M. Mussey, at Exeter, N. H., produced a loom capable of weaving, but possessing no claim as a labor-saving machine. About the same time a vertical loom was made at Dorchester, and Mr. Batchelder saw another in operation at Dedham, weaving about twenty yards of coarse cloth per day. Neither of these was, however, superior to the hand-loom in economical results.

The following memoranda of various attempts to weave by power in Rhode Island during the years of the war, when cotton manufacturing was making its first extraordinary advance in that State, have been furnished for this work by the Hon. Zachariah Allen, of Providence:

"In March, 1812, John Thorpe, of Providence, obtained a patent for a vertical power-loom, and put it in operation in the mill of Henry Franklin at Johnston. About the same time Samuel Blydenburgh made and put in operation at the Lyman Mill, in North Providence, twelve power-looms for weaving cotton cloth.

"Thomas R. Williams soon after (1813) followed, putting in operation several looms.

"Mr. Elijah Ormsbee constructed several power-looms near Providence in 1814.

"Mr. Silas Shepherd, of Taunton, states that he constructed an experimental power-loom in 1811, and, in the winter of 1812, commenced making them for sale in connection with John Thorpe.

"But all of these looms failed of successful operation on account of the imperfect system of dressing and beaming the warps, and also for want of a device to prevent the smashing the warp when the shuttle failed to go through the web to its place in the box.

"Mr. Francis C. Lowell introduced power-looms into the Waltham Mill, operated by a cam and weight to act on the lay to beat in the filling. This pattern of loom was copied from the work on weaving by John Duncan, Plate XIV. These looms were put in operation in 1814, and all the operations of making the yarn, dressing it, and weaving were performed in superior manner, taking precedence.

"The first cotton mill in which all parts of the manufacture were accomplished to delivery of the finished cloth, in Rhode Island, was in Olneyville, belonging to Henry Franklin and John Waterman.

"The first wide looms for weaving woollen broadcloth were put in operation in Allendale, North Providence, in the year 1826."

To two very progressive manufacturers, Mr. Francis C. Lowell of Boston, and Judge Lyman of Providence, the development of weaving by power was mainly due. Mr. Lowell visited Europe in 1810-11, and, if he did not see the Scotch loom in operation, was doubtless acquainted with its results and general principles. Returning to America, he organized the Boston Manufacturing Company in February, 1813, and late in the same year completed the erection at Waltham of a factory of seventeen hundred spindles. In 1814 he devised, constructed, and put in successful operation a power-loom differing essentially from the Scotch loom, but accompanied by the dressing machine of Horrocks, which Mr. Lowell had procured drawings of, and materially improved upon.

In the perfection of the Waltham loom, Mr. Batchelder remarks that application was made to Shepherd, of Taunton. Capt. Shepherd, one of the oldest manufacturers of cotton machinery in the country, was believed by David Anthony to have been the first who experimented upon the production of a power-loom.

The Waltham loom was a satisfactory success, and the mill in which it was operated was the first in the United States, and possibly in the world, conducting all the operations of converting the raw cotton into finished cloth. Lowell, who was as remarkable for his projecting and organizing capability as for his inventive genius, died in 1817 at the early age of forty-two. When Nathan Appleton and others of his associates in the Waltham enterprise, a few years after his death, were beginning on their land at East Chelmsford the immense industries which for many years constituted the largest cotton-manufacturing centre in America, they paid only a worthy tribute to his extraordinary merit in naming the future city Lowell.

Hardly more than a year (September, 1816) subsequent to the Waltham invention, the Scotch loom was introduced in this country by William Gilmore, a Scotch machinist, who was thoroughly acquainted with the original construction of Cartwright, and the various improvements which had rendered it a practical machine. Of Gilmore, Mr. Allen's memoranda says: "The principal great impulse given to power-loom weaving was accomplished by William Gilmore, who came from Scotland with the latest improved Scotch loom, warper, and dresser, in 1815. He built several looms at the Lyman factory in North Providence."

Gilmore's first communication with manufacturers in New England was at Slatersville with John Slater. Mr. Slater was in favor of accepting his proposition to construct the Scotch loom for his company, but, in the depression of business, his partners were averse to any new investment of capital. At this time fortunately, Judge Lyman, who had employed Blydenburgh to put up several looms in his mill, which did not operate satisfactorily, heard of the foreign machinist, and at once employed him to build twelve machines. They were completed fully to the satisfaction of the patron, and successfully operated early in 1817.

This was the first introduction of the crank-loom in this country, the maker receiving fifteen hundred dollars for his services—a most inadequate recognition, if we consider the enormous benefits accruing to the industry from its results.

"Mule-spinning," says Mr. Batchelder, "having been introduced in Rhode Island, the building of the power-loom by Gilmore completed the manufacturing system of that State within about three years from the time when the power-loom was put in operation at Waltham.

"It was not until ten years after the crank-loom had been in use in Rhode Island that it was adopted at Waltham or Lowell, and in neither place, nor in any of the mills that followed their system, was mule-spinning introduced until after 1830."

The last important advance in mill machinery through the introduction of the self-acting mule of Sharp & Roberts will be noticed at length in the history of Fall River cotton manufacture.

With the completion of the processes of cloth-making, within the factory, by the introduction of the power-loom, the industry became permanently established in the United States. Notwithstanding the unstable policy of parties upon the question of tariffs and imports, the number of mills was constantly increasing, and, as they began to be built on a larger scale, the number of spindles was likewise even more largely extended.

From the statistics of cotton manufacturing embodied in the census of 1820 the following statement is extracted:

STATES.	POUNDS OF COTTON ANNUALLY SPUN.	NUMBER OF SPINDLES.	STATES.	POUNDS OF COTTON ANNUALLY SPUN.	NUMBER OF SPINDLES.
Maine	56,500	3,070	Pennsylvania	1,067,753	13,776
New Hampshire	412,100	13,013	Delaware	423,800	11,784
Massachusetts	1,611,796	30,304	Maryland	849,000	20,245
Rhode Island	1,914,220	63,372	Virginia	3,000	
Connecticut	807,335	29,826	North Carolina	18,000	288
Vermont	117,250	3,278	South Carolina	46,449	588
New York	1,412,495	33,160	Kentucky	360,951	8,097
New Jersey	648,600	18,124	Ohio	81,360	1,680

This estimate, showing a material falling off from the figures presented to Congress in 1815 by the Committee on Manufactures, was evidently inadequate. In 1821, as will appear, the amount of cotton consumed in domestic manufacturing was 20,000,000 lbs.

In 1825, the number of spindles operated in the United States was estimated at 800,000, and the cotton worked up, 100,000 bales. The average price per pound was 11 cents. The average price of the prints of the Merrimac Company at Lowell was 25.07 cents per yard.

In 1826, quoting Bishop's *History of American Manufactures*, the number of distinct factory buildings in New England was estimated at 400, averaging 700 spindles each, or 280,000 in all. The new ones were very large, the old ones quite small. Each spindle was presumed to consume about one half a pound of cotton per day, or 140 pounds per annum, which, for 280 days' work, gave 39,200,000 pounds, or about 98,000 bales for the year's consumption. About one third of the buildings employed power-looms, one third hand-looms, and the others spun yarn and twist for the Middle and Western States. The factories were distributed about as follows: In Massachusetts, 135; Rhode Island, 110; Connecticut, 80; New Hampshire, 50; Maine, 15; Vermont, 10. The number of cotton factories in all the other States was estimated at 275, of the same average size, which would make the total annual consumption about 150,000 bales, or 60,000,000 pounds.

In 1831, in the midst of the heated controversy between not only parties, but individual thinkers, upon the proper and just tariff policy, a convention of prominent promoters of domestic industry was held in the city of New York on the 26th of October. This convention included over five hundred delegates from the Eastern and Middle States, Virginia, Maryland, and Ohio, and its discussion elicited correct and reliable statements of the condition and relative importance of "the various pursuits of domestic industry." The subjoined summary of the report of the Committee on Cotton Manufacture is copied from Mr. Bishop's History:

"From the best information that could be obtained, the Committee on Cotton, of which P. T. Jackson, of Massachusetts, was chairman, estimated the crop of the United States, after the year ending October 1, to be, in the Atlantic States, 486,103 bales of 306 pounds each, equal to 148,747,518 pounds, and in the Southern and Western States, 552,744 bales of 411 pounds, equivalent to 227,177,784 pounds, giving a total crop of 1,038,847 bales, or 375,925,302 pounds. The domestic consumption amounted to more than one fifth of the whole crop; and the value of the product, allowing it to be increased four-fold in the process of manufacture, probably four fifths that of the cotton crop, and equal to the value of the whole quantity exported.

"The following is a summary of the detail of the cotton manufacture in the twelve Eastern and Middle States, including Maryland and Virginia. But owing to misapprehension of the question respecting capital, only that employed in fixtures was returned, and some manufacturers were reluctant to give the details of their business, for which reasons it was thought that one fourth to one third might be safely added to the account. The statement was exclusive of no less than thirty establishments returned from the Southern and Western

States, from which no accurate details were received, and also of family manufactures. The cotton mills in the twelve numbered seven hundred and ninety-five.

	Total in Cotton Mills.	Machine Shops.	Bleacheries.	Printeries.	Total.
Capital (principally in fixtures) in dollars	40,614,984	2,400,000	900,000	1,000,000	44,914,934
Spindles in operation	1,246,503	......	......	......	......
Yards of cloth made	230,461,900	......	......	......	......
Pounds of yarn sold	10,642,000	......	......	......	......
Pounds of cotton used (214,822 bales)	77,757,316	......	......	......	......
Hands employed (females, 38,927)	62,157	3,200	738	1,505	67,600
Pounds of starch used	1,641,253	......	429,625	......	2,070,873
Barrels of flour for sizing	17,245	......	......	1,300	18,455
Cords of wood	46,519	......	......	30,000	76,519
Tons of coal	24,420	......	19,250	2,250	45,920
Bushels of charcoal	39,205	......	......	......	......
Gallons of oil	300,338	......	......	2,800	303,138
Value of other articles in dollars	599,223	1,960,212	276,625	935,585	3,766,283
Spindles building	172,024	......	......	......	......
Hand weavers	4,760	......	......	......	......
Total dependents	117,625	9,600	1,403	2,860	131,489
Annual value in dollars	26,000,000	3,500,000	1,036,760	1,500,000	32,036,760
Aggregate wages	10,294,944	1,248,000	209,814	402,965	12,155,723

From 1831 to 1836 a large increase of the capacity of distinct mills was observed, the new erections averaging from five to six thousand spindles. This enlargement of mill capacity continued with the growth of the industry, but is now believed to have reached its maximum.

It is unfortunately impossible to furnish an exact statement of the number of mills engaged in the various branches of cotton manufacture in the United States. In 1850 they numbered 1094, employing 92,286 hands, consuming 288,558,000 pounds of cotton, and realizing a product worth 865,501,687 upon a capital invested of $74,500,931. In 1860, there were 1091 mills of 5,235,727 spindles, employing 122,028 hands, consuming 422,704,975 pounds of cotton, producing $115,681,744 of goods, on an invested capital of $98,585,269. In 1870 the number of distinct producers had fallen off to 956; but this does not indicate a diminution in the industry, the estimate of spindles operated being 7,132,415; the hands employed, 135,369; cotton worked up, 409,899,746 pounds; capital invested $140,706,291; and the value of product, $177,489,739. The foregoing figures are taken from the census reports for the several decades. The report of the amount of cotton worked up in 1860 is obviously an error, and is more correctly estimated by Mr. Nourse at 364,036,123 pounds.

The subjoined summary of the strictly cloth-producing business of the country was made up in November, 1874, by the thorough statistician of the *New York Commercial and Financial Chronicle*, and its tables republished in 1875 as a correct exhibit of the industry.

STATEMENT OF THE NUMBER AND CAPACITY OF COTTON MILLS IN THE UNITED STATES AND THE CONSUMPTION OF COTTON FOR THE YEAR ENDING JULY 1, 1874.

NORTHERN STATES.	No. of Mills.	No. of Looms.	No. of Spindles.	SOUTHERN STATES.	No. of Mills.	No. of Looms.	No. of Spindles.
Maine	24	12,415	609,898	Alabama	16	1,360	57,594
New Hampshire	42	20,422	855,189	Arkansas	2	28	1,256
Vermont	10	1,274	58,948	Georgia	42	2,934	137,330
Massachusetts	194	71,202	3,769,292	Kentucky	4	42	10,500
Rhode Island	115	24,706	1,336,842	Louisiana	3	300	15,000
Connecticut	104	18,170	908,200	Mississippi	11	348	15,150
New York	55	12,476	580,917	Missouri	4	382	18,656
New Jersey	17	2,000	150,968	North Carolina	30	1,055	55,498
Pennsylvania	60	9,772	452,964	South Carolina	18	1,238	62,872
Delaware	8	796	47,976	Tennessee	42	1,014	42,058
Maryland	21	2,399	110,260	Texas	4	230	10,225
Ohio	5	236	20,410	Virginia	11	1,664	56,490
Indiana	4	618	22,988				
Minnesota	1	24	3,400				
Total	660	176,480	8,927,754	Total	187	10,495	487,639

RECAPITULATIONS.

	No. of Mills.	No. of Looms.	No. of Spindles.	Average Size of Yarn. No.
Total Northern	660	176,480	8,927,754	28.56
Total Southern	187	10,495	487,569	12.50
Grand Total	847	186,975	9,415,323	27.73

COTTON USED.

	Lbs.	Bales.
Northern States	507,790,099	1,094,387
Southern States	59,793,775	128,526
Total	567,583,873	1,222,913

We have seen that the number of spinning spindles in the United States on the 1st of July, 1874, was 9,415,383 against 7,114,000 at the same date of 1870, and 6,763,557 at the same date of 1869, as follows:

1874.	Looms.	Spindles.
North	176,480	8,927,754
South	10,495	487,629
Total 1874	186,975	9,415,383
1870.		
North	147,682	6,851,779
South	5,852	262,221
Total 1870	153,534	7,114,000
1869.		
North	....	6,538,494
South	....	225,063
Total 1869	....	6,763,527

The above records a very rapid progress since 1870, being about 33 per cent in the number of spinning spindles.

GOODS MANUFACTURED THIS YEAR.

No portion of our inquiry has been more difficult than the obtaining of statistics with regard to production, and no one, of the results reached, possesses more interest. The most notable feature is the enormous production of print cloths. It is to be regretted that we have no figures for previous years with which to make comparisons, or by which we could show the growth of this branch of manufacture, but it is well known they have increased rapidly of late years. Of course we do not claim that these results of quantities and kinds of goods are as exact as the returns of consumption ; but we believe they are as close an approximation as the nature of the case will permit.

STATEMENT OF THE KINDS AND QUANTITIES OF COTTON GOODS MANUFACTURED IN THE UNITED STATES FOR THE YEAR ENDING JULY 1, 1874.

	New England States.	Middle and Western States.	Total Northern States.	Total Southern States.	Total United States.
Threads, yarns, and twines, lbs.	32,000,000	99,000,000	131,000,000	18,000,000	149,000,000
Sheetings, shirtings, and like plain goods, yards	520,000,000	90,000,000	610,000,000	97,000,000	707,000,000
Twilled and fancy goods, Osnaburgs, jeans, etc., yards	204,000,000	80,000,000	284,000,000	22,000,000	306,000,000
Print cloths, yards	481,000,000	107,000,000	588,000,000	......	588,000,000
Gingham, yards	30,000,000	3,000,000	33,000,000	......	33,000,000
Ducks, yards	14,000,000	16,000,000	30,000,000	......	30,000,000
Bags, No.	5,000,000	1,000,000	6,000,000	......	6,000,000

Besides the above, there is a large production of hosiery and knit goods, made of cotton by itself or mixed with wool, of which we are able to give no satisfactory statement. Another year we hope to push our investigations as to production in every direction.

The exportation of cotton cloth was an important feature in the commercial relations of the country at a comparatively early period of the industry. The goods first made at Waltham were heavy sheetings, of the kind which has since been the staple production, and under the name of "American domestics," won and retained the preference for excellence of quality in every market of the world. The superiority of this branch of American production was soon recognized by the British manufacturers, and the dangerous competition threatened therein was very seriously discussed by the commercial and practical writers of England. So great was the alarm of the cotton interest of Manchester, that it resorted not only to furtive attempts to create a public sentiment in this country antagonistic to protection, but adopted trade-marks, mill-tickets and stamps similar to the American, and in every possible way sought to imitate the production of the New England mills. So persistent was this effort, that in 1827 the demand for American domestics in Brazil was considerably affected by the competition of a lower grade of goods, pretending to be New England fabric, but made in Manchester, and offered at a less price. The efforts of Manchester to substitute its inferior cloth, though pursued with desperation of purpose, were, however, only temporarily successful, the American exportation constantly increasing. Dr. Livingstone, who was in his youth a weaver, in his first published record of travel, speaks of finding in the hut of a negro king a piece of Manchester cloth labelled New York Mills—so wretched an imitation of the well-known fabric it claimed to be, that he seems to wonder at the attempted deception even in the wilds of Africa.

In 1835 the exportation had attained a really respectable position, promising, if continued, to consume a considerable proportion of the entire production. Of this period Mr. Bishop remarks:

> "The quantity of cotton long cloths imported this year from the United States into China was 134,000 pieces, and of cotton domestics 32,743 pieces; while of cotton goods the whole importation into that country in British vessels was only 75,922 pieces. The importation of American piece goods was nearly double that of the previous year, amounting to 24,745 pieces. An extensive manufacturer of Glasgow, who had for several years supplied Chili with cotton domestics, spun and woven in his own works to the best advantage, had latterly been obliged to abandon the trade to American competition. At Manilla, 35,240 pieces of thirty-inch and 7000 pieces of twenty-eight-inch American gray cottons were received, and only 1832 pieces of Belfast manufacture. The ports of Rio de Janeiro, Aux Cayes, of Malta, Smyrna, and the Cape of Good Hope, were also overstocked with American unbleached cottons, to the exclusion of British goods, which they undersold."

The terribly disastrous effects of the civil war, almost sweeping American commerce from the seas, at last gave to the British manufacturer the advantage he was unable to secure in a legitimate competition. Up to the appearance of rebel privateers upon the ocean, our domestic production in nearly every foreign market was preferred to the British, and in China had well-nigh driven it from the field. Mr. Eli T. Sheppard, United States Consul at Tien-tsin, the principal port of entry for cotton fabrics, in a communication to the State Department, October 10, 1872, in regard to the relative position of American and British stuffs, remarks as follows:

"The importation of American cotton manufactured goods into China is worthy of our most earnest consideration. Ever since the British plenipotentiary, who signed the treaty at Nankin in 1842, informed his countrymen that ' he had opened up a country to their trade so vast that all the mills in Lancashire, by running night and day, could not make stocking-stuff enough for one of its provinces," the question of supplying China with manufactured cottons has been one of the most absorbing interest for the wisest statesmen and political economists of Great Britain.

"During the year 1861, before the civil war in America had seriously crippled our commerce and manufactures, 133,401 pieces of American drills and jeans were sold in Tien-tsin, netting in gold $583,223. So great, indeed, had become the demand for American cotton fabrics, that the demand far exceeded the supply.

"Against the 133,401 pieces of American goods imported at Tien-tsin in

1861, the number of pieces of English drills imported was only 3599 pieces for the same period. In other words, the trade at this port in American cottons was, in round numbers, forty times that of English manufactured articles of a like character. During the war the imports of American cottons became merely nominal, while a corresponding increase of English fabrics supplied the market. From this I infer that there is no good reason why American manufactured cotton goods should not again resume their place in the markets of China.

"Cotton manufactures form at present the largest part of the direct trade between England and China, and Tien-tsin has already become the largest importer of these articles in the empire."

In 1859 and 1860, preceding the war, there were severally shipped from the port of New York alone to China and the East Indies 53,662 and 47,735 packages. In 1861, the effect of the war not yet being seriously felt, the amount fell off to 31,911 packages. In 1862 to 1865 the exportation was entirely cut off, and the Chinese market virtually lost to American industry. Since the close of the internecine struggle, efforts have been made to re-establish the trade, the shipments from New York in 1866 being 6,972 packages; but it is a difficult undertaking to build again both trade and commerce.

Meanwhile the competitors of the United States in China, the English and Dutch manufacturers, had enjoyed the trade without even a contest; the former not only, in the forced absence of his old antagonist, still pursuing the dishonest practice of assuming his trade-marks, and using every means to counterfeit his production in appearance, but resorting to a fraudulent debasing of the fabric in both material and finish that has threatened to close the Eastern market to all European as well as American enterprise. This pernicious policy of the Manchester cotton interest was manifested to some degree in the early period of competition, English cloth having always discovered a proportion of foreign matter in its material when tested by washing. Within the present decade, the practice of introducing clay and other matter to increase the weight, and exaggerating the "sizing" far beyond the requisite degree needed to dress the warp properly, has, however, reached a point at which adulteration is a mild term to apply to it. The fraud had in 1873 become so flagrant as to force the British merchants in China to memorialize the Manchester Chamber of Commerce upon the subject, and the *London Times* to utter the protest of honest industry as follows:

"It seems a pity that the present exhibition was not made the opportunity of instructing the public in that dark chapter of the cotton manufacture known as the 'sizing' question, concerning which a memorial went up to the Government last year from the weavers of Todmorden, and has been followed this year by a very clear and emphatic report from Dr. Buchanan, a Government officer commissioned to make inquiries. This matter of the 'sizing' of cotton lies in a nutshell, and we will state it shortly for the information of those who are not likely to see Dr. Buchanan's temperate but decided report. Up to twenty years ago fermented flour and tallow were used in the cotton manufacture to give tenacity to the warp and to lessen the friction in weaving. It was then found that the brown color imparted to the cloth by size made from cheap and bad flour could be corrected by china clay added to the size, and furthermore that this clay lessened the amount of tallow needed in the size. The clay came thus into use, and its use became still more general when the Russian war raised the price of tallow. Presently came the American war of secession, and the manufacturers were forced to put up with bad, short-fibred cotton, difficult to weave. It was then further found that a free use of size gave to poor sorts of cotton the needful tenacity of twist, and, weight for length being the test of good cloth, it was also evident that the more the size used the greater the weight. Thus very soon a practice crept in, and has now spread largely over the cotton trade, of unwarrantably loading cotton with quantities of size laid on to the warps to the extent of forty, sixty, and even, as the weavers assert, one hundred per cent of their original weight. This practice of deliberate adulteration has become in the cotton trade a recognized detail of manufacture; but, however it may be viewed by those interested in the practice, it must still seem a downright dishonesty to the outer world. But the dishonesty of this practice is not the worst part of it, for the weavers suffer far more than the public, being compelled to inhale the dust of the clay as it rises from the warps. The Government report shows this 'heavy sizing' process has thus converted weaving from a healthy into an unhealthy occupation; that it has made the weaving-room more dusty than the carding-room, and that it has sensibly increased among weavers in the clay-using mills lung diseases and the death-rate. It is intolerable that operatives should thus suffer because their employers choose to indulge in a questionable practice, and we trust that in the name of common humanity and commercial morality some speedy stop may be put to a state of things so deeply scandalous."

In March, 1874, Mr. Sheppard, the very intelligent representative of the United States at Tien-tsin, in his official report to the State Department, referred at length to the adulteration fraud, accompanying his document with copious extracts from the *North China Herald* and other public expressions, indicating the disgust of all European residents in the Celestial Kingdom:

"Although the raw material used in manufacturing these fabrics, consumed by China, is chiefly produced in the United States, yet American cotton must now pass through the looms of England and Holland before it can find a market in China. The superior quality of American cotton is well known to Chinese traders. Our cotton goods, by reason of their cheapness before the war, supplied the China markets to the exclusion of all others, and created a demand that, since our war, has steadily increased to its present imposing magnitude. The superiority of our cotton still remains an enduring advantage possessed by American fabrics over all others; but this important advantage is now almost entirely neutralized by their high cost, as compared with those others.

"One material advantage reaped, and still enjoyed, by England from the civil war in the United States, was the monopoly of supplying China with manufactured cotton goods. Cheap labor was unquestionably the cause of this; but after the monopoly of this trade had been fully secured to England as a consequence of our war, English manufacturers did not rest satisfied with the single advantage sustaining their monopoly—cheap labor—but resorted to counterfeiting American trade-marks that had become popular among the Chinese. The end in view was duly attained, by successfully palming off inferior English cotton fabrics upon unsuspecting native merchants as American manufactures, and thus our share in this trade was still further effectually reduced to its present insignificant proportions. As might be expected, deception was not confined to counterfeiting trade-marks and the names of American mills; a wider field was opened for its practice, and the system of over-sizing or weighting the cotton goods with worthless substances, such as clay, etc., was commenced by English manufacturers shortly after our war, and has since developed into what it is at present—a gigantic fraud.

"By this practice cotton goods, which are sold by the piece, weighing a certain number of pounds, are so prepared by manufacturers as to reduce the proper amount of cotton from one third to one half; and this deficiency in weight is made up by worthless rubbish, which does not outlast the first washing to which the cloth is subjected by the native consumer, who is deceived in buying it.

"Although our interest in the trade is now so small, it is well to mention here that this fraudulent practice is receiving the countenance of American trade-marks, which are still extensively used by English manufacturers; and thus the injury which American trade at first suffered through counterfeiting is now aggravated by the further dishonesty of adulteration.

"It is a question whether this fraudulent practice of over-sizing would have occasioned so much outspoken condemnation among those who are interested in the English trade, excepting manufacturers, had it not been that an unlooked-for result of over-sizing—namely, mildew, made its appearance to such an extent that a large proportion of English cotton goods sent to China was, and is still, found to be unmerchantable as sound goods on reaching this country. Hence, over-sizing, or weighting, is now better and less offensively known as the 'mildew question.' The English manufacturers and merchants appear to have joined issue on this question. The merchants and their agents accuse the manufacturers of dishonesty, and the latter rejoin that merchants encourage and sustain the practice of weighting by buying goods so prepared in preference to honest goods. Meanwhile the trade continues, and weighting increases, and is likely to continue so long as the Chinese consumer is the chief sufferer.

"But the iniquities of the English trade in cotton goods are working its disorganization, and perhaps destruction. When, after having fatally overreached themselves, those interested in the trade are found, as they now are, each enjoining upon his neighbor one of the first principles of morality taught in the maxim that 'honesty is the best policy,' there is ground for hope that honesty will be allowed to prevail over deceit and fraud. But an honest trade implies honest competition; and honest competition in the foreign cotton goods trade in China would result in the ascendency of American interests, and a complete reversing of the present huge and unnatural disproportion between American and English trade in China."

It is of course understood that the bulk of American exportation of cotton manufactured is of the "domestic" article, in which the raw material enters more largely into the product. The balance of trade in cloth is largely against the United States, England still finding with us a market for her very finest fabrics, and France and England both sending us enormous quantities of prints. In 1874, for instance, while our total of exports was but $3,091,332, our total of imports of manufactured cotton was $28,183,878. During the twelvemonth now closing the outward movement of American "domestics" has been extraordinary, the largest in many years, and hopeful augury for the future is justifiable. It is also gratifying that in our own market American prints have begun to secure the permanent approval of their merits which is really due to their quality and finish, and that consequently the year's close will show an importation largely decreased from previous annual summaries.

The following tables of exports from the ports of New York and Boston, of manufactured cotton, from 1849 to 1876 inclusive, compiled by the New York *Journal of Commerce*, will be found both interesting and valuable. The statement for 1876 includes only the shipments reported up to the week ending November 18th, inclusive.

DESTINATION.	1849.	1850.	1851.	1852.	1853.	1854.	1855.
	Packages.	Packages.	Packages.	Packages.	Packages.	Packages.	Packages.
Mexico	1,920	2,463	820	1,479	8,765	1,713	2,972
Dutch West Indies	359	289	352	321	292	306	337
Swedish West Indies	51	16	24	21	3	3	6
Danish West Indies	116	56	261	70	82	147	284
British West Indies	19	131	131	131	89	903	499
Spanish West Indies	97	129	132	77	13	69	1,143
St. Domingo	324	1,208	1,895	736	292	208	411
British North America	4	47	195	108	56	54	16
New Granada	163	206	153	643	396	112	131
Brazil	1,783	1,478	3,178	3,281	1,194	2,682	2,764
Venezuela	548	990	865	865	462	988	1,094
Argentine Republic	957	249	86	1,475	250	1,445	468
Cisplatine Republic	....	....	....	....	....	....	....

Destination.	1849.	1850.	1851.	1852.	1853.	1854.	1855.
	Packages.	Packages.	Packages.	Packages.	Packages.	Packages.	Packages.
Central America	354	607	1,218	653	713	43	495
West Coast South America	2,603	3,426	1,395	2,743	1,642	809	1,152
Honduras	859	101	150	246	179	276	401
Africa	475	538	1,772	3,405	1,239	1,007	1,324
Australia	....	....	....	....	200	529	1,908
East Indies and China	13,143	20,091	27,002	38,413	18,889	12,436	11,929
All others	231	130	31	25	82	550	251
Total packages shipped from New York	24,006	32,155	40,560	54,692	34,828	24,280	27,585
Add packages shipped from Boston to all ports	41,344	34,307	46,589	59,295	54,729	35,428	34,093
Total packages from both ports	65,350	66,462	87,149	113,987	89,557	59,708	61,678

Destination.	1856.	1857.	1858.	1859.	1860.	1861.	1862.
	Packages.	Packages.	Packages.	Packages.	Packages.	Packages.	Packages.
Mexico	4,897	2,084	2,446	2,475	4,873	2,766	2,427
Dutch West Indies	151	581	317	531	664	569	84
Swedish West Indies	10	....	4	....	47	38	....
Danish West Indies	427	564	691	696	952	522	316
British West Indies	880	207	219	227	497	537	165
Spanish West Indies	151	223	358	366	193	374	140
St. Domingo	228	591	262	977	2,169	1,257	484
British North America	25	42	14	18	10	60	23
New Granada	949	560	627	767	1,381	2,005	609
Brazil	3,756	2,751	4,466	3,637	8,103	5,400	953
Venezuela	335	268	523	919	1,328	1,421	141
Argentine Republic	590	90	328	903	1,111	430	145
Cisplatine Republic	....	....	....	....	....	....	....
Central America	190	101	200	55	53	23	1
West Coast South America	158	3,710	4,195	6,606	13,291	5,299	1
Honduras	160	170	436	259	389	245	12
Africa	1,874	1,414	1,200	323	1,406	876	49
Australia	2,060	418	109	135	323	180	3
East Indies and China	17,674	12,676	43,419	53,662	47,735	31,911	187
All others	267	203	180	1,793	1,793	1,823	47
Total packages shipped from New York	34,782	26,653	59,994	74,549	86,318	55,736	5,787
Add packages shipped from Boston to all ports	37,880	26,000	29,875	31,661	33,588	18,146	4,238
Total packages from both ports	72,662	52,653	89,869	106,210	119,906	73,882	10,625

Destination.	1863.	1864.	1865.	1866.	1867.	1868.	1869.
	Packages.	Packages.	Packages.	Packages.	Packages.	Packages.	Packages.
Mexico	1,886	849	112	282	1,090	1,837	1,496
Dutch West Indies	9	3	....	42	133	157	310
Swedish West Indies	....	....	....	....	....	....	....
Danish West Indies	29	1	8	16	33	87	170
British West Indies	149	24	9	58	254	399	335
Spanish West Indies	66	86	30	22	292	140	273
St. Domingo	63	12	....	9	244	69	138
British North America	16	....	....	3	....	14	30
New Granada	356	83	11	423	575	253	1,083
Brazil	86	4	....	261	2,343	1,716	1,494

COTTON AND ITS MANUFACTURE.

Destination.	1863.	1864.	1865.	1866.	1867.	1868.	1869.
	Packages.	Packages.	Packages.	Packages.	Packages.	Packages.	Packages.
Venezuela	32	9	4	35	116	303	84
Argentine Republic	13	2	17	77	551	529	1,377
Cisplatine Republic	19	8	3	59	399	121	247
Central America	1	6	....	....	3	3	49
West Coast South America	....	2	....	293	1,024	207	667
Honduras	5	4	....	5	47	121	38
Africa	11	24	....	807	2,016	2,700	2,255
Australia	....	....	....	....	....	....	....
East Indies and China	5	7	....	6,972	4,558	15,677	10,471
All others	30	8	....	52	197	1,715	485
Total packages shipped from New York	2,776	1,132	194	9,416	13,875	26,048	21,047
Add packages shipped from Boston to all ports	421	264	308	6,802	9,031	11,422	7,185
Total packages from both ports	3,197	1,396	502	16,218	22,906	37,470	28,232

Destination.	1870.	1871.	1872.	1873.	1874.	1875.	1876.
	Packages.	Packages.	Packages.	Packages.	Packages.	Packages.	Packages.
Mexico	680	1,948	1,593	1,402	1,529	1,230	1,635
Dutch West Indies	270	339	329	330	318	194	95
Swedish West Indies	....	....	....	....	....	....	....
Danish West Indies	285	139	281	161	139	178	194
British West Indies	261	241	348	323	438	329	723
Spanish West Indies	543	731	646	610	409	328	780
St. Domingo	1,698	829	625	1,376	1,123	2,867	1,027
British North America	48	43	32	93	81	664	825
New Granada	1,139	1,464	785	643	1,012	1,224	4,156
Brazil	1,712	2,431	2,886	2,879	3,699	5,320	4,831
Venezuela	164	381	458	252	708	1,276	1,880
Argentine Republic	617	85	472	1,194	285	1,000	523
Cisplatine Republic	256	317	255	745	671	73	505
Central America	54	4	44	252	148	77	310
West Coast South America	624	387	336	972	....	990	425
Honduras	39	81	164	136	195	298	607
Africa	1,927	1,524	1,563	1,024	1,049	2,614	2,757
Australia	....	....	....	....	....	....	68
East Indies and China	3,174	5,488	1,798	2,302	6,349	10,017	13,415
All others	1,051	583	510	2,382	4,704	8,886	27,172
Total packages shipped from New York	14,482	17,049	13,045	17,281	23,047	37,574	63,828
Add packages shipped from Boston to all ports	7,550	11,157	4,889	7,442	13,876	16,935	24,392
Total packages from both ports	22,032	28,206	17,934	24,723	36,923	54,509	87,220

The cotton manufacture of Europe and America at the close of 1874 is shown in the subjoined table:

	No. of Spindles.	Pounds per Spindle.	Total Pounds.	Bales of 400 Pounds.	Average per Week.
England	37,515,000	32	1,259,836,000	3,149,590	60,569
United States	9,415,383	65	522,378,200	1,305,943	25,114
Russia and Poland	2,500,000	60	150,000,000	375,000	7,212
Sweden and Norway	305,000	65	19,825,000	49,562	913
Germany	4,650,000	55	255,750,000	639,375	12,296
Austria	1,555,000	67	104,185,000	260,463	5,009

	No. of Spindles.	Pounds per Spindle.	Total Pounds.	Bales of 400 Pounds.	Average per Week.
Switzerland	1,850,000	25	46,250,000	115,625	2,223
Holland	230,000	60	13,800,000	34,500	663
Belgium	800,000	50	40,000,000	100,000	1,923
France	5,000,000	42	210,000,000	525,000	10,096
Spain	1,750,000	46	80,500,000	201,250	3,870
Italy	800,000	56	44,800,000	112,000	2,154
Totals	66,370,383	..	1,747,324,200	6,868,308	142,042

The four principal centres of the manufacture are in Massachusetts and New Hampshire. The first factory was started in Fall River in 1813. At Amoskeag Falls, New Hampshire, a mill was operated in 1804, but the large enterprise of Manchester dates from 1831. The first cotton mill in Lowell, then East Chelmsford, was established in 1822, and the first in Lawrence in 1849. Fall River is at present, and promises to continue to be, the chief seat of the manufacture in the United States.

In 1837 the Secretary of State of Massachusetts was instructed by a concurrent vote of the Legislature to prepare a statistical exhibit of the several conspicuous industries of the Commonwealth. The following statement of the cotton manufacture, tabulated by counties, was embodied in his report:

COUNTIES.	No. of Mills.	No. of Spindles.	Pounds of Cotton consumed Y'rly.	Yards of Cloth man'fd Yearly.	Value of Cotton Goods man'fd Y'rly. Dollars.	Males em- ploy'd	F'mles em- ploy'd	Capital invested in the Cotton mnfr Dollars.
Suffolk	..	......	......	......	......	..	..	......
Essex	7	13,300	804,222	2,301,520	372,972	115	402	337,500
Middlesex	34	165,868	17,696,245	52,860,194	5,071,172	1054	6435	6,900,000
Worcester	74	124,720	5,292,018	20,250,312	1,991,024	1384	1998	2,015,100
Hampshire	6	8,312	563,000	1,574,000	176,060	72	233	216,000
Hampden	20	66,552	4,727,302	15,107,583	1,504,896	626	1886	1,698,500
Franklin	4	5,024	135,045	1,081,140	76,125	48	140	90,000
Berkshire	31	35,260	1,390,162	7,530,667	575,087	339	766	633,725
Norfolk	32	25,782	1,365,953	4,953,816	509,383	280	583	609,500
Bristol	57	104,507	4,814,238	18,382,828	1,678,226	987	2015	1,622,778
Plymouth	15	13,298	480,884	2,052,061	182,474	85	279	230,616
Barnstable	2	1,508	6,848	195,100	19,240	7	20	7,000
Dukes Cou..ty	..	......	......	......	......	..	..	......
Nantucket	..	......	......	......	......	..	..	......
Total	282	565,031	37,275,917	126,319,221	13,056,659	4997	14,757	14,369,719

In comparison with the figures of this report of the cotton manufacture of Massachusetts in 1837, Fall River makes the following exhibit in 1876:

No. of Mills.	No. of Spindles.	Pounds of Cotton Consumed Annually.	Yards of Cloth Manufactured.	Employés.	Capital Invested.
33	1,258,508	58,050,000	340,000,000	14,000	$30,000,000

The extraordinary development of Fall River has been effected by several causes. Baines attributed the origin and growth of Manchester to the fortunate location of the place in the centre of a district rich in "water-power, fuel, and iron," possessing "ready communication with the sea by means of its well-situated port, Liverpool," and early enjoying the "acquired advantage of a canal communication." These tributary circumstances are generally wanting in the case of Fall River, which possesses neither iron nor fuel in close proximity to its demands, and reaps no appreciable advantage from its water beyond its use in the engine-rooms and the bleaching processes. Yet in several respects the location of the city is favorable to the prosecution of its great industry. Its relation to the sea, more immediate than that of its great rival, is a positive aid, the depth of water at its wharves admitting the loading and discharging not only of coasting craft, but of large ships. Thus the coal absolutely necessary for the fuel of the mill engines, and the iron worked up in its machine shops and foundries, are conveyed from the mines, in most cases, entirely by water carriage, reducing the cost of freightage to the *minimum* figure, and giving the hive of industry on Mount Hope Bay a superiority over manufacturing towns situated inland and obtaining their supplies by railroad.

In the relation of Fall River to the sea exists likewise a circumstance favorably affecting the manufacture of cotton. One of the traditional claims of England to an advantage over other countries in this pursuit has been its "sea-girt" position, which assures a constant humidity, that is an essential, in a greater or less degree, in all the stages of cloth production. Of course, the atmosphere of the region in and about Fall River has far from the same degree of moisture that is permanent in England, and a still less constituent proportion than that of the Irish coast, exposed immediately to the dense fogs of the Gulf Stream, and especially created (if we may credit the superstition of the Belfast people) by a beneficent Providence for the fabrication of linen; yet, with its slight remove from the ocean, whose moist breath is softened by its passage up the inland estuary, while the English air carries the extreme of humidity to the spinning and weaving processes, that of the great American manufacturing district probably enjoys the really proper mean of temperature. In this connection an extract from recent statements of the Coast Survey officials regarding the relative temperatures of New England localities is of interest: "Locally there are some important modifications of this general character, chief of which is the softening of the extremes of heat and cold on the islands and coasts of the south-east, Nantucket, Barnstable, and Bristol counties. The well-known mildness of Newport continues all along the coast, and the difference" (between it and the extreme cold of interior Massachusetts) "in winter is very marked. The Gulf Stream comes near enough to be sensibly felt, in addition to the general modifications" (of the inland rule of extreme heat or cold) "caused by the extension, as it may be called, of these districts into the sea. Though storms are very violent off

Cape Cod, and the long circuit southward of Nantucket, the temperature is still so much modified as to be 7° warmer for the mean of the winter months at Nantucket than at Cambridge, and nearly 5° warmer at New Bedford, Williamstown" (Berkshire County) "is 7° colder than New Bedford for the average of the winter months."

It will be remembered that New Bedford and Fall River are closely contiguous points, bearing about the same relation to the sea.

The internal administration of a Fall River industry is not essentially different from that in other advanced centres of cotton manufacturing, treasurers, agents, and superintendents of mills exercising the duties conventionally attaching to those offices. But, unlike other centres, the treasurers are invariably residents, and generally the subordinate offices are filled by persons immediately interested in the business. The stockholders likewise are, in a much greater proportion than governs elsewhere, "native there, and to the manner born." This is a very great, indeed, an almost incalculable factor in the general development. Absenteeism, the curse of most large congregations of industry, is unknown and, happily, unfelt in its baleful influences. The community itself, in its integral construction and outward manifestation, is one of active, interested workers, the owners and projectors breathing the same atmosphere with the operatives, who, in their turn, under such a system, may also become, by diligence and temperance, owners and projectors. From this condition of the community results the intensely practical spirit that pervades and controls the place, and assures conservatism of management and wise husbandry of resources through the control and under the watchfulness of a universal intelligence. Too much importance can not be ascribed to this most fortunate sympathy of the social and economical constituents of any population; but its largest uses and richest results are manifested in the great cotton-manufacturing centres.

To the conservatism and practical nature of the people of Fall River is due the fact that the history of the place shows so insignificant a number of industrial disappointments. In 1871-2, when mills were springing up in number like a forest, the business world was dazed by the extraordinary spectacle, and wiseacres, who did not know its people, began to mutter, "Fall River is mad, downright crazy." The event has not, however, justified the censures of the cynics or the croakings of the seers. On the contrary, the statisticians have discovered that the number of spindles added to the productive force was demanded by the development of trade, and that what appeared to be the inspiration of an inflated unreason was really the movement of a calm and intelligent calculation. Speculative ideas and business charlatanry, so far from being encouraged, are not even entertained by these practical schemers, and the result is that no place in New England, within our ken, has so very small a grave-yard of deceased enterprises, great expectations that have died of slow consumption or sudden collapse.

What the future has in store for Fall River, if we study simply its past, need not be answered indefinitely. To-day not a spindle in its mills, nor a granite block in their walls, is weighted with a mortgage. It is the first city in the extent of its cotton manufacture in the United States, and second only to Manchester in the world. Its resources are within its own community, and the market for its production is the whole globe. So long as the same conservative enterprise, honest purpose, and harmony of effort, which have established its fortunes, are the distinctive qualities of its people, it will continue to be, as it now is, the finest monument of American industry.

PROGRESS OF INVENTIONS IN COTTON MACHINERY.

Anno Domini.
- 1765. Fly Shuttle (John Kay) and Drop Box (Robert Kay).
- 1767. Spinning Jenny—Patented in 1770—Hargraves.
- 1769. Spinning Frame—Arkwright. Wyatt's Patent was in 1738, but was not put into practical operation.
- 1775. Mule—Jenny and Frame combined—Crompton.
- 1785. Power Loom—brought into general use in 1820—Cartwright.
- 1792. Cotton Gin—Whitney. American.
- 1797. Cards—Whittemore. American.
- 1797. Reeds—Wilkinson. American.
- 1807. Steam Engine—Wyatt and Fulton. American.

MACHINES
AND
PROCESSES OF MANUFACTURE.

THE perfection of machine process which has been reached in the production of a single yard of cotton cloth is one of the best illustrations of the attainment possible to patient study and indefatigable experiment. Baines, the Lancashire historian of cotton manufacture, already quoted, who wrote in 1835, after rehearsing the train of processes, cannot forbear exclaiming: "It is by iron fingers, teeth, and wheels, moving with exhaustless energy and devouring speed, that the cotton is opened, cleaned, spread, carded, drawn, rove, spun, wound, warped, dressed, and woven. The various machines are proportioned to each other in regard to their capability of work, and they are so placed in the mill as to allow the material to be carried from stage to stage with the least possible loss of time; all are moving at once—the operations chasing each other; and all derive their motion from the mighty engine, which, firmly seated in the lower part of the building, toils through the day with the strength of perhaps a hundred horses. Men, in the mean while, have merely to attend on this wonderful series of mechanism, to supply it with work, to oil its joints, and to check its slight and infrequent irregularities; each workman performing, or rather superintending, as much work as could have been done by *two or three hundred men sixty years ago.*"

Yet all this perfection of machine process is only the attainment of many years, half a century at least, and of the worn-out lives of a legion of workers. Brains and hands, working hopelessly in too many instances, were two or three decades in labor before the spinning-frame was evolved, and it is to-day even in doubt to whom the original credit of that great invention belongs. From Crompton's mule to the improved mule of Roberts, fifty years intervened. The Scotch loom of the clergyman Cartwright was invented in 1785, and though it was the original suggestion of all power-weaving processes, the inventor would hardly recognize his idea in the improved machine of the present day. While the principles involved were all suggested in the first constructions, time has wonderfully developed their perfection and magnified both the extent and the quality of their results, so that, what with an enlarged experience and advanced practical science, the model mill of the present must indeed be pretty near the culminating point of excellence in location, structure, labor organization, and mechanical equipment.

PROCESSES OF MANUFACTURE.

To explain satisfactorily, for the comprehension of the general and unpractical reader, the elaborate operation through which a yard of cotton cloth is produced, would be impossible by means of ordinary letterpress, a patient inspection of processes from stage to stage, and story to story, in the mill, being the only mode of imparting a knowledge that involves so much beauty of theory and ingenuity of application. The following bare and superficial suggestion of the processes of manufacture may not, however, be without its value to the reader.

Among the more recently erected mills of Fall River there are probably three or four—possibly a larger number—superior in organization of labor and machine process to any in the world. As the most recent constructions, they not only possess the very latest practical features of perfection in all details of equipment, but are the best efforts of the wisest brains of a community of experts. The general production of the Fall River mills is print cloth, and when we state the probable and generally conceded fact that a yard of print cloth costs to produce in that city less than the same yard costs to produce in any other manufacturing district in the United States, the inference is obvious as to the relative capability of production.

In print-cloth *parlance* the standard of extras—as the marketable first quality goods are termed—is a piece or cut 28 inches in width and 45¼ yards in length, having 64 threads per inch running lengthwise, and 64 threads running crosswise, the cloth—that is, the goods have a standard fineness of 64 threads, or 64 by 64. The longitudinal threads are called the warp and the transverse threads the weft.

In the production of a yard of cotton the first stage regards the preparation of the raw material for the machining into threads. Every mill has its cotton house, conveniently located as is possible, fire-proof so far as ordinary care will secure that qualification, and dry. In a few of the later Fall River structures, where the location has permitted, the basement, but partially sunk, is used for storage of the raw material. The average stock carried by a mill is one thousand bales. Two thirds of the cotton worked up in Fall River is purchased directly for account of the mills, in the South. The grade runs from good ordinary to low middlings. Gulf and bottom-land cottons are much preferred, although it is brought to the city from every part of the producing region. No day passes that a Fall River mill treasurer has not an opportunity to purchase stock, and that quotations from every cotton centre in the country are not presented by the local brokers.

The first introduction of the raw cotton to its new life is its conveyance to the mixing-room, where the bagging and hoops that it put on in the Southern cotton-press are removed. An average quantity of twenty-five tons is assorted ready for the subsequent operation of cleaning. Here we have our initial glance at the white mass, and can imagine, or attempt to, the myriad myriads of fibres in that fleecy pile. Taking a tiny lock between finger and thumb and pulling the staple, what a delicate filmy nothing is the cotton fibre! It would beggar fancy, could we estimate the infinity of fibres in that mountain of twenty-five tons, reflecting that one week's work of the six towering stories demands that all the fibres of three such mountains shall be cleansed, dusted, straightened and laid out side by side, roved and twisted, and finally elongated into miles on miles of thread of warp and weft, to be interlaced and woven into 250,000 yards of cloth.

Manufacturing conventionalism has originated many expressions strange to well-disciplined terminology, and one of these is the word *bing*. The *bing* is the heap of cotton after it is mixed.

In all well-ordered factories it is considered of large importance to constitute the bing of fair proportions of all the bales. The wool from each bale is evenly spread in a layer upon a perfectly clean floor, so that when the whole number of bales are opened a section cut through from top to bottom will include a contribution from the whole stock. As the cotton in one bale may, notwithstanding the most careful discrimination, be superior or inferior in part or whole, this procedure is obviously important to assure uniformity of the character of yarn, which is a prime quality. No small skill or judgment is exercised in the mixing operation, in order to improve a weak stapled quality and make it work into good yarn. Cottons differing at all considerably in their length of staple and form of fibre lack the elements of strength and tenuity, and the careful manufacturer regards this difficulty with the utmost jealousy, often using fingers and sometimes the microscope to determine characteristics of his raw material. It is said that cotton-brokers—and why not mixers—in exceptional instances, can detect the original locality and year of a bale of cotton, blindfolded, by the simple pull of staple and feel of fibre in their fingers.

Having been mixed, the first introduction of the fleecy bing to its new life is at the eight-inch orifice of a tin or sheet-iron tube. A man sitting at the mouth of the tube does nothing the live-long day but throw armful after armful of cotton into it, a strong inhalation drawing it through as fast as it is served. Urged swiftly along its dark passage, the cotton is precipitated upon and into a revolving cylinder, having an inner bottom wall of fine screen-work and an internal mechanism of moving arms. During its revolution it is beaten and whipped violently by the active arms, the consequent agitation together with a strong air-current forced into the cylinder, separating the usual constituents of dust, sand, and other foreign matter, and driving it through the screen, to which the main body clings till thrown from an extended apron in fleecy masses on the floor.

There now remains a proportion of seeds, nubs, and leaves yet to be expelled. This is the office of a train of pickers, from each of which, as it moves along, the cotton issues cleaner and cleaner. The pickers first receive the cotton between revolving fluted rolls, from which it is torn into minute fragments by the swiftly operating blades of what is termed the beater, the object being to loosen the hard-packed filaments of the pressed bale, and still farther disintegrate the foreign material. Conveniently situated at this point is an aperture through which enters a powerful draught, which seizes the light fibres as they are torn by the flat blades of the beater, and lodges them on the face of a revolving screen, at the same time expelling the more palpable dirt and leaves from the machine. Carried on the exterior of the screen, the cotton is next introduced to another set of rollers, beaters, and screens, until, free from all its plantation and press-room vices, it emerges in a coil of broad laps of proper weight and uniform thickness, ready to be subjected to the operation of the carding-machines.

The office of the carding engines—generally two, a breaker and finisher—is to still farther separate the filaments and to complete the work of the pickers, and to turn out the cotton, straightened in parallel direction of staple and fibre, in an ultimately continuous strand. If we look in our Webster Unabridged at the common word *sliver*, which from time immemorial is associated with the wounded fingers of childhood, many of us will be able to catch the meaning of a term that the agent of a Fall River mill uses with an entire correctness of original phraseology and application that must be conceded, but a disregard for the pronunciation of the outside world which is at least startling. The *sli-ver* of the cotton-manufacturer's terminology is a provincial English word, and expresses the condition of cotton in a straight strand or ribbon; and it is the business of the carding-room to perform the operation upon the raw material which shall entitle it to this appellation.

Uncurled from the roll of laps by a movement so slow as to be imperceptible to the eye, within the grasp of fluted iron rolls, the cotton is now exposed to the revolving surface of a large cylinder, as thickly studded with minute, exquisitely fine, and hook-pointed teeth as the drum of a music-box. Caught by this legion of tentacles—and it seems impossible for a single particle, however insignificant, to elude them—every fibre is torn individually from every other fibre, and from all foreign substances. The bunch or seed that may have escaped the picker, essays in vain a farther intimacy with the cotton. It can not hide itself away among the interstices of the teeth, but, left on the surface, is at once caught up in a series of "top slats," also armed with tentacles, which cover the upper periphery of the machine. Opposite to the side of the carding cylinder, at which the cotton lap attaches to it, is another cylinder, some 16 to 18 inches in diameter, called the doffer, whose office is to receive the carded, straightened body of dismembered filaments and roll it out in a fleecy sheet, combing delicately but decidedly the fibrous constituents into a uniform direction.

The extreme tenuity of the sheet as it falls from the doffer may be inferred from the fact that it is only a hundredth part the thickness of the lap which entered the main cylinder.

This thin sheet, as it proceeds from each doffer, is made to pass through an elliptical orifice, and is thus formed into the *sli-ver* or strand, about an inch broad and perhaps one eighth of an inch thick. The cards are worked in gangs, twelve or thirteen of them together, usually placed in a row, and each deposits its charge upon an endless belt, which traverses their united frontage, gathering up the combined production, and finally delivers it to the curious and clever process of the railway head.

The duty of this machine is to transform the bulky mass of fibre coming from the thirteen cards into a small, even, and manageable strand. The railway head is a series of rolls, kept in proper relative contiguity by weighting, to which converge, by means of the belt above referred to, the ribands of cotton from the rank of cards. The stream of ribands, ten inches broad and an inch thick apparently, enters the rolls, and, coming out so thin as to almost resemble cloth of the same width, is swept into a trumpet, delicately poised on springs and having an elliptical aperture hardly one eighth by half an inch in dimensions. Through this small aperture passes the entire product of thirteen cards. The function of the trumpet is double, it being not only to govern the confluence of these distinct streams of machine fibre and reduce them to an approximate stage of their subsequent proportion, but also to correct any errors of weight due to an occasional default of its principles. To the observer's eye it has a generally swaying motion; a downward deflection indicating overweight in the coincident delivery, and an upward the opposite. As soon as it discovers a discrepancy, however, it automatically increases or slackens the speed of the delivery roll, and thus regulates the excess or deficiency.

From the mouth of the trumpet the strand of sli-ver is coiled in a cylindrical case, standing ready to receive it. In the average Fall River mill there are twelve of these gangs or sections of cards, six of which treat the cotton which goes into the warp, and the same number that for the weft. In England, previous to the invention of the railway head, which was originated at the cotton factories in Matteawan, N. Y., each card delivered into its individual can, and an independent process was requisite to unite the products in one strand.

We have now arrived at the first form of the thread. We have the cotton clean, the fibres straight and parallel, but the thread is much too large, and altogether lacks strength, being nothing more than a spongy continuity, held together by the mere coherence of its staple. To reduce it to a suitable size and impart the needed degree of strength, are problems next claiming our attention, the solution of which calls for two processes of drawing, three of speeding, and finally the function of the mule, or yarn finishing proper.

Twist is the element which adds strength to sli-ver, by compactly twining about each other the cotton fibres. In the drawing-frames no twist is imparted; in the speeders, or roving-frames, only so much as will afford enough strength to uncoil itself for each succeeding process; but in the mule all the twist is furnished that a perfect and enduring thread demands. From each consecutive stage of the process of manufacture we are now considering, the strand gradually emerges smaller and smaller, nearer and nearer approaching the yarn, which is our objective.

The process of drawing is conducted by machines involving the same principle as the railway head, and not unlike it in general design, having rollers and funnel preserving the same relations to each other. In the first process three separate strands, the product of the railway head, are drawn down by the action of fluted rolls, and then united through a trumpet or funnel in one strand. The second process is an exact copy of its precedent, the same number of strands emerging from the first train of drawing-rolls being subjected to a second operation of union. The effect of this machining has been not only to reduce the relative bulk of the sli-ver, but to perfect the straightening of filaments, and by associating ribands of sli-ver to strengthen the whole.

The strand is now ready for the action of the speeders. These are three in number, namely, the slubber, intermediate, and jack. The processes of these machines are all similar, the work being simply a series of stages. As in the drawing-frames, the grooved rolls are still essential features, reducing gradually the volume of the strand. But, as twist is first here introduced, an entirely new feature is now for the first time found, in the presence of the spindle.

From the cans containing the product of the drawing-frames, the sli-ver is first subjected to the train of rolls, and then passes automatically on its way till seized by a bifurcated attachment of a revolving spindle, of which there are generally thirty to each slubber or coarse-roving frame. The spindle likewise carries a wooden bobbin or spool, the flyer, as the bifurcated attachment is called, setting over it on the spindle. The strand, in the grasp of one of the arms of the flyer, is swung round and round by its revolution, and thus compelled to assume a regular degree of twist, while, directed by the other arm, it is wound about the convenient bobbin in layers of coil.

The rolls through which the strand is fed, and the spindle which carries both flyer and bobbin, have each their regular and certain speed of revolution, but, while the flyer revolves with the spindle, the bobbin has its independent motion and different in speed from that of the flyer. This variance of velocities is necessary, since, if both revolved with the same speed, the small periphery of the bobbin could not take up the full measure of roving, as the strand is called after twisting, fed to it by the extended arm of the flyer. To meet this exigency has required no especial skill in mechanical movements, but a second difficulty presented itself, much more serious. This discovered itself in the increasing surface of the bobbin, its volume enlarging with every additional coil of roving, while the stream itself was not at any time accelerated or slackened. The result was that the bobbin must have what may be termed a speed varying from itself, a velocity of rotation in inverse ratio to its increase of periphery. The solution of this problem, for a time baffling the inventive powers of many excellent machinists, was at last achieved by Mr. Henry Houldsworth, of Manchester, England, who devised an equational motion, by which every exigency was allowed for. It may well be called the differential calculus applied to mechanism; a more beautiful device certainly is not known in the whole range of cotton machinery.

The slubber, or coarse-rover, is followed by the intermediate. This machine has just half the number of bobbins of its predecessor, two bobbins in the former delivering strands to one in the latter frame. The same process is pursued with the jack or fly-frame, which is the last of the train of roving-machines.

The bobbins of the fly-frame represent the finished product of the carding-room. All the stages of the manufacture so far described are under the direction of one man, who employs about sixty operatives to perform his work in all its branches.

From the processes of the three speeders, the sli-ver, or, under its new appellation, *roving*, receives just so much twist, and no more, as is essential to enable it to unwind, without impairing its uniformity. Having still to undergo a process of elongation and consequent attenuation, a proportionately increasing union of filaments is obviously demanded.

The finishing and spinning stage of the cotton thread is now reached. The machine by which these final operations are performed is termed a mule. The name of a hybrid animal was probably given to the machine at its birth, because it had two distinct functions—to subject the cotton strand to its extreme tension, and thus draw it down to the constituency of thread, and to exert upon it the maximum torsion required to give it a permanent twist, and thus, by the perfect implication of its filaments, to assure its strength.

The mule is the most ingenious and complex machine used in cotton manufacturing. If it possesses no isolated feature as curious as Houldsworth's exquisitely clever application of equational mechanism to the speed of the bobbin, in the antecedent process, it is the combination of numberless adroit achievements and ingenious devices, contributed by as many inventive hands almost as its whole has parts. No man can claim as his own invention the machine as it now is, the growth of many brains and product of many inventions.

Twenty years ago the hand mule was not infrequently met in American factories—a machine which could not perform its work without manual assistance in its regular and necessary changes. The self-acting mule of to-day operates of and through itself, and embodies the poetry of manufacturing. Six or eight hundred spindles, and sometimes even a thousand, set in a carriage, moving backward and forward automatically, hum busily around at a speed of 6000 revolutions in a minute. On these spindles is built the cop, or conical ball of thread spun by the two-fold operation.

Like the drawers and speeders, a mule has its essential train of rolls. The roller-beam may be imagined occupying the background of the machine. The bobbins, bearing the accumulations of the last speeder's work, are set in a creel back of the roller-beam, and their strand ends inserted between the rolls. In the foreground of the machine, perhaps five feet from the rolls, and parallel with them, are the spindles, in regular alignment, close ranked together. This rank of spindles, actuated by the will of the tender, travels forward to the roller-beam and backward to its own position, its carriage, not obvious to the view, running upon three or more ground rails. The spindles are first run up to the roller-beam to receive the ends of the bobbin strands. These attached, the farther operation is thus described by Dr. Ure: "When the spinning operations begin, the rollers deliver the equally attenuated rovings as the carriage comes out, moving at first with a speed somewhat greater than the surface motion of the front rollers. The spindles meanwhile revolve with moderate velocity, in order to communicate but a moderate degree of twist. When the carriage has advanced through about five sixths of its path, the rollers cease to turn or to deliver thread. The carriage thenceforth moves at a very slow pace, while the speed of the spindles is increased to a certain pitch, at which it continues till the carriage arrives at the end of its course. The spindles go on revolving till they give such an additional twist to the thread as may be desired, the degree of twist being greater for warp than for weft. The spindles then stop, and the whole machine becomes for a moment insulated from the driving-shaft of the factory. Now the delicate task of the spinner begins. First of all he causes the spindles to make a few revolutions backward. In this way he takes off the slant coils from their upper ends, to prepare for distributing the fifty-four or fifty-six inches of yarn just spun properly on their middle part. He, using the *faller-wire* with his left hand, gives it such a depression as to bear down all the threads before it to a level with the bottom of the cop, or conical coil, of yarn formed, or to be formed, round the spindles. Under the control of an experienced eye, his right hand at the same time slowly turns the handle of a pulley in communication with the spindles, so as to give them a forward rotation, and his knee pushes the carriage before it at the precise rate requisite to supply yarn as the spindles wind it on. As the carriage approaches to its primary position, near to the roller-beam, he allows the faller-wire to rise slowly to its natural elevation, whereby the threads coil once more slantingly up to the tip of the spindle, and are thus ready to coöperate in the twisting and extension of another stretch of the mule."

Dr. Ure's description gives a correct idea of the general operation of the mule as it was in England in 1865. Improvements made since the issue of the volume from which quotation is made, and due to American ingenuity, have, however, still farther developed the self-acting nature of the machine, till it is now indeed, in all respects, automatic. In the perfected mule of American production—which, made by Hawes, Marvel & Davol, of Fall River, and other manufacturers of spinning machinery, is now generally purchased for the equipment of mills—instead of the one faller-wire indicated by Ure, there are two, the upper, or faller proper, which leads the thread and forms the cop, and the lower, or counter-faller, which stiffens the thread and assists the operation of its companion. These wires, supported by curved arms or hooks, placed at intervals along the rank of spindles, are extended parallel with the spindles at a distance of about three eighths of an inch. The hooks, actuated by a weight, incline downward when the carriage is nearly run out, thus dropping the wire to the base of the spindle and pressing down the thread. When the carriage retires, the hooks rise again, elevating the wires and relieving the cops. The wires can be controlled by hand, but this is unnecessary, and when their action is wholly automatic the cops are better than those produced by the most experienced spinners. In this respect the improvement is a very valuable one, while there is the still farther important advantage gained by the automatic process, that the spinner, relieved of his constant care of the faller-wires, has only to watch the general operation of the mule, preserve the continuity of threads, and repair those that are broken.

Looking at the spinning process, in which sometimes a thousand spindles are twisting, stretching, and winding up a thousand threads, the mule of mechanism seems much more like a sentient organization than the mule of nature.

In the average Fall River mill, 40,000 of these spindles run back and forth, in industrious locomotion, all day long, as busy as the ant of fabled story.

The same machine can be adapted for the production of warp or weft, the former being coarser and requiring more twist. The weft on leaving the mule is ready for the loom, the warp still requiring some preparatory attention before it is in condition. The thread in both cases, however, is all right, as the stage of manufacturing ended with the spinning process.

Our yard of print cloth, it will be remembered, is 28 inches broad, having 64 threads to the inch, and consequently 1792 threads of warp must be used to constitute its whole width. It is obvious that the yarn-beam, which is to furnish the material for the loom's consumption, must, therefore, hold 1790 threads, the weft forming the two outside threads. The operation of transferring the thread from the cops to this beam is not direct, there being intermediate stages worthy our notice.

In the first place, the warp cops are wound on spools, 6 inches long and 4 inches in diameter. These spools, 358 in number, are then arranged in a creel or stand, and subjected to the warping-machine, an ingenious contrivance credited to the eccentric Jacob Perkins, inventor of the steam-gun, which detaches their threads and winds them, each distinctly, the whole number preserving an exactly parallel alignment, on its beam. Five of these beams thus freighted are then taken to the slasher, or dressing-machine, where they are all wound on to the main yard-beam for the loom. During its passage through the slasher, the yarn is stretched and ironed, and also measured into sections of forty-five and one quarter yards, the points being indicated by a red, blue, or yellow dye, where the weaver is to take off a cut. The Fall River mills weekly consume 50,000 lbs. of potato starch in dressing their yarns.

The yarn-beam, 34 inches in length, has now wound upon it 1790 parallel coils, each something more than 15,000 feet, and together forming a body of warp, as the thread is now termed, 18 inches in diameter.

The weft-thread requires no dressing, or even manipulation, after the finishing stage in the mule, being at once taken, cop by cop, and placed in the shuttle to do its duty as an individual thread in the weaving process.

If we reflect that the function of a shuttle in a loom is the same as that of a needle in a woman's fingers, it is obvious that the warp must be made to assume some shape different from a web of 1790 threads, stretched upon a perfectly even plane. In the process of darning, the sempstress's intelligent and habile fingers direct the needle over and under the threads of the fabric she works upon. The shuttle has to darn, but has no sentient intelligence to direct its point, and is obliged to run its course to and fro in the loom, whether it passes a thread or not. This being the case, it is necessary to arrange the warp threads so that the shuttle, carrying its thread of weft, will pass over one and under the next, and *vice versâ* across the web. To effect this, recourse is had to the harness.

The harness, or heddle, as it is called in England, was a necessary fixture of the original hand-loom, and, until some more clever and convenient device shall supplant it, will remain a fixture of the power-loom so long as men weave cloth. Possessing neither mechanical beauty nor the least degree of ordinary inventive ingenuity, its place is permanent and its function indispensable.

The harness is a web of varnished hempen twines, running perpendicularly and quite close together, enclosed in a framework just heavy and strong enough to give it permanent shape. In forming the web, each couple of twines by a system of knotting is furnished with an eyelet, or small loop, so that the harness has a row of eyelets crossing its entire length. The pair of harness are separately suspended by pulleys from an arched beam of iron which rises over the loom—one a little lower than the other, so that the ranks of eyelets will be on a different level—and passing down into the loom, are secured to the machinery of a set of treadles, by which they receive such upward and downward play as the work demands.

Before placing the yarn-beam in its position on the back of the loom it is necessary to pass its threads through the two harnesses that are required in the production of plain cloth. This is done in the web-drawer, which separates the 1790 ends of thread, and puts half of them through the eyes of one harness, and half through the eyes of the other. The beam is now set in its place and the harnesses suspended from their iron archway. The next operation is to take the ends of each pair of threads, held by the loops of the harnesses, and insert them in the dents of the reed, a light framework of wood, after passing through which they are finally secured to the cloth-beam, which is situated on the front of the loom, relatively opposite to the yarn-beam. If the reader has been able to follow this description of the arrangement of the warp, he will see that after passing the loops of the harnesses it is divided into two webs, or banks of web, the threads of which have an upward and downward play through the harnesses, actuated by their treadle connection. The space thus opening and constantly changing for the race of the shuttle, and with each motion offering a thread alternately above and below its plane, is termed *shed*. With every play of the shuttle crosswise, its coadjutor, the reed, vibrates backward, *beating up*, or forcing the threads of weft to close together, and then, resuming its position, gives place for the return of the busy worker. This is, roughly and superficially sketched, the process of the loom, utterly prosaic and destitute of the fine mechanical achievement and the poetry of motion discovered in the spinning stage, yet a veritable realization in its operation of the cognate process pursued by human fingers.

The foregoing summary of the different stages of manufacture, though without the assistance of illustrative cuts to make its details clear to the unpractised contemplation, will still impart a general idea of the operation through which the raw material from the Southern cotton-press is spun and woven into 64 by 64 print cloth in the Northern mill.

How long a period is consumed in the passage of the raw material through the consecutive processes, is a question that may suggest itself to the curious mind. It is not so easy to answer this question in the regular operation of a mill, but assuming a new grade of cotton to be put into a mill, furnishing the entire preparation for the looms, it would require fully seven weeks to work up the whole bing, though within ten days a portion of it should have issued in the shape of cloth. The latter period may therefore be accepted as a fair length of time to go through all the processes, under good average working conditions.

The manufactured cloth is conventionally allowed to weigh seven yards to the pound of cotton consumed; that is, one yard weighs one seventh of a pound, or $2\frac{89}{100}$ ounces. This does not of course represent the entire weight of cotton as taken from the bale for the specific yard, there being an unavoidable waste in the various operations; and practically, calculating the proportional weights of hoops and bagging for which the mill has to pay, about three ounces gross weight in the bale is the equivalent of the yard of Fall River print cloth. The estimate is also somewhat affected by the grade of cotton used (some grades showing much less foreign matter and making less waste than others), and by the care taken to utilize the waste. The first figures given of the weight allowed ($2\frac{29}{100}$ ounces) to each yard indicate a waste of $\frac{19}{100}$ ounces in the gross amount. The value of this waste is realized by selling it, and by so much diminishes the gross amount, leaving a net waste relatively small. Manufacturers of print cloth, out of every gross pound of the grades commonly put in, expect to obtain from 5 to $5\frac{1}{2}$ or $5\frac{5}{8}$ yards of fabric.

The waste per gross pound is now estimated at about fifteen per cent in the New England mills. In 1831 it was perhaps twenty per cent.

The experience of the Fall River cotton manufacturers has led them to the conclusion that the most desirable size of a mill, for the manufacture of print cloths, is one of 30,000 spindles. In such a mill, the different parts balance each other to the best advantage; that is, if properly arranged, the looms will just take care of the preparation—the carding, spinning, dressing, etc.—with no surplus or deficiency. It is also about as large as a superintendent can handle easily, by keeping up the different ends, and having everything run smoothly, without hitch or break.

Such a mill, according to the Fall River standard, should be built of stone or brick, 300 feet long, 72 feet wide, five stories high, with hip or flat roof, the latter more desirable on account of fire. It will have a capacity of 30,000 spindles and 800 looms, will employ 325 to 350 operatives, and use about 3500 bales of cotton in the production of 9,000,000 yards of print cloths per annum. A capital of $500,000 would probably be required to pay the cost of the mill and machinery (which are generally reckoned in the proportion of two fifths and three fifths), and allow a small margin for working capital. From four to ten acres is generally allowed for a mill site, varying according to the number of tenements put up for the operatives.

There are some twelve general departments in a mill of from 30,000 to 40,000 spindles, and employing from 350 to 450 persons. These are divided as follows: 8 pickers, 8 card-strippers and grinders, 4 drawing-tenders, 24 speeder-tenders, 30 other card-room hands, 32 spinners, 36 other hands in spinning-room, 28 spoolers, 6 warpers, 3 slashers, 11 web-drawers, 200 in the weaving department, and some forty on miscellaneous work. Each department is necessary to every other, and all act as forwarders of the general work. If one department, though never so small, becomes disarranged from any cause, the result is a disarrangement of all the other departments of the mill. Hence the necessity that the mill "when wound up," as it is called, should have all the departments balance each other in their production, and that the superintendent should be a man of skill and judgment, and of sufficient capacity to keep the whole machine well in hand.

Of course a very important factor in the perfect organization of a cotton factory is the arrangement of the different departments of machinery. The system pursued in Fall River disposes of the five stories allotted to manufacture, as follows: The first and second floors are used for weaving, the third for carding, and the fourth and fifth for spinning. The engine is placed in an ell, running from the centre of the rear of the mill and generally opposite to the tower, which furnishes the main ingress and egress on the front. The main driving-wheel, from which proceed all the belts transmitting the power to the various departments, is entirely within the basement of the main structure, thus bringing the source of transmission in the closest possible relation to its work. This ell, usually three stories high, is occupied by the mixing-room and the picking-room, the latter on a level with the third story of the mill, so that the picking stage delivers its cotton on the same level to the carders, where it is divided, a part led off in one direction to form the warp and the remainder in the opposite direction to form the weft. After undergoing the various processes of the carding-room, the preparation, still preserving its newly assumed relations, passes up through elevators located at each end of the mill, to the stories occupied by the spinning machinery, whence the cops are lowered, when finished, to the weaving floor. In the factories of New England, at the period of Mr. Montgomery's visit and description, the second story was used for the carding, the third the spinning, and the fourth and attic the weaving and dressing.

The cotton is generally stored in a separate building, though in occasional new mills of six stories the ground floor is, by a very convenient and economical arrangement, devoted to this purpose.

The average wages for operatives of all ages are a trifle above those of Lowell and Lawrence, and while Fall River has to compete on short tenhour time directly with the Rhode Island mills, not regulated as to hours of labor, the former makes a better showing in the remuneration accorded to its operatives.

The operatives employed in Fall River are mostly foreigners, but the American, French, and Irish elements are well disposed as a rule, and give little trouble except when led by the English (Lancashire) operatives, who, having come from the most discontented districts of England, have brought their peculiar ideas and the machinery of their home style of agitation along with them. This system is not relished by the other operatives, but so potent has been the influence of the active element that it has sometimes held the others in awe, and in times gone by has even been so powerful that if one of the trades-union men went into a mill and held up his hand, all the operatives at once, quitting their machines, left the mill, and went outside to find out why it was that they left their work. But it is hoped that the day of this style of terrorism and despotism has gone by, and that the compulsory system of school education, now in force in Massachusetts for factory children, will put them in a position to control their own motions, rights, and interests.

STATISTICS OF COTTON MANUFACTORIES IN FALL RIVER.

	Corporation.	Number of Mills.	Location.	Capital.	Spindles.	Looms.	Style of Goods.	Incorporated.	Bales Cotton used per annum.	Yards of Cloth manufactured per annum.	No. hands employ'd	Monthly Pay Roll.
1	American Linen Co.	2	Ferry Street.	$800,000	92,512	1,956	Print Cloths.	1852	8,500	21,000,000	1,000	$22,000
2	Annawan Manufactory.	1	Annawan Street.	160,000	10,016	192	" "	1825	1,000	2,150,000	140	2,800
3	Barnard Mfg. Co.	1	Quequechan St.	350,000	28,401	768	" "	1874	3,500	9,000,000	340	8,500
4	Border City Mills.	2	North Main Road	1,000,000	72,144	1,760	" "	1872	8,250	20,500,000	980	22,000
5	Chace Mills.	1	Rodman Street.	500,000	13,480	1,056	" "	1871	4,500	11,000,000	425	11,000
6	Crescent Mills.	1	Eight Rod Way.	500,000	33,286	684	Yd.-wide fine g'ds.	1871	3,250	5,750,000	340	9,000
7	Davol Mills.	2	Hartwell Street.	500,000	30,496	730	Sheet'gs & Silesias.	1867	3,500	5,000,000	375	11,000
8	Durfee Mills.	2	Pleasant Street.	500,000	87,424	2,064	Print Cloths.	1866	9,500	23,000,000	950	22,500
9	Fall River Manufactory.	1	Pocasset Street.	150,000	25,092	600	" "	1813	3,000	7,000,000	330	7,000
10	Fall River Merino Co.	1	Alden Street.	90,000	1,560	15	Merino Underwear	1875	750		60	2,000
11	Fall River Print Works.	1	Pocasset Street.	200,000	13,600	300	Print Cloths.	1848	1,350	3,500,000	175	4,750
12	Flint Mills.	1	Alden Street.	600,000	45,360	1,008	" "	1872	4,750	12,500,000	450	11,000
13	Granite Mills.	2	Twelfth Street.	400,000	76,920	1,868	" "	1863	9,000	21,500,000	900	22,000
14	King Philip Mills.	1	Laurel Lake.	500,000	37,440	776	Yd.-wide fine g'ds.	1871	3,000	5,500,000	425	12,000
15	Mechanics' Mills.	1	Mechanicsville.	750,000	53,712	1,248	Print Cloths.	1868	5,750	14,000,000	550	14,500
16	Merchants' Mfg. Co.	2	Fourteenth Street	800,000	55,570	1,942	" "	1867	9,250	22,500,000	500	21,000
17	Metacomet Mill.	1	Annawan Street.	250,000	23,340	591	Bags, Duck & Bats.	1847	2,500	2,000,000	275	7,250
18	Montaup Mills.	1	Laurel Lake.	250,000	7,200	216	Shirtings.	1871	750	1,225,000	125	3,000
19	Mount Hope Mill.	1	Bay Street.	200,000	9,024	675	Print Cloths.	1867	3,250	8,250,000	325	8,000
20	Narragansett Mills.	1	North Main Road	400,000	27,920	700	" "	1871	3,250		325	8,000
21	Osborn Mills.	1	Laurel Lake.	500,000	37,232	930	" "	1871	4,250	11,000,000	425	11,000
22	Pocasset Mfg. Co.	2	Pocasset Street.	800,000	36,744	918	Sheetings & Shirtings	1822	3,150	7,500,000	550	12,000
23	Richard Borden Mfg. Co.	1	Rodman Street.	500,000	42,528	1,032	Print Cloths.	1871	4,500	12,000,000	450	11,500
24	Robeson Mills.	1	Hartwell Street.	250,000	21,632	552	" "	1867	2,500	6,500,000	275	7,000
25	Sagamore Mills.	1	North Main Road	500,000	37,672	990	" "	1872	4,000	10,500,000	425	10,000
26	Shove Mills.	1	Laurel Lake.	550,000	37,504	960	" "	1872	4,250	11,500,000	425	11,000
27	Slade Mills.	1	Laurel Lake.	550,000	37,040	860	" "	1871	4,000	10,000,000	350	9,500
28	Stafford Mills.	1	Quarry Street.	550,000	34,928	860	" "	1871	4,000	10,000,000	350	9,500
29	Tecumseh Mills.	1	Hartwell Street.	500,000	42,166	1,014	" "	1866	4,500	12,000,000	400	12,000
30	Troy C. & W. Manufactory	2	Troy Street.	300,000	38,928	933	" "	1814	4,000	10,250,000	400	10,500
31	Union Mill Co.	2	Pleasant Street.	500,000	44,784	1,050	" "	1859	5,000	12,000,000	475	13,500
32	Wampanoag Mills.	1	Quequechan St.	400,000	27,920	704	" "	1871	3,250	8,250,000	325	8,000
33	Weetamoe Mills.	1	Mechanicsville.	550,000	34,080	840	" "	1871	4,000	10,000,000	350	9,250
		43		$14,735,000	1,369,048	30,144			139,175	343,375,000	14,270	$359,550

ORGANIZATION OF CORPORATIONS.

AMERICAN LINEN COMPANY.

President: Jefferson Borden.
Clerk and Treasurer: Walter Paine 3d.
Directors: Jefferson Borden, Philip D. Borden, Richard B. Borden, George B. Durfee, Walter Paine 3d.
Annual Meeting—2d Wednesday in February.

AMERICAN PRINT WORKS.

President: Jefferson Borden.
Clerk: Thomas J. Borden.
Agent and Treasurer: Thomas J. Borden.
Directors. Thomas J. Borden, Jefferson Borden, Nathan Durfee, George B. Durfee, John S. Brayton.
Annual Meeting—1st Tuesday in August.

ANNAWAN MANUFACTORY.

President: Jefferson Borden.
Clerk and Treasurer: Thomas S. Borden.
Directors: Holder B. Durfee, Jefferson Borden, Wm. H. Durfee, Wm. Valentine, R. B. Borden.
Annual Meeting—1st Tuesday in August.

BARNARD MANUFACTURING COMPANY.

President: Louis L. Barnard.
Clerk and Treasurer: Nathaniel B. Borden.
Directors: L. L. Barnard, Stephen Davol, Wm. H. Jennings, A. D. Easton, Arnold B. Chace, Robert T. Davis, Simeon Borden, James M. Aldrich, N. B. Borden, Alphonso S. Covel, John Campbell, Jos. A Bowen, Wm. H. Gifford.
Annual Meeting—3d Thursday in January.

BORDER CITY MILLS.

President: S. Angier Chace.
Clerk and Treasurer: George T. Hathaway.
Directors: S. A. Chace, David T. Wilcox, Job T. Wilson, Chas. P. Stickney, Elijah C. Kilburn, Chester W. Greene, Geo. T. Hathaway, James A. Hathaway, Isaac Smith, George Parsons, H. B. Durfee.
Annual Meeting—4th Wednesday in October.

CHACE MILLS.

President: Augustus Chace.
Clerk and Treasurer: Joseph A. Baker.
Directors: Augustus Chace, Cook Borden, James Henry, George W. Grinnell, Robert K. Remington, Edward E. Hathaway, William Mason, Charles P. Stickney, Joseph A. Baker.
Annual Meeting—In October.

CRESCENT MILLS.

President: Benjamin Covel.
Clerk and Treasurer: Alphonso S. Covel.
Directors. Benjamin Covel, Daniel A. Chapin, Wm. B. Durfee, Alphonso S. Covel, Griffiths M. Haffards, Joseph Brady, David F. Brown, John F. Nichols, Lafayette Nichols.
Annual Meeting—2d Wednesday in February.

DAVOL MILLS.

President: William C. Davol.
Clerk and Treasurer: Wm. C. Davol, Jr.
Directors: William C. Davol, Chas. P. Stickney, Foster H. Stafford, Frank S. Stevens, Jonathan Slade, John P. Slade, Wm. W. Stewart, Edward E. Hathaway, W. C. Davol, Jr.
Annual Meeting—in April.

DURFEE MILLS.

President: John S. Brayton.
Clerk: Hezekiah A. Brayton.
Treasurer: David A. Brayton.

Directors: John S. Brayton, David A. Brayton, Israel P. Brayton.

Annual Meeting—2d Wednesday in October.

FALL RIVER BLEACHERY.

President: Jefferson Borden.
Clerk and Treasurer: Spencer Borden.
Directors: Jefferson Borden, Spencer Borden, Richard B. Borden, Philip D. Borden, Bradford D. Davol, Charles P. Stickney, Thomas Bennett, Jr., George B. Durfee, Crawford E. Lindsey.

Annual Meeting—last Monday in May.

FALL RIVER IRON WORKS COMPANY.

President: Jefferson Borden.
Clerk and Treasurer: Robert C. Brown.
Directors: Jefferson Borden, Holder B. Durfee, John S. Brayton, William B. Durfee, Richard B. Borden.

Annual Meeting—1st Tuesday in August.

FALL RIVER MANUFACTORY.

President: Holder B. Durfee.
Clerk: John S. Brayton.
Treasurer: S. Angier Chace.
Directors: Holder B. Durfee, John S. Brayton, S. Angier Chace, Christopher Borden, James M. Anthony.

Annual Meeting—2d Tuesday in March.

FALL RIVER MANUFACTURERS' MUTUAL INSURANCE COMPANY.

President: Stephen Davol.
Secretary and Treasurer: Isaac B. Chace.
Directors: Stephen Davol, S. A. Chace, D. A. Brayton, T. J. Borden, Jefferson Borden, Wm. H. Durfee, Jennings, Walter Paine 3d, I. B. Chace, P. D. Borden, R. B. Borden, E. C. Kilburn, Andrew G. Pierce, George T. Hathaway, T. F. Eddy, George B.

Annual Meeting—1st Wednesday in March.

FALL RIVER MERINO COMPANY.

President: Frank S. Stevens.
Clerk and Treasurer: Seth H. Wetherbee.
Directors: Frank S. Stevens, Foster H. Stafford, Robert T. Davis, Wm. Mason, Samuel M. Luther, Danforth Horton, John D. Flint, Samuel Wadington, Samuel W. Flint, S. H. Wetherbee

Annual Meeting—4th Thursday in January.

FALL RIVER PRINT WORKS.

President: Linden Cook.
Clerk and Treasurer: Andrew Robeson.

Directors: Linden Cook, Charles P. Stickney, Andrew Robeson.

Annual Meeting—4th Wednesday in January.

FALL RIVER RAILROAD.

President: Joseph R. Beauvais.
Clerk and Treasurer: Thos. B. Fuller.
Directors: J. R. Beauvais, C. R. Tucker, G. A. Bourne, Geo. Wilson, G. S. Phillips, L. L. Kollock, W. R. Wing, of New Bedford; R. T. Davis, J. D. Flint, of Fall River; L. S. Judd, of Fairhaven; and J. H. Perry, of Boston.

Annual Meeting—1st Wednesday in December.

FALL RIVER SPOOL AND BOBBIN COMPANY.

President: Cook Borden.
Clerk: Bradford D. Davol.
Treasurer: Nathan B. Everett.
Directors: Cook Borden, F. H. Stafford, Wm. H. Jennings, Stephen Davol, David Bass, Jr., Wm. Lindsey, Walter Paine 3d, Joseph Healy, Geo. T. Hathaway, S. A. Chace, Aug. Chace.

Annual Meeting—last Tuesday in October.

ORGANIZATION OF CORPORATIONS.

FALL RIVER STEAMBOAT COMPANY.

President: Charles P. Stickney.
Clerk: Thomas J. Borden.
Treasurer: Charles P. Stickney.
Directors: Charles P. Stickney, Stephen Davol, Philip D. Borden, S. Angier Chace, Daniel Brown, Augustus Chace, T. J. Borden, Walter Paine 3d, Robert K. Remington, Geo. B. Durfee.
Annual Meeting—1st Tuesday in February.

FALL RIVER, WARREN AND PROVIDENCE RAILROAD COMPANY.

President: Onslow Stearns.
Clerk: John S. Brayton.
Treasurer: John M. Washburn.
Directors: Onslow Stearns, Chas. F. Choate, Boston; J. S. Brayton, T. J. Borden, Fall River; Benj. Finch, Newport; E. N. Winslow, Hyannis.
Annual Meeting—2d Monday in March.

FLINT MILLS.

President: John D. Flint.
Clerk and Treasurer: Geo. H. Eddy.
Directors: John D. Flint, Wm. H. Jennings, Simeon Borden, Wm. Carroll, Frank L. Almy, William T. Hall, Gardner T. Dean, George H. Eddy, Junius P. Prentiss, Samuel W. Flint, Danforth Horton.
Annual Meeting—1st Monday in November.

GRANITE MILLS.

President: William Mason.
Clerk and Treasurer: Charles M. Shove.
Directors: Wm. Mason, Edmund Chase, Chas. P. Stickney, John S. Brayton, Iram Smith, John P. Slade, Charles M. Shove.
Annual Meeting—4th Monday in October.

KING PHILIP MILLS.

President: Crawford E. Lindsey.
Clerk: Azariah S. Tripp.
Treasurer: Elijah C. Kilburn.
Directors: C. E. Lindsey, Jonathan Chace, Jas. Henry, S. Angier Chace, Edwin Shaw, Philip D. Borden, E. C. Kilburn, Benj. A. Chace, Simeon Borden, Chas. H. Dean, William Lindsey.
Annual Meeting—last Thursday in October.

MANUFACTURERS' BOARD OF TRADE.

President: Walter Paine 3d.
Vice-President: Geo. T. Hathaway.
Secretary: Simeon B. Chase.
Treasurer: Isaac B. Chase.
Annual Meeting—3d Friday in January.

MANUFACTURERS' GAS COMPANY.

President: ———— ————
Clerk and Treasurer: Chas. P. Stickney.
Directors: S. Angier Chace, ———— ————, Augustus Chace, Chas. P. Stickney, David A. Brayton, Wm. C. Davol, Jr., Foster H. Stafford, Thomas F. Eddy, Joseph A. Baker.
Annual Meeting—3d Monday in June.

MASSASOIT STEAM MILLS.

President:
Clerk: Charles Durfee.
Treasurer: Holder B. Durfee.
Directors: ———— ————, S. Angier Chace, Holder B. Durfee.
Annual Meeting—3d Monday in May.

MECHANICS MILLS.

President: Stephen Davol.
Clerk: James M. Morton, Jr.
Treasurer: George B. Durfee.
Directors: Stephen Davol, Job B. French, Thos. J. Borden, George B. Durfee, Tillinghast Records, Southard H. Miller, James M. Morton, Jr., John B. Hathaway, F. S. Stevens.
Annual Meeting—1st Thursday in February.

MERCHANTS MANUFACTURING COMPANY.

President: James Henry.
Clerk and Treasurer: Wm. H. Jennings.
Directors: James Henry, Wm. H. Jennings, Augustus Chace, Robert S. Gibbs, Chas. H. Dean, Crawford E. Lindsey, Jas. M. Osborn, Richard B. Borden, Robert T. Davis.
Annual Meeting—4th Wednesday in January.

METACOMET MILL.

Agent: Thomas S. Borden. | Owned by the Fall River Iron Works Co.

MONTAUP MILLS.

President: Geo. B. Durfee.
Clerk and Treasurer: Isaac Borden.
Directors: Geo. B. Durfee, Isaac Borden, Thos. J. Borden, Wm. L. Slade, Holder B. Durfee, William Valentine, Bradford D. Davol, Weaver Osborn, Geo. H. Hawes, Wm. H. Ashley, Benj. Hall.
Annual Meeting—4th Monday in October.

MOUNT HOPE MILL.

Agent: Jefferson Borden, Jr. | Owned by American Print Works.

NARRAGANSETT MILLS.

President: Holder B. Durfee.
Clerk and Treasurer: James Waring.
Directors: Holder B. Durfee, James Waring, Foster H. Stafford, Daniel McCowan, David T. Wilcox, Samuel Watson, James P. Hillard, Robert Henry, Samuel Wadington, Wm. Beattie, Geo. W. Nowell.
Annual Meeting—In October.

OLD COLONY RAILROAD COMPANY.

President: Onslow Stearns.
Clerk: George Marston.
Treasurer: John M. Washburn.
Directors: Onslow Stearns, Uriel Crocker, Chas. F. Choate, F. B. Hayes, Boston; Benj. Finch, Newport; Oliver Ames, Easton; Samuel L. Crocker, Taunton; Jacob H. Loud, Plymouth; J. S. Brayton, T. J. Borden, Fall River, R. W. Turner, Randolph; E. N. Winslow, Hyannis; P. S. Crowell, Dennis.
Annual Meeting—4th Tuesday in November.

OLD COLONY STEAMBOAT COMPANY.

President: Onslow Stearns.
Clerk: Chas. F. Choate.
Treasurer: John M. Washburn.
Directors: Onslow Stearns, C. F. Choate, Silas Pierce, Jr., Boston; Benj. Finch, Newport; T. J. Borden, C. P. Stickney, Fall River; Albert Terrill, Weymouth; Oliver Ames, Easton; Wm. Borden, New York.
Annual Meeting—4th Tuesday in June.

OSBORN MILLS.

President: Weaver Osborn.
Clerk and Treasurer: Joseph Healy.
Directors: Weaver Osborn, Frank S. Stevens, Charles P. Stickney, Joseph Osborn, John C. Milne, Joseph Healy, Edward E. Hathaway, Geo. T. Hathaway, Benj. Hall, George W. Gibbs, Chas. H. Dean.
Annual Meeting—last Tuesday in April.

ORGANIZATION OF CORPORATIONS.

POCASSET MANUFACTURING COMPANY.

President: Samuel R. Rodman.
Clerk and Treasurer: Bradford D. Davol.
Agent: Stephen Davol.
Directors: Stockholders, who meet quarterly.
Annual Meeting—last Monday in January.

RICHARD BORDEN MANUFACTURING COMPANY.

President: Thomas J. Borden.
Clerk and Treasurer: Richard B. Borden.
Directors: Richard B. Borden, Thomas J. Borden, Philip D. Borden, A. S. Covel, Edward P. Borden.
Annual Meeting—2d Tuesday in November.

ROBESON MILLS.

President: Charles P. Stickney.
Clerk and Treasurer: Louis Robeson.
Directors: Charles P. Stickney, Wm. R. Robeson, Linden Cook, Wm. C. Davol, Jr., Frank S. Stevens, Samuel M. Luther, Louis Robeson.
Annual Meeting—1st Monday in February.

SAGAMORE MILLS.

President: Josiah C. Blaisdell.
Clerk and Treasurer: Geo. T. Hathaway.
Directors: J. C. Blaisdell, L. L. Barnard, John D. Flint, James W. Hartley, Geo. T. Hathaway, Jos. McCreery, James A. Hathaway, Job T. Wilson.
Annual Meeting—4th Monday in October.

SHOVE MILLS.

President: John P. Slade.
Clerk and Treasurer: George A. Chace.
Directors: John P. Slade, Geo. A. Chace, William Mason of Taunton, Edmund Chase, Lloyd S. Earle, Josiah C. Blaisdell, Isaac W. Howland, Charles M. Shove, H. B. Allen, Asa Pettey, Joseph E. Macomber, Clark Shove, George W. Slade.
Annual Meeting—in February.

SLADE MILLS.

President: William L. Slade.
Clerk: John C. Milne.
Treasurer: Henry S. Fenner.
Directors: Wm. L. Slade, S. Angier Chace, Jerome Dwelly, Wm. Valentine, Frank S. Stevens, Richard B. Borden, Benj. Hall, James M. Osborn, Jonathan Slade, John C. Milne, Daniel Wilbur.
Annual Meeting—last Tuesday in January.

STAFFORD MILLS.

President: Foster H. Stafford.
Clerk and Treasurer: Shubael P. Lovell.
Agent: Foster H. Stafford.
Directors: F. H. Stafford, Wm. C. Davol, Chas. P. Stickney, Robert T. Davis, Edmund Chase, Danforth Horton, Wm. L. Slade, Weaver Osborn, Wm. Mason.
Annual Meeting—4th Tuesday in January.

TECUMSEH MILLS.

President: Augustus Chace.
Clerk and Treasurer: Simeon B. Chase.
Directors: Augustus Chace, Cook Borden, Jona. T. Lincoln, Andrew M. Jenning, Samuel Wadington, D. T. Wilcox, John Southworth, S. B. Chase.
Annual Meeting—4th Tuesday in October.

TROY COTTON AND WOOLEN MANUFACTORY.

President: Jefferson Borden.
Clerk and Treasurer: Richard B. Borden.
Directors: Jefferson Borden, Stephen Davol, Thos. J. Borden, John S. Brayton, Richard B. Borden.
Annual Meeting—1st Tuesday in February.

UNION BELT COMPANY.

President: Richard B. Borden.
Clerk and Treasurer: A. S. Covel.
Agent: William H. Chace.

Directors: R. B. Borden, W. Paine 3d, B. D. Davol, Wm. H. Chace, A. S. Covel, E. C. Kilburn, T. J. Borden.

Annual Meeting—3d Thursday in January.

UNION MILL COMPANY.

President: John B. Anthony.
Clerk and Treasurer: S. Angier Chace.
Directors: John B. Anthony, S. Angier Chace,

Wm. Mason, Elijah C. Kilburn, Charles P. Dring, Foster H. Stafford,

Annual Meeting—3d Monday in January.

WAMPANOAG MILLS.

President: Robert T. Davis.
Clerk and Treasurer: Walter C. Durfee.
Directors: Robert T. Davis, W. C. Durfee, John

D. Flint, Stephen Davol, Foster H. Stafford, Wm. H. Jennings, Geo. H. Eddy, Lloyd S. Earle, Simeon Borden, Alphonso S. Covel, John H. Boone.

Annual Meeting—4th Monday in January.

WEETAMOE MILLS.

President: Job B. French.
Clerk: John E. Blaisdell.
Treasurer: William Lindsey.
Directors: Job B. French, Elijah C. Kilburn,

Josiah C. Blaisdell, Francis B. Hood, Henry C. Lincoln, Wm. Lindsey, John P. Slade, Wm. H. Ashley, Charles H. Dean.

Annual Meeting—4th Wednesday in January.

SKETCH OF EACH CORPORATION.

The following somewhat detailed notices of the different corporations, embodying facts, figures, and general information, which could not well be introduced in the course of the narrative, it is believed will be of value as well as of interest.

THE FALL RIVER MANUFACTORY.

As full an account as was possible of the organization of this mill, which shares with the Troy Cotton and Woollen Company the credit of initiating the manufacture in Fall River, has been given in preceding pages. The factory erected in 1813 was enlarged in 1827, and again in 1839. In 1868 it was entirely destroyed by fire. During the next year the present mill, considerably larger than the original structures, was erected.

The Fall River Manufactory was incorporated in 1820, with a capital of $150,000. The destruction of the records unfortunately prevents the same detail of its first year's experience that has been furnished of the Troy. Dexter Wheeler, who was David Anthony's most active associate in putting up and equipping the first factory, was a mechanic of very good ability. He died in 1836, at the age of fifty-nine. It is unfortunate that memory preserves no more facts of a man who is regarded by many as having exerted a paramount influence in developing the early enterprise of the place. That he was something of an inventor as well as machinist, the contrivance and actual operation of the power-looms made by him sufficiently evidence. During his practical solution of the weaving problem, tradition says, he labored so incessantly, giving neither mind nor body rest for consecutive days, that a temporary aberration was the result.

The present factory of this corporation is of stone, 275 feet long, 73 feet wide, and five stories high, with a flat roof. It is built directly across the stream, and utilizes the fall by two turbine wheels of 140 horse-power each. As a supplementary motor the mill also operates a Corliss engine of 300 horse-power, fed by two upright boilers. The mill contains 600 looms and 25,992 spindles. Its production is print cloth, of which 7,000,000 yards are annually made, consuming 3000 bales of cotton. Provision is made against fire by the constant readiness of two large force-pumps, and stand-pipes and hydrants connected with the city water-works.

The present list of stockholders of this company numbers forty-seven. The company owns thirty-eight tenement houses for its operatives. Dr. Nathan Durfee was president of the company up to the time of his death.

THE TROY COTTON AND WOOLEN MANUFACTORY,

incorporated in 1814, has a capital of $300,000. The several alterations of the mill structures have been fully detailed. The factories of the Troy Company front on Troy street, running from Bedford to Pleasant street, and occupy half of the block upon which the United States Government is now erecting a fine public building for the post-office and other purposes. The number of looms operated is 932, and of spindles 38,928, producing 10,250,000 yards of print cloth, and working up 4000 bales of cotton in a year.

THE POCASSET MANUFACTURING COMPANY

has a present capital of $800,000. As the third cotton-manufacturing enterprise in the place, its large agency in the general development has been frequently observed in the course of the general narrative.

The original stockholders of the Pocasset were eight in number, namely, Samuel Rodman, Abraham Bowen, Oliver Chace, Clark Chase, William Slade, Nathaniel B. Borden, Nathaniel Wheeler, and Edward Bennett. The capital was fixed at $400,000, but was increased to $800,000 in 1849. The company own two factories, namely, the Quequechan Mill for the manufacture of print cloths, and the Pocasset Mill, for the manufacture of sheetings and shirtings.

The Quequechan Mill commenced operation in 1826. It is built of stone, 319 feet long, 48 feet wide, and five stories high, with a pitch roof, and contains 16,392 spindles and 492 looms.

The Pocasset Mill commenced running in 1847. It is also built of stone, 208 feet long, 75 feet wide, and five stories high, with a pitch roof and a square tower on the end which fronts the street. It was the first of the wide mills, so called, and contains 20,352 spindles and 422 looms. The machinery is run by a Corliss engine and three turbine wheels. The fire apparatus consists of two force-pumps, stand-pipes, hydrants, sprinklers, and complete connections with the city water-works. The company owns fifty-four tenements and employs 550 operatives.

The present number of stockholders is twenty-one.

THE ANNAWAN MANUFACTORY.

Abraham Wilkinson, Benjamin Rodman, Bradford Durfee and their associates were incorporated February 8, 1825, under this name, which claims historic interest as that of one of King Philip's most famous captains. One of the lower water privileges on the Fall River stream was purchased of the Fall River Iron Works Company, and a brick mill, with finished stone in the lower stories, immediately erected under the supervision of Major Bradford Durfee. This mill building, extending from bank to bank of the stream, is still standing, and is 181 feet long by 46 feet wide, and five stories high, including basement. The machinery is run by a turbine wheel, assisted occasionally by a small engine of 50 horse-power. The Annawan contains 10,016 spindles and 192 looms, and works up about a thousand bales of cotton annually in the production of 2,150,000 yards of print cloth. Its fire apparatus consists of one rotary force-pump, hydrants, and connections with the city water-works. It is lighted by gas from the works of the Fall River Gas Company. Thirty-two tenements are provided for the accommodation of the operatives. The capital stock was originally divided into thirty-two shares, and taken by thirteen subscribers. The present number of stockholders is twenty-eight.

THE METACOMET MILL,

owned exclusively by the Fall River Iron Works Company, was erected in 1847. The factory is placed on the west bank of the Fall River stream, just below the lower fall. It is built of stone, 247 feet long, 70 feet wide, and five stories high, with basement and a barn roof. The machinery, of which about two thirds is American, is arranged for the manufacture of print cloths 64 by 64. It contains 23,840 spindles and 591 looms, and manufactures about 6,500,000 yards of cloth annually, from 2500 bales of cotton. The motive power is a single Corliss engine, rated at 375 horse-power, and turbine wheels which carry about one third of the machinery. The steam is generated in three upright boilers of 180 horse-power each. Protection from fire is furnished by a steam pump, wheel pump, stand-pipes, and connections with the city water-works. The mill is lighted by gas from the Fall River Gas Works. The company owns fifty-six tenements.

THE AMERICAN LINEN COMPANY,

incorporated in 1852, for the manufacture of linen fabrics, owns two mills, both built of Fall River granite. The No. 1 Mill, 301 feet long, 63 feet wide, and four stories high, with a barn roof, was erected in 1852, and designed for the manufacture of linen fabrics. In 1858 it was decided to change the production to cotton print cloths, and the mill was accordingly enlarged by the addition of another story, the other dimensions remaining as before. The No. 2 Mill, built in 1866, was 393 feet long, 72 feet wide, and five stories high, with basement, and a barn roof. On the 29th of June, 1876, a destructive fire broke out in the fourth story of this mill, used as a mule-room, and before it could be mastered burned out the upper two stories, besides occasioning considerable damage to the lower rooms. Immediate preparations were made for rebuilding, and within four months the mill was in operation again. A flat roof was substituted for the barn roof, which had proved so dangerous in case of fire.

The mills contain 82,512 spindles and 1956 looms. Each mill is dependent on the other—the No. 1 Mill, not being suited to the long mules used in the manufacture of cotton goods, is occupied for the carding, warping, spinning, and spooling processes, while in the lower three stories of the No. 2 Mill is done all the weaving, and in the upper two stories the weft spinning, etc.

The machinery is driven by two double and one single Corliss engine, the steam for which is furnished by sixteen tubular boilers.

Eight thousand five hundred bales of cotton are worked up annually into 21,000,000 yards of print cloths, 64 by 64. The company employs 1000 hands, and has provided 110 tenements for the accommodation of their families.

Protection against fire is furnished by two powerful steam pumps, standpipes, hydrants, and sprinklers in each mill; connections with city water throughout, and a hose company detailed from the operatives in the mill.

James P. Hillard has been superintendent for many years.

The present number of stockholders is seventy-five.

THE UNION MILL COMPANY,

incorporated in 1859, will be remembered as the first result of a movement to establish industries upon the basis of general subscriptions of the community. At this period steam had been introduced as a motive power into but few mills in Fall River.

In the summer of this year, Mr. Hale Remington conceived an enterprise which developed into the organization of the Union Mill Company and the erection of the No. 1 Mill of that corporation.

Mr. Remington invited Mr. David Anthony, Mr. S. A. Chace, and Mr. Oliver Chace to join him. Mr. Anthony was quite advanced in years. He had been one of the early manufacturers of the town, but had retired from active business. He was of sound judgment, and his early experience made him a good adviser.

These gentlemen together fully decided upon the practicability of the movement. Mr. Oliver Chace owned a large tract of unimproved property in the southerly part of the city. He wished the mill located upon it. This land was carefully inspected, but no site was found quite satisfactory to Mr. S. A. Chace.

The latter then looked over the town and selected the site upon the Quequechan River, and having taken his associates to that location, they at once agreed with him in his choice.

Mr. Oliver Chace fully concurred in the wisdom of the choice, but withdrew because he wished all his investments to benefit his landed estate.

The other gentlemen purchased the land and matured their plans for the erection of a print-cloth mill of about 15,000 spindles, and the organization of a corporation with a capital of $175,000, in shares of $1000 each. This stock was soon pledged by about twenty gentlemen, whose subscriptions varied from one share to twenty. Mr. Josiah Brown was employed as architect and draftsman, and much advice was given by Mr. William C. Davol.

The erection of the mill building was commenced in the month of August and was completed in December. The cotton machinery was built by Marvel, Davol & Co., of Fall River, and William Mason, of Taunton; the engines by the Corliss Steam Engine Company, of Providence. The whole establishment was completed and in operation early in March, 1860.

The corporation was organized under the General Statutes on the 31st day of December, 1859, by the election of S. Angier Chace, president; David Anthony, treasurer; Simeon Borden, clerk; and S. A. Chace, David Anthony, Hale Remington, William Mason, Charles O. Shove, and Charles P. Dring, directors.

The enterprise proved signally successful, and has led to the starting in Fall River of more than 1,000,000 cotton spindles, and a relative growth of the city in every direction.

In 1865 the company erected its No. 2 Mill, of about 30,000 spindles, without any increase of the capital stock. Twenty shares of the stock have since been purchased by the company, and the capital reduced to $155,000.

The present number of stockholders is thirty-one.

THE GRANITE MILLS,

so called from the material of their two fine structures, was the first enterprise established during the dark days of the war.

For several years, Charles O. Shove, Esq., had contemplated the erection of a cotton-mill. In the early part of 1863, with the co-operation of Edmund Chase (with whom he had had many conferences upon the subject) and others, he took the preliminary steps for the organization of a company with a capital of $225,000, divided into shares of $1000 each.

A charter was secured under date of March 3d, 1863, by which William Mason, Southard H. Miller, Charles O. Shove, and their associates were incorporated as the "Granite Mills."

William Mason was elected president ; Charles O. Shove, treasurer ; and William Mason, Lazarus Borden, Edmund Chase, Samuel Hathaway, Charles O. Shove, and Charles P. Stickney, the first board of direction.

A mill site was purchased, comprising the lot fronting on Twelfth street, and extending from Pleasant to Bedford street, and the construction immediately commenced of a factory 328 feet long by 70 feet wide, and five stories high, with a barn roof. Prudential considerations, due to the uncertainty which prevailed in business circles at the time, led the managers to contract at first for machinery for but half of the mill. In May, 1864, however, it was determined to increase the capital stock to $400,000, and to put the whole mill into complete running order. Two months later (July, 1864), the stock was further increased to $415,000, but reduced again in 1871 to $400,000. The plans, specifications, drawings, and indeed the estimates for the establishment in its entirety, were tabulated by Mr. Shove, the prime mover of the enterprise.

Owing to some delay in receiving the machinery, and the enormous price to which cotton advanced, the mill did not commence running until January, 1865, and the first lot of cotton manufactured into print cloths netted the company a loss of $60,000. But better times soon dawned, the mill began to run at a profit, paid up its indebtedness, remunerated its stockholders handsomely, and in 1871 it was determined to build a new structure on land bought on the north side of Bedford street, and quite contiguous to their first purchase.

This mill, also of granite, is 378 feet long, 74 feet wide, and five stories high, and when finished was considered one of the most perfect in the city, harmonious in proportions, stately in appearance, and complete in detail. Every provision for the comfort and safety of the operatives, and the manufacture of the raw cotton into the finished cloth, that industrial science could suggest, was adopted, and experts regarded the two mills as models and standards of excellence. But experience, "that dear school for learners," taught that perfection had not yet been attained. On the morning of September 19th, 1874, a fire started in the mule-room of the No. 1 Mill, which soon got beyond control, and the dense black masses of smoke, terrifying the operatives in the upper stories, created a panic, which prevented their using the means of escape at hand, and numbers threw themselves from the upper story to the ground. Twenty-three persons were killed and thirty-three wounded in this dreadful calamity. The upper stories of the mill were burned before the fire was subdued.

As soon as the débris could be cleared away, the mill was rebuilt with a flat roof, however, instead of the barn roof, which through its inaccessibility had proved itself a very fire-fiend, and every additional safeguard furnished that experience or wisdom could suggest. Five distinct means of escape are now provided on every story of the mill. Tanks of water are placed overhead, and sprinkler pipes liberally distributed to every part of the structure. There are five stand-pipes to each mill, and hydrants connected with the city water-works, besides two powerful force-pumps, one in each building, connected by a pipe underground, so that both can be used on one mill should necessity require. The recurrence of another such calamity thus seems to have been put beyond the possibility of a contingency.

The company owns about eleven acres of land, and has built nearly one hundred tenements for the accommodation of its operatives. The machinery of the No. 1 Mill, mostly of American manufacture, is propelled by a double Corliss engine of 650 horse-power, fed by twenty-four cylinder boilers. Water for steam purposes is drawn through a canal from the upper Fall River stream. The engine of the No. 2 Mill is also a double Corliss engine of 750 horse-power, with twenty-four cylinder boilers for the generation of steam. The machinery, spinning-mules, and fly-frames are English, the remainder American. The No. 1 Mill contains 33,856 spindles and 860 looms; the No. 2 Mill, 44,664 spindles and 1008 looms Nine thousand bales of cotton are used in the annual production of about 21,500,000 yards of print cloths, 64 by 64. The company employs 900 operatives, with a monthly payroll of $22,000. The mills are lighted by gas from the Fall River Gas Works. The present number of stockholders is sixty. In July, 1875, Charles O. Shove, the originator of the enterprise, who had managed the manufacturing and financial departments of the company from the beginning, died after a short illness, and his son, Charles M. Shove, was elected his successor.

THE ROBESON MILLS.

For some years previous to the death of Andrew Robeson, Sr., in 1862, the subject of a cotton-mill to be erected at some future time was frequently discussed by himself, William R. Robeson, Samuel Hathaway, and Linden Cook. The idea did not assume tangible form, however, until some years after the death of Mr. Andrew Robeson, Senior. In 1865, it was determined to realize the project, and to erect a mill upon land belonging to the Rodman estate on Hartwell street, a short distance above the upper or Troy dam. A meeting for organization was held December 1st, 1865, at which a board of directors was chosen, consisting of Andrew Robeson Jr., Charles P. Stickney, Samuel Hathaway, William C. Davol, Jr., Linden Cook, Samuel Castner, and Josiah Brown. Samuel Hathaway was elected president, and Linden Cook treasurer. The new corporation took the name Robeson Mills, from Andrew Robeson, Sr., and was duly incorporated February 20, 1866. A brick mill, three stories high, with a French roof, 222 feet long and 76 feet wide, was erected during the year 1866, after plans furnished by Josiah Brown, architect. It was filled with American machinery, and commenced running in March, 1867. In 1875 the mill was considerably enlarged, by taking off the French roof, carrying up the walls two stories higher, and finishing with a flat roof. The mill now runs 21,632 spindles and 552 looms, and manufactures annually 6,500,000 yards of print cloths 64 by 64, from 2500 bales of cotton. The motive power is furnished by two Corliss engines, a high-pressure of 160 horse-power and a low-pressure of 217 horse-power. The steam is generated by eighteen cylinder boilers. Water is conveyed directly to the mill by a canal dug from the stream. The mill is lighted by gas from the Manufacturers' Gas Company. The fire apparatus consists of two force-pumps, stand-pipes, hydrants connected with the city water-works, and sprinklers distributed through the three upper stories and picker-house. The company owns about seven acres of land, and has provided thirty-three tenements for its operatives. The present number of stockholders is twenty-five.

THE TECUMSEH MILLS.

The demand which arose at the close of the war for cotton fabrics of all kinds gave an immense stimulus to the business, and led to the enlarging of the mills already in existence and to the building of still others. The "Tecumseh Mills" was a direct outgrowth of this demand and the improved prospect for all business enterprises. Some steps looking to the formation of the company were taken in the latter part of 1865, but the first regular meeting for organization was not held until February 17, 1866. An act of incorporation, under date of February 8th, 1866, had been secured, by which Augustus Chace, James W. Hartley, John P. Slade, and their associates were incorporated as the "Tecumseh Mills Company," with a capital of $350,000 in shares of $1000 each. This stock was taken by eighty-nine subscribers. Land was purchased on Hartwell street, bordering also on the Quequechan River, a short distance above the upper or Troy dam, and immediate steps taken for the erection of a mill of about 20,000 spindles. Augustus Chace was elected president, Isaac B. Chace treasurer, and the following board of direction, namely: Augustus Chace, James W. Hartley, Louis L. Barnard, Lazarus Borden, Jonathan T. Lincoln, Cook Borden, and Danforth Horton. The necessary contracts were made, and in the course of the year the mill was erected, filled with machinery, and put in operation.

In 1872 it was determined by the corporation to build another mill of about the same capacity as the first, on land bought for the purpose on Eight Rod Way. This project was also consummated, and the mill started up in 1873. The company now owns two mills, built of granite, for the manufacture of print cloths 64 by 64. The No. 1 Mill contains 20,480 spindles and 480 looms, and is 196 feet long, 72 feet wide, and five stories high, with a pitch roof. The machinery is mostly of foreign make, and is driven by a Corliss engine, built at Taunton, of 400 horse-power. Steam is supplied by four tubular boilers.

The No. 2 Mill contains 21,686 spindles and 534 looms, and is 200 feet long, 74 feet wide, and five stories high on the south, six on the north, with a pitch roof. The machinery is also mostly of foreign manufacture, and is driven by a Corliss horizontal engine of 400 horse-power. Steam is generated in fifteen cylinder boilers.

The production of both mills is about 12,000,000 yards of print cloths per annum. The consumption of cotton is 4500 bales. Four hundred operatives are employed, with a monthly pay-roll of $12,000. The company has all the best and most recent improvements for the prevention of fire, including force-pumps, stand-pipes, hydrants, sprinklers, and connection with the city water-works. The mills are lighted by gas from the Manufacturers' Gas Company. The company owns nine acres of land and fifty-three tenements. The present number of stockholders is ninety-nine.

THE DURFEE MILLS

probably present the finest view to the eye that seeks something like artistic effect in this great congregation of factories. They consist of two very large

five-story structures at right angles with Pleasant street, occupying a large square beautifully grassed, and fronted by a handsome iron fence. The buildings, including a spacious office structure which stands between them, are of granite. The company was organized in 1866, with a capital of $500,000, and named after Major Bradford Durfee, whose son, since deceased, was the principal stockholder and original president. Mill No. 1 was erected the same year, and its companion in 1871. The company runs 87,424 spindles and 2064 looms, being the largest capacity of any corporation in Fall River. Its production is print cloth, of which 23,000,000 yards are annually made, consuming 9500 bales of cotton, and employing 950 operatives. The number of stockholders is seven.

THE DAVOL MILLS COMPANY

was organized December 1st, 1866—nineteen persons contributing the entire capital of $270,000—and named after one of the conspicuous promoters of cotton manufacturing, William C. Davol. A site was selected above the dam and on the west side of the pond, in such proximity to the latter as to assure a convenient supply of pure water for steam purposes. Ground was broken for the foundation, April 1st, 1867, and on the 11th of March, 1868, the first yard of cloth was woven. The mill structure is essentially different in design and material from the Fall River type of long, straight granite factories. The mill proper forms two sides of a quadrangle, the picker, engine, and boiler houses constituting the remainder. The mill and out-buildings are of brick, the former four stories high, flat roof, and with its two sections 457 long and 73 feet broad. The machinery is entirely of American manufacture.

The production of the Davol Mills is shirtings, sheetings, silesias, and fancy fabrics. The shirtings stand very high in the retail market, and at the Centennial Exhibition elicited not only the highly commendatory award of the Commissioners, but the admiration of the visitors and particularly of the European experts. The company now numbers thirty-five stockholders.

THE MERCHANTS MANUFACTURING COMPANY,

organized October 24th, 1866, operates the largest distinct mill in Fall River, and few larger are known to us in New England. The promotion of this conspicuous enterprise was due to the great business energy and tact of Mr. William H. Jennings, who, after digesting carefully his scheme, secured all the capital ($800,000) in the brief period of two days. The site selected for the factory was the lot now bounded by Bedford and Pleasant, and Thirteenth and Fourteenth streets, then owned by the heirs of N. B. Borden and other parties. This property was purchased in preference to the Wardrope estate, at first decided upon, but finally considered to be too limited in area.

On the 2d November, a permanent organization of the company was arranged, W. H. Jennings being chosen treasurer and corporation clerk, and James Henry, W. H. Jennings, Augustus Chase, L. L. Barnard, Robert S. Gibbs, Charles H. Dean, Crawford E. Lindsey, Robert K. Remington, and Lafayette Nichols, directors. At a subsequent meeting James Henry was made president, and Mr. Jennings, clerk.

Ground was at once broken for the erection of a factory, Lazarus Borden superintending the design as building architect, Tillinghast Records being master mason, and James B. Luther, master carpenter. The design contemplated a structure of Fall River granite, 397 feet long by $92\frac{8}{12}$ broad, six stories in height, including a Mansard roof, with a capacity for 54,324 spindles and 1242 looms. The work of building pushing on rapidly, in January, 1867, Mr. Jennings, accompanied by Lazarus Borden, embarked for England, for the purpose of purchasing the picking, speeding, and spinning machinery in Manchester. The mill was completely finished during the last days of 1867—the English machinery arriving coincidently—turned out its first cloth in February, 1868, and in the early fall was in full operation. Its production has been print cloth, 64 by 64.

In connection with building matters, the company purchased twelve additional acres of land on Pine, Davis, Plane, Cherry, and Locust streets, and on a part of it erected one hundred tenement houses for its operatives.

The business proving successful, at a special meeting, January 2, 1871, the stockholders authorized their directors to proceed at once to the erection of an addition to the mill structure, it being considered better to enlarge the original building than to build a distinct mill. The new erection was commenced early in the spring, Samuel Luther supervising the masonry, and David G. Baker the wood work. Early in 1872, the addition was completed and filled with English machinery in full operation. The Merchants Mill, thus extended, contains, under one roof, 85,570 spindles and 1942 looms.

The Merchants, in all features of perfection, the structure of the mill, the excellence and amplitude of its machinery, the simplicity for so immense an establishment of its labor organization, and the admirably devised and sustained economy of its successive stages of production, is a superb example of the industrial triumphs of Fall River. The number of its stockholders is two hundred and fifty.

THE MECHANICS MILLS

claims attention as the enterprise next following the Merchants, in the print-cloth production, and particularly by its location in the extreme northern district of the city, founding a new colony and setting the first example of erecting a mill at any distance from the stream.

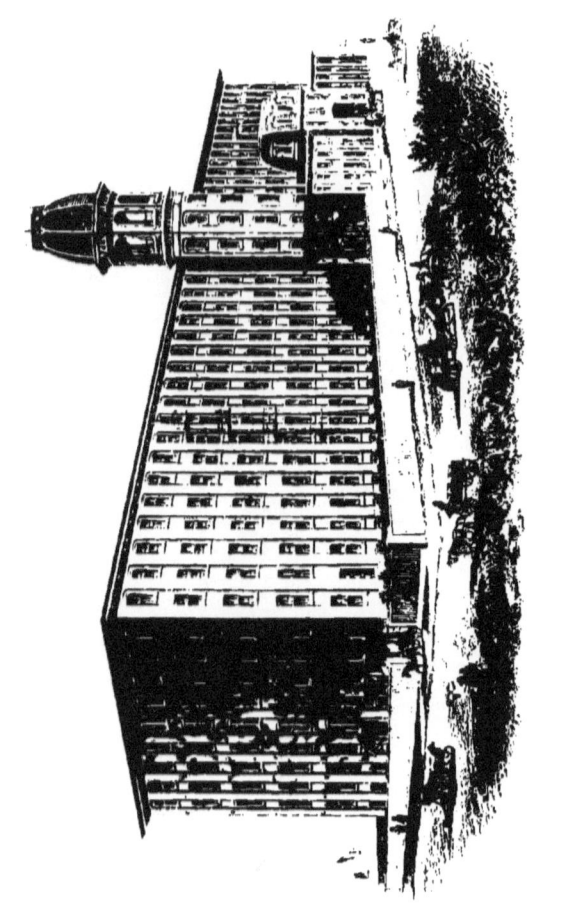

By a special charter granted by the Legislature of Massachusetts, May 25th, 1868, Thomas J. Borden, Stephen Davol, Lazarus Borden, and their associates were incorporated as the Mechanics Mills.

The charter was accepted, and the corporation organized July 1st, 1868, and the following officers were chosen, namely: President and agent, Thomas J. Borden; clerk and treasurer, D. H. Dyer; directors, Thomas J. Borden, Stephen Davol, Lazarus Borden, Job B. French, Southard H. Miller, B. M. C. Durfee, Tillinghast Records, James M. Morton, Jr., and A. D. Easton.

The original scheme was to build a mill 375 feet long, 92 feet wide, and three stories high. At a meeting of the stockholders, held July 9th, 1868, it was determined to increase the size of the mill by the addition of two stories in height, and a wing on the rear for opening and picker rooms, engine-room, and boiler-house, the mill to contain 53,712 spindles and 1248 looms. The capital stock was fixed at $750,000, divided into 7500 shares of $100 each. The stock was largely distributed among parties of small means, there being in all 328 stockholders, 188 of whom owned from one to ten shares each, and 73 owned from eleven to twenty-five shares each, making 261 stockholders, no one of whom owned over $2500 of the stock, and averaging less than $1000 each. The organization of the Merchants Manufacturing Company in 1867, with a capital of $800,000, and about 250 stockholders, and of the Mechanics Mills in 1868, with a capital of $750,000, and 328 stockholders, were the development of a new feature in the ownership of manufacturing property in Fall River, all previous enterprises of the kind having been associations of parties of considerable wealth, while these two were the result of bringing together in large amounts the funds of parties of very moderate capital, and enabling them to receive all the advantages in the conduct of the business that persons of ample means, associated together in small numbers, derived. The Mechanics Mills scheme was in other aspects somewhat of an innovation upon the previous practice in Fall River. All of the cotton-mills of any magnitude previously built had been located near, and took their supply of water, either for power or for making steam, from the outlet of Watuppa Lake to tide-water. The location selected for the Mechanics Mills was in the northerly section of the city, bordering upon the Taunton River, at its junction with Mount Hope Bay, about one and a half miles north of the outlet of the Quequechan River.

This section had previously been occupied solely by private residences there having been no mechanical or manufacturing establishments in the vicinity. A wharf, about 400 feet long and 100 feet wide, was built at the westerly side of the mill site, where all coal for the use of the mill is landed within a few rods of the boilers.

Water for the boilers was obtained by digging a well 18 feet diameter, inside, and of sufficient depth to secure a permanent supply.

For two or three years this mill was entirely isolated from the other manufacturing establishments of the city, and was regarded by the operatives as being quite out of town, but the rapid extension of the cotton industry has resulted in the erection of five other mills still farther north, making six factories in that neighborhood, aggregating 225,528 spindles and 5448 looms. This colony of mills is about two miles north of those lying along the stream, and constituting the central group. As a third group of five mills is located in the vicinity of Laurel Lake, about the same remove south of the centre of the city, the extreme distance from the most northerly to the most southerly mills of the city is over four miles.

The location of this northerly group of mills being two and a half to three miles from the granite quarries in the easterly part of the city, and very accessible either by rail or tide-water to the brick-yards of Taunton, all of these six mills have been built of brick.

The Mechanics Mills was the first new mill in the country provided with slashers for dressing warps—a system which has since almost entirely superseded the old method of dressing, as it can be operated for about one quarter the expense, a larger percentage of reduction in cost of production than has been made in any other department of cotton manufacturing since the invention of the self-operating mule.

The following changes have occurred in the officers of the corporation since its original organization:

February 3d, 1870, James M. Morton, Jr., was chosen clerk; February 2, 1871, Thomas J. Borden was chosen treasurer, and resigning the office of president, Stephen Davol was chosen to that position; February, 1876, Thomas J. Borden resigned the office of treasurer, and George B. Durfee was elected to fill the vacancy.

Two of the original directors, Lazarus Borden and B. M. C. Durfee, have died, and Mr. A. D. Easton resigned. These vacancies have been filled by the election of John B. Hathaway, George B. Durfee, and Frank S. Stevens.

The erection of the mill commenced in the summer of 1868, and was completed and the machinery set up by June, 1869, the establishment being in full operation in December. The company has about twelve acres of land, exclusive of mill site and wharf, and has built one hundred and twenty-six tenements. The fire-prevention of the mill is ample, comprising Parmelee's automatic sprinklers in the upper three stories and the opener and picker rooms, connected with the city water-works, as well as stand-pipes, front and rear, one each side of the tower and one in the tower, extending to the roof, all operated by a powerful force-pump. In addition to this extraordinary provision, the mill yard has its hydrants, always in working order, and a large supply of hose and apparatus is in easy recourse.

The "Stafford Mills"

was organized under the General Statutes of Massachusetts, December 12th, 1870, with a capital of $500,000, in shares of $100 each. Foster H. Stafford was elected president and agent, and Shubael P. Lovell clerk and treasurer, with the following board of directors: F. H. Stafford, Samuel Hathaway, Charles P. Stickney, Robert T. Davis, William C. Davol, William L. Slade, Danforth Horton, Edmund Chase, and Weaver Osborn.

On the 18th of March, 1871, this corporation was dissolved, and the subscribers, twenty-two in number, reorganized under a special charter granted by the commonwealth to Charles P. Stickney, Samuel Hathaway, Foster H. Stafford, and their associates, as the "Stafford Mills," with a capital of $550,000. The persons chosen officers in the first organization were elected to the same positions under the special charter.

The company assumed the name of "Stafford Mills," in honor of their president, who was the projector of the enterprise, and whose long experience, untiring devotion to the business, and proved skill and success had justly earned him the confidence and esteem of his associates.

Mr. Stafford is one of the few practical manufacturers of to-day, whose life has compassed almost the whole range of cotton manufacture from its beginning in this country.

Having entered the mill when a boy, scarcely more than seven or eight years of age, he has been connected with it in various capacities for more than fifty years. Coming to Fall River in 1842, he was for ten years the superintendent of the old Fall River and Annawan manufactories. When Mr. Lazarus Borden resigned the superintendency of the Metacomet Mill, that, too, was joined to these, and he continued in the charge of all three until 1859. Desiring then to enter into business for himself, he removed to Pawtucket, and with his brother commenced the manufacture of thread. In 1859 the new enterprise of the Union Mill was projected, and the managers, in casting about for some one to superintend the operations, speedily placed themselves in communication with Mr. Stafford, and the success of that experiment was due in no small degree to the practical knowledge and skill of Mr. Stafford. After ten years' service at the Union Mills, during which a second mill was built, of twice the capacity of the first, without any increase of capital or assessment on the stockholders, dividends paid amounting to several times the original subscription, and the stock increased more than five-fold in value, leading the way for many enterprises of a similar character which have followed. Mr. Stafford resigned his position, and with Mr. Samuel Hathaway and others organized and put into successful operation the new enterprise of the "Stafford Mills."

Land was purchased at a spot known as White Brook, at the junction of the old Bedford road and Pleasant street, not far distant from the upper part of the Quequechan River. Work on the foundation was begun in April, 1871, and some portions of the machinery were started the next January. The mill is built of granite, 374 feet long, 70 feet wide, and five stories high, with an L for engine-house, boilers, picker-house, etc. Stairways are placed at each end, and thus the whole space is rendered available, while safe means of ingress and egress are afforded. As Mr. Stafford quaintly says, "Towers don't pay dividends"—the tower was omitted. The machinery is partly foreign, and occasioned considerable delay in starting up the mill on account of its non-arrival. The engine is a double Corliss of 600 horse-power, and is supplied with steam by twenty-four cylinder boilers. Water is drawn from the Quequechan River, the Brook water not proving quite clear enough generally for manufacturing purposes, though it could be used if a better supply were not near at hand.

The mill contains 34,928 spindles and 860 looms, and manufactures 10,000,000 yards of print cloth, 64 by 64, per annum. It is lighted by gas from the Manufacturers' Gas Company, and has all the modern appliances for protection against fire.

The company, instead of buying land and building tenements for their operatives, adopted the plan of loaning the necessary capital to those owning land in the neighborhood and taking leases of the houses erected by them; thus securing the accommodations required, helping the land-owners near by, and saving so much of an investment in unproductive real estate and depreciation in buildings. One hundred and twenty-four tenements were built and leased on these terms, and within a few years the money loaned was repaid, and the ownership fully vested in the original proprietors of the land—a specimen of co-operative ownership which might perhaps be profitably followed in other communities and in other departments of trade. The company now owns about fifteen acres of land, including its mill site. The present number of stockholders is forty.

The Weetamoe Mills Company

is the outgrowth of the prosperity of the mills of the decade of 1860 to 1870. The first steps in the organization of the company were taken by D. Hartwell Dyer, Esq., who opened the books for subscription to a capital stock of $550,000. He met with such success that $100,000 was offered in excess of the amount named. The first meeting for organization was held December 29th, 1870, and the following board of direction chosen: L. L. Barnard, Job B. French, Jonathan I. Hilliard, Josiah C. Blaisdell, William Lindsey, Francis B. Hood, Henry C. Lincoln, E. C. Kilburn, and D. H. Dyer. L. L. Barnard was elected president, and D. H. Dyer treasurer. The act of incorporation is dated February 24th, 1871. The number of original subscribers was two hundred and seventy-five. Land for a mill site was purchased on the banks of Taunton River, near Slade's Ferry, and the new corporation assumed the name of "Weetamoe," after the Queen of the Pocassets, who was drowned near by, in crossing the river. Another tract of land, north of Mechanicsville, was purchased for tenement houses. Work on the mill building was begun in March, 1872, and within ten months the looms were running off cloth. The plans were all drawn by Mr. Dyer, who, more or less connected with cotton-mills from his boyhood, in later years had turned his attention to the architecture of mill buildings, and the preparation of plans and specifications for the same.

The mill is of brick, 320 feet long, 74 feet wide, and five stories high with basement. It has a flat roof, and an L for engines, boilers, etc. Most of the machinery, looms, spoolers, cards, etc., is American, but a small portion English. The engine is a double Corliss of 500 horse-power, and steam is furnished by five sections of the Harrison boiler. The water for steam purposes is supplied by wells dug on the premises. The mill is lighted by gas from the Fall River Gas Works. There are sixty-five tenements, the outer walls of brick, for the accommodation of the operatives. The company owns nine acres of land, together with a fine wharf privilege, which is utilized for the landing of coal, cotton, building material, and supplies. The present number of stockholders is three hundred.

The Slade Mill

is noteworthy as the first erected of the group of factories located in the southern district of Fall River. The enterprise was initiated by the owners of a large tract of unimproved land a few rods south of the Globe Village, on and about what is known as Cook's Pond (or Laurel Lake)—Messrs. William L. and Jonathan Slade, Benjamin Hall, and the Dwelly heirs—who entered into a joint agreement, on the 1st of May, 1871, to sell their real estate for the erection of a mill thereon. Before the day was concluded every share of the stock had been subscribed, and probably double the amount could have been raised. The original subscribers were but twenty-seven in number, conspicuous in the list, in addition to those already mentioned as owners of the one hundred and fifty acres of land conceded to the company, being Frank S. Stevens, John C. Milne, W. and J. M. Osborn, Richard B. and Thomas J. Borden, S. Angier Chace, David A. Brayton, B. M. C. Durfee, and William Valentine. On the 13th of May a permanent organization was formed, Mr. William L. Slade being chosen president and James M. Osborn treasurer. Ground was at once broken for a mill, and the structure of brick rapidly pushed forward.

The effect of this new industrial movement was phenomenal. Real estate in the vicinity took an instantaneous upward turn, plots of unoccupied land in every proximate direction being picked up by eager purchasers almost before the owners could name a price, acres that were not valued a few years previously at $200 going off for $10,000. The shares of the new company rose from par ($100) to $172, before the foundation of the factory had been completely laid.

In the midst of this activity—so surely does one enterprise beget others—other companies were formed, and the King Philip, Osborn, and Montaup Mills soon in process of erection on portions of the land originally owned by the Slade corporation.

The result of this pioneer enterprise has been the establishment of a new village, adding probably 5000 to the population of Fall River, and over $2,000,000 to its production. One of the finest public-school edifices in the city has been erected on Main street, near the mills, known as the Slade school, and a new church has likewise been built for the Catholic community. The highways, thrown open on its real estate by the company, have been accepted by the city.

The Slade Mill produces print cloth. Its capacity is 10,000,000 yards annually, consuming 4000 bales of cotton. It runs 37,040 spindles and 860 looms. The present number of stockholders is seventy.

THE RICHARD BORDEN MANUFACTURING COMPANY

was initiated early in 1871. The entire capital of $800,000 was taken by twelve individuals, and May 19th the charter was accepted. At the first meeting of organization, Thomas J. Borden was elected treasurer and corporation clerk, and Richard Borden, Philip D. Borden, Thomas J. Borden, Richard B. Borden, and A. S. Covel, directors. Richard Borden was chosen president at the subsequent board meeting. At the same meeting it was voted to purchase of Colonel Richard Borden the real estate owned by him, and known as the Borden farm, lying east of the Eight Rod Way and south of the Quequechan, as well as two acres belonging to Cook Borden, adjacent. Portions of the land were afterwards sold for the erection of the Chace and Tecumseh Mills.

The mill, which is one of the most perfect structures for manufacturing purposes in the country, was erected and "wound up" under the personal supervision of Thomas J. Borden, who made the plans of construction and machine equipment. It started full operation in February, 1873, the present number of spindles (1536 having been added to the original design) being 44,064, with 1032 looms. Its production annually is 12,000,000 yards of print cloth. The present number of stockholders is fifteen.

Colonel Richard Borden dying in February, 1874, his son, Richard B. Borden, was elected president, and continued in that office until the early part of 1876, when, by the resignation of his brother Thomas J., he was called to the more active duties of treasurer. Thomas J. Borden is now the president of the company.

THE WAMPANOAG MILL COMPANY

was the result of a preliminary meeting on the 23d of May, 1871, at which Stephen Davol, J. D. Flint, William H. Jennings, L. S. Earl, Walter C. Durfee, and R. T. Davis were associated for the purpose of projecting a new corporation. On the 31st of the same month, the capital of $400,000 having all been taken up, a meeting of stockholders was held to organize the company, at which Walter C. Durfee was elected treasurer and corporation clerk, and R. T. Davis, J. D. Flint, Walter C. Durfee, Stephen Davol, Foster H. Stafford, Simeon Borden, George H. Eddy, A. L. Covel, L. S. Earl, William H. Jennings, and John H. Brown, directors. At a subsequent meeting R. T. Davis was chosen president.

The land for the mill site was purchased of Messrs. Davis and Flint, fifteen acres in extent, and the construction of the factory at once proceeded. On the 1st of April, 1872, within ten months of laying the first stone, cloth was woven in the mill. The company now owns eighteen acres of land, and has erected thereon ten large tenement houses admirably planned, and a dwelling for its superintendent. The mill has a run of 28,000 spindles and 704 looms, producing 8,000,000 yards of print cloth per annum. Its provision against fire consists of two powerful force-pumps, besides the usual quota of hydrants, all connecting with the city water-works. The present number of stockholders is ninety-eight.

THE NARRAGANSETT MILL

was the third erection of the group in the northern district. Its original promoters were Daniel McCowan, James Waring, A. D. Easton, and others. The capital, originally $350,000, was on the acceptance of the charter, July 6th, 1871, increased to $400,000. At the meeting of organization, July 12th, James Waring was chosen treasurer, and A. D. Easton president. The mill was finished and wound up for operation by the latter part of December in the following year. Its capacity is 27,920 spindles and 700 looms, producing print cloth and corset jeans. Its real estate on the east side of North Main street, twenty-one acres, including a tract, also, on the west side of that thoroughfare, was purchased of Job T. Wilson and others. Its present stockholders number two hundred and forty.

THE KING PHILIP MILLS COMPANY.

In the spring of 1871, Messrs. C. E. Lindsey and E. C. Kilburn of Fall River, and Jonathan Chace of Valley Falls, R. I., had several interviews with reference to building a cotton-mill for the manufacture of fine cotton fabrics. Believing that there was an opening for an enterprise of that class, they decided to test the practicability of the scheme by opening books for subscriptions to a capital stock of $500,000, contemplating a mill of about 36,000 spindles. The matter was put in charge of Mr. E. C. Kilburn, and within a fortnight the whole amount of $500,000 was taken by forty-seven responsible persons, and an additional $160,000 asked for. But at the first meeting of the subscribers, held July 14th, 1871, for organization, it was decided to limit the capital stock to $500,000. A code of by-laws was adopted, and the first board of directors elected, consisting of Jonathan Chace, James Henry, S. Angier Chace, C. E. Lindsey, Philip D. Borden, Charles O. Shove, E. C. Kilburn, A. S. Tripp, Benjamin A. Chace, Simeon Borden, and Charles H. Dean. E. C. Kilburn was elected treasurer, and A. S. Tripp clerk of the corporation. At the first meeting of the board of directors, held the same day, Crawford E. Lindsey was elected president of the corporation.

The act of incorporation bears date September 15th, 1871.

It was at first decided to erect the mill on a tract of land belonging to the late Oliver Chace and his children, situated on the corner of Middle and Bay streets and on Sprague street, containing about twelve acres. But upon digging a well to test the supply of water requisite for steam purposes, it was found entirely inadequate, and the treasurer was instructed to look up other locations. At a meeting of the directors, held September 4th, 1871, negotiations were approved, which resulted in the purchase of twenty-one acres of the

Dodge Farm, so-called, and fifteen acres of the Slade Mills land adjoining, making a tract extending from Laurel Lake on the east to South Main Road on the west, and comprising about thirty-seven acres. Preparations were immediately made for putting in a foundation, and work continued until cold weather put a stop to out-door operations. It was resumed the next April, and the mill carried forward to completion.

The mill building, located on the west shore of Laurel Lake, is constructed of granite, most of which was taken from a ledge on the premises, and is 320 feet long by 92 feet wide, four stories high on the front and five on the rear. The engine and picker house, attached to the main building at the south-east corner, is three stories high, 65 feet long, and 50 feet wide; the boiler-house, on the north side of the picker-house, is one story high, 98 feet long, and 50 feet wide.

The mill was built under the superintendence of the treasurer, assisted by W. F. Sherman and F. P. Sheldon, architects and draftsmen. The mason work was done by A. T. Pierce of Dighton, and the carpentry by L. T. Miller of Fall River. Machinery began to be introduced in October, 1872. The mules were built by Parr, Curtis & Madeley, and the speeders and roving-frames by Howard & Boullough, of Accrington, England. The card and spinning frames were furnished by the Saco Water-Power and Machine Company, of Biddeford, Maine, the looms and shafting by Kilburn, Lincoln & Company, of Fall River.

The mill started up in January, 1873, but on account of delays in receiving machinery from England, was not in full running order until late in the summer. The panic of 1873 occurred just as the first finished goods were put into the agent's hands, but notwithstanding the depression and falling market, they were well received, soon made for themselves a name, and have since maintained an honorable reputation with old and well established manufactories of like productions.

The regular makes are now " King Philips" fine wide sheetings, $\frac{4}{4}$, $\frac{7}{8}$, and $\frac{4}{4}$; " King Philips" fine cambric muslins, and " King Philips" jaconets. There are also manufactured " Laurel Lake Sheetings," and various other kinds of brown sheetings and umbrella goods. The mill runs 37,440 spindles and 776 looms, and works up some 3000 bales of cotton annually in the production of 5,500,000 yards of cloth. It requires about 425 hands to operate its machinery, while its monthly pay-roll amounts to $12,000. The engine is a Harris-Corliss of 550 horse-power, made by Wm. A. Harris, of Providence, R. I. Twenty-four cylinder boilers are in constant use to furnish the necessary steam. Abundance of water is supplied by the lake, from which a canal leads directly into the engine-room. The fire apparatus consists of two of the largest size Fulton steam-pumps, and the mill is also connected with the Slade Mills, not far distant, by a six-inch iron pipe, to which the pumps of each mill are attached, so that in case of fire the one can assist the other. The mill is lighted by gas furnished by the Slade Mills, and conveyed through the pipe above referred to, which thus answers the double purpose of a gas conduit, or, in case of fire, by shutting off the gas, it becomes a water conduit. Stairs are at each end of the mill building, and fire-escapes are attached to each story, front and rear. The company owns six houses with four tenements in each, and two blocks with twenty-eight tenements each, making in all eighty tenements; also a house for the superintendent, connected with the mill by a bell, to be used by the watchman in any sudden emergency at night. Mr. B. W. Nichols was appointed superintendent in October, 1872, a position he has filled honorably and successfully to the present time. The stockholders of the King Philip Company number one hundred and forty.

THE CRESCENT MILLS CORPORATION

was organized October 25th, 1871, with a capital stock of $500,000. The original stockholders numbered thirty. Ground was broken for foundation in the same month, and the work rapidly pushed forward till cold weather, when operations were suspended until spring. The main building is of granite, 339 feet by 74, four stories and attic above the basement. The picker-house building in rear is 85 by 50 feet, three stories high. The first cotton was put in December 21st, 1872, and the first cloth produced February 8th, 1873, and the entire mill was in full operation August 30th, 1873.

The picker-house machinery and roving-frames were built by Messrs. Walker & Hacking, Bury, Lancashire, Eng. The cards, mules, looms, and spinning-frames were built by William Mason, of Taunton, Mass.

The engine was furnished by the Foundry and Machine Company of Taunton, Mass. It is of the Corliss pattern, having the cylinder 26 inches diameter by 5 feet stroke, and working up to 450 horse-power. The twenty-four boilers, cylinder pattern, were made by the Fall River Iron Works Company, and are 30 feet long by 30 inches in diameter. The mill contains 33,280 spindles and 744 looms, manufacturing ¼ fine brown sheetings and special styles of fine goods for printing and converting. Three thousand five hundred bales of cotton are used annually, producing 6,000,000 yards of cloth.

The original officers of the corporation were: Benjamin Covel, president; Lafayette Nichols, treasurer; and Benjamin Covel, L. Nichols, D. A. Chapin, William B. Durfee, J. F. Nichols, Joseph Brady, David F. Brown, G. M. Haffards, and A. S. Covel constituted the board of directors.

Mr. Nichols served as treasurer until November 12th, 1873, when he resigned, and was succeeded by Mr. R. B. Borden. Mr. Borden filled the position until the annual meeting, February 9th, 1876, at which time he also resigned, and Mr. A. S. Covel, the present treasurer, was elected to fill the vacancy.

The land purchased for the mill site is bounded by the Quequechan River, Eight Rod Way, and Pleasant street. It contains about twenty-five acres, and is the centre of a circle of eighteen large mills, and was chosen on account of the valuable water-front, its proximity to so many large corporations, and its consequent prospective value as an investment. Already the Fall River Railroad Company has a large tract of this land for their terminus, and several large lots have been leased to parties for different branches of business. The company numbers ninety-four stockholders.

THE MONTAUP MILLS

was projected by Josiah Brown, Esq., of Fall River. In following his business as a civil engineer, Mr. Brown had been brought in contact in various parts of New England with mills for the manufacture of bags, duck and cotton bats, and conceived the idea that in Fall River, with its numerous cotton-mills, there was an excellent opening for such an enterprise. Having put his ideas in form, and broached the subject to several of his friends, he found them ready to make the necessary investment, and within a week after the books were opened, the whole amount was subscribed, and the preliminary steps taken in the formation of the company. The first meeting was held November 14th, 1871, by the original subscribers, thirty-five in number, and the following board of directors chosen: Josiah Brown, Bradford D. Davol, George B. Durfee, A. D. Easton, William L. Slade, Isaac Borden, George H. Hawes, William Valentine, Holder B. Durfee, and Thomas J. Borden. Josiah Brown was elected president, and Isaac Borden treasurer and clerk of the corporation. The capital was fixed at $250,000, and the name of "Montaup Mills" adopted as the corporate name, suggested by the Indian name of "Mount Hope." The act of incorporation bears date December 1st, 1871.

Between eight and nine acres of land were bought on the northern shore of Laurel Lake, and as soon as the plans could be drawn, work was begun on the foundation. The mill is built of brick, 242 feet long and 74 feet wide, and four stories high, with a flat roof. An L for a picker-house projects on the east, 77 feet long by 29 feet wide, three stories high. On the west is another L, 30 by 20, two stories high, occupied as an engine and boiler house. Josiah Brown was the architect; John O. Chace, the mason; and W. T. Wood, the carpenter. The cards were furnished by William Mason, of

Taunton; the drawing-frames by the Whitin Machine Company, of Whitinsville, Mass.; the speeders by Parr, Curtis & Madeley, of Manchester, England; the spinning-frames by Fales & Jenckes, of Pawtucket, R. I.; and the looms by the Lewiston Machine Company, of Lewiston, Maine.

Operations on the foundation were begun February 13th, 1872, and the work advanced with such rapidity that the engine was started January 2d, 1873, and the weaving February 7th, 1873, or in a little less than a year from the first breaking of ground.

The company entered immediately upon the manufacture of first quality seamless bags, cotton bats and duck, running 7200 spindles and 112 looms, from which it can produce 600,000 bags (two-bushel) annually. The company employs 125 hands, and its pay-roll is $3000 per month. The works are run by a single engine, of 350 horse-power, made by the Corliss Steam Engine Company, of Providence, R. I. Steam is furnished by three upright boilers of 150 horse-power each. A canal from the lake conveys the water directly into the engine-room. The mill is lighted by gas made from oil, and manufactured on the premises. Two Fulton steam pumps, and connections with the city water-works, give ample protection against fire. Fire-escapes upon the front and rear of the mill, and stairways at each end, give ready means of exit in any sudden emergency. The company owns six houses, containing thirty-six tenements, which are rented at moderate rates to the operatives. Mr. John F. Hamlet has filled the office of superintendent since the organization of the company, and has brought to his position a large and skilled experience in this particular branch of cotton manufacture. The company numbers seventy-five stockholders.

THE OSBORN MILLS

enterprise was due to the suggestion of Weaver Osborn, Esq., who, in consultation with Messrs. Easton & Milne and Joseph Healy, proposed the formation of a company with $500,000 capital for the manufacture of print cloths. The books were opened, and *before night* the whole amount was subscribed, and the same evening "rights" sold at three per cent premium. The first meeting of the original subscribers, thirty-five in number, was holden October 9th, 1871, and the company organized with the following board of directors: Weaver Osborn, Joseph Healy, James T. Milne, Benjamin Hall, Andrew J. Borden, Joseph Osborn, Joseph E. Macomber, George T. Hathaway, John C. Milne, D. H. Dyer, and Edward E. Hathaway. Weaver Osborn was subsequently elected president, and Joseph Healy treasurer and clerk of the corporation. The capital was fixed at $500,000, and the name of "Osborn Mills," in honor of the president, selected as the corporate name. The act of incorporation bears date February 1st, 1872.

A tract of land on the eastern shore of Laurel Lake, comprising about fifteen acres, was secured as a mill site, and a smaller lot of five acres, near by, purchased for tenement houses. Plans for the mill were drawn during the winter by D. H. Dyer, architect, and work begun on the foundation April 4th, 1872. The mill is built of granite, from a ledge on the south shore of the lake, and is 318 feet long by 74 feet wide, five stories high, with a flat roof and a basement. A finely proportioned tower at the centre affords means of entrance and exit. An L, on the west, 90 feet by 40, and three stories high, serves as an engine and picker house, to which is attached a boiler-house, 41 feet by 42, two stories high. The mason work was done under the direction of William M. Manley, and the wood work by David D. Grinnell, both of Fall River. The looms and cards were furnished by William Mason, of Taunton; the mules and speeders by Walker & Hacking, of Manchester, England; the spoolers by Payne & Matthewson, of Pawtucket; the warpers by the Hopedale Machine Company, of Hopedale, Mass.; the drawing by the Whitin Machine Company, of Whitinville, Mass., and the shafting by William Sellers & Co., of Philadelphia. The mill building was put up, the machinery placed in position, and weaving commenced (March 10, 1873) in less than a year from the time of beginning work on the foundation. The mill was "wound up" for the manufacture of print cloths 64 by 64, and contains 37,232 spindles and 930 looms. Four thousand two hundred and fifty bales of cotton are used per annum in the production of 11,000,000 yards of cloth. Four hundred and twenty-five hands are employed, and the monthly pay-roll amounts to $11,000. The motive power is furnished by a double steam-engine of 500 horse-power, made by the Corliss Steam Engine Company, of Providence, R. I. Four upright boilers, 12 feet in diameter, supply the steam, while an abundance of water is secured by a canal from the adjacent lake. The mill is lighted by gas from the Fall River Gas Works. The fire apparatus consists of two Niagara force-pumps, with two stand-pipes and two hydrants connected with the city water-works. The company has provided for its help thirteen houses, containing forty-nine tenements. Mr. Joseph Watters has proved an efficient and practical superintendent from his first appointment, at the formation of the company. The stockholders are two hundred and six in number.

THE CHACE MILLS COMPANY

was organized in 1871-2, the original promoters of the enterprise being Augustus Chace, George W. Grinnell, and J. M. Earl. The first suggestion of the new corporation was the effort of a few gentlemen, associated with Mr. John P. Slade, to start a mill a considerable distance south, on the shore of the Quequechan Pond. The locality proposed being considered too far removed from the city, the undertaking resolved itself into another enterprise, which terminated in the formation of the Chace Company.

The Chace Mill, located on Rodman street, is a granite structure, 377 feet long by 74 feet wide, and six stories elevation. The engine-house and picker-room occupy an **L**, three stories high, in the rear. In this mill the basement, a full story, remarkably dry, airy, and light, is used for cotton storage.

At the first meeting of organization, Augustus Chace was chosen president, and Joseph A. Baker treasurer. The superintendent, George H. Hills, though probably the youngest man in the vocation in Fall River, has had an exceptionally thorough experience, having, with an early prepossession for cotton manufacture, perfectly acquainted himself with all the details of the industry by entering a mill while yet a boy, and successively working his way up to overseer in every department. This is a very unusual tuition, but it has given Mr. Hills a knowledge of cloth production in all its stages that cannot be too highly appreciated.

This mill contains 43,480 spindles and 1056 looms, producing 12,000,000 yards of print cloth out of 4500 bales of cotton. The company has a capital of $500,000, distributed among one hundred and ninety stockholders.

THE FLINT MILLS

was organized in February, 1872, with a capital of $500,000, which was increased to $600,000 in October of the same year. The act of incorporation bearing date February 28th, 1872, names John D. Flint, Stephen C. Wrightington, Simeon Borden, and William H. Jennings, their associates and successors, as the new corporation. The number of original subscribers was about two hundred. John D. Flint was elected president, Stephen C. Wrightington treasurer, and J. D. Flint, Robert T. Davis, Stephen Davol, William H. Jennings, William T. Hall, Daniel McGowan, Gardner T. Dean, S. C. Wrightington, William Carroll, and Cornelius Hargraves, the board of direction. Mr. Wrightington resigned in March, and George H. Eddy was elected treasurer to fill the vacancy. The organization assumed the name of Flint Mills, in honor of its president, and the village which has since grown up in the vicinity of the mill, is known locally as "Flint Village." Land for a mill site and tenements was purchased on the upper part of the stream, near where it issues from the South Pond, and before frost was out of the ground operations were begun for the foundation of the mill. The

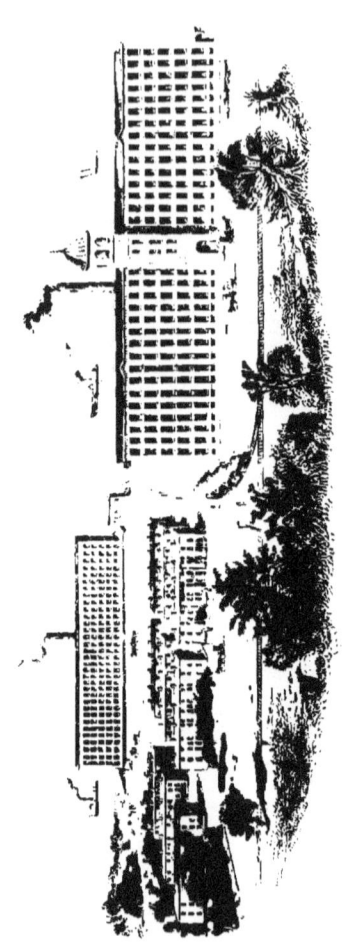

mill is built of stone, in accordance with plans drawn by D. H. Dyer, architect, and, unlike most of the cotton-mills in the city, is a wide mill, after the English style, being 300 feet long by 94 feet wide, instead of the usual width of 72 to 74 feet. It is five stories high, with a flat roof, and a finely proportioned tower in front. The machinery is mostly American, and arranged for the manufacture of print cloth 64 by 64. The mill commenced running in April, 1873, and manufactures 12,500,000 yards of print cloths per annum. It contains 45,360 spindles, 1008 looms, and employs 450 operatives, with a monthly pay-roll of $11,000. The machinery is driven by a double Corliss engine of 650 horse-power. Steam is supplied by five upright boilers of 170 horse-power each. Water is taken directly from the stream by a canal dug for the purpose. The mill is lighted by gas made from petroleum, and furnished by the Wampanoag Mills near by. The fire apparatus consists of two large force-pumps, stand-pipes, hydrants, sprinklers, and connections with the city water-works; also a large tank in the back tower. The company owns forty-two tenements, and about sixty-two acres of land. The present number of stockholders is two hundred and fifty.

The Border City Mills

is the project of George T. Hathaway, Esq., who, after consultation with Messrs. S. Angier Chace and Chester W. Greene, of Fall River, and James A. Hathaway, of Boston, solicited subscriptions to a corporation of one million dollars capital. The stock was taken by about one hundred and fifty subscribers.

The first meeting for organization was held April 29th, 1872, at which the following gentlemen were elected a board of direction: S. Angier Chace, Stephen Davol, Chester W. Greene, E. C. Kilburn, Charles P. Stickney, A. D. Easton, George T. Hathaway, John M. Dean, William E. Dunham, James E. Cunneen, Horatio N. Durfee. S. A. Chace was subsequently elected president, and George T. Hathaway treasurer. An act of incorporation was secured under date of June 3d, 1872, and the name of "Border City Mills" adopted —a name often applied to Fall River because of its proximity to the State of Rhode Island.

It was at first contemplated to erect a single mill of some 75,000 spindles, but the experience of the past seemed to indicate that such a number of spindles could be handled better in two mills than in one, and the final decision was given for the erection of two mills, of about 35,000 spindles each. Thirty acres of land were purchased in the north part of the city, at a point known as Wilson's Cove, on the east bank of Taunton River, and immediate preparations were begun for the erection of the No. 1 Mill. The site chosen had admirable facilities for the transaction of business, a good depth of water on the west, where a wharf was easily constructed for the reception of building material, coal, cotton, freight, etc., while on the east was the Old Colony Railroad, from which a spur was built directly past the doors of the mills to the wharf, and by which cloth and supplies could be readily shipped north or south.

The mills are built of brick. The No. 1 Mill was located near the shore, and work begun on the foundation in June, 1872, from plans furnished by Josiah Brown, architect and civil engineer. It is 318 feet long, 73 feet wide, and five stories high, with an L for engine and boiler room. It was filled with machinery, mostly of American manufacture, and started up in June, 1873. The No. 2 Mill was located some distance east, quite near the railroad. It was also built of brick, 329 feet long, 73 feet wide, five stories high, with basement and L, and started up in March, 1874. The motive power of each mill is furnished by a double Corliss engine of 565 horse-power. The steam is generated in the No. 1 Mill by four upright boilers, while the No. 2 is provided with twenty-four cylinder boilers. Water is drawn from wells dug on the premises. Both mills are lighted by gas furnished by the Fall River Gas Company. The No. 1 Mill contains 35,632 spindles and 880 looms, and the No. 2 Mill, 36,512 spindles and 880 looms. They consume about nine thousand bales of cotton annually, in the production of 20,500,000 yards of print cloths 64 by 64. Each mill is provided with two large force-pumps, together with sprinklers in each room, as well as stand-pipes and hydrants connected with the city water-works. The company owns twenty blocks, containing one hundred and fifty-eight tenements. James E. Cunneen has been superintendent of the mills since the organization of the company. The present number of stockholders is three hundred and fifteen.

THE SAGAMORE MILLS.

The first meeting for the organization of the Sagamore Mills was held March 6th, 1872. The number of original subscribers to the capital stock, of $500,000, was one hundred and seven. An act of incorporation was soon after secured, and on the completion of the organization, L. L. Barnard was elected president, Francis B. Hood treasurer, and the following board of direction: L. L. Barnard, F. B. Hood, Josiah C. Blaisdell, James W. Hartley, Charles McCreery, Jonathan I. Hilliard, Joseph Borden, William M. Almy, D. Hartwell Dyer, and Job T. Wilson. A tract of land on the borders of Taunton River, a little north of Slade's Ferry, was purchased, and work on the foundations of the mill begun in July, 1872. The mill is built of brick, from plans drawn by D. H. Dyer, architect, and is 320 feet long, 73 feet wide, and five stories high, with a flat roof, tower, and basement.

The machinery was started in July, 1873, and is about half American and half English. The engine is of 400 horse-power, the boilers (six sections of the Harrison boiler) of about 50 horse-power each. Water is supplied by wells dug on the premises. The mill is lighted by gas, furnished by the Fall River Gas Company. The fire apparatus consists of two steam pumps, stand-pipes, hydrants, sprinklers, and connections throughout with city water. The company owns thirty-five acres of land and forty-eight tenements. The mill contains 37,672 spindles and 900 looms, and works up annually 4000 bales of cotton into 10,500,000 yards of print cloths. It employs 425 operatives, with a monthly pay-roll of $10,000. The present number of stockholders is two hundred and sixty-eight.

THE SHOVE MILLS.

The first steps in the formation of the Shove Mills were taken by John P. Slade, Esq., and it was mainly through his instrumentality that the organization was finally effected, a charter secured, and the project brought to a successful issue. During the early stages of the movement, he had frequent consultation with Messrs. Charles O. Shove, George A. Chace, and Joseph McCreery.

The first meeting of the subscribers, thirty-one in number, for the organization of the company, was held March 4th, 1872. The act of incorporation is dated April 2d, 1872. The capital was fixed at $550,000, and the name of "Shove Mills" assumed as the corporate name, in honor of Charles O. Shove, a prominent cotton manufacturer of the city, and the first president of the new corporation. John P. Slade was elected treasurer, and the following board of direction: Charles O. Shove, Joseph McCreery, George A. Chace, Lloyd S. Earle, William Connell, Jr., Nathan Chace, Isaac W. Howland, Josiah C. Blaisdell, and John P. Slade.

Land for a mill site was purchased on the western shore of Laurel Lake, just within the line of boundary between Massachusetts and Rhode Island, and further purchases beyond the boundary line were made for tenement blocks.

No active steps towards building the mill were taken until the fall of 1873, when a foundation only was put in. Work was resumed in the spring of 1874, and the building carried forward to completion, and filled with machinery. The mill is a handsome granite structure, 339 feet long, 74 feet wide, and five stories high, with a basement, a flat roof, and a large square tower running up at the centre. The machinery is mostly American, and commenced running in April, 1875. The engine is a Harris-Corliss, of 500 horse-power. Steam is generated in twenty-four cylinder boilers, and abundance of water is furnished by the neighboring lake. The mill contains 37,504 spindles and 960 looms, and manufactures 11,500,000 yards of 64 by 64 print cloths per annum. Four hundred and twenty-five operatives are employed, with a monthly pay-roll of $11,000. The mill is heated by steam, and lighted by gas made from petroleum and manufactured on the premises. The company has provided ample protection against fire, by two force-pumps, stand-pipes and hydrants, front and rear, and sprinklers within the mill. Fire-escapes are placed on the ends and at other convenient places about the mill, thus affording, with the tower, rapid and safe means of exit in any sudden emergency. The company owns forty-eight tenements and one hundred and twenty-two acres of land. The number of stockholders is one hundred.

THE BARNARD MANUFACTURING COMPANY

was projected in October, 1873, by L. L. Barnard, Stephen Davol, W. H. Jennings, and N. B. Borden. At the meeting of organization, on the 14th of that month, Mr. Barnard was chosen president. N. B. Borden treasurer and corporation clerk, and L. L. Barnard, Stephen Davol, W. H. Jennings, A. D. Easton, R. T. Davis, Simeon Borden, J. M. Aldrich, N. B. Borden, A. B. Chace, A. S. Covel, John Campbell, Cornelius Hargraves, and W. H. Gifford directors. A site was secured for the erection of a mill in the eastern part of the city, on the Quequechan River, and in convenient proximity to the New Bedford Railroad, which was then in contemplation.

On the 20th of October foundations were commenced for the engine and boiler houses and continued seven weeks, until suspended by the approach of unfavorable weather. During the ensuing winter the plans for factory and machine equipment were carefully perfected and the machinery contracted for. On the 2d of April, 1874, work was resumed, William R. Huston, of Providence, taking the contract for building the mill structures.

The mill was not entirely wound up and all the machinery in operation before April 7th, 1875, though weaving on a partial scale commenced on the 9th of January. The longer period, however, was but one year exactly from the day upon which the contractor commenced his building operations. The mill has a capacity of 28,400 spindles, with 768 looms, producing 9,000,000 yards of print cloth annually, and working up 3500 bales of cotton. The mill structure is of granite, presenting a fine appearance, and possessed of the amplest and most improved safeguards against fire. The capital of $350,000 is owned by sixty-nine stockholders.

The Fall River Bleachery.

Up to that extraordinary year in the progress of Fall River (1872) the cloth production of the city had lacked one important element of a business perfect in all its stages—the immediate neighborhood of a bleachery. During the remarkable industrial development of that twelvemonth, however, attention was naturally drawn to an enterprise so obviously essential to local business. Among those who took particular interest in the establishment of bleaching works was happily one exceptionally suited to fashion and conduct a project of the kind—Mr. Spencer Borden. Mr. Borden, the eldest son of Jefferson Borden, one of the two conspicuous original promoters of local progress surviving, had enjoyed advantages for acquainting himself with the technical and scientific branches of manufacture of an exceptional character, having, after two years' tuition in the dye and color department of the American Print Works, spent a like period in Europe, inspecting the advanced systems of Manchester and Mulhouse, and studying applied chemistry and other arts used in cloth production, both at Paris and London.

Early in 1872, Mr. Borden prepared a carefully digested and elaborated scheme for a bleach works, and first submitted it to the owners of the great Wamsutta Mills in New Bedford. It was not only cordially received by them, but when, by their then agent, Mr. Thomas Bennett, Jr., laid before other local capitalists, very favorably entertained by them likewise. Large manufacturers in Rhode Island, and every mill in Fall River that bleached or was likely to bleach its cottons, also welcomed Mr. Borden's suggestion, and every thing seemed to indicate the time had come when this important adjunct of large cotton-manufacturing interests should be called into existence.

Committees to secure a site were appointed, and visited every stream of importance in Fall River, Tiverton, Somerset, and as far off as the Bridgewater ponds, gauging and analyzing the water, and examining the water-shed and freighting facilities.

It was finally decided that the lower privilege of the so-called Sucker Brook, about two miles from the City Hall on Stafford road, near the Rhode Island line, was the most available situation.

The following reasons led to this decision: Upon gauging the stream in May, it was found there were 1250 cubic feet per minute flowing in this brook to the Watuppa Pond. At the time when the people of Fall River desired to introduce water into the city, Stafford Pond, the source of this brook, was found to be the purest water examined, or whose examination was recorded in any of the water reports of the country. This beautiful sheet of water, lying 225 feet above Mount Hope Bay, has no stream flowing into it, is fed entirely by boiling springs at its bottom, and is so clear that fish swimming far beneath the surface can be plainly seen from above. Its only outlet is the Sucker Brook, which flows a mile and a half, falling 75 feet in the distance, to the site decided upon for the new industry. Again, coming from another valley to the east of Stafford road, a very pure stream flowed into the same hollow land as the Sucker Brook. This, upon being traced to its source, was found to issue from a collection of about twenty springs situate on the so-called Newhall and Dickinson Farms.

Having decided upon this location for the bleachery, the lower twenty-five acres of the Israel Buffington or Howard Farm, including the site of the old batting-mill, run formerly by Mr. Buffington, on this brook, were bought by some of the more prominent promoters of the enterprise. To this were afterwards added the three acres on Newhall Farm, where the springs were situated, a strip ten feet wide connecting that with the first purchase, and, still later, about twenty-five acres of the farm of Isaac Cook: thus securing the whole valley lying along the Sucker Brook, and the brook itself, from the lower side of the Job Estes privilege nearly to Watuppa South Lake, with right to deepen the brook even to the lake.

The books of the company were then opened and the stock so quickly subscribed, that before a stone had been laid it was quoted at 110 in the market. Prominent among the subscribers were Messrs. Jefferson, Philip D. and Richard B. Borden, Stephen Davol, Frank Stevens, C. E. Lindsey, C. P. Stickney, George B. Durfee, Walter Paine (3d), of Fall River; Messrs. Thomas Bennett, Jr., William J. Rotch, Edward D. Mandell, Edward C. Jones, William W. Crapo, Charles L. Wood, Andrew G. Pierce, Joseph Arthur Beauvais, Edward L. Baker, Jonathan Bourne, Jr., Charles L. Hawes, David B. Kempton, of New Bedford; Messrs. T. P. Sheperd & Co., John O. Waterman, George Bridge, and Arnold Peters, of Rhode Island; and Mr. Dempsey, of Lewiston, besides others.

A meeting of the stockholders being held, Jefferson Borden was chosen president, Spencer Borden, agent and treasurer, and Messrs. Thomas Bennett, Jr., Richard B. Borden, Bradford D. Davol, Crawford E. Lindsey, Philip D. Borden, George B. Durfee, and Charles P. Stickney, with the president and treasurer, directors of the corporation. Plans for the proposed bleachery were drawn by the agent and accepted by the directors, Mr. Walter J. Paine performing the architect's functions, the mason work being done by Slade W. Earle, and the carpentry and joinery by Obadiah Pierce.

It was decided to build of stone, and of this material enough fine granite was found on the premises to answer the requirements of construction.

A level having been determined for the ponds, which were to be raised, the site of the building was excavated thirteen feet below this point, to allow of this grand fall of water into the washing machines, and to fill the kiers and boilers without pumping.

Two entirely separate ponds, of five acres each, varying from eight to eleven feet in depth, were raised—one for the water of Stafford Lake, the other for that from the springs. The buildings were so placed that the front toward the west made the back wall of the Stafford-water dam, that toward the south the back of the spring-water dam, and these walls were built seven feet thick, and laid in cement to the top of the dam, which is thirty feet wide.

Workmen then went to the Newhall Farm, cleared and stoned the springs, and run-ways from them into a stone reservoir one hundred feet square, where they were all collected. Earthenware pipes twelve inches in diameter were laid thence to conduct this water one quarter of a mile to the spring-water pond already mentioned. Meanwhile other gangs of men, with hoes and shovels, cleaned all the mud and stumps out of this spring pond, wheeling every thing that could contaminate the water out upon firm land—a labor which cost above $4000. As a final precaution against defilement of the pure water needed in bleaching, brick filters were built in each pond, as follows: An arch, of four feet radius and sixteen to twenty feet long, was first laid in good hard body brick. Six inches outside of this another arch was started, and as it rose, charcoal of the size of robins' eggs carefully put into the space between the two arches. The ends were then built up solid, and all water that enters the pipes of the Fall River Bleachery, besides its perfect natural purity, is filtered through two courses of brick and six inches of fine gravel or charcoal. A sixteen-inch pipe supplies the boilers, kiers, and first six washing machines from the Stafford-water pond. A ten-inch pipe of spring water supplies the two final washers, the eight rinse boxes—a feature peculiar to this works and the Lewiston Bleachery, the invention of Mr. Dempsey, of Lewiston—the mangles, sprinklers, and water for the paper-collar combining, of which more later.

Not to go further into minute details, the bleachery was built with twelve kiers, or a capacity of twelve to thirteen tons per diem, all the other machinery being in the proportion necessary to take care of this amount of cloth, and including all that was late and desirable in bleaching and finishing machinery. Besides the experience acquired by the agent in his survey of European works and his scientific studies, the company was most fortunate in the acquisition, before the works started, of Mr. Michael Partington as superintendent—a man whose years of practical intimacy with the business and ability to manage men have been of immense advantage to the undertaking.

The boilers are of Corliss' upright pattern, he being also builder of the engine. This is high-pressure, and with the exhaust steam the kiers are boiled. The dry-sheds at this works are the only ones where cloth is never handled either in hanging or taking down, the whole being done by machinery. They are also the only ones entirely independent of the weather a very important desideratum in a place where one of the first articles of faith with the management is that no satisfactory finish can be gotten upon any cloths but those dried by hanging in air.

The buildings are arranged so that the capacity of the works can be doubled—to twenty-four tons per diem—without additional construction, excepting that of dry-sheds. Already the desire of the managers to please the public is appreciated, and no finish is more popular in market than that of the Fall River Bleachery.

In ten months from the time the axe was applied to the forest, stately buildings rose, ponds were made, and cloth put through the bleaching process. In three of the hardest years the business of the country ever labored under, meeting a panic the first year of its existence, the bleachery has made friends enough to more than fill the machinery it started with, and already kiers, boilers, and folding machines have to be added.

Not only so, but in this Centennial year a new industry has been added to their already large business. Having concluded that a bleachery was the place where paper-collar stock could be most advantageously handled, it was decided to add machinery for this purpose. Usually, goods have been sent to a bleachery brown, gone through the bleaching process, and, when starched and finished, packed in rolls of—say 1000 yards each. In this condition they are shipped to the "combiners," where they are united with paper, and the combined stock calendered until highly finished. The great advantage of doing this at a bleachery is the saving in extra packing and transportation of the white cloth to the combiners. Moreover, when the whole business is done under one roof, certain processes, usually applied before the bleached goods are shipped away, may be omitted without detriment to the quality of stock when combined.

The paper-collar stock finished by this bleachery has met with so good a reception in market, that the company is adding new and more complete machinery to that already in position, the entire paper-collar floor, when complete, being intended to produce 15,000 to 20,000 yards of yard-wide stock per diem. The new machinery is also intended to combine cloth as wide as $\frac{4}{5}$ to $\frac{5}{8}$, which will be of immense advantage to the manufacturer of paper collars and cuffs, allowing him to get a greater number of the strips from which these articles are cut, with only the edge waste incident to all yard-wide muslin.

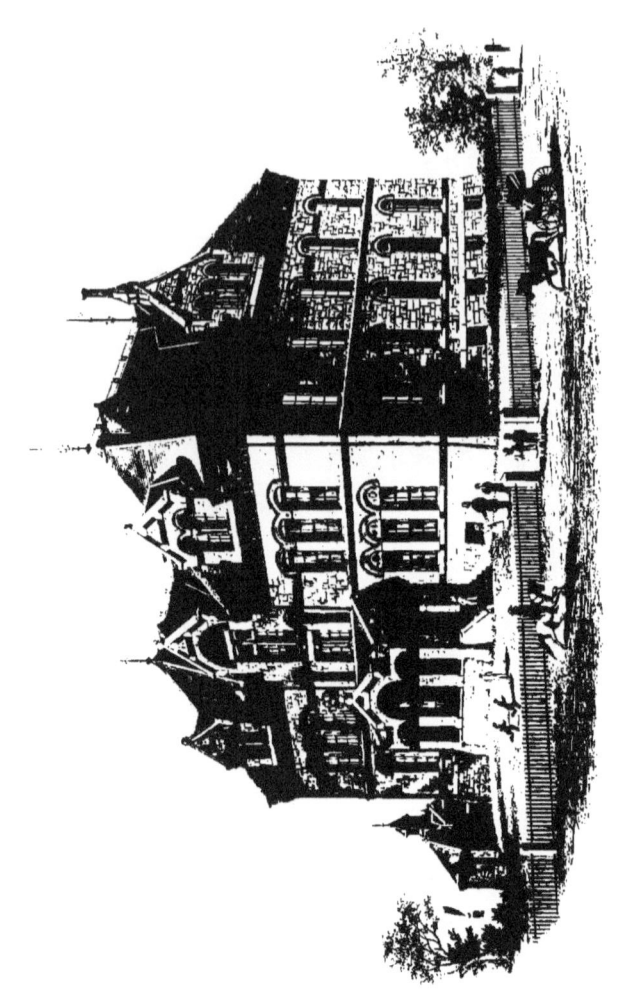

FALL RIVER:

ITS

EDUCATIONAL, RELIGIOUS, MUNICIPAL, AND FINANCIAL FEATURES.

SO far as the mental and moral elevation of their work people is concerned, the manufacturers of Fall River have spared neither cost nor effort, fully realizing the value to their individual interests, as well as to the social economy of their city, of an intelligent and hopeful community of operatives. In every direction this desire of the promoters of the local industry has shown itself. The apartments of the Christian Association are nightly filled with the mill-workers, both male and female, and the same assertion is true of other reading-rooms, opened by benevolent enterprise in less central districts. In some of the companies the list of stockholders includes quite a respectable proportion of operatives, and the policy of securing such an interest among the workers is earnestly pursued.

The system of local instruction, ordered by the admirable educational laws of the State, is thoroughly organized and generously sustained, general tuition being provided in 1 high school, 19 grammar schools, 26 intermediate, 57 primary, and 2 evening schools. The report for 1876 shows a force of 131 teachers and an attendance of 4,918 pupils, the total expenditure of the municipality for educational purposes being $134,964, of which $76,163 was teachers' wages.

The city is provided with a free public library and several circulating libraries, all of which are well supplied with the most recent publications, and are accessible to all. There are also numerous private and society libraries and local book-clubs, and it is a well-authenticated fact that Fall River has a much greater proportion of readers than is commonly found outside of the larger and wealthier cities.

In its secular and religious teachings, Fall River appears determined, notwithstanding all obstacles, to maintain a good moral reputation in the community. The great evil with which all manufacturing cities and towns have to contend, at the present day, especially, is the indiscriminate sale and use of stimulants, and with this evil the moral and sober-minded people of Fall River are constantly battling. It is worthy of note, however, as being somewhat at variance with the commonly received opinion concerning ignorance and crime, that there is much less punishable vice and criminality in Fall River than in most manufacturing places. There is comparatively little violence, pilfering, or prostitution. Although poor and ignorant, the new population of Fall River is industrious, and shows no serious proclivity to offend against good order. One reason for this prevalence of good order is doubtless the policy of the manufacturers to secure for operatives men and women with families, and not a mere shifting class, moving from one manufacturing town to another as their necessities require.

While the principal manufacturing business of Fall River consists in the production of print cloths, its industrial activity is also largely engaged in the printing of calicoes, in the manufacture of iron, in the forms of hoops, rods, nails, castings, etc., and of machinery. In the various machine shops of the city is manufactured machinery of every description, though mostly confined to cotton machinery. No better cotton machinery is found in the country than that made at Fall River.

The harbor formed at the mouth of Taunton River is safe, commodious, easy of access, and deep enough for ships of the largest class. The navigable interests of the city are by no means inconsiderable, and besides the vessels owned in the place and engaged in the coasting trade, many, and some of them of a large class, are annually chartered to bring from foreign and domestic ports lumber, coal, iron, and various other articles required for local consumption.

The district of Fall River includes the ports of Taunton, Dighton, Somerset, Freetown, and Swansea. The registration includes 92 sailing vessels, with a tonnage of 11,733; 23 steamers, with a tonnage of 15,025; and 6 barges, with a tonnage of 1,974; or a total measurement of 28,732 tons.

The city has within its borders, and in its immediate vicinity, an inexhaustible supply of fine granite, equal in quality to any in the country. This granite is extensively wrought, giving employment to and affording support for numerous persons. The fortifications at Newport, R. I., and the foundations of the State House at Albany, N. Y., were constructed mainly with granite obtained from these quarries, and it has been used largely for building purposes in the city itself.

Of fine public buildings there are comparatively few, but the elegant, commodious new Central Church, built of brick and sandstone in the Victorian early English Gothic style, stately in proportions, complete in detail and reputed to be one of the most perfect ecclesiastical structures in New England; the Episcopal Church, unique, yet chaste and beautiful with its rough ashlar work and brick trimmings; the substantial and massive Borden Block, containing the Academy of Music and numerous fine stores and offices; together with the Fall River Savings and Pocasset Bank buildings, the older Granite Block and City Hall, recently transformed at large expense into a noble edifice of modern style, give a foretaste of what may be expected in this direction when capital is a little more at leisure.

Fall River includes the localities popularly known as Copicut, Globe Village, Mechanicsville, Mount Hope Village, New Boston, and Steep Brook.

The municipality is divided into six wards, and is governed by a mayor, a board of aldermen of one member and a common council of three members from each ward. It is the seat of the Second District Court of Bristol County, and has a police force of 70 members, under the city marshal.

Fall River is 49 miles south of Boston, 183 miles north-east of New York, 17 miles south of Taunton, 18 miles south-east of Providence, 14 miles west of New Bedford, and 18 miles north of Newport. Daily lines of steamers connect Fall River, Providence, Newport, and New York, while three lines of railways give ample passenger and freight communications inland. Fourteen passenger trains pass to and fro between Fall River and Boston daily.

Public Library.

A free public library, where the people of both sexes and all classes may have easy and constant access to a large and well-stored treasury of the world's lore in literature, science, and art, is the crowning glory of that system of public education which has been, from her earliest history, the pride of Massachusetts. The system of public instruction in the common schools, excellent as it is, closes with the period of childhood. The great and important work of educating the people demands an agency which shall continue its operation after the school-days are over, and when the active duties of mature age have been reached. To meet this demand, the system of public libraries was inaugurated, the first institution of the kind known to the world being established in Massachusetts in 1853.

In 1860, an ordinance was passed by the City Government of Fall

River for the establishment of a free public library, and an appropriation made for its maintenance. A library room was provided in the City Hall, building, and properly fitted for the purpose. The Fall River Athenæum, established in 1835, transferred to the city its collection of some 2400 volumes, other contributions were made by associations and individuals, and the library was opened to the public May 1st, 1861. During the first year, the subscribers numbered 1,248, to whom were delivered 30,252 volumes, at an average of nearly 100 volumes per day.

The successful experience of each year since its organization has afforded conclusive evidence of the usefulness and stability of the institution. For the year ending August 1st, 1876, there were issued 130,717 volumes, at a daily average of 437 volumes, and also for the same period 67,960 periodicals, at a daily average of 227. The number of subscribers was 5,299, and the total number of books in the library was 14,448 volumes.

The original space assigned to the library soon became too limited for its use, and various expedients were resorted to for temporary relief, but no adequate provision was made until the completion of the alterations of the City Hall building (1872-3), when the whole lower floor was arranged and fitted with every convenience for the purposes of a library and reading-room. The latter is one of the finest in the State, being light, pleasant, cheerful, and spacious, and easy of access to the public. The government of the library is vested in a board of trustees consisting of the mayor, *ex officio*, and six other citizens.

CHURCHES.

There are in the city twenty-six churches, well arranged and commodious, supplied with well-educated and talented preachers, and attended by fair-sized and some of them by large congregations. Mission schools, shedding the kindly influence of Christianity here and there, have been established in various parts of the city, and, under the care of devoted and self-sacrificing teachers, have continued from year to year with growing numbers and increasing usefulness.

First Baptist Church.—Organized, 1781. Church on North Main Street, corner of Pine Street. Built, 1850. Pastors: Revs. Amos Burroughs, 1783-4; James Boomer, 1795-1803; Job Borden, 1795-1833; Arthur A. Ross, 1827-29; Bradley Minor, 1830-33; Seth Ewer, 1830-33; Asa Bronson, 1833-44; Velona R. Hotchkiss, 1845-49; A. P. Mason, 1850-53; Jacob R. Scott, 1853-4; P. B. Haughwout, 1855-70; Daniel C. Eddy, D.D., 1871-73; Albion K. P. Small, 1874-.

First Congregational Church.—Organized, 1816. Church on North Main Street, corner of Elm Street. Built, 1832. Pastors: Revs. Augustus B. Reed, 1823-25; Thomas M. Smith, 1826-31; Orin Fowler, 1831-50; Benjamin J. Relyea, 1850-56; J. Lewis Diman, 1856-60; Soloman P. Fay, 1861-63; William W. Adams, 1864-.

Society of Friends.—Organized, 1819. Church on North Main Street, between Pine and Cherry streets. Built, 1836. Overseer in Fall River, Nathan Chace. The first meetings of the Society of Friends in Fall River were held about the year 1812, the attendants coming mostly over the river from Swansea and Somerset.

First Methodist Episcopal Church.—Organized, 1826. Church on South Main Street, opposite Borden Street. Built, 1844. Pastors: Revs. N. B. Spaulding, E. T. Taylor, E. Blake, D. Webb, J. M. Bidwell, S. B. Hascall, M. Staples, J. Fillmore, H. Brownson, P. Crandall, previous to 1840. Revs. Isaac Bonney, 1840; Thomas Ely, 1842; George F. Pool, 1844; James D. Butler, 1845; David Patten, 1847; Daniel Wise, 1849; Frederick Upham, 1851; Elisha B. Bradford, 1853; John Howson, 1855; Thomas Ely, 1857; Andrew McKeown, 1859; Chas. H. Payne, 1861; Henry Baylies, 1863; Joseph H. James, 1865; John D. King, 1867; S. L. Gracey, 1870; Alfred A. Wright, 1871; Ensign McChesney, 1874.

First Christian Church.—Organized, 1829. Church on Franklin Street, corner of Purchase Street. Built, 1844. Pastors: Revs. Joshua V. Hines, Benjamin Taylor, H. Taylor, James Taylor, Simon Clough, M. Lane, A. G. Cummings, Jonathan Thompson, previous to 1840; Revs. P. R. Russell, 1841; A. M. Averill, 1843; Elijah Shaw, 1845; Charles Morgridge, 1847; Stephen Fellows, 1848; David E. Millard, 1852; B. S. Fanton, 1855; Thomas Holmes, 1863; Hiram J. Gordon, 1865; S. Wright Butler, 1866.

Unitarian Church.—Organized, 1832. Church on North Main Street, between Cherry and Locust streets. Built, 1860. Pastors: Revs. George W. Briggs, 1834-1837 A. C. L. Arnold, 1840; John F. W. Ware, 1843; Samuel Longfellow, 1848; Josiah K. Waite, 1852; W. B. Smith, 1860; Charles W. Buck, 1864; Joshua Young, 1869; Charles H. Tindell, 1875-1877.

Church of the Ascension (Protestant Episcopal).—Organized, 1836. Church on Rock Street, between Franklin and Pine streets. Built, 1875. Rectors: Revs. P. H. Geeenleaf, 1836-1837; George M. Randall, 1838-1845; Amos D. McCoy, 1845-1847; Emery M. Porter, 1849-1862; A. M. Wylie, 1863-1868; John Hewitt, 1870-1872; Henry E. Hovey, 1872-1873; William McGlathery, 1874-1876; William T. Fitch, 1877.

Central Congregational Church.—Organized, 1842. Church on Rock Street, between Bank and Franklin streets. Built, 1875. Pastors: Revs.

Samuel Washburn, 1844-1849; Eli Thurston, 1849-1869; Michael Burnham, 1870.

Second Baptist Church.—Organized, 1846. Church on South Main Street, between Annawan and Spring streets. Built, 1838. Pastors: Revs. Asa Bronson, 1846–1857; Charles A. Snow, 1858–1864; John Duncan, D.D., 1865–1870; Frank R. Morse, 1871–1873; Henry C. Graves, 1874.

United Presbyterian Church.—Organized, 1846. Church on Pearl Street, corner of Annawan Street. Built, 1851. Pastors: Revs. David A. Wallace, 1851–1853; William Maclaren, 1854–1867; Joshua R. Kyle, 1869–1875; James H. Turnbull, 1876.

St. Paul's Methodist Episcopal Church.—Organized, 1851. Church on Bank Street, between Main and Rock Streets. Built, 1852. Pastors: Revs. Ralph W. Allen, 1851; John Hobart, 1853; M. J. Talbot, 1855; Samuel C. Brown, 1857; J. B. Gould, 1859; J. A. M. Chapman, 1861; Samuel C. Brown, 1863; Alfred A. Wright, 1865; George Bowler, 1866; Francis J. Wagner, 1868; Emory J. Haynes, 1870; George E. Reed, 1872; George W. Woodruff, D.D., 1875.

Brayton Methodist Episcopal Church.—Organized, 1854. Church on Globe Street, Globe Village. Built, 1850. Pastors: Revs. A. H. Worthing, 1855; C. A. Merrill, 1857; A. U. Swinerton, 1859; Elihu Grant, 1861; William P. Hyde, 1869; George H. Lamson, 1871; Charles S. Morse, 1873; Edward A. Lyon, 1875.

Church of the New Jerusalem.—Organized, 1854. Church on Rock Street, between Cherry and Locust streets. Built, 1869. Leader, John Westall.

North Christian Church.—Organized, 1842. Church on North Main Road, Steepbrook. Pastors: Revs. William Shurtleff, 1861; Moses P. Favor, 1866; Charles T. Camp, 1872; O. P. Bessey, 1874; O. O. Wright, 1876.

North Methodist Episcopal Church.—Organized, 1859. Church on North Main Road, Steepbrook. Built, 1854. Pastors: Revs. Philip Crandon, 1861; George H. Manchester, 1863; John Gifford, 1865; John Q. Adams, 1867; J. G. Gammons, 1869; Philip Crandon, 1871; R. W. C. Farnsworth, 1873.

Quarry Street Methodist Episcopal Church.—Organized, 1870. Church on Quarry Street, between Bedford and Pleasant streets. Built, 1870. Pastors: Revs. Samuel M. Beal, 1873; Richard Povey, 1875.

Third Baptist Church.—Organized, 1871. Church on Brownell Street, Mechanicsville. Pastors: Revs. Ambler Edson, 1872-1873; Frederick A. Lockwood, 1874-1876.

Third Congregational Church.—Organized, 1874. Church on Hanover Street, corner of Maple Street. Built, 1874. Pastors: Revs. Leander S. Coan, 1874; Calvin Keyser, 1875.

Terry Street Methodist Episcopal Church.—Organized, 1875. Church on North Main Road corner of Terry Street. Built 1875. Pastor, Rev. William B. Heath, 1875.

Central Mission Sabbath School.—Organized, 1854. Chapel on Pleasant Street, corner of Sixth Street. Rev. Edwin A. Buck, missionary.

Columbia Street Mission (Baptist).—Organized, 1859. Chapel on Columbia Street, corner of Canal Street.

New Boston Chapel, New Boston Road.—Organized, 1860. Pastor, Rev. James L. Pierce.

King Philip Mission (Congregational).—Organized, 1874. Rev. Robert F. Gordon, missionary, 1875-1876.

St. Mary's Church (Roman Catholic).—Organized, 1836. Church on Spring Street, between Main and Second streets. Pastors: Revs. John Corry, Richard Hardy, Edward Murphy, 1840; Assistant Pastors: Revs. John O'Connell, Cornelius McSweeney, 1875.

Church of the Sacred Heart (Roman Catholic).—Organized, 1873. Church on Linden Street, between Bank and Pine streets. Pastor, Rev. Mathias McCabe, 1875; Assistant, Rev. James Masterson, 1875.

St. Ann's Church (French Catholic).—Organized, 1873. Church on Hunter Street, corner of William Street. Pastor, Rev. A. de Montaubricq, 1873.

St. Joseph's Church (Roman Catholic).—Organized, 1874. Church on North Main Road, opposite North Cemetery. Pastor, Rev. William H. Bric, 1874.

St. Patrick's Church (Roman Catholic).—Organized, 1874. Church on Slade Street, Globe Village. Pastor, Rev. J. Kelley, 1874.

Our Lady of Lourdes (French Catholic).—Organized, 1874. Church on Bassett Street, corner of Ashton Street, Flint Village. Pastor, Rev. P. J. B Bedard, 1874.

CEMETERIES.

Oak Grove Cemetery occupies an elevated spot in the north-easterly section of the city. The land for this purpose, purchased in 1855, originally comprised a lot of forty-seven acres, which was enlarged in 1866 by the purchase of twenty-eight acres adjoining. The ground is well laid out with gravelled walks and roadways, and its natural beauties enhanced by a tastefully ordered profusion of trees, shrubbery, and flowers. Numerous monuments of artistic design have already been erected. A shrewd philosopher in social science has said, " Let me see the burial-place of a people and I can tell the degree of taste, refinement, and kindly feeling that exists among them." In the application of such a test, Fall River has little to fear, Oak Grove, though limited in extent, being already one of the most beautiful cemeteries in New England.

The North Cemetery, upon North Main Road, was for many years the principal burial-place of the city. After the purchase and laying out of Oak Grove Cemetery, the remains of many persons there interred were transferred to the new grounds. Quite contiguous to the North Cemetery is another cemetery owned and occupied by the Roman Catholics, this denomination also owning other cemeteries in the outskirts north and south of the city.

Parks.

Fall River possesses so large and uninterrupted a prospective of surrounding land and water, that the absence of a specially ordered and arranged area of pleasure-ground in the very centre of industry and life might easily be pardoned. Ten or, at the most, twenty minutes' walk in any direction will take one into the country or bring him to the shores of the beautiful bay, while many parts of the resident region, with their broad avenues and well-shaded open spaces, fairly justify at least the suggestion of *rus in urbe*. With such immediate land and sea scape, a more sordid municipal organization would not have been seriously blamed if large and valuable territory, now allotted to the uses of relaxation and pleasure, had been put to business purposes and covered with mills, shops, or dwellings. The brains that planned and the capital and enterprise that have promoted the growth of Fall River have happily entertained a more generous and humanitarian view of their trust. Appreciating the gregarious nature of a community of working people, the first thought was to provide an easily accessible ground for their assemblage and enjoyment out of labor hours. The initial step in this direction was taken in 1868, the municipal government securing two areas of unimproved land, one in the north-east and the other in the southern part of the city. The former, comprising some fifteen acres, includes a fine natural plantation, previously known as Ruggles's Grove, and, in the possession of such sylvan attractiveness, required little if any additional outlay to render it a charming and salubrious resort. The growth of trees is luxuriant and the contour of the land comely, so that, with the exception of a very few private properties, this little territory is one of the most lovely spots in the city. The larger and more pretentious ground in the southern limits stretches from

CITY OF FALL RIVER
GENERAL PLAN FOR LAYING OUT THE PARK
AS PROPOSED BY
OLMSTED, VAUX & CO., LANDSCAPE ARCHITECTS

MAY 1871

Main Street to the Bay. It is sixty acres in area, having a length of 3,800 and a breadth of 800 feet. The eastern part, bounded by Main Street, is high table-ground, affording a view of the city to the north and the river with Mount Hope and Somerset shore to the west. Gradually sloping down to the water, it is superficially well adapted for grading and ornamentation. Though originally lacking the umbrageous beauties of the "Grove," the large number of trees which have been set out on its borders promise before many years to supply this serious deficiency, and, when the designs of the eminent landscape artists charged with its laying out have been executed, the new park will be a superb pleasure-ground for the community.

Drives.

The city possesses not a few beautiful drives, some of which cannot be excelled, especially those on the outskirts of the city proper. Highland Avenue stretches off along the margin of the hills to the north, affording numberless fine views up the river, and down the bay, and over the country beyond. "Eight Rod Way," so called because its width is just eight rods, is a pleasant avenue on the south, stretching along the margin of the South Watuppa, giving a fine view of the great granite factories along its borders, thence over the hill to Laurel Lake beyond, a beautiful sheet of water, around whose northern shore may be seen another cluster of mills, huge, substantial structures, alike noble and grand in appearance.

Broadway, leading from the south, also affords excellent views of the city, the bay, the opposite shores, and of Taunton River winding down from among the hills to the north; while for calm, quiet country views, close at hand or stretching off miles in the hazy distance, the equal of North Main Road, on a bright sunny day, cannot often be found. To these may be added the longer drives—Bell Rock Road, the Pond Road, Stone Bridge Road, and the Ferry Road (to Somerset), each having its own peculiar attractions of quiet country life, of hill and dale, of meadow, brook, and woodland, or the more stirring scenes of the seashore, with the white glistening sails of the shipping, the swiftly gliding steamers, and the rush of the railway cars.

Local Nomenclature.

Many of the corporations, banks, associations, and local institutions have assumed Indian names peculiar to the neighborhood. The following is a list of such names, with a brief explanation of the origin and meaning of each.

ANNAWAN—1600 (?)-1676. "An officer." A Wampanoag, one of King Philip's most famous captains.
CANONICUS—1557 (?)-1647. Chief of the Narragansetts ; a friend of Roger Williams.
CORBITANT—1590 (?)-1624. Sachem of Pocasset tribe ; chief residence at Gardner's Neck, Swansea.
KING PHILIP—1628 (?)-1676. English name of Metacomet, youngest son of Massasoit, and his successor, in 1662, as chief of the Wampanoags.
MASSASOIT—1581-1661. Sachem of the Wampanoags and chief of the Indian confederacy formed of tribes in Eastern Massachusetts and Rhode Island. A staunch friend of the English.
METACOMET—Indian name of King Philip, second son of Massasoit.
MONTAUP—" The Head." Indian name of Mount Hope.
NARRAGANSETT—" At the Point." Indian tribe on west side of Narragansett Bay.
NIANTIC—" At the River Point." Sub-tribe of the Narragansetts.
POCASSET—" At the opening of the Strait"—*i.e.*, Bristol Ferry into Mount Hope Bay. Indian name of territory now including Fall River and Tiverton.
QUEQUETEANT—" The place of falling water." Indian name of Fall River.
QUEQUECHAN—" It leaps or bounds." Indian name of the stream—Fall River—signifying falling water or quick-running water.
SAGAMORE—" A leader." Title of Indian chief.
TECUMSEH—1770-1813. Chief of the Shawnees ; distinguished for his eloquence, bravery, and manly virtues. Prominent on the Western frontier in the war of 1812.
WAMPANOAG—" East landers"—*i.e.*, east of Narragansett Bay. Indian tribe dwelling north and east of Narragansett Bay, west of Mount Hope Bay.
WAMSUTTA—1625 (?)-1662. English name, Alexander. Eldest son and successor of Massasoit in 1661.
WATUPPA—" Boats or the place of boats." Name of the ponds east of the city.
WEETAMOE—1620 (?)-1676. "Wise, shrewd, cunning." Daughter and successor of Corbitant as sachem of the Pocasset tribe ; residence at Fall River ; drowned while crossing Slade's Ferry.

Water Works and Fire Department.

The system of public water works, regarded by engineers as one of the most perfect, both in design and construction, in the Union, is justly a constant cause of self-congratulation to the residents of Fall River. The natural resources of the district in which the city has grown up, almost unique in the wealth and purity of their treasure, hardly need be suggested to the reader who has formed his own conception of the eastern plateau, extending parallel with the community of mills and residences, and bearing in its bosom the long chain of spring-fed lakes. Farther on will be given a comparative view of the enormous volume of water which this unequalled natural reservoir contains. The value of Watuppa to the city, regarded simply as an element in its industrial progress, is very great, but when its more recent service, as a sure and powerful antagonist of fire, and a never-failing purveyor of health, cleanliness, and comfort in every household, is considered, its worth is really beyond our powers of estimate.

The editor is indebted to William Rotch, Esq., the superintendent and engineer of the Water-works Board, who has been actively identified with the projection and construction of the system, for the following detailed account of this most important public enterprise :

Fall River is fortunate in the possession of a beautiful lake of fresh water within two miles of the centre of the city, whose purity is unsurpassed by any other public water supply equally extensive and so easily attainable, and yet whose advantages were so little appreciated a few years ago, that some persons gravely suggested that Fall River might find it necessary to go to the Middleborough ponds in order to obtain a sufficient supply of water.

Watuppa Lake, the source of supply for the water-works, and also for eight mills that run by water-power, on the lower part of Quequechan River—the outlet of the lake—is seven and two thirds miles in length, with an average width of about three quarters of a mile. It is fed principally by springs and small streams, which collect the water from the surrounding hills. The drainage area is sparsely settled, and covered principally by a young growth of oak, interspersed with pine and chestnut; and the soil is exceedingly favorable for the collection of a pure and abundant water supply, being composed principally of sand, gravel, and gravelly loam, interspersed with numerous boulders, and resting generally on a solid stratum of granite rock.

The whole area included by the water-shed contains about 20,000 acres, or 31.25 square miles, and is capable of furnishing a daily supply equal to half the amount of water used by the city of Paris, or about double the quantity used by the city of Boston; so that even if the rapid growth of Fall River during the last half-dozen years should continue during the next half century, the supply of water would still be comparatively inexhaustible, so far as the demands of the city are concerned.

In fact, the lake is capable of furnishing a daily supply of about 35,000,000 gallons, and of this the water-works took less than 1,000,000 gallons per day during the year 1875, and about 1,500,000 gallons per day during the excessively dry season in the summer of 1876. The daily average for the whole of the year 1876 will undoubtedly be less than one and a quarter millions.

According to the analysis made by Prof. John H. Appleton, in 1870, the water of Watuppa Lake is remarkably pure, there being but 1.80 grains of solid matter per gallon; while the Cochituate and Croton waters, as analyzed by Prof. Silliman, in 1845, contained respectively 3.37 grains and 10.60 grains per gallon. Later analyses indicate that the water supplied to New York is, however, purer than when analyzed by Prof. Silliman. The water of the Schuylkill, analyzed by Prof. Silliman, contains 5.50 grains per gallon; the Pawtuxet, at Providence, contains 2.14 grains per gallon; and the average amount of solid matter in the water furnished to London by nine different companies is about 20 grains per gallon.

The nature of the soil around Watuppa Lake, and the fact that the neighboring country is very thinly settled, will make it impossible for many impurities to reach the lake, and will insure the purity of its waters for many years.

In the spring of 1871 the first Board of Water Commissioners was appointed by the City Council, and in the fall of the same year work was begun upon a road which it was necessary to construct for a distance of nearly a mile and a half to give access to the place selected for a pumping station.

During the year 1872 the foundations of the engine-house, boiler-house, and coal-house were built, and the superstructure was completed the following year, being constructed of granite quarried in the immediate neighborhood, on the lot bought by the city for the pumping station and reservoir.

The gate-house, where the water is taken from the lake, was built 225 feet from the shore, where the depth of water is ten feet; so that in years of extreme drought, when the lake is sometimes five feet below high-water mark, there is a depth of at least five feet of water at the gate-house and four feet in the pump-well.

The engine-house was made large enough for four engines—two for the high-service and two for the low-service—which it was thought the increasing wants of the city would ultimately require.

The first engine was built in 1873 by the Boston Machine Company, and was put in operation January 5th, 1874, the first water being supplied to the city on January 8th. This engine is a double horizontal condensing engine, similar to the engines at Boston Highlands, which were built by the same company, and consists of two pumps 16 inches in diameter, and two steam cylinders 28 inches in diameter, both cylinders and pumps having a stroke of 42 inches, and working from one crank-shaft with one fly-wheel, 15 feet in diameter, and weighing 15 tons. The engine possesses one important advantage—which on several occasions, while the community was dependent on its unassisted efforts, has proved very useful and essential—the fact that its two parts are symmetrical, and, although designed to work together, capable of being run separately, and one half stopped if it is necessary to make any repairs or to adjust or replace the valves.

This engine pumps directly into a 24-inch force-main, extending from the engine-house to the centre of the city at the corner of Main and Bedford streets, a distance of a mile and three quarters, and this force-main supplies the low-service—that is, all those portions of the city which can be satisfactorily supplied with an adequate pressure from a reservoir, which is intended to be constructed at some future time on the hill near the pumping station, where the elevation of the highest point is 256 feet above tide-water.

The remainder of the city, comprising about one quarter of the whole area, and situated principally on two hills on either side of the Quequechan River, forms the high-service, and is supplied by a distinct system of pipes fed by a 16-inch force-main, extending a distance of a mile and a quarter from the engine-house to Robeson and Twelfth streets, from which place lateral pipes are laid to the two hills above referred to.

The high-service is supplied directly by an engine built in 1875 by Henry R. Worthington, of New York ; but cross-pipes with suitable gates are arranged at the engine-house, so that either or both services can be supplied by either or both engines, which is an important provision in case of an accident to one of the engines, or in case of a large conflagration necessitating more than the capacity of a single engine. The guaranteed capacity of the Boston engine is 3,000,000 gallons in twenty-four hours, but at the time of the fire at the American Print Works, December 8th, 1874, it pumped for an hour or more at the rate of 4,000,000 gallons in twenty-four hours.

The guaranteed capacity of the Worthington engine is 5,000,000 gallons in twenty-four hours, but during the fire at the American Linen Mill, June 29th, 1876, it pumped for a time at the rate of 5,500,000 gallons in twenty-four hours. This engine, known as the "Worthington Duplex Pumping Engine," consists of two horizontal, direct-acting steam engines, of equal dimensions, placed side by side, and so connected that the motion of one will operate the steam valves and change the motion of the other. Each engine works a separate pump, and has two steam cylinders, one high and one low pressure, the two pistons being connected with the same rod, which is prolonged into the pump cylinder to form the pump rod. The low-pressure piston is connected with the main rod by means of a cross-head and two small rods with outside stuffing-boxes, thus avoiding the danger of leakage through an inside stuffing-box between the two cylinders.

The smooth and noiseless action of the engine, and the ease with which it performs its work, are very striking, and it is difficult to realize that the piston-rods, which seem to move so easily, are really working against a resistance of about fifteen tons.

The principal dimensions of the engine are as follows :

```
Diameter of high-pressure steam cylinders.........29 inches.
    "       " low      "        "       "  .........50½   "
    "       " pump plunger (air-pump side).........22    "
    "       "   "      "    (north side)............22¼  "
    "       " piston-rod for water cylinders........ 4   "
Maximum length of stroke........................50        "
Diameter of air-pumps....................,27 and 29⅞    "
Stroke     "    "       .........................23      "
```

The contract horse-power of the engine is 176, equivalent to raising 5,000,000 gallons 200 feet high in twenty-four hours, with a plunger speed not exceeding 110 feet per minute. Several trials have been made to test the capacity of the engine, and it has been found to exceed the contract guarantee in this respect.

Besides this guarantee of "capacity," the engine was guaranteed to show a "duty" of 65,000,000 - that is, to be capable of raising 65,000,000 pounds of water one foot high with 100 pounds of coal; and October 4th, 1876, a trial took place, with the following result:

> Duration of trial, 13 hours.
> Total number of strokes, 31,376.
> Average number per minute, 40.23.
> Average length of stroke, 49.7 inches.
> Capacity of pump per stroke, 82.3 gallons.
> Total amount of water pumped, 2,582,245 gallons, or 22,535,932 pounds.
> Total lift, including friction in force-main, 217.52 feet.
> Total weight of coal burned, 6600 pounds.
> Duty, 70,977,177, showing an excess of 9 per cent above the guarantee.

The amount of water pumped during each year since the water-works have been in operation is as follows:

Year.	Total No. of Gallons pumped.	Average per Day.	Each Inhabitant per Day.	Each Consumer per Day.
1874............	185,116,305	507,168	11.65	84.53
1875............	296,007,606	810,980	18.02	70.83
1876 (to October)	297,658,014	1,086,343	24.69	49.38

The extreme drought during the summer of 1876 increased the consumption for a short time to 1,800,000 gallons per day, but this was caused, to a great extent, by the large amount used by some of the mills that were unable to obtain the usual supply from the pond, which, during the month of October, fell to within a few inches of the lowest point recorded during the last forty years.

The number of pipes laid and gates set, previous to September 1st, 1876, will be found in the following table:

Size.	Pipes (lineal feet).	Gates.
24 inch	11,488	12
20 "	21,317	24
16 "	26,823	40
12 "	17,799	36
10 "	18,801	30
8 "	52,246	100
6 "	89,789	249
Total..............	238,263 (or, 45.13 miles).	491

The number of flush hydrants in use September 1st, 1876, was 291, and the number of post hydrants 170, making a total of 461.

The number of service-pipes at the same date was 1440, and the number of meters 484.

The amount of rock encountered in laying the main pipes has averaged 21 per cent of the total amount of trenching, or about nine and one quarter miles out of forty-five, and this item alone has increased the cost of the work at least $100,000.

One of the most conspicuous features of the water-works is the tower, containing two stand-pipes, three feet and six inches in diameter, one for the high-service and one for the low-service. The top of the low-service stand-pipe is 48 feet above the highest point of the 24-inch force-main, and it is provided with two waste outlets, one 3 feet below the top, and the other 13 feet below. The top of the high-service stand-pipe is 88 feet above the highest point of the 16-inch force-main, and it is likewise provided with two waste outlets, one 3 feet and the other 23 feet below the top. The lower outlet is provided with a gate, which, on ordinary occasions, is kept open, the height of this outlet being sufficient to give all the pressure required for the regular supply in the higher portions of the city, but in case of fire this gate can be closed, and the water will then rise to the upper outlet, giving 20 feet additional head for the fire streams.

The two outlets of the high-service stand-pipe are connected with a pipe leading into the top of the low-service stand-pipe, and while the daily consumption in the city is comparatively small, it is found to be more economical to run but one engine, and pump all the water into the high-service stand-pipe, the low-service being supplied through the waste-pipe of the high-service.

The tower is built entirely of granite, quarried upon the spot, with the exception of a part of the cornice, some of the "quoins" and some of the arch stones over the doors and windows, which are made of a handsome blue stone, found in the immediate vicinity. Most of the work is "rough ashlar," the buttresses, window-caps, etc., being left with "quarry face," and there is very little hammer-dressed stone in the building.

The base is 21 feet square to a height of 22 feet 6 inches, surmounted by an octagonal shaft 60 feet 6 inches high, with an outside batter of half an inch per foot. The inside diameter is 15 feet 6 inches at the bottom, and 12 feet 9 inches at the top. The pipes occupy the centre of the tower, and around them is a circular iron stairway leading to the top.

At a height of 72 feet above the base of the tower, and 324 feet above the sea-level, is a balcony, 3 feet wide, on the outside of the tower, furnishing a most extended view in every direction, comprising the cities of New Bedford, Taunton, and Providence, and most of the country within a radius of twenty miles. The whole height of the tower from the base to the vane is 121 feet.

The total cost of the water-works, up to October 1st, 1876, is $1,328,456.14.

The cost of maintenance and the revenue for the first two years after the introduction of water was as follows:

ITEMS.	1874.		1875.	
	Total.	Per 1000 gallons pumped.	Total.	Per 1000 gallons pumped.
	$	cts.	$	cts.
Interest on bonds, per annum	57,694 67	31.16	67,660 00	22.86
Management and repairs	15,328 19	8.29	18,917 24	6.39
Cost of pumping	7,933 52	4.28	10,504 52	3.54
Total cost of maintenance, per annum	80,956 38	43.73	97,081 76	32.79
Revenue, per annum	24,336 95	13.15	41,139 19	14.00
Excess of revenue over management, repairs, and pumping	1,075 24	0.58	12,017 43	4.07

From January 1st to October 1st, 1876, the revenue has been $43,142.51, and this will probably be increased to $50,000 by the end of the year. The cost of management, repairs, and pumping will be about $25,000, so there will be a balance of about $25,000, to go towards paying the interest on the bonds. This balance will go on increasing every year, and, provided a proper policy is pursued with regard to water rates and the use of meters, the water-works should, in a few years, be entirely self-supporting; for if the city can receive payment at the rate of three cents per hundred gallons, as allowed by the Ordinance, for all the water pumped, the revenue will, in a short time, exceed the total cost of maintenance. This can be done by preventing water from being wasted without being paid for, and to accomplish this, no way is so efficient as to make the use of meters as universal as possible.

It has been the endeavor of the Water Board to encourage the use of meters in all cases, for such a policy is beneficial both for the city and for the consumer, because not only is the cost of measured water in most cases less than by the ordinary rates, but a large amount of waste is prevented, and the cost of pumping diminished.

The Fall River Water Works have been constructed in the most substantial and durable manner, with a liberal allowance for the probable growth of the city. The main and distributing pipes are of ample size and strength, the fire hydrants are placed at frequent intervals, and the pumping machinery,

Engine House

boilers, and force-mains are duplicated, so that nothing but an extraordinary concurrence of circumstances could cut off the supply of water. Taking into consideration the thoroughness with which all parts of the work have been planned and executed, the high price of labor and materials during the years when most of the work was done, and the unusually large amount of rock encountered in laying the pipes, the cost of the work will not appear excessive; while the purity, abundance, and favorable location of the source of supply make it probable that Fall River will find its water-works satisfactory and adequate for all the wants of the city for many years to come.

The Fire Department of Fall River has necessarily been for many years a conspicuous feature of the municipal organization. Aside from the very large proportion of wooden domiciles, the value of the mill structures and machinery in the city—at a low calculation, $25,000,000—and the immense loss that would fall upon the community by their destruction, have not only inspired a more than ordinary spirit of precaution in this particular, but enlisted and retained in the ranks of the department the sterling and responsible residents. As a consequence of this last circumstance, the several companies are composed of the most worthy young men of the city, and the department has been generally superintended by some prominent citizen, whose pronounced executive ability and large material interest in the general safety against conflagration have especially commended him for the position.

The present chief of the department, for instance, is William C. Davol, Jr., the treasurer and agent of the Davol Mills. Two years since the position was ably filled by Holder B. Durfee, treasurer of the Massasoit, and for several terms by Thomas J. Borden, whose active interest in the department will not soon be forgotten.

With the completion of the water-works, extraordinary resources for the prompt extinguishment of fire were at once assured. The system of hydrants, judiciously disposed, in every part of the city, has rendered these resources available for any unusual exigency.

The fire department consists at present of seven very powerful steamers, each with a complement of sixteen men and three horses; one extinguisher engine, nine men and one horse; two hook-and-ladder trucks, eighteen men and two horses; and one hose company, nineteen men and one horse.

Notwithstanding the heterogeneous population of a considerable part of the city, and the want of proper conservation perhaps to be inferred, the fires in Fall River are few in number, and show a relatively small annual average of loss. In 1875 the department was called out by genuine alarms but 37 times, and the total loss for the year was $162,052, of which $157,987 was covered by insurance.

The efficiency of the Fire Department has been greatly enhanced within the past few years by the erection of engine-houses in different sections of the city, so distributed as to make every point easily accessible by at least two steamers with their trained corps of firemen. The latest of these buildings, and most complete in all its appurtenances, is the engine-house upon Eight Rod Way. It is constructed of brick, with granite trimmings from the local quarries, and has within spacious rooms for a hook-and-ladder truck and a steam fire-engine. The large basement, extending under the whole building, is used for storage, heating apparatus, coal, etc., and contains a tank sixty feet long, for washing hose. The second story contains the reception-rooms, bath-rooms, sleeping-bunks, etc. The tower, one hundred feet high, is used for drying hose, and for suspending the alarm-bell. A stable in the rear connects directly with the rooms containing the fire apparatus, the first stroke of the alarm opening the stall doors (fastened by springs) and allowing the horses to take their respective positions with the least possible delay. The building, as completed, cost about $20,000, and, like the other engine-houses in the city, possesses all the latest conveniences and improvements for the expeditious use of the apparatus in case of fire.

BANKS AND SAVINGS INSTITUTIONS.

THE FALL RIVER NATIONAL BANK.

Charter—Original, 1825 ; *National,* 1864.

The first meeting of the citizens of Fall River to take into consideration the expediency of establishing a bank in the village was held at the office of James Ford, Esq., January 18th, 1825. The record reads as follows:

"At a meeting of the citizens of the village of Fall River, at the office of James Ford, Esq., January 18th, 1825, pursuant to previous notice, to take into consideration the expediency of establishing a bank in said village, David Anthony being called to the chair and James Ford appointed secretary, it was

"*Voted and Resolved,* That a petition be presented to the Legislature, at their present session, for a charter for a bank ;

"That a committee of five be appointed to receive subscriptions for the stock, and to cause the petition to be presented ;

"That Oliver Chace, David Anthony, Bradford Durfee, Richard Borden, and James Ford be this committee ;

"That five cents on a share be paid by the subscribers to defray the expenses that may accrue in obtaining an act of incorporation;

"That Oliver Chace be treasurer to receive the above money.

"A true copy.   Attest : M. C. DURFEE."

The act of incorporation contains the names of Oliver Chace, David Anthony, Bradford Durfee, Richard Borden, Nathaniel B. Borden, John C. Borden, Lucius Smith, Samuel Smith, Clark Shove, Harvey Chace, Edward Bennett, Arnold Buffum, James Ford, James G. Bowen, William W. Swain, Benjamin Rodman, William Valentine, and Holder Borden.

At the first meeting of the stockholders, April 7th, 1825, Oliver Chace David Anthony, Bradford Durfee, Sheffel Weaver, Edward Bennett, Gideon Howland, Benjamin Rodman, John C. Borden, and Richard Borden were elected directors, and at a subsequent meeting of the directors, May 3d, 1825, David Anthony was chosen president and Matthew C. Durfee cashier.

One of the present officers of the bank, whose father was an original stockholder, recollects, as a boy, riding on horseback from Freetown to bring the specie, in bags, to pay for his father's stock. Having hitched his horse to a pair of bars where the Stone Church now stands, he then, with his heavy load, trudged down into the village, which seemed quite a distance away. It was the only bank of discount and deposit in the village for twenty years.

David Anthony, after a service of forty years, resigned the office of president, on account of ill-health, in 1865, and was succeeded by Colonel Richard Borden, who, having deceased in 1874, was succeeded by Guilford H. Hathaway.

Matthew C. Durfee continued as cashier until 1836, when he resigned and was succeeded by Henry H. Fish, who served twenty-seven years, resigning in 1863. George R. Fiske was elected his successor and served until 1873, when he resigned and was succeeded by Ferdinand H. Gifford.

The first banking house of the Fall River Bank was a brick building, erected in 1826, on the corner of Main and Bank streets. It was destroyed by the great fire in 1843, but rebuilt of the same material the same year.

The Fall River Bank started with a capital of $100,000, which was increased to $200,000 in 1827, and to $400,000 in 1836. In 1844 it was reduced to $350,000, but increased again to $400,000 in 1864, when it was incorporated as The Fall River National Bank, No. 590. The management of its business has been conservative and far-sighted, resulting in continued prosperity. It is also a fact worthy of note that, taking into account the many years of its existence, the changeable condition of trade, the monetary crises, etc., which it has experienced, this institution has never been obliged to pass a dividend.

The Fall River Savings Bank.

Incorporated in 1828.

The first savings bank in the United States was established at Philadelphia, in the year 1816. The second was organized in Boston in the same year, and during the next ten or twelve years several were established in different parts of the commonwealth. The intensely practical and sagacious men who had to do with the early business interests of Fall River quickly discerned the advantages of such institutions to a community largely made up of day-laborers and people of small means, and accordingly made application for a charter for a savings bank. A charter was granted March 11th, 1828, by which Oliver Chace, James Ford, Harvey Chace, Bradford Durfee, John C. Borden, Clark Shove, and Hezekiah Battelle were constituted a corporation by the name of "The Fall River Institution for Savings."

The declared object of the institution was "to provide a mode of enabling industrious manufacturers, mechanics, laborers, seamen, widows, minors, and others in moderate circumstances, of both sexes, to invest such part of their earnings or property as they could conveniently spare in a manner which would afford them profit and security." The organization of the new institution was speedily completed by the election of Micah H. Ruggles as president, Harvey Chace secretary, and a board of eighteen trustees, viz.: David Anthony, Samuel Chace, Nathaniel B. Borden, John C. Borden, Harvey Chace, Joseph Gooding, James Ford, Bradford Durfee, Richard Borden, John S. Cotton, Clark Shove, Philip R. Bennett, Joseph C. Luther, Jesse Eddy, Enoch French, Hezekiah Battelle, Matthew C. Durfee, and Wm. H. Hawkins. James Ford was elected treasurer, and Enoch French, David Anthony, Matthew C. Durfee, Jesse Eddy, and Harvey Chace a board of investment.

On May 28th, 1828, the bank was opened for business, and $65 was deposited on that day by four depositors. During the first year, there was $3224 received from 58 depositors, but of this amount $518 was withdrawn. The first dividend was made in October, 1828, amounting to the sum of $13.04. From 1828 to 1837, $181,276 was received and $85,764 was withdrawn, leaving less than $100,000 on deposit. The dividends for the same period were at the rate of from 5 to $5\frac{1}{2}$ per cent per annum. From 1836 to 1842, the semi-annual dividends ranged from 3 to $3\frac{1}{2}$ per cent, and as they increased so also did the deposits, which in 1842 amounted to $350,000. The next ten years the increase was much more rapid, so that, in less than twenty-five years succeeding the organization, the deposits exceeded a million of dollars, a very large amount for those days.

Fall River Savings Bank

Since the opening of the institution, with the exception of the years ending with March, 1849, '58, and '62, there has been an annual increase. For four or five years succeeding the latter date, the increase was over $100,000 annually. The dividends from April, 1837, to October, 1866, amounted to $1,819,162.31; and of this sum, $1,255,483.63 was accredited to depositors and the balance paid out as stock dividends. During these thirty years, $8,006,834.63 was credited to deposits and $6,322,881.69 paid out on deposit or dividends account. While these amounts would not, perhaps, attract special attention at a day when moneyed transactions are reckoned in millions and even billions, in the period mentioned they were regarded with both surprise and curiosity. Since 1867, the business of the institution has advanced even more rapidly, for several years gaining from half to three quarters of a million annually, and in one year (1870) showing a total increase for *six months* of $500,000, a sum almost inconceivably large, taking into consideration the size of the city and the character of its population. There is little cause for wonder that, with such an exhibit, the name and credit of the bank should spread abroad, and its reputation for careful management and sound investment bring to it deposits from every one of the New England and some of the Middle States.

A careful comparison of the several savings banks in Massachusetts shows that this bank has paid more interest on the same amount of deposits for a term of years than any other in the State. It can also be said, without fear of contradiction, that no savings bank in the State has been conducted with so little expense. For the first fourteen years of its existence, the whole amount paid to the several treasurers for services, office-rent, fuel, lights, and stationery, which in those days were required of the treasurers, was but $3762.52, or an average of but little more than $250 per year, while the average amount of deposits for the same time was more than $100,000,

The practice of rigid economy in the expenses of the bank, instituted at the very beginning of the enterprise, is illustrated by the following minute of record, under date of April 2d, 1829: "*Voted*, That the treasurer be allowed *fifteen dollars* for his services for office-rent, etc., for the year past." And again, under date of April 7th, 1834, we find: "*Voted*, That sixty-two and a half dollars be appropriated to the treasurer for his services, office-rent, and stationery for the past year."

As the bank commenced so has it continued, and it is doubtful if another institution of the kind can be found whose percentage of expense account will average so small as compared with the amount of business transacted.

Another feature—perhaps not peculiar to this bank alone, but accounting in some measure for its remarkable and long-continued prosperity—is the fact that every loan is required to be guaranteed by two sureties, even though the principal may have given a mortgage or collateral to secure the final payment of the loan. As a result of this doubly secure method of conducting its business, the bank, with one or two minor exceptions where the amount paid *plus* the interest has more than equalled the principal, has never lost a dollar of its loans in the long half-century of its existence, during which its operations have amounted to thousands of millions of dollars.

The first act of incorporation of the Fall River Institution for Savings provided for its continuance for a term of twenty years. In April, 1847, by special vote of the Legislature, the act was continued without limitation. In April, 1855, the name of the bank was changed to "The Fall River Savings Bank."

The bank has had but three presidents, viz.: Micah H. Ruggles, from 1828 to 1857; Nathaniel B. Borden, from 1857 to 1865; and Job B. French, from 1865 to the present time. Its original place of business was in the office of James Ford, the first treasurer. In 1830 it was removed to the store of Hawkins & Fish, south-east corner of Main and Bedford streets, Mr. Wm. H. Hawkins having succeeded Mr. Ford in the office of treasurer. In July, 1833, Mr. Hawkins was succeeded by Mr. Henry H. Fish, who was in turn succeeded in 1836 by Mr. Joseph F. Lindsey. Mr. Lindsey devoted the best years of his life to the interests of the bank; and upon his retirement in 1877, after forty years' service in an office which he had conducted with marked honesty, ability, and courtesy, was complimented with the appointment of vice-president of the corporation. His successor as treasurer was Mr. Charles A. Bassett.

The bank continued in Mr. Fish's store till some time in 1841, when an increase of business demanded more room, and a small building in the rear of the old Post Office on Pocasset Street was procured. It remained here about a year and was then removed to the basement of a house on North Main Street, owned and occupied by Dr. Nathan Durfee. This house was destroyed in the great fire of July, '43, and a private dwelling was occupied by the bank until the next January, when the Mount Hope House Block was completed on the site of the former office. The bank was then moved into the office in the south-west corner of this block, where it remained until the completion of its own banking house on North Main Street, opposite the head of Elm Street, in March, 1869.

Thus for forty years the bank carried on its business with no special conveniences for office work,—sometimes quite otherwise. On several occasions committees were appointed to take the matter into consideration, but without definite result. In 1867, however, the urgent necessities of the bank compelled the appointment of a committee, the result of whose efforts is apparent in the present symmetrical and elegant building.

The building is rectangular in form, its dimensions being 43 feet by 66 feet in the main walls, exclusive of belts or projections. Its height is 40 feet at the front and 39 feet at the rear. The walls are of faced brick, 20 inches thick, while the steps, buttresses, and underpinning are of fine hammered granite. The banking room, upon the lower floor, is airy, spacious, and provided with everything that can render it convenient. The entire inside finish, including shutters and sheathing, is of butternut, with black-walnut bases and mouldings. The banking room is entered through a vestibule having two sets of fly-doors with black-walnut frames, and sashes glazed with the finest quality of plate glass. The counter, semi-circular in form, sweeps well out into the centre of the banking room, and has convenient openings, plainly marked, for the different branches of business. During the building of the banking house, the vault was constructed in the best and most approved manner which knowledge or experience could suggest, being as strong as granite, iron, and brick combined could possibly make it. The different locks on the vaults and chests are burglar proof and of high cost. As new and later improvements have been devised they have been added, and no expense has been spared to insure the greatest safety and security to the books, funds, and other representatives of value deposited. Adjoining and connected with the banking room are two ante-rooms for the use of the trustees and treasurer, carpeted and neatly furnished. Gas is carried throughout the building, and both the upper and lower halls are perfectly adapted for the purposes for which they are designed. The upper hall is occupied by the Mount Hope and King Philip lodges of Free and Accepted Masons, being arranged and finished in an elegant and convenient manner. Between the upper and lower stories there is no connection. The building taken as a whole is complete in all its parts, and is a credit to the architect and builders, the institution itself, and the city which contains it.

The bank has fully realized the hopes of its founders, proving a blessing to thousands of the moderately conditioned citizens, men, women, and children of Fall River. The policy of the bank has always been liberal, as becomes the conservator of the savings of the people; the surplus of good times has been treasured up for the wants of hard times; the earnings of health placed in security against the necessities of sicknesss; the accumulations from self-denial added to by loan, for the purchase of a house and home for the family. The bank has also been a conservator of the business interests of the place, its board of investment consistently aiming to strengthen the hands of industry at home, to make loans among the constituents of the bank, rather than to invest their funds in public stocks and national enterprises. Especially has the wisdom of this policy been exemplified in sudden emergencies resulting in monetary crises, when distrust and alarm have spread throughout business circles. The consciousness of the substantial basis of their loans and the visible evidences of property have inspired a mutual trust and confidence which has proved a source of strength to the bank and indirectly given steadiness to the whole community. Some of the strongest enterprises of to-day have been tided over difficulties and helped to their present secure standing at home and abroad by this conservative management of the trustees.

Hence, as a result, in the half-century of existence of this institution, it has steadily risen in local esteem as a model of careful management and judicious investment; it has been a training-school for the officers of some of the banks of this and other cities, and by its age and character has commanded the respect and interest of similar institutions throughout the country.

The National Union Bank.

Charter—*Original*, 1823; *National*, 1865.

Reckoning by years, "The National Union Bank" is the oldest bank in the city, having been chartered as "The Bristol Union Bank," of Bristol, R. I., in 1823. Its authorized capital was $50,000, with the privilege of increasing the same to $200,000. The shares were placed at $100 each. It began business in January, 1824, with a paid-in capital of $10,000, which was increased within the next two years to $40,000. The bank has undergone many changes in its various departments during the half century of its existence, as indicated by the following table:

	Name.	Capital.	President.	Cashier.	Location.
1823	Bristol Union Bank	$10,000			Bristol, R. I.
1824		30,000	} Barnabas Bates } Parker Borden {	Nath'l Wardwell	
1825		40,000		Josiah Gooding	
1826				Wm. Coggeshall	
1830					Tiverton, R. I.
1831	Fall River Union Bank				
1834		100,000			
1838			David Durfee		
1846		200,000	Nath'l B. Borden		
1856					Fall River, R. I.
1860				Daniel A. Chapin	
1862					Fall River, Mass.
1865	National Union Bank		Jesse Eddy		
1866		300,000			
1874			Cook Borden		

In 1830, Fall River, Mass., affording a more promising field for banking operations, the bank was removed from Bristol and located in Tiverton, just over the line from Fall River, and its name changed to the Fall River Union Bank. Its office was on South Main Street, opposite the head of Columbia Street. In 1837 the bank erected for its accommodation the brick building corner of South Main and Rodman streets, and removed its office to the lower floor, where it continued its business until 1862. In that year, by the change of boundary line, Fall River, Rhode Island, became Fall River, Massachusetts, and the bank was removed to the office in the south-west corner of the market building, now City Hall.

In June, 1865, the bank became a national banking association, under the name of "The National Union Bank," No. 1288. In 1872 the office of the bank was removed to No. 3 Main Street, opposite the Granite Block, where it has a well-lighted and easily-accessible banking room for the transaction of its business.

THE MASSASOIT NATIONAL BANK.

Charter—Original, 1846; National, 1864.

The Massasoit Bank was organized June 2d, 1846, with an authorized capital of $100,000. Jason H. Archer was elected president, Leander Borden cashier, and Jason H. Archer, Oliver S. Hawes, Azariah Shove, Nathan Durfee, Henry Willard, Iram Smith, and Benjamin Wardwell a board of directors. The bank commenced business in December, 1846, with a paid-up capital of $50,000, which was increased in the following March to $100,000. In January, 1854, the capital stock was again increased to $200,000.

In October, 1852, Dr. J. H. Archer, having removed from the town, resigned his office as president, and Israel Buffinton was chosen his successor. In October, 1864, Charles P. Stickney was elected president, *vice* Israel Buffinton, resigned. No change of cashier has been made since the original appointment of Leander Borden.

In December, 1864, the bank was converted into a national banking association, under the name of "The Massasoit National Bank," No. 612. It was also made a depository and financial agent of the United States. Regular semi-annual dividends have been made uninterruptedly since its organization in 1846. Sixty dividends have been paid, as follows: 15 of 3%, 8 of 3½%, 13 of 4%, 1 of 4½%, 13 of 5%, and 10 of 6%. In addition to dividends paid, municipal taxes assessed to shareholders during the last three years have also been paid to the amount of $14,446.

The bank when first established occupied rooms in the north end of the

Mount Hope Block, corner of Main and Franklin streets. It continued here for thirty years, or until 1876, when it was removed to its more commodious and convenient banking house at the Four Corners, the north-east corner of Main and Bedford streets.

CITIZENS' SAVINGS BANK.

Incorporated in 1851.

In 1851 the October session of the General Assembly of the State of Rhode Island passed an act incorporating " The Savings Bank" to be located in Tiverton. Oliver Chace, Jr., Cook Borden, Thomas Borden, Clark S. Manchester, and their associates and successors were created a body politic under the name and style of "The Savings Bank," with perpetual succession. The amount of deposits to be received was limited to $400,000.

The bank was organized November 15th, 1851, by the election of Joseph Osborn president, Charles F. Searle secretary, Wm. H. Brackett treasurer, and a board of fifteen trustees. Cook Borden, Oliver Chace, Jr., Weaver Osborn, William C. Chapin, and Samuel Hathaway were chosen a board of investment. The bank was opened for business December 1st, 1851, at the office of the Fall River Union Bank, and on that day the first deposit was made.

In June, 1854, the bank was removed to the office in the south-west corner of the Fall River Union Bank building on South Main Street, corner of Rodman Street, and continued there until the change in the boundary line between Rhode Island and Massachusetts, March 15th, 1862, when it became a Massachusetts institution under the name of the Citizens' Savings Bank, and was removed with the Pocasset Bank to the north-west corner of the market building, now City Hall. In January, 1873, the bank was again removed to the office prepared for it, in connection with the Pocasset National Bank, in the latter's new building, erected for a banking house and other purposes, on the corner of Main and Bedford streets.

In December, 1862, Wm. H. Brackett resigned the office of treasurer on account of removal to another city, and Edward E. Hathaway was elected to fill the vacancy.

The first dividend was declared June 4th, 1852, viz.: three per cent for the preceding six months. There have been fifty semi-annual dividends declared, up to the first of December, 1876, and the average annual per cent paid has been 6.68 per cent.

The Metacomet National Bank.

Charter—Original, 1853; *National,* 1865.

The Metacomet Bank was incorporated by the Legislature of 1852–3 with a capital stock of $400,000. It was organized in the summer following, by the choice of Jefferson Borden as president, Azariah S. Tripp cashier, and a board of nine directors, viz.: Jefferson Borden, Nathan Durfee, William Lindsey, Philip D. Borden, Thomas J. Borden, Daniel Brown, William Carr, William Marvel, and Joseph Crandall. The bank was located in the brick building opposite the American Print Works, corner of Water and Pocasset streets, and commenced business in December, 1853.

A few months' operations were sufficient not only to vindicate the judgment of its founders, that another banking institution was needed in the town, but to demonstrate that still further bank accommodation was required to quicken local industries and develop business resources, which the more discerning felt had been only partially employed. By these clear results of their short experience, the managers of the bank were assured that it could profitably use a larger capital. Application was accordingly made to the Legislature, at its next session, for authority to increase the capital stock to $600,000, which was granted. The new capital was mostly subscribed by the old stockholders, and all paid in the same year, 1854. The capital was then as large as that of any bank in the commonwealth outside of Boston.

In 1865 the institution was converted into a national banking association, under the name of "The Metacomet National Bank of Fall River," No. 924. After having been located twenty-three years on the boundary of the "Border City," it removed in 1876 to the commodious apartments and eligible situation for banking purposes now occupied by it in the Borden Block, corner of South Main and Pleasant streets.

The operations of well-managed banks furnish very little material for local annals. They are not instituted to pioneer business enterprises or to stimulate new adventures, but are subsidiary in their scope and object. When kept within their "true sphere," they erect few visible monuments to indicate the part they have taken in building up and developing the resources of a manufacturing and commercial city. The history of the Metacomet Bank, covering the period of the greatest business development and growth of Fall River, is no exception to this recognized view of the province of a bank. For nearly a quarter of a century it has quietly and sucessfully prosecuted legitimate banking unvexed by dissensions within, undisturbed by misfortunes without.

Few changes have taken place in its management, and in this particular, at least, the bank has been most fortunate, perhaps,—a rare exception. Since only the experience and established character which mature age alone can give is thought eligible to official position in moneyed institutions, it is quite remarkable that the same president and cashier and a majority of its nine directors respectively hold, in the twenty-fifth year of its organization, the positions to which they were chosen when the bank first commenced business. The records also show that in fifteen consecutive annual elections of officers, the board of directors chosen consisted of the same nine individuals. Such a record is specially interesting and noteworthy in view of the fact that at the beginning of this period the average age of the nine was nearly fifty years, and is an unusual instance of exemption from the visitation of Him who waits on all and only passes by the most favored for a few short years. The first death occurring in the board of directors was that of the late Dr. Nathan Durfee, after twenty-three years of official service.

THE POCASSET NATIONAL BANK.

Charter—Original, 1854; *National*, 1865.

The Pocasset Bank was incorporated by the General Assembly of the State of Rhode Island in May, 1854, Moses Baker, Oliver Chace, and Joseph Osborn being named in the charter. The bank was organized June 3d, 1854, by the choice of Oliver Chace, Samuel Hathaway, Weaver Osborn, Gideon H. Durfee, and Moses Baker of Tiverton, and John C. Milne and Wm. H. Taylor of Fall River, Mass., as directors. Oliver Chace was elected president and Wm. H. Brackett cashier.

The bank was located in the Fall River Union Bank building, corner of South Main and Rodman streets, then in Tiverton, R. I. In 1856 the town of Tiverton was divided, and that part wherein the bank was located became Fall River, R. I. In 1862 the boundary line between Rhode Island and Massachusetts was changed, Fall River, R. I., being set off to Massachusetts, and the bank, by authority of the Legislature, became a Massachusetts institution and was removed to the office in the north-west corner of the market building, now City Hall, on Main Street.

February 1st, 1865, the bank was organized as a national bank under the title of "The Pocasset National Bank," No. 679. In 1872 the bank purchased the lot on the south-east corner of Main and Bedford streets, and erected on this elegible site (it being one of the Four Corners, so called) a fine building of dressed granite, three stories high, with a Mansard roof. In

January, 1873, the office of the bank was removed to the convenient and well-arranged banking rooms provided on the lower floor of this building.

January 7th, 1862, Oliver Chace resigned the presidency, and Samuel Hathaway was elected to fill the vacancy. December 9th, 1862, Wm. H. Brackett resigned as cashier, and Edward E. Hathaway was elected in his place. April 15th, 1873, Weaver Osborn was elected president to fill the vacancy occasioned by the death of Samuel Hathaway.

The bank has been a success from the first, as indicated by the fact that it has never passed a dividend and has a growing surplus account.

THE FALL RIVER FIVE-CENT SAVINGS BANK.

Incorporated in 1855.

This institution was the development of a desire to encourage the individual commencement of saving. Its promoters recognized the fact that a large part of the population attracted to the city by its industrial occupations, untaught in New England thrift but used to living from hand to mouth and spending at once the earnings of the week, whatever their amount, might be induced to save little by little, if the sanctuary for small offerings were established in their midst. Other banks, already many years in existence, would take care of the dollars; one that would receive and cherish the pennies was the desideratum. The excellent results of the dime and half-dime savings institutions of other and larger communities were noted with delighted approval, and the conclusion was soon reached that a bank for such humble deposits must be started in Fall River. During the winter of 1855, a positive move was made towards the realization of this essentially benevolent design. In an act of incorporation dated April 10th of that year, Messrs. S. Angier Chace, Hale Remington, Walter C. Durfee, James Buffinton, E. P. Buffinton, B. H. Davis, Asa P. French, and Alvan S. Ballard were named as incorporators. The institution was organized on the 25th of the succeeding October, its officers being S. Angier Chace, president, Hale Remington, secretary, Charles J. Holmes, Jr., treasurer, and S. Angier Chace, Asa Eames, E. P. Buffinton, Abner L. Westgate, and Robert K. Remington, a board of investment. A board of trustees of twenty-six members was likewise chosen. A very earnest interest in the success of the new enterprise was entertained by the promoters, and few public objects have elicited a larger or more practical sympathy. At the outset, one gentleman offered the use of a convenient banking room, rent free for a year, while three others supplied all the furniture of the institution, including a safe and account-books.

The bank was opened for the transaction of business January 1st, 1856, and its first dividend was paid in June of the same year, at the rate of six per cent per annum. The dividends of the bank have been as follows, viz.: 3 at the rate of 5 per cent per annum (i.e., during the war, 1862–'3), 12 at the rate of 6 per cent, 19 at the rate of 7 per cent, and 7 at the rate of 8 per cent. The operations of the bank have been eminently successful and satisfactory to its projectors and present managers.

The office of the bank has always been located in the south end of the Mount Hope Block: from 1856 to 1869 at No. 55 North Main Street, and from 1869 to the present time two doors south, at No. 53, it being the office on the corner of North Main and Bank streets.

THE SECOND NATIONAL BANK.

Charter—Original, 1856 ; *National,* 1864.

The Second National Bank was originally incorporated June 4th, 1856, as the Wamsutta Bank. The corporators were S. Angier Chace, Hale Remington, and William Mason, second, and the capital was fixed at $100,000. S. Angier Chace was elected president, Charles J. Holmes, Jr., cashier, and S. A. Chace, Hale Remington, Jas. B. Luther, Brownell W. Woodman, E. C. Kilburn, Thos. F. Eddy, and Thos. Almy a board of direction. The office of the bank was located in the Mount Hope Block, North Main Street, second door north from Bank Street.

In May, 1864, the corporation became a national banking association, under the name of the Second National Bank of Fall River, No. 439. The capital was increased to $150,000. The bank has proved a profitable investment for its stockholders, having paid dividends as follows, viz.: 12 of 3 per cent, 1 extra of 5 per cent at the time of the increase of the capital stock, 22 of 5 per cent, and 1 of 6 per cent. The present capital is $150,000, with a surplus account of $50,000. In 1869 the office of the bank was removed one door south, to the corner office of the Mount Hope Block, which had been conveniently arranged and fitted for a banking house with ante-rooms, vault, and other necessary accessories.

THE FIRST NATIONAL BANK.

Date of Charter, January, 1864.

The First National Bank of Fall River was organized January 23d, 1864. It was the first bank in this section of Massachusetts established under the National Bank Act. Its number is "No. 256," only that number of national banks, being in existence in the United States at the time of its organization. Its capital was fixed at $200,000. Hon. John S. Brayton was elected president and Mr. Charles A. Bassett cashier. In March, 1865, the capital stock was increased to $400,000, which is its present figure. From the date of organization until 1870, it was a United States depository and financial agent. The bank was located at No. 14 Granite Block, on the corner of Main and Central streets, the south-west of the Four Corners, so called. There has been no change in its location up to the present time. Mr. Chas. A. Bassett, cashier, having in 1877 been elected treasurer of the Fall River Savings Bank, was succeeded by Mr. Hezekiah A. Brayton.

THE UNION SAVINGS BANK.

Incorporated in 1869.

The Union Savings Bank was incorporated April 24th, 1869, with Gardner T. Dean, Edwin Shaw, and Lafayette Nichols as corporators. An organization was immediately effected by the choice of Augustus Chace president, James M. Morton, Jr., secretary, D. A. Chapin, treasurer, and a board of twenty-five trustees. The board of investment consisted of Cook Borden, William B. Durfee, Gardner T. Dean, Lafayette Nichols, and Alphonso S. Covel.

The bank opened for business in May, 1869, having its office in the south-west corner of the market building, now City Hall. In 1872, having purchased the estate on Main Street, midway between Bedford Street and Market Square, it removed to its own convenient and well-arranged banking rooms, where it has since continued, doing a safe and profitable business with an accumulating amount of deposits and an increasing number of depositors.

BANKS OF THE CITY OF FALL RIVER, MASS., FROM THE OFFICIAL REPORTS, JAN., 1876.

NAME.	ESTAB.	PRESIDENT.	CASHIER.	CAPITAL	SURPLUS AND INT.	DIS'CT DAY.
Fall River National Bank....	1825	G. H. Hathaway......	F. H. Gifford....	400,000	156,960	Mon.
National Union Bank........	1830	Cook Borden........	D. A. Chapin....	300,000	66,535	Fri.
Massasoit National Bank.....	1846	Chas. P. Stickney....	L. Borden......	200,000	162,141	Wed.
Metacomet National Bank....	1853	Jefferson Borden.....	A. S. Tripp.....	600,000	337,108	{ Mon. / Thu.
Pocasset National Bank......	1854	Weaver Osborn.......	E. E. Hathaway.	200,000	104,738	Tues.
Second National Bank,......	1857	S. Angier Chace......	C. J. Holmes...	150,000	65,323	Thurs.
First National Bank.........	1864	John S. Brayton......	C. A. Bassett,...	400,000	431.018	Daily.
				2,250,000	1,324,123	

SAVINGS BANKS OF FALL RIVER, MASS., FROM THE OFFICIAL REPORTS, JAN., 1876.

Name.	Incor	Treasurer.	Deposits.	Deposi- tors.	Disc't Day.	Dividends.	
Fall River Savings Bank.	1828	J. F. Lindsey.	6,099,863 59	11,585	Tues.	Apr.	Oct.
Citizens' Savings Bank.	1851	E. E. Hathaway.	1,940,356 72	2,885	Fri.	June.	Dec.
Five Cent Savings Bank.	1856	C. J. Holmes.	1,488,818 62	5,752	Mon.	June.	Dec.
Union Savings Bank.	1869	D. A. Chapin.	661,527 68	1,440	Fri.	Nov.	May.
			10,190,566 61	21,622			

United States Custom-House and Post-Office.

The increasing business of the port of Fall River, and the rapid multiplication of its manufactories, necessitated the procurement of larger and more convenient accommodations for the offices of the general government. The proper representations were accordingly made to Congress by the faithful member from the district, Hon. James Buffinton, and through his instrumentality an appropriation of $200,000 was secured in the year 1873, and a commission of leading citizens appointed to select a suitable building site. The lot finally chosen for the purpose was situated on Bedford Street, corner of Second Street, it being a central location and convenient to all parts of the city.

In 1875 a further appropriation of $40,000 was made by Congress, and in 1876 additional sums of $25,000 and $20,000, making a total of $285,000. The building was designed and the plans completed in 1875 by Mr. William A. Potter, supervising architect, to whose professional ability it is certainly very creditable. Labor upon the foundation was begun in September, 1875, under direction of Mr. Edward T. Avery, superintendent of construction, and it is expected that the building will be ready for occupancy early in 1879.

The government structure has a frontage on Bedford Street of 125 feet, and on Second Street of 84 feet. It is three stories elevation, with a steep, high roof, the total height from street curb to line of roof being 92 feet. At the two flanks, and facing on Bedford Street, are circular pavilions which project from the body of the building, and between these, on the ground-floor, are the entrances to the post-office, through five broad archways. The main features here are the large monoliths of polished red granite, each in one block, 5 feet by 3 feet 6 inches, finished by elaborately-carved capitals of gray granite. A noticeable amount of carved work of a high order is displayed upon the Bedford Street front, in red and some in gray granite.

On the Second Street frontage, the entrance to the custom-house is the prominent feature of the design. This entrance-way, with its arches, polished columns, massive buttresses, corbels, crockets, copings, etc., is a masterpiece

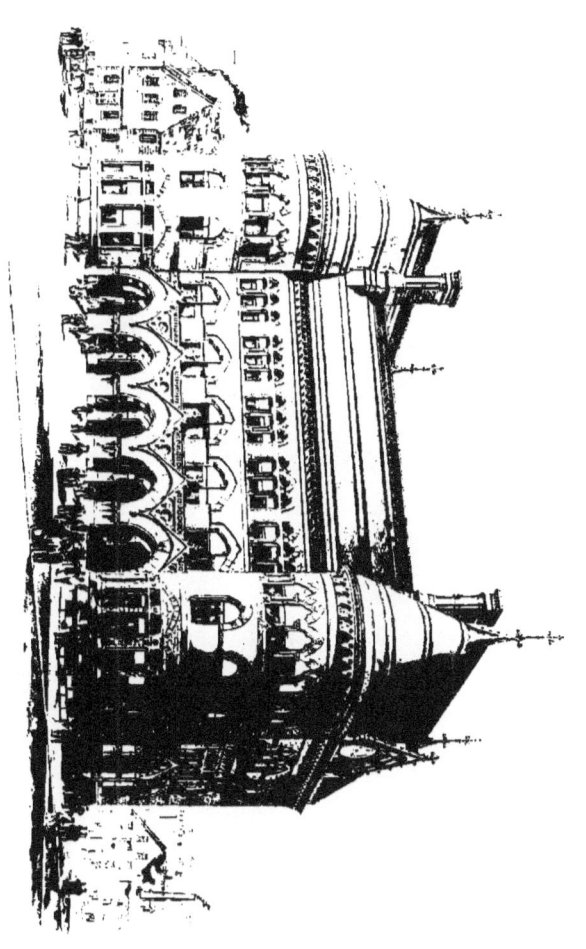

of architecture, occupying a space 29 feet in breadth and two stories in height. The main body of the building is gray rock-faced ashlar, laid in regular courses. The mullions and reveals of the windows, the interior of the arcade entrances to the post-office, and other prominent points are of gray granite, finely dressed. The band courses, sills, lintels, cornices, water-tables, etc., are of red granite, similarly face-finished.

The entire ground-floor is occupied by the post-office, the second floor by the custom-house, while the third floor can be used for the United States courts whenever required. The construction is fireproof throughout, the floor being of iron, concrete, and brick, and the roof of iron, concrete, copper, and slate. All interior walls are of brick, all exterior of granite; the flooring of the corridors, etc., is covered with marble and tiles laid in cement. The basement-floor is also cemented, and the foundations rest on a solid bed of concrete. The cost of the building, with furniture complete, is estimated at about $350,000, the land costing $132,000. The new structure, when fully completed, will be one of the greatest ornaments of the city.

CITY HALL.

The first town house was established at Steep Brook, the then centre of business, in 1805. In 1825 a new town house was erected on land now occupied by the North Cemetery. In 1836 this building was removed to Town Avenue, and occupied until the completion of the new town hall and market building, erected, after the great fire, on Main Street. In 1845-6 the present City Hall building, built of Fall River granite, was erected in Market Square, at an expense of $65,000, including lot, foundation, sidewalks, furniture, etc. It was considered a model public building for the time, solid and substantial in its construction, and judiciously arranged with a lock-up or town prison in the basement, a market on the first floor, and a large town hall, with offices in front, upon the second floor. The hall was one of the best in the State, and more commodious even than the far-famed Faneuil Hall of Boston. With the growth of the city, however, more office accommodation was required, and in 1872-3 the building was entirely remodelled (the original walls only being left) and rebuilt, with the addition of a Mansard roof, tower, clock, bell, etc., at a cost of $200,000.

The present noble edifice, from its positon and fine proportions, is an architectural ornament to the city, and will furnish, for many years to come, ample room for the use of all departments of the government. The Public Library and Reading Room occupy the main lower floor, the second is devoted to offices for the heads of departments, while upon the third are spacious chambers for the boards of aldermen and common councilmen, with ante-rooms attached. From the tower is obtained a fine bird's-eye view of the whole city, the harbor, and bay, together with the country beyond. It is a worthy monument of public spirit, taste, and utility, and in its solid and substantial proportions an object of pride to the citizens.

FALL RIVER:

ITS

NEWSPAPERS AND STEAM MARINE.

OUR country had reached its semi-centennial before a newspaper was published in Fall River, and not until twenty-three years after the settlement of the town did any one have the courage to venture out upon the sea of journalism. The first number of the *Fall River Monitor* was issued January 6th, 1826, by Nathan Hall. The town was then under the corporate name of Troy, although the name of Fall River, by which it was first called and to which it was changed back in 1834, still existed as the name of the village, the place of the publication of the paper. The office of publication was in a brick building on Bedford Street, south side, about midway between Main and Second Streets. The size of the paper was 19 by 24 inches, four pages, and four columns to a page. The first post-office antedated the paper some fifteen years, and the first two cotton mills by thirteen years. The paper was printed on a Ramage press similar to the one used by Franklin. The ink was distributed upon the type by balls, the very ancient style of the art.

The following detailed history of Fall River journalism is part of an interesting contribution to the local annals from the pen of a veteran citizen, whose professional experience is older than that of any still living representative of the Massachusetts press. Of the *Monitor* he observes:

"The publisher in his opening article 'feels assured that it [the paper] will receive a liberal patronage, provided it be conducted on fair principles and contain that variety of intelligence which subscribers have a right to demand.' Still he adds, ' The number of patrons at present are not sufficient to warrant the undertaking. We hope, however, that our paper will not be found entirely without merits.' Even at this early period, he finds it necessary to add that among the obstacles to be met with is the fact that ' our country abounds in public journals, which are daily increasing; they are managed by able hands, and have opportunities of news which we cannot immediately possess.' He hopes that 'these difficulties may be obviated by an extensive correspondence and increasing facilities of intercourse which pervade almost every part of our land.' He alludes to the 'genius and enterprise of the native citizens, and the knowledge and skill of strangers whom Providence has brought within its borders, which has raised it to a rank hardly second in the county of Bristol.'"

"The ludicrous side of life was then as apparent as now, for we find the veritable sea-serpent was seen in those days fully as large as these, besides it was the common practice of about all the dealers in groceries to dispense the ardent liquid which we fear has introduced a most dangerous serpent into many families, the fruits of which their descendants are still reaping to their sorrow and disgrace. The lottery was a fashionable institution, and some of our prominent citizens were agents for the same.

"At this time (1826) there were ten factories on the stream, six of which were in operation with 10,000 spindles, one iron and nail manufactory, a furnace, and a forge. The mills gave employment to about 1300 persons. There were only four churches in existence here. The Congregationalists, with Rev. Mr. Read pastor, worshipped in a house which stood where is now situated the Annawan Street school-house, and the Baptists still worshipped in the old meeting-house near the buttonwood-tree, with Rev. Job Borden pastor. The Methodists held meetings in the old school-house on the corner of South Main and Annawan Streets. Of the place of worship of the other religious society we are not advised. A writer who sailed up the river to Somerset speaks of Fall River as 'a city of the wilderness, rising in the midst of hills, trees, and water-falls and rural scenery.'

"It contained thirty-six stores, a tavern with a stone post thirty-six feet high, three physicians, one attorney, one brick-yard, and one bank with a capital of $100,000. This writer well says, 'Industry is the presiding goddess of Fall River; an idle man could no more live there than a beetle in a bee-hive.' Well has it maintained its reputation from that day to this.

"The number of advertisements, though quite limited, was respectable for this early period of our history as a town. Among these we note that John S. Cotton offers a variety of goods at his store, at the old stand at the corner formerly occupied by the Fall River manufactory, viz.: Dry goods, groceries, crockery, glassware, and hardware. John Southwick was also a dealer in the same articles. J. & D. Leonard supplied the people with paints and oils, but as nothing is said about paper hangings, we infer that Fall River people had not attained to the style necessary to make them a profitable commodity. Bennett & Jacobs were prominent dealers in West India goods and groceries, as also was Hiram Bliss. Enoch French & Sons supplied the people with boots, shoes, and leather, which, by the way, is the only store which has remained till this day, the same being continued by one of the sons, and a grandson, under the firm name of Job B. French & Son, at or near the old stand, but with greatly increased facilities. Samuel Shove & Son were engaged in the dry goods business, also including in their stock crockery, earthen and glass ware. Blake & Nichols were dealers in staple goods. Peleg H. Earl was the merchant tailor. James Ford dispensed the law. Joseph Luther and J. Ames taught private schools

Benj. Anthony and John Southwick were the auctioners. James G. Bowen was the Postmaster. Matthew C. Durfee was the only bank cashier. Susan Jennings was the tailoress, and Mrs. Hannah Allen the mantua-maker. David Anthony was agent for a Boston insurance company. John C. Borden and David Anthony were among the principal owners of real estate, and the former was Justice of the Peace, his name appearing occasionally as officiating at marriage ceremonies. A Masonic lodge was in being here at this early day, of which Rt. W. Leander P. Lovell was master, and John C. Borden was secretary and tyler, with Rev. A. B. Read as chaplain.

"Benjamin Earl entered the office of the *Monitor* as an apprentice late in the fall of 1826. After serving three years and continuing labor in the office some six months longer, he purchased the office with all its materials, including the good-will and list of subscribers, and commenced its publication on the 1st of July, 1830, continuing it until 1838, when the business was sold out to Tripp & Pearce. During the last year or two of Mr. Earl's connection with the office, J. S. Hammond was associated with him in that and other business.

"James Ford, Esq., officiated as editor of the *Monitor* during the most of the period of its publication by Mr. Earl.

"During the publication of the *Monitor* by Mr. Earl, the Morgan excitement on Masonry and anti-Masonry sprung up and waxed hot and bitter between the contending adherents on either side; and also the "great Hodges and Ruggles' contest," as it was afterward called, for Congressional appointment, which finally terminated in the election of Hodges on the *seventh* ballot. The *Monitor* took the Masonic side of the question in controversy, and this gave to its publisher the cognomen of 'Jack-mason.'

"In March, 1838, Earl & Hammond sold out their interest in the paper to Messrs. N. A. Tripp & Alfred Pearce. Their partnership continued but three months, when Mr. Henry Pratt assumed the obligations which Mr. Pearce had thrown off. Thus for many years the publishers were Messrs. Tripp & Pratt. In 1850 Mr. Tripp went out of the firm, and in 1857 engaged in the publication of the *Daily Star*, which soon after came into existence.

"For many years previous to the fire of 1843, the *Monitor* was published in the Exchange Building, which stood where the City Hall building is now located. After the fire it sought temporary quarters in the rear of Mrs. Young's residence, on North Main Street, until the Borden Block, which stood where the new one is now erected, was finished, when the office was removed thither. When the Pocasset House was rebuilt, the office was removed to its present quarters, where it has remained ever since.

"In 1841 Wm. S. Robertson, the present proprietor, entered the office to serve an apprenticeship, after concluding which he continued in the employ of Mr. Henry Pratt, the publisher, most of the time till about 1855, when he engaged in business himself. In December, 1868, he assumed the publicacation of the *Monitor*, which had been suspended for some months. For two years it was run as a free paper. January 1st, 1871, it was enlarged, a small subscription price charged, and it has undoubtedly now a far wider circulation than at any period in its history. It has always been issued as a weekly paper. The names of those who at various times have wielded the editorial pen in its columns are in their order as follows: Joseph Hathaway, Esq., Charles F. Townsend, Matthew C. Durfee, James Ford, Esq., Hon. Joseph E. Dawley, and William. S. Robertson, the present publisher and proprietor.

Contemporary Papers.

"While the *Monitor* has lived through this long period, there have come into existence many newspapers, both daily and weekly. Some of them were short-lived, merely giving a flickering light and expiring, while others have continued until this day. The first of these was the *Moral Envoy* (anti-Masonic), which was started in 1830 by George Wheaton Allen, a native of Batavia, N. Y. This journal continued to be published about a year, when in 1831 it was succeeded by the *Village Recorder*, Noel A. Tripp publisher. This was issued once a fortnight from the same office as the *Monitor*, for a short time, until 1832, when it came out weekly. After running nearly three years, the *Recorder* was merged in the *Monitor*.

"In 1836 there was started the first Democratic paper, a weekly, called the *Patriot*. The publisher was William. N. Canfield. It was edited a few months by B. Ellery Hale, after which the editorial work was mostly performed by a coterie of writers, among whom were the late Dr. P. W. Leland, Dr. Foster Hooper, Jonathan Slade, and Louis Lapham, Esq. These were the "forty fathers," so termed by James Ford, Esq., who at this time edited the *Monitor*. The *Patriot* was a journal of considerable ability, and did good service for the Democracy. It lived four or five years, and was succeeded by the *Archetype*, which was started in 1841, under the management of Messrs. Thomas Almy and Louis Lapham. After one brief year's existence it succumbed to an inevitable fate, and was followed by the *Gazette*, published by Abraham Bowen, and edited by Stephen Hart. This was also short-lived, when the *Argus*, a new candidate for public favor, sprung up under the editorial supervision of Jonathan Slade, with Thomas Almy as publisher. The office being destroyed in the great fire of 1843, the paper was suspended. About this time was issued the *Flint and Steel*, a small weekly sheet edited by the late Dr. P. W. Leland. It was in the interest of the Democracy, and gave full scope to the talent possessed by the Doctor in making the sparks of criticism and sarcasm fly thick and fast.

"At its demise, various ventures in journalism were made, among them *The Mechanic*, by Mr. Thomas Almy, the *Wampanoag*, and some others we do not now recall. The *Weekly News* was started in 1845, with Messrs. Almy & Milne as publishers. The paper is still published in connection with the *Daily News* by Messrs. Almy, Milne & Co. Since the date of that publication we have had the *All Sorts*, by Abraham Bowen, published occasionally, *Journal*, weekly, by George Robertson, *People's Press*, tri-weekly, by Noel A. Tripp. The *All Sorts* and *Journal* lived for a season. The *Press* was published five years, and then, in 1865, was merged into the *Monitor*.

"The *Labor Journal*, published by Henry Seavey, was started in 1873, and is still in existence. The *L'Echo du Canada*, an organ of the French

Canadians, was started in 1873, and lived about two years. The *Saturday Morning Bulletin*, a free paper weekly, started in 1872, is still issued."

Daily Papers.

"The first daily paper was *The Spark*, published in 1848, a small campaign paper, under the editorial supervision of Louis Lapham, Esq., which lived, but a few weeks. The first daily paper that survived was the *Daily Evening Star*, started in 1857, by Mr. Noel A. Tripp, afterward, in 1858, called *The Daily Beacon*, and edited by Louis Lapham, Esq. It continued one year, when it was purchased by Messrs. Almy & Milne, by whom it is still published under the firm name of Almy, Milne & Co. It is now called the *Fall River Daily Evening News*. The daily *Border City Herald* is now in the fourth year of its existence. Previous to this, the *Monitor* published a daily edition in 1865 for nine months, and in 1868 the *Daily Times* was published from the *Monitor* office for about eight months."

Journalism in Fall River cannot have lacked in variety, however unfruitful it has been in enriching the publishers. Certainly no class have labored with greater zeal to attain success. That they have not reached to the standard of metropolitan journalism is not their fault. Though the prophet might go to Mahomet, Mahomet could not go to the prophet. The tendency to monopolies has not left journalism untouched, and, outside of the great cities, there are few journals which attain sufficient patronage to cope with them. But that the citizens of Fall River have given some sort of support and encouragement to newspapers is manifest by the number and variety of undertakings in this line during the half century whose record is presented in these pages.

Mount Hope Bay and its Steam Marine.

This beautiful estuary, some nine to ten miles in length, and varying from three to five miles in breadth, is the right arm of the larger Narragansett, through which, on the west side of Rhode Island and the narrow and deep Seaconnet on the east, it empties into the Atlantic the combined tributes of the Taunton, Cole's, Lee's, and Kickamuit rivers. Among our Eastern bays there is certainly none more charming in situation and outline than Mount Hope, and had it the same surroundings of palm and flower-covered hills, the same city of centuries in the background, and an Italian sun in a concave of blue overhead, the comparison which returned tourists are fond of making for it with the Bay of Naples would not be unfair, or at all pretentious. The calm loveliness of this picturesque water, though recognized and amply appreciated by the industrious communities upon its shores, is not the distinctive merit suggesting our present consideration. As a harbor or roadstead, easily made in whatever weather, broad enough to shelter navies upon its unbroken expanse, sufficiently deep for the passage of the largest ships, and by its landlocked position protected from storms in all directions, Mount Hope Bay is of the largest value to Fall River and its people.

In the course of the purely narrative part of this work, allusions have been made to the local advantages of Fall River, and in their proper connection brief notices incorporated of the means of communication with other business centres. The commercial facilities afforded by the situation of the city, upon so secure and spacious a sheet of water, are of inestimable account to its future. Between New York and Boston, with the possible exception of New Bedford, there is no harbor possessing the number and excellence of features that this landlocked bay can claim, all others either lacking in room, ease of access, or sufficient depth. The singular availability of Fall River as a location for bonded warehouses, its docks and piers possessing a draught of water adequate to the approach of the largest vessels, and its railroad and marine communication offering the best freight carriage north and south, has not infrequently drawn the attention of engineers and capitalists. The railroad features of the place may be said to be unique in one important respect—that the main line from Boston, following the shore of the bay, admits of dock connections at any desired point along the whole water-front, and the New Bedford line entering the very heart of the city, and landing goods almost at the doors of the mills, though constructed fifty years after the laying out of the highways, crosses but one public street. The exceptional advantages of the location as an industrial centre, due to the cheap transportation of coal, cotton, iron ores, and other raw material, at its command, constitute an important integer in the general enterprise and prosperity. Should foreign commerce, in some not far distant day, appropriate to its uses the remarkable advantages already largely enjoyed by domestic trade, such a result would be neither illogical nor surprising.

Occasional suggestions have been afforded in the preceding history of the early modes of travel and freight carriage established between Fall River and Boston, New York and Providence. A more complete record of the progress of communication in those directions, prepared by a careful hand, is embodied in the following pages.

Early communication with the neighboring places was limited to private conveyance, until the establishment in 1825 of a stage line for passengers between Fall River, Providence, and New Bedford, the terminus of each line being at Slade's Ferry, where the only means of crossing was by sail or row boat. Isaac Fish, who also ran coaches to Boston, Bristol, and Newport, *via* Bristol Ferry, was the proprietor of the Providence line, and I. H. Bartlett had control of the New Bedford line. In 1826, a horse-boat was put on at Slade's Ferry, so that the stages could come over to the village. This simple craft ran satisfactorily for many years, but in January, 1847, was superseded by the steam ferry-boat Faith, which in turn made way for the Weetamoe, in March, 1859. The completion of the new iron railroad bridge in 1875, erected by the Old Colony Railroad Company at this point of the river, with carriage road included, rendered the ferry, which for generations had been a great public convenience, useless, and the boats were accordingly withdrawn.

As business advanced, and there came the necessity of more frequent intercourse with the neighboring towns and of transportation to and fro of merchandise, corn, grain, provisions, etc., the convenience of water communication was noted, and efforts made to realize the marine advantages of the locality. At first, sailing craft of greater or less capacity were employed, the Irene and Betsey, a two-masted lighter, and the sloops Fall River and Argonaut, each of thirty or forty tons, being the first to ply regularly on the waters of the Mount Hope and Narragansett bays. Soon sailing packets began stated trips to New York, Albany, Newport, and Providence; and then came the Eudora, a propeller built expressly to run between Fall River and New York as a freight boat. She was the first propeller in use here or on any of the adjoining waters, and was commanded by that veteran captain of the Sound boats, William Brown.

THE PROVIDENCE LINE.

Shortly after the organization of the Fall River Iron Works Company, with Colonel Borden as managing agent and treasurer, a regular line of communication by water between Fall River and Providence was established under its auspices. The early experience of the Colonel in shipbuilding and boating well fitted him for further and more extensive enterprises in such direction, and, with the advent of steam-power in navigation, a steamer was purchased and placed upon the route. The first boat was the Hancock, built in Castine, Maine, in 1827, and brought to Boston, where she was purchased by Mr. Holder Borden, soon after her arrival. She measured 98 tons, was 89 feet long, 18 feet beam, and about 6 feet depth of hold. The Hancock was commanded by Captain Thomas Borden, who went to Boston to bring her to this port, and, in coming through the draw at Stone Bridge, encountered considerable difficulty on account of the width of the steamer and the narrowness of the draw. She began running regularly between Fall River and Providence in September, 1828, occupying about three hours in the trip. A picture of her is still in existence, but so blackened that the outlines only can faintly be traced. The picture, which is a painting, was discovered a few years since covering a chimney flue, where it had been placed by one who failed to appreciate its value. A number of figures are to be seen on the open deck of the boat, appearing to an ordinary observer like very black gentlemen wearing extremely angular coats and enormous hats.

The Hancock was succeeded in 1832 by the King Philip. She was built in New York, and measured 169 tons. Her length was 120 feet, breadth 20 feet, and depth 7½ feet. She also was under the charge of Captain Borden, and for more than a dozen years made her trips regularly between the two ports, without accident or noticeable incident.

In 1845, the Bradford Durfee was placed upon the route, the King Philip being used as a supplementary boat. She was named for one of the most active and most energetic business men of his time, largely concerned in manufacturing pursuits, and having much to do with out-door affairs, especially in shaping and erecting the earlier docks and wharves of the city. The Bradford Durfee has been kept in good repair, is still in active service, and appears to be as strong and as safe as ever. She has a square engine—a style peculiar to the earlier New York boats—which has done excellent service.

The staunch and noble Canonicus was next added to the list of steamers owned by this company. Built in 1849, and commanded by Captain Benjamin Brayton, she was run for a few years between Newport and Providence, *via* Fall River and Bristol, and subsequently as an excursion boat to different points. In 1862, she was sold to the United States Government, to be used as a transport; in 1865, bought back again by the Iron Works Company, she is now employed for extra service and occasional trips to Rocky Point, Newport, Block Island, and other resorts during the summer months. "None know her but to love her," and she has ever proved one of the most popular and reliable boats on these waters.

In 1854, the Metacomet appeared in the bay, a very beautiful steamer, owned by the same company; she was built in New York, was 170 feet long, 26 feet beam, and 9 feet depth of hold, being about the same size as the Canonicus. She also was disposed of in the early days of the rebellion, transformed into a gunboat, named the Pulaski, and finally wrecked on the coast of Mexico. In 1874, the steamer Richard Borden was placed upon the route. She is one of the fastest, if not the fastest, boats in either Mount Hope or Narragansett bays, having travelled the distance, about thirty miles, in one hour and a half, including stoppages. She, with the Bradford Durfee, now forms a line of two boats, each day, one leaving either city in the morning and returning in the afternoon.

One of the peculiarities of this line is that it has been absolutely changeless. It was owned at the outset by the Fall River Iron Works Company, and they own it now. Security and stability have ever been its characteristics. There has never been any decided opposition. One or two boats have made a few trips between Providence and Fall River, but they were soon withdrawn. The boats have landed at their present wharves in Fall River and Providence for many years. The Iron Works Company own the wharf at which the boats land in Bristol, and they hold the wharf at Bristol Ferry almost in perpetuity. Even the running time has changed but little, about two hours being the average, summer and winter.

In the summer of 1829, a Liliputian steamer, called the Experiment, made occasional trips upon the Providence River and between Taunton and Newport, sending a boat ashore with passengers at Fall River. Other steamcraft, the Babcock, the Rushlight, and the Wadsworth, at sundry times attempted to establish communication between Fall River and neighboring ports, but with only partial or no success. In 1847, the Perry, a steamer looking much like the Canonicus, was built for Rufus B. Kinsley, to run between Newport and Fall River. She made three trips a week to Fall River, running alternate days to Providence. In June, 1848, she began running to Fall River in the morning, and to Providence in the afternoon, but, her owners soon finding that two trips daily to Providence would be more profitable, she was withdrawn entirely from the Fall River route.

In May, 1827, the Marco Bozzaris, a steamer, was advertised to run between Dighton and New York, stopping at Fall River—" Passengers to be taken by stage from Dighton to Boston." Whether any trips were ever made, cannot now be stated with certainty, but the project thus boldly put forth was realized twenty years later, with only this change—that Fall River became the grand centre of transfer from water to land transportation.

THE NEW YORK LINE.

In 1847, shortly after the completion of the Fall River Railroad opening direct railway communication with Boston, the Bay State Steamboat Company was formed with a capital of $300,000, and in the spring of that year, the steamer Bay State, built expressly for the line, commenced her regular trips between Fall River and New York. Many citizens will remember the May morning when she proudly entered the harbor, an event signalized by the firing of guns, ringing of bells, and the, if possible, more demonstrative shouts and cheers of the excited people, who crowded the high bluffs along the shore, or pressed forward upon the wharf which was henceforth to be her point of arrival and departure. She was the pioneer of a noble and eminently successful enterprise.

The Bay State proved worthy of her name. She was commanded by Captain Joseph J. Comstock, who was subsequently captain of the ocean steamer Baltic, and always the same popular and gentlemanly commander. The length of the Bay State was 320 feet; her tonnage, 1600. Until the completion of the Empire State, of equal size and power, the steamer Massachusetts was chartered as alternate boat, and commanded by that long-experienced veteran, Captain William Brown. In 1854, the mammoth Metropolis, the most superb steamboat of her period, was added to the facilities of this admirably conducted line. Built and equipped solely from the profits of its business, she was as strong as wood and iron combined could make her, and elegantly furnished throughout, eliciting among the townspeople almost as much excitement and commotion on her arrival as was awakened by her predecessor, the Bay State. Her length was 350 feet, breadth of beam 82 feet, and depth of hold 15 feet. Her capacity was 2200 tons.

The conception of the organization of this favorite through route of travel between Boston and New York, *via* Fall River, was largely due to Colonel Richard Borden, by whom also the railroad was projected and mainly constructed. Other business men were interested in this latter movement and aided in its development, among whom were Andrew Robeson, Sr., who was its first president, his successor, Hon. Nathaniel B. Borden, and David Anthony, who was treasurer. Jefferson Borden was also most prominent in the management, and shared with his brother Richard in the organization of the steamboat line. Until 1846, there had been no communication direct from Fall River by steam or rail with either Boston or New York, although the traveller might, by going to Providence or Stonington, catch a train or boat.

The Bay State Steamboat Company in course of time passed into the control of the Boston, Newport and New York Steamboat Company, and, the Old Colony Railroad Company having in the meantime extended their road from Fall River to Newport, that city (1864) was made the eastern terminus for the boats of the line. Soon came another change, the steamers becoming the property of the Narragansett Steamship Company, then under the control of Messrs. Fisk and Gould, of New York, and the eastern terminus was re-established (1869) at Fall River, the conviction having forced itself upon all, whether travellers or proprietors,—that there was the most convenient and popular point of ingress and egress.

A year or two more, and this favorite line of travel became the property of the Old Colony Steamboat Company, forming, in connection with the Old Colony Railroad, then running by a new and shorter line, *via* Taunton, to Boston, the safest, the most delightful in point of scenery, and by far the most comfortable route between the commercial centre of the nation and New England.

The older steamboats having had their day, including the Governor, the Senator, and the Katahdin, which were chartered from time to time and used as winter boats, as also the State of Maine, purchased about 1850 and proving one of the best sea boats ever in Eastern waters, the Old Colony Steamboat Company is now equipped with the staunch and beautiful steamers, Newport and Old Colony, as winter craft, and the truly magnificent floating palaces, Bristol and Providence, for the milder and pleasanter portions of the year. The latter steamers, built in 1867, each 373 feet long, 83 feet beam, 16¼ feet draught, and 3000 tons measurement, excel all other steamers afloat in elegance of finish, furniture, and appointments. They each have 240 staterooms, and sleeping accommodations for 800 to 1000 passengers. The officers and crew of each comprise 130 persons. The most experienced and cautious pilots are employed, every precaution is taken to guard against casualties of all sorts, and ample provision is made for the welfare and safety of passengers should disaster occur. One of the later features of the line, of a rather æsthetic character, is an evening concert in the saloon by a fine band. It is so highly appreciated as to be considered now well-nigh indispensable.

This route, "The Old Fall River Line," has continued for thirty years *the* favorite of the travelling public, on account of its certainty, and its uniform speed and safety. Among the hundreds of thousands of people transported by this line during the Centennial year, not one received injury. That this route to New York, for comfort, convenience, and beauty of scenery, far excels all others, there is no question. Passengers leaving Boston in the early evening, have a delightful view of the harbor, with its islands, shipping, and way out to the sea; pass through numerous towns and villages, and an everchanging landscape; and then, for a score of miles, sweep along the banks of Taunton River to Fall River, a distance by rail of 48 miles, travelled in an hour and fifteen minutes, in spacious and elegant cars, over a road-bed smooth and even, laid with steel rails the entire distance. From the decks of the steamers, as they pass down the bay in the still hours of twilight, may be seen one of the finest and most varied panoramic views in New England, rich in historic and natural interest. At the start is Fall River, with its church spires and mammoth manufactories, rising abruptly from the bay on the east; the bare, bald summit of Mount Hope, the seat of the Indian sachem King Philip, a little farther down on the west; while the islands and softly undulating waters of Mount Hope and Narragansett bays stretch away towards the south until Newport is reached. Passengers by this route secure a good night's rest, and arrive in New York or Boston in ample season for extended travel south, or north and east, and for all business purposes.

FREIGHT LINES.

In 1866, the transportation of freight to and from Fall River had increased to such dimensions, that enterprising gentlemen obtained a charter and organized the "Fall River Steamboat Company." The propellers Albatross and United States, each between 400 and 500 tons measurement, were purchased and placed upon the route to New York, running two trips each, weekly, between the two ports. Upon the formation of the Old Colony Steamboat Company, comprising some of the gentlemen connected with this line, the boats were sold to the new company, and are now run in connection with the larger steamers for the transportation of freight.

In the spring of 1865, the Fall River and Warren Railroad, connecting with the Providence and Bristol line at Warren, being ready for travel, the steamer Oriole was put on as a ferry-boat, connecting this road at its eastern terminus, opposite the city, with the Old Colony Railroad at their depot on Ferry Street. On the completion of the new bridge at Slade's Ferry, the railroad, having in the meantime been purchased by the Old Colony Railroad Company, was extended and brought over the river into the city, thus dispensing with the ferry-boat and inaugurating a route for freight as well as for passengers between Fall River, Providence, and further west. Several large coal steamers, bringing 1000 tons of coal each trip, arrive weekly at this port, and there are besides other steam-craft used for freight, excursions, and tugboat purposes. A large fleet of tugs used in the fishing business are wholly or in part operated by citizens of Fall River, and belong to the steam marine of Mount Hope Bay.

THE CLYDE LINE.

In March, 1876, the proprietors of the Clyde line of steamers, perceiving the natural advantages and facilities for business afforded by Fall River, determined to make that port the eastern terminus of a line of freight propellers to Philadelphia. They placed two boats upon the route, the Norfolk, of 411 tons burden, and the Defiance, of 381 tons, each capable of carrying the contents of thirty-five railway cars. Connections were made with the Old Colony Railroad, thus opening up a new and direct route from Boston to Philadelphia, and avoiding the perils of Cape Cod and Vineyard Sound on the one hand, or the intricate windings, shoals and shallows, rocks and sand-bars of inland river navigation on the other.

The venture proving unexpectedly successful, and verifying the wisdom of the movement, the next year the company added to the line the Vindicator, a propeller of 1021 tons burden, one of the largest on the coast, and capable of stowing 4000 bales of cotton, or the contents of one hundred cars.

Applying here the truth, " coming events cast their shadows before," it may not be too much to predict that active business men in Fall River of to-day will, in their time, witness the arrival and departure of steamships from their harbor on lines to be established direct between Fall River and foreign ports.

FALL RIVER:

ITS

HISTORICAL, POLITICAL AND SOCIAL PHASES.

THERE is still treasured by a very few of our oldest citizens, a modest pamphlet, coverless, not exceeding twelve pages, and altogether unpretentious in typographical execution, yet exceedingly valuable for its true picture of the settlement as it was about the middle of the last century, and for the record of local patriotism it has preserved. Its author, referred to in the early pages of our narrative, was a conspicuous citizen, identified with the original industrial enterprise of the settlement (then Tiverton, R. I.,) as the projector of the first spinning factory, and noted for his intelligent and comprehensive observation. In 1834, still possessing a vivid recollection of the incidents of his youth and maturer years, he wrote the interesting, though much too brief, record of local events, which is here reproduced in its entire volume.

REMINISCENCES OF COL. JOSEPH DURFEE,

RELATING TO THE

EARLY HISTORY OF FALL RIVER, AND OF REVOLUTIONARY SCENES.

"Joseph Durfee was the eldest son of the late Hon. Thomas Durfee. He was born in April, in the year 1750, in what is now the city of Fall River. At that time, and until within a few years, the Fall River stream was owned by the Bordens. Much of what now is the city, where are elegant buildings and a dense population, was then a wilderness, where the goats lodged in the winter seasons. The Bordens and the Durfees were then the principal proprietors of the Pocasset Purchase, and owners of the land on the south side of what is now Main Street, for more than a mile in length. Thomas and Joseph Borden owned the south side of the stream, and Stephen Borden owned the north side. Thomas Borden owned a saw-mill and a grist-mill at that time, standing where the old saw and grist mills stood near the iron-works establishment.

"Thomas Borden left a widow and four children, viz.: Richard, Christopher, Rebecca, and Mary. Joseph Borden, brother of Thomas, owned a fulling-mill, which stood near where the Pocasset Factory now stands. He was killed by the machinery of his fulling-mill. He left four children, viz.: Abraham, Samuel, Patience, and Peace. Patience was my mother. Stephen Borden, who owned the north side of the stream, had a grist-mill and a saw-mill, standing near where the woollen establishment has since been erected. He left six children, viz.: Stephen, George, Mary, Hannah, Penelope, and Lusannah.

"The widow of Joseph Borden was afterwards married to Benjamin Jenks, by whom she had six children—John, Joseph, Hannah, Catherine, Ruth, and Lydia. The widow of Stephen Borden was married to John Bowen, by whom she had two sons—Nathan and John.

"At that time, and until within a few years, there were but two saw-mills, two grist-mills, and a fulling-mill standing on the Fall River. There are now about forty different mills on the river. The stream was very small; but the falls were so great that there was little occasion for dams to raise a pond sufficient to carry the wheels then in operation. A small foot bridge, which stood near where the main street now crosses the stream, afforded the only means of passing from one side to the other of the stream, except by fording it. There was formerly a small dam near where the Troy Factory now stands, over which the water flowed the greater part of the year. When it failed, those who owned the mills near the mouth of the stream hoisted the gates at the upper dam and drew the water down. It was no uncommon thing, twenty-five or thirty years ago, for the water to be so low and the river so narrow at the head of the stream, that a person might step across without difficulty. It was frequently not more than six inches deep. At one time there was a foot bridge of stepping-stones only across the Narrows between the North and South Ponds.

"Our country has been involved in three wars since my recollection. The first was with the French and Indians—when we fought for our lives. The French offered a bounty for every scalp which the Indians would bring them. It was therefore certain death to all who fell into the Indians' hands. I distinctly recollect the time when General Wolfe was killed—and of seeing the soldiers on their march to reinforce the army. I saw many men enlist into the service, and among them, Joseph Valentine, father of William Valentine, of Providence. I was then about ten years of age.

"The second war was with Great Britain, during the greater part of which I was actively engaged in the service of my country. We then fought for our liberty. We were divided into two parties, called Whigs and Tories—the former, the friends of liberty and independence; the latter, the enemies of both. Before the Revolution broke out, the Whigs were busy in making saltpetre and gunpowder, in making and preparing small arms, in training and learning the art of war. At this time, we of this State were British subjects, and constituted what was then called the Colony of Massachusetts. Conventions were held in the colony to transact the business and consult upon the affairs of the colony. At one of these conventions I received a captain's commission, signed by Walter Spooner, Esq., and took the command of a company of minute men.

"British ships, commanded by Wallace, Asque, and Howe, early in the Revolution, were off our coast, in the river and bay, harassing and distressing the towns of Newport, Bristol, and other towns on the river. I was called upon with my company and such others as could be mustered to guard the shores and prevent the British from landing, until the colony could raise a force sufficient to protect the inhabitants from their depredations.

"In 1776, after the battle on Long Island, a reinforcement was called for to cover the retreat of the American troops. I was ordered to take the command of a company of sixty men and march forthwith to the army then retreating from New York. These orders were promptly obeyed. With the company under my command, I joined the regiment commanded by Colonel Thomas Carpenter, and by a forced march we reached the army a few days before the battle at the White Plains. In that engagement I took an active part.

"Soon after my return home from the battle at the White Plains, the British landed at Newport, on Rhode Island, and took possession of that town. I was called upon to proceed immediately with my company to assist in covering the retreat of the small forces then commanded by Colonel John Cook from the island of Rhode Island. This was effected without loss, though attended with difficulty and delay, as there was then no bridge from the island to the mainland. At that time, the inhabitants in the south part of Massachusetts and Rhode Island were in a critical situation. They were nearly surrounded with British emissaries. A part of the English squadron lay off our coast, and their troops had possession of the south part of Rhode Island. Both were harassing our towns, destroying property, and making prisoners of the inhabitants. In addition to this, we had Tories at home, enemies in disguise, who were aiding and abetting the British, while they professed friendship for the cause of liberty, and for those who were shedding their blood to obtain it.

"Early in the spring of 1777, I received a major's commission, and was stationed at Little Compton, in the State of Rhode Island, in the regiment under the command of Colonel John Hathaway, of Berkley, Mass. At Little Compton and in that neighborhood I continued several months on duty with the regiment, often changing our station, to repel the invasions of the enemy and to protect the inhabitants from their frequent depredations. In the fall of 1777, I returned home to Fall River. I found the citizens, among whom were my relatives and best friends, exposed and continually harassed by the enemy. I applied to several of the leading and influential men of this place, and proposed raising a guard for the safety and protection of the inhabitants.

They coincided with my views, and the necessity of a guard to protect our defenceless inhabitants. I went to Providence to consult General Sullivan, who was commander-in-chief of all the forces raised in this section of the country, and to obtain assistance from him. He approved of my plan of raising a guard, and gave me an order for two whaleboats, and an order also for rations for twenty men, drawn upon the commissary, then at Bristol. I soon raised a guard, procured the store now standing at the end of the Iron Works Company's wharf in this place for a guard-house, where we met every day, called the roll, and stationed sentinels for the night to watch the movements of the enemy and give the alarm when approached. The orders of the sentinel were peremptory—that if a boat was seen approaching in the night, to hail them three times, and if no answer was received to fire upon them. It was not long before one of the guard, Samuel Reed, discovered boats silently and cautiously approaching the shore from the bay. The challenge was given but no answer received. He fired upon the boats. This created an alarm, and the whole neighborhood were soon in arms. I stationed the guard behind a stone wall, and kept up a constant fire upon the enemy until they brought their cannon to bear upon us, and commenced firing grapeshot amongst us—when, as we were unable to return the compliment, it was deemed advisable to retreat. Two of the guard were sent to remove all the planks which laid over the stream for foot people to cross upon, and to cut off, as far as possible, every facility for crossing the stream, except the upper bridge. We then retreated slowly until we reached the main road, near where the bridge now crosses the stream. I then gave orders to form and give them battle. This was done, and never were soldiers more brave. So roughly were the enemy handled by our little band of Spartans, that they soon beat up a retreat, leaving behind them one dead and another bleeding to death, besides the wounded, whom they carried away.

"The wounded soldier, left by the enemy, before he expired, informed me that the number of the enemy who attacked us was about 150, commanded by Major Ayers. When the enemy landed, they set fire to the house of Thomas Borden, then nearly new. They next set fire to a grist-mill and a saw-mill, belonging to Mr. Borden, standing at the mouth of the Fall River. These buildings I saw when set on fire. When the British troops retreated, as they were compelled to do, from the shots of our little band of volunteers, they set fire to the house and other buildings of Richard Borden, then an aged man, and took him prisoner. We pursued them so closely in their retreat, that we were enabled to save the buildings which they had last fired. The British were frequently fired upon and not a little annoyed by the musketry of our soldiers, as they passed down the bay in their boats on their retreat. Mr. Richard Borden, whom they took prisoner, was in one of their boats. Finding themselves closely pursued by a few American soldiers, who from the shore poured in their shot and balls upon them as fast as they could load and fire, and finding themselves in danger from the musketry of these few brave Whigs who pursued them, they ordered Mr. Borden, their prisoner, to stand up in the boat, hoping that his comrades on the shore would recognize him and desist from firing upon them. But this he refused to do; and threw himself flat into the bottom of the boat. While laying there, a shot from the Americans on shore killed one of the British soldiers standing by his side in the boat. Mr. Borden was obstinately silent to all the questions which were asked him; so that not being able to make any profitable use of him, they dismissed him in a few days on parole. This engagement took place of a Sabbath morning, on the 25th of May, 1778. The two British soldiers killed in this engagement, were buried at twelve o'clock on the same day of the battle, near where the south end of the Massasoit Factory now stands.

"During a considerable part of the month of August following, we were busily engaged in procuring arms, ammunition, and provisions for the soldiers, and in building flat-bottomed boats and scows for the troops to cross over the river on to Rhode Island, with a view to dislodge the British army, who then had possession of the island. A barn, now standing near the Stone Bridge, was occupied for a commissary store, of which I had the charge until things were in readiness and the troops prepared to cross over to the island, when I left the store in charge of my friend and relative, Walter Chaloner.

"In the fore part of August, 1778, the American troops embarked in the boats and scows prepared for them, and landed on Rhode Island, where I joined them, having been appointed a major in Colonel Whitney's regiment. Our troops were then marched to a spot but a short distance to the north of what is called Butts' Hill, where they encamped for the night with but the canopy of heaven for a covering and the ground for our beds. But we were animated with the hope of liberty—with a belief that we were engaged in a righteous cause—and that He who sways the sceptre of the universe would prosper our undertaking. At this time we were anxiously looking for the French fleet, from which we hoped for assistance against the enemy, whose numerous bodies of troops were before us. Soon the French fleet hove in sight, when the British set fire to the shipping in the harbor and blew up most of the vessels within their reach. Not long after the French fleet came up, the British fleet appeared in the offing. Immediately the French fleet tacked about, went out and attacked the British squadron, when broadsides were exchanged, and a bloody battle ensued. A tremendous storm came on, long remembered as the August storm, in which the two fleets were separated, and many who had escaped the cannon's mouth found a watery grave. The French fleet, or so much of it as survived the storm, went into Boston to repair, and the remnant of the British fleet went into New York.

"Soon after this storm, our troops marched in three divisions towards Newport—one on the East road, so called, one on the West road, and the brigade commanded by General Titcomb moved in the centre—until we came in sight of Newport, when orders were given to halt, erect a marquee, and pitch our tents. General orders were issued for a detachment from the army of three thousand men, our number being too small to risk a general engagement with the great body of British troops then quartered on the south end of the island. Early on the next morning a detachment of troops, of which I was one, was ordered to proceed forthwith and take possession of what was called Hunneman's Hill.

"The morning was foggy, and enabled us to advance some distance unobserved by the enemy; but the fog clearing away before we reached the hill, we were discovered by the British and Tory troops, who commenced such a heavy cannonade upon us, that it was deemed expedient by the commanding officers, to prevent the destruction of many of our brave troops, that we should fall back and advance under the cover of night. Accordingly, when night came, we marched to the hill undiscovered by the enemy. We immediately commenced throwing up a breastwork and building a fort. When daylight appeared, we had two cannon mounted—one twenty-four pounder, and one eighteen—and with our breastwork we had completed a covered way, to pass and repass without being seen by the enemy. The British had a small fort or redoubt directly under the muzzles of our cannon, with which we saluted them, and poured in shot so thick upon them that they were compelled to beat up a retreat. But they returned again at night to repair their fort, when they commenced throwing bombshells into our fort, which, however, did but little damage. I saw several of them flying over our heads, and one bursting in the air, a fragment fell upon the shoulder of a soldier and killed him.

"At this time we were anxiously waiting the return of the French fleet from Boston, where they had gone to repair. But learning that they could not then return, and knowing the situation of the British troops, that they were enlarging and strengthening their forts and redoubts, and that they had reinforcements arriving daily from New York, it was deemed expedient by our commanding officers, Lafayette, Green, and Sullivan, all experienced and brave Generals, that we should retreat to the north end of the island.

"Accordingly, on the 29th day of August, early in the morning, we struck our marquee and tents and commenced a retreat. The British troops followed, and soon came up with our rear-guard and commenced firing upon them. The shots were briskly returned and continued at intervals, until our troops were joined by a part of our army a short distance to the south of Quaker Hill, so called, when a general engagement ensued, in which many lives were lost on both sides. At night, we retreated from the island to Tiverton. On the following day we left Tiverton, crossed over Slade's Ferry and marched through Pawtucket and Providence to Pawtuxet, where we remained until our time of service expired.

"Some time after this, I received a lieutenant-colonel's commission, and took the command of a regiment to guard the sea-shores, and a part of the time my regiment was stationed at Providence. I soon received orders from General Gates, who at that time was principal in command, to march with my regiment to Tiverton and join General Cornell's brigade. The war now raged throughout the country. Old and young, parents and children, all, excepting the Tories, were engaged in the common cause of their country —in breaking the shackles of Colonial bondage—in obtaining her liberty and achieving her independence. Old England now began to examine the prospects before her. She found after a bloody contest, what she might and ought to have known before, that her rebellious colonies, as she was pleased to term them, could be ruled, but not ridden upon; that by mild and liberal measures she might have retained a valuable part of her kingdom. She discovered her error too late to profit by it. The brave people of her colonies were resolved to throw off the yoke, and themselves be free.

"On the 29th day of October, 1779, the British troops left Rhode Island, and the American troops, under the command of Generals Gates and Cornell, marched on to the island and took possession of the town of Newport. On the 29th day of December following, my time of service having expired, I returned home to my family. This was the coldest winter known during the last century. The river and bay were frozen over so thick, that people with loaded teams passed all the way from Fall River to Newport on the ice. I continued in the service of my country until about the close of the Revolutionary war, when I removed from Fall River to Tiverton, in the State of Rhode Island, where I lived about thirty years. During this time, I was elected by my fellow-citizens to several offices in town, and was a member of the General Assembly for many years.

"When Thomas Jefferson was elected President of the United States, in 1801, and the Democratic fever raged to the highest pitch, I was what was then called a Federalist, and having repeatedly sworn to support the federal Constitution, could not consent to turn my coat wrong side out. I was therefore not permitted to hold any office for some time after. But in time this party fever abated, and finally the people united in electing Mr. Monroe, under the general appellation of Federal Republicans. Attempts have since been made to alter the Constitution, that noble fabric reared by the Revolutionary patriots, and should they succeed, it will be in my estimation like sewing new cloth to an old garment."

FALL RIVER IN THE CIVIL WAR.

At the outbreak of the rebellion Fall River had been a municipality exactly seven years, its city charter dating April 12th, 1854, and the attack upon Fort Sumter having occurred April 12th, 1861. Although possessing less than one third of its present population, and hardly a quarter of its taxable valuation, it was still an important city, and had just begun, perhaps, to show promise of the high rank since attained as a cotton-manufacturing centre. The incorporation of the Union Mill Company in 1859, and its very successful inauguration, had given a new and popular impetus to the manufacture of cotton cloth, heretofore confined to corporations that had been established many years. The moment seemed to be ripe for somewhat of a departure from the old-time, conservative, and, in a sense, monopolizing influences that had long prevailed, and business men were looking forward to new ventures and undertakings. The general aspect of the place was thriving. The wheels of manufacture and of trade were in motion, and the city was alike active and prosperous. Its population in 1861 was 14,026, and its valuation $11,261,065.

The news of the firing upon Fort Sumter quickened all the loyal and patriotic impulses of the citizens, and stirred them into immediate effort. The children proved worthy descendants of their sires, for as the inhabitants of Fall River, then Freetown, declared for the Independence of the Colonies July 15th, 1776, but a few days after the Declaration of Independence of the United States, so the citizens of Fall River pronounced at once and with no uncertain utterance for the preservation and maintenance of the Union. A call, signed by Hon. N. B. Borden, James Ford, Hon. James Buffinton, Hon. E. P. Buffinton, and twenty-eight other prominent residents, was immediately issued for a public meeting. The opening words of the call had the true ring of patriotism. "Be this our motto," it said, "Our God and our country. War is proclaimed; rebellion stalks abroad as yet unscathed; the enemy is plotting the nation's destruction, and fight or fall is now the inevitable result." The meeting, convened at the City Hall on the evening of April 19th, 1861, was one of the largest and most enthusiastic ever there assembled. The attack upon the Massachusetts soldiers in the streets of Baltimore, on that day, and the intense and bitter feeling consequent upon this and other acts of the rebels and their sympathizers, had thoroughly aroused the citizens. The meeting was called to order by Hon. N. B. Borden, who read the call, was chosen chairman, and made the opening address. Speeches were also made by David Anthony, James Ford, Hon. James Buffinton, Dr. Foster Hooper, John Collins, John Westall, J. C. Blaisdell, R. T. Davis, and Walter C. Durfee. Dr. Hooper offered the following resolutions, which were adopted by acclamation :

"*Resolved*, That the Government of the Union shall be sustained.

"That the city government be requested to appropriate $10,000 in aid of those who may volunteer, and for the support of their families.

"That each volunteer be paid the sum of twenty dollars per month from the city treasury, in addition to what is paid by the Government."

On April 24th, the committee of the City Council to whom these resolutions were referred, reported as follows :

"*Whereas, etc.*, in the southern section of our country public law is disregarded, the authority of the United States set at defiance, and armed forces have been, and are, organizing with the avowed purpose of overthrowing the government as formed by our Revolutionary fathers, and of establishing a new government, in which freedom of the press, of speech, and of the individual man shall be more restricted—in a word, a government for the perpetuation of slavery ; and

Whereas, etc., for the repelling of such forces the standing army being inadequate, the President of the United States has made requisition on the several States for militia ; therefore, to the end that said requisition may be more readily answered.

Ordered, That to each of our citizens who may join a militia company of our city, organized according to law, pledged to render military service whenever and wherever required, whether by authority of the State or the United States Government, there be paid from the city treasury the sum of fifteen dollars for outfit, when such company shall be mustered into service; and thereafter, for a term not exceeding three months, fifteen dollars a month, the latter to be applied for the support of the family or dependants, as the soldier may direct; and if, at the expiration of the service, a balance, or the whole, shall remain unpaid, then payment to be made to the soldier in person, or his legal representatives: these payments to be made in addition to compensation that may be realized from the United States Government."

The order was adopted by the City Council, and $10,000 were appropriated in accordance therewith. Meanwhile, enlistments were rapidly going on. A company was already partly formed, under Lieutenant Cushing, who had seen service in the Mexican war, and a rifle company, composed of some of the best young men in the town, was being organized under Captain, afterwards Lieutenant-Colonel, C. W. Greene. Fall River was the third in the list of applicants in the commonwealth to Governor Andrew for permission to raise military companies. April 29th, the mayor was requested to apply to the State authorities to furnish two hundred (200) muskets for the two companies organized in the city. These were mustered into the United States service June 11th, 1861, and formed companies A and B of the Seventh Massachusetts Regiment of Volunteers, commanded by Colonel, afterwards General, D. N. Couch, of Taunton, and by Lieutenant-Colonel Chester W. Greene, of this city. Besides the above-mentioned companies, a third was formed, composed mainly of "adopted citizens." It was not deemed expedient, however, for them to be mustered into service at the time, and June 5th, 1861, the city government voted that twelve dollars be paid to each member, and they were disbanded. In September, 1861, a bounty of fifteen dollars was authorized to be paid to each volunteer who should join a company then forming, which was afterwards mustered into active service.

The first Fall River soldier who fell in the struggle for the nation's life was Nathaniel S. Gerry, a private in Company A, Seventh Regiment Massachusetts Volunteers; and the first commissioned officer was Lieutenant Jesse D. Bullock, of the same regiment, who died June 25th, 1862, from wounds received at the battle of Fair Oaks. The City Council, as a mark of respect to their memories, attended the funerals of those patriot soldiers in a body, and a deep sense of sadness was manifested throughout the community.

As the war was prosecuted with greater strength and vigor on the part of the Government, the energies put forth by Fall River did not flag. The

President having called for three hundred thousand more men, a public meeting was held July 11th, 1862, at which it was recommended to pay each volunteer for three years' service a bounty of one hundred dollars. The following resolution among others was adopted:

"*Resolved*, That our old men contribute of their substance, and our strong young men tender their services; remembering that if in ancient times 'for a good man some would even dare to die,' surely for the necessary support of a righteous cause there should be no hesitancy because life would be attended with hazard." The resolutions were adopted the next day by the city government, and the mayor was directed to make arrangements for enlisting men. On the 14th of August, 1862, another citizens' meeting was held, at which it was resolved that "the patriotism of Massachusetts will sustain the Government in putting down the rebellion at any cost of men and money." It was also voted to raise, by subscription, money sufficient to add one hundred ($100) dollars to each volunteer's bounty. A resolution was passed to aid the Rev. Elihu Grant to raise a military company for active service. September 1, 1862, the city government voted to pay a bounty of two hundred ($200) dollars to each volunteer for nine months' service, when credited to the quota of the city, and forty-five thousand ($45,000) was appropriated for the purpose.

Thus the work went on, the succeeding years until the close of the war witnessing no diminution in the loyalty or energy of the people. The city furnished 1845 men to aid in trampling under foot the rebellion, which was a surplus of 21 over and above all demands. Thirty-seven of these were commissioned officers. It is hardly within the scope of this chapter to give the names of those who went from this city, or to follow them in their various battles upon the land and sea. They bravely acquitted themselves wherever they were called, many of them cheerfully giving up fine prospects and more than comfortable homes at the behest of patriotism and duty. The roll of 163 names of fallen heroes on the soldiers' monument in Oak Grove Cemetery shows in part only the sacrifice in human life made by Fall River in the struggle for national existence.

The following is a summary of the different regiments in which Fall River men served, and will give a correct idea of the extent of their services. In the three years' regiments of Massachusetts volunteers, the city furnished Companies A and B, of the Seventh Regiment; Company G, Twenty-sixth Regiment; a large portion of Companies F and G, Fifty-eighth Regiment; and a number of men for the Ninth, Eleventh, Twelfth, Sixteenth, Seventeenth, Eighteenth, Nineteenth, Twentieth, Twenty-second, Twenty-fourth, Twenty-fifth, Twenty-eighth, Twenty-ninth, Thirty-second, Thirty-third,

Thirty-seventh, Thirty-ninth, Fortieth, Fifty-fourth, and Fifty-seventh regiments of infantry; also for the Fifth and Sixth Batteries of Light Artillery, Second and Third regiments and First Battalion of Heavy Artillery; and for the First, Second, Fourth, and Fifth regiments of cavalry. Besides the above, Fall River men also served in the Regular Army, General Service, Signal Service, and in regiments from Rhode Island, Connecticut, New York, and Illinois. Four hundred and ninety-seven men from Fall River also served in the United States Navy. In the short-term service the city furnished companies C and D, Third Regiment (9 months), also a number for the Eighth, Forty-third, Forty-sixth, Forty-seventh, and Forty-eighth Regiments, (9 months); for the Sixty-first Regiment (1 year); Company D, Sixteenth Regiment (100 days); Fifth Unattached Company (90 days); Twenty-first Company (100 days); and also men for the Fifth, Fifteenth, Eighteenth, and Twenty-fourth Unattached Companies (100 days).

The amount of money appropriated and expended by the city on account of the war, exclusive of State aid, was one hundred and seven thousand eight hundred and twenty-eight dollars, and three cents ($107,828.03). The sums of money raised and expended by the city during the years of the war for State aid to soldiers' families, and which were repaid by the Commonwealth, were: In 1861, $7,262.25; in 1862, $29,771.67; in 1863, $36,476.10; in 1864, $34,000; in 1865, $20,000. Total amount, $127,510.02.

The city was fortunate in having for municipal officers, as well as in other places of power and trust, men of high integrity and undoubted patriotism. During the whole war, the city government was especially active in striving to promote the public weal. Its members worked hand in hand with the soldiers, encouraging them with words of sympathy and cheer, and by many tokens of material aid. The mayor, through the entire crisis, was Hon. E. P. Buffinton. He was thoroughly acquainted with, and commanded the confidence of the people. His labors were incessant and untiring. Ready in emergency, quick to note the public pulse, a keen observer of men and things, he controlled the masses, and imbued them with his own blunt, unswerving loyalty. He was emphatically the friend of the soldiers, doing all within his power, as chief magistrate, to provide for their needs and to further their interests. Large in stature, his heart corresponded to his physical proportions. His private generosity was as unostentatious as it was unstinted. His services to the city and to the nation were great, and deserve lasting remembrance. The aldermen during the years of the war, all of whom were substantial and trustworthy citizens, and steadfastly coöperated with the mayor in his labors, were: In 1861, George H. Eddy, Nathaniel B. Borden, Asa Pettey, Jr., John Mason, Jr., James Ford, Job B. Ashley; in 1862, Joseph

Borden, Nathaniel B. Borden, Asa Pettey, Jr., John Mason, Jr., James Ford, Job B. Ashley; in 1863, Samuel Hathaway, Joseph Borden, Nathaniel B. Borden, Benjamin Covel, Charles O. Shove, Walter Paine, 3d; in 1864, Weaver Osborn, Joshua Remington, Nathaniel B. Borden, Daniel Stillwell, Walter Paine, 3d, Philip D. Borden; in 1865, James Henry, Joshua Remington, Nathaniel B. Borden, Daniel Stillwell, Walter Paine, 3d, Philip D. Borden.

The member of Congress from this district during the war, and to whom the city is as largely indebted, perhaps, as to any one man, was Hon. James Buffinton. Mr. Buffinton enlisted as a private in Company "A," Seventh Massachusetts Regiment, at an early hour of its organization, and positively declined to be elected to any office therein. He took part in its preparatory drills and movements, marching in the ranks, and went with it when it was mustered into service. At Camp Brightwood, Washington, he was appointed adjutant of the regiment, under Colonel Couch. He performed the duties of his position until the fall session of Congress in 1861, when his constituents demanded his discharge, and the resumption of his seat in Congress. The first mayor of Fall River, and an old resident, he was thoroughly informed concerning the city and its surroundings. The work done by Mr. Buffinton for his soldier constituents was enormous. He was the friend and counsellor of them all. In camp, in hospital, in field, he watched over them. He gave to them without stint, time, labor, money, and unbounded sympathy. When the hills around Washington were white with the tents of the nation's defenders, and when the mails were overflowing with correspondence to their homes, Mr. Buffinton would, after a hard day's work, sit far into the night, until perforce his hand refused longer to write his name, franking the thousands of soldiers' letters brought to him. In every way in his power, he gave comfort and cheer. His influence smoothed rough places and overcame obstacles. Many of the enlisted men and officers from his district were sons of his old friends, and he was to them, away from their homes, at once a father and companion.

In Congress, Mr. Buffinton's course was far-seeing, sagacious, patriotic. He was not gifted with the graces of oratory, and he was seldom heard on the floor of the House; but he had great personal influence and magnetism. Dignified, affable, of commanding presence, intimately acquainted with the prominent men of the time, he seldom failed in accomplishing the things he undertook. Quick to discern, he was prompt to act. He had the quiet persistency, the calm self-possession, that achieves success. Sprung from the good old Quaker stock, that so moulded and shaped events in the early history of Fall River, Mr. Buffinton inherited many of the qualities of his ancestry. He was like them in his methods and habits. The teachings and examples of such men as Oliver Chace, Sen., Edmund Chace, Sen., Daniel Buffinton, and other Quaker settlers here, had left their impress on him; and, although he had grown away, perhaps, from the tenets of their religious faith, the virtues inculcated in his early training steadfastly remained. At the capital, Mr. Buffinton's counsel was much sought by the leading men, and for years he was a colleague of many of the most prominent statesmen of the country. With them he put forth every endeavor for the suppression of the rebellion and preservation of the Union he loved. Citizens and soldiers of Fall River and of New England have abundant reason to cherish his worth and honor his memory, for he gave the best years of his life to the service of his city and his country, and at times, moreover, when that service was fraught with difficulty and peril.

At one of the public meetings held here, it was resolved that "our old men contribute of their substance and our young men tender their services." This resolution was fully carried out. The elderly men did contribute abundantly of the sinews of war, and the young men went forth to fight the battles. The old families, the Bordens, Durfees, Chaces, Buffintons, Davols, were public-spirited and patriotic. They were ready in every emergency with material as well as with moral aid. As a representative man, Colonel Richard Borden was prominent in all loyal endeavors. His influence was as great as his generosity was unbounded. Advanced in years, engrossed in the charge of large manufactures, he nevertheless always answered the numerous calls upon him in his country's behalf. Quiet and retired by nature and disposition, domestic in his habits, his frequent presence at the public assemblages was hailed with enthusiasm. His house was the abode of hospitality, open to statesman, executive, officer, soldier, alike. Fall River, by reason of its prominence as a steamboat connection between New England and New York, was a great centre of transportation. Many regiments from various States passed through the city on their way to or from the capital. Colonel Borden, as agent of the steamboat company, was always ready with his boats at the demand of State or Government officials, and he acquired a reputation far and wide as a prompt and excellent business man.

His private liberality was very large. The soldiers' monument in Oak Grove Cemetery was presented by him, and his deeds of generosity to soldiers and their families were manifold. A rare old man, his memory will ever be green in the hearts of those who knew him.

No allusion to Fall River in the Civil War would be in any sense complete without referring to the noble part acted by her clergy. One and all they were intensely patriotic, and the churches were fortunate in being presided over by men of vigorous loyalty. Especially is the city indebted to the services of Rev. Eli Thurston and Rev. P. B. Haughwout. Mr. Thurston's voice was heard on every public occasion. Who that listened to him can forget his ringing utterances! Strong, logical, incisive, both in thought and speech, he dealt scathing blows at the rebellion and the causes whence it came. His church was always kept, so to speak, attuned to the key-notes of patriotism and duty. He manifested an interest in every public act. A great reader of the press, in the crises of peril he haunted the periodical stores to obtain the latest news. He liked to read the *New York Tribune*, and the stirring appeals of its editor, Horace Greeley, whom in the strong and forcible qualities of his mind Mr. Thurston much resembled. The New York papers were then received the day after their publication, and the Saturday's issue did not arrive till Sunday morning. Mr. Thurston's copy was left at his house, and he used to state in private conversation that he could not resist the temptation to look it over before the morning sermon. But oftentimes the reading so worked upon him, that he had to discontinue the practice, in order to keep his mind calm and free for the duties of the day. Brave preacher of the gospel of truth, champion of liberty, defender of freedom, with him faith has indeed given place to sight.

Mr. Haughwout was a worthy compeer of Mr. Thurston. Quick in action, intense in thought and speech, he too was highly strung to loyalty. He was always eloquent in behalf of his country. He could brook no delay. He was often impatient at men and things. Like Joshua, he would have commanded circumstance and compelled success. He had an intuitive perception of the country's danger, and his historical learning and great research often led him far in advance of the experience of the hour. The eloquent words he uttered in pulpit and on the rostrum will long be remembered. He appealed to every loyal emotion; he kept to glowing heat the fires of patriotism; his sentences were breathing brilliant heart-throbs, animated with love for country and devotion to the cause. He, too, has gone to his reward. The other clergymen were also strenuous in devotion. Rev. Mr. Adams, Rev. Mr. Snow, who afterwards became chaplain in the Third Mass. regiment, Rev. Mr. Chapman, and others, performed well their parts. The Catholic priest, Rev. Edward Murphy, was unsparing in his efforts. His people were taught the strict line of patriotism. Having lived here almost a generation, Father Murphy, as he is lovingly called was really a father to his flock. He loved his people and was loved by them, and he held them with firm, unwavering hand to the path of duty.

The women of Fall River during the struggle were worthy of the city and of the cause. They were constant with their help and loving work.

As early as April 27th, 1861, a ladies' sewing society was organized. For six weeks the members met daily, working from morning until evening, and afterwards they usually came together one afternoon in each week. Many other meetings were held for work and consultation, and several ladies did their work for the society at their own dwellings. Mrs. Richard Borden was the president, Mrs. Avis Ames, vice-president, and Miss A. C. G. Canedy, secretary. The Committee of Arrangements comprised twenty-two of the prominent ladies of the town, and the society retained its organization from April 27th, 1861, to July 28th, 1865, with some change in its officers, although Mrs. Borden remained its president during the entire period. Miss Caroline Borden, the treasurer, Mrs. Ames, Mrs. William Munday, Mrs. S. Angier Chace, Mrs. Mary A. Brayton, Mrs. Mary Young, Mrs. Foster Hooper, Mrs. Mary Durfee, and many other ladies rendered valuable services. The society received during the time of its existence $33347.76 in cash, which was properly expended for materials to be made up for the soldiers. Among the articles furnished were 200 soldiers' uniforms, 231 bed-sacks, 131 bed-quilts, 365 bed-comforters, 87 blankets, 355 sheets, 262 pillows, 307 pillow-cases, 167 cushions for wounds, 90 dressing-gowns, 380 cotton shirts, 292 flannel shirts, 284 shirts, 209 drawers, 1164 pairs woollen hose, 1365 handkerchiefs, 2246 towels, 5589 yards, 323 rolls, 1 box and 4 bundles of bandages, 127 boxes of lint, and a great number and variety of other articles, including pin-cushions, wines, jellies, pictures, newspapers, books, etc., etc. These articles were generally sent to the front through the agents of the Sanitary and Christian commissions. A great number of valuable donations were sent to Portsmouth Grove Hospital, in Rhode Island, only a few miles south of this city, including a Thanksgiving dinner. In November, 1863, a fair was held at the City Hall, extending through several evenings, in the management of which the ladies were very successful. A children's lint society was also kept up during the war, alternating its meetings at the different homes of the children. On the whole, the patriotic devotion of the ladies of Fall River was worthy of great praise.

In the space devoted to this chapter but a general idea can be given of the part Fall River took in the civil war, and it has only been the intention to touch upon the salient points and features of the history of the city during the momentous struggle. The unwritten experience of good deeds done by city and citizen alike is a part of the common heritage. The names of the brave men who went from this city at their country's call, the acts of heroism they performed, the sacrifices they made, the wounds they suffered, the glorious deaths they died, may not be recounted here. These will live in the hearts of their posterity, and are memorials more enduring than any chiselled in granite or sculptured from marble.

Fall River's "West End."

The following description of the principal street and residences of Fall River, about the middle of the fourth decade of this century, is from a paper prepared by one of our older citizens some years since. It embodies his recollections and impressions of those early days, and will doubtless bring to mind many pleasant memories to a few now living, as well as convey some rather surprising information to those younger in years.

Every considerable city or town has usually its West or Court End, so called. Fall River once had a West End. But who, at the present day, walking through Central Street would imagine it was ever the Court End of the town? Let us take a walk down this avenue, noting on either hand the stores, residences, and their occupants as we pass toward the river.

At the south-west corner of Main and Central streets was "Cotton's Corner," so called. The store on this corner, owned by John S. Cotton, was *the* store of the place. The shelves were well filled with a mixed medley of goods—ribbons, tapes, galloon, needles, pins, cambrics, muslins, sheetings, shirtings, factory checks, molasses, butter, cheese, flour, spices, powder, hardware, ox-yokes, plows, stick-baskets, and various other goods—all ready to supply the townspeople and "over the pond-ers." Behind the counter stood the very obliging clerk, John B——, his face full of smiles, ready to anticipate your every want. In front of the store was the market-stand, where the wagons from the country might be seen at early dawn, well supplied with the substantials of life.

On the opposite corner (where is now Durfee Block) was B. W. Chace's store, filled with domestic goods, groceries, crockery, and hollow-ware, where the ladies went to get a new bake-pan, or cover, should the old one be cracked, and where friend Chace was ever ready to give directions how to boil the covers in lye to prevent their cracking. In those days a cracked bake-pan cover, a leaky tea-kettle, and green, round pine-wood were the greatest evils of housekeeping.

Passing westward, the eye was first caught by a building whose basement was used for many years as the Congregational meeting-room, and next by Dr. Durfee's brick-front drug-store, where the Doctor greeted all with a smile and a welcome, while his genteel and polite clerk, H. R——, stood behind the counter to supply customers with pills, or plasters, or whatever they wanted most. Then came the stately residence of Major Durfee, kept as the crack hotel of the place, where the upper ten secured a temporary home. Across the street was the house of Esquire Ford in which Aunt Dorcas kept a lady's shop, where the ladies of the town got all their fine fixings, and found their hearts' desire in things tasty, unique, or antique. Next was I. & D. Leonard's paint-shop. They were the only persons then in town to make the houses shine inside or out. Close by was Messrs. Wilcox & Wardwell's tin-shop, and then S. & J. Smith's meat-market, where the best of steaks were sold for 6¼ cents per pound, and thought high at that. The fish-market was nearly adjoining, so that within a few feet could be obtained fish, flesh, or fowl suited to every appetite. After the Dunbar House came that of Mr. Horton, who kept a stock of West India goods, and whose daughters were the belles of the place. When he died he possessed quite a competence, and from the proceeds of his estate was built, in the old burying-ground, a fine tomb, the first ever erected in this vicinity.

The next structure (Burroughs') was kept as a genteel boarding-house for the overseers, engravers, and clerks of Robeson's Print Works. No gentleman could get boarded for less than *two dollars* per week, and no lady for less than *a dollar and a quarter*.

Crossing the street, and stepping a short distance northward, we enter Stone Lane, on the westerly side of which were several stone cottages, mostly used as boarding-houses for those working in the satinet factory of Samuel Shove & Co., later J. & J. Eddy, and the machine-shop and cotton-mill of O. S. Hawes & Co. A little further along, on the easterly side, was the residence of Aunt Hannah Durfee, in which several young men boarded, who, becoming sometimes a little too boisterous in the exuberance of youthful spirits, were quieted with the threat of being reported to her brother, the Major.

Still further westward, on the north side of Central Street, was a neat little cottage occupied by S. K. Crary, Esq., town clerk, public instructor, and a prominent citizen in other relations. Next came another small cottage; but not so small were the occupants, for the united weight of the two heads of the family was something over a quarter of a ton.

On the south side of the street, standing a little in from the sidewalk, was the Methodist meeting-house, a fine, commodious wooden structure, where gathered weekly crowds of waiting souls to hear the stirring words of truth from the lips of Father Taylor. Occasionally he might be seen leading a band of joyful converts down to the river's edge, there to receive the sacred rite of baptism.

On the north side of the street stood the smithy and dwelling of Father Healy. The smithy was one of the institutions of the day; and especially was the house well *manned*, since the injunction laid down in Genesis 1 : 28 had been faithfully obeyed by Father Healy and his consort. But a short distance off was the hotel of Captain Sanford, furnishing entertainment for man and beast. The captain was a frank, open-hearted man, and studied well the wants of his numerous customers. For their social enjoyment, he built a ten-pin alley under a row of apple-trees in his orchard west of the house, where they exercised their athletic powers without molestation.

Across the street was the Marshall Warren house, a large, square dwelling overlooking the harbor and the mouth of the creek, the descent to which was short and abrupt and not always free from danger.

A few years later, near the junction of Central and Main streets, Mr. Samuel Shove built a large, showy drug-store, with enormous bow-windows, and from these at night shone forth with dazzling lustre the globes of vari-colored waters. This was the store resorted to by the young men of the place for their supplies of the best Spanish-American cigars and mintdrops. Then, too, came the famous store of Messrs. Lovell & Durfee, filled with the choicest groceries to be dealt out to the élite of the West End by Cotton's custom-drawing clerk, the smiling and ubiquitous J. B——.

Such were the residences and attractions, such the style, of Fall River's "West End" in 1834.

SETTLEMENT OF STATE BOUNDARIES—1862.

The territory embracing the present city of Fall River was included in that part of New England subsequently known as Plymouth Colony. Its charter was granted in 1629, and by it one half the waters mentioned as the Narragansett River formed her western limit. The first charter of Rhode Island, granted to Roger Williams in 1643, did not conflict with the claims of Plymouth, but a succeeding one issued by Charles II., in 1663, extended some parts of the eastern boundary of the former three miles to the east and north-east of Narragansett Bay. Plymouth immediately took measures to secure her rights, and, on the report of a special commission appointed by the king, her claims were confirmed.

Until 1740, the boundaries of Plymouth, as established by her original charter of 1629, were recognized as the true boundary between Massachusetts and Rhode Island. In that year, however, Rhode Island sought to have the question reopened, and a commission appointed by George II. rendered a decision which was immediately appealed from by both provinces. The award, nevertheless, was confirmed by the king in 1746. The lines thus decreed were run *ex parte* by Rhode Island. Massachusetts, having good reason to suppose that the boundaries had been marked in accordance with the decree of the king, took no measures to have them examined until 1791, when, on account of renewed difficulties, the *ex-parte* lines of Rhode Island were properly examined, and found in every case to infringe upon Massachusetts territory.

One of the decrees in the king's award mentioned "a certain point four hundred and forty rods to the southward of the mouth of the Fall River,' from which a line was to be run three miles towards the east, forming the northern boundary of that part of Rhode Island. In measuring this four hundred and forty rods, the *ex-parte* commissioners of 1746 " measured round a cove or inlet, and followed the sinuosities of the shore" until they reached a point from a quarter to a half mile further north than if the same distance had been measured in a straight line. From this point they extended the three-mile line, running it through the southern part of the village of Fall River at the old Buttonwood Tree, so called, on Main street, a little north of the present line of Columbia Street. No definite decision of the question in dispute was reached at the time, and in 1844 another commission was appointed, which in 1848 made a report to their respective legislatures.

In a matter so seriously affecting the interests of Fall River, it was deemed expedient to appoint a committee, consisting of Rev. Orin Fowler, Dr. Foster Hooper, and Dr. Phineas W. Leland, to petition the Massachusetts Legislature not to allow any settlement of the boundary line less advantageous than that granted by George II. in 1746. This committee claimed, and gave good reasons therefor, that George II. designed that the point from which to run the three-mile line should be 440 rods in a *direct* line from the mouth of the Fall River. They showed that in making these measurements as they had, "the Rhode Island commissioners added to their State a thickly-settled territory with about 1500 inhabitants, and a taxable property valued at nearly half a million of dollars, when, if the measurements had been made in straight lines, not only would the design of George II. and his commissioners have been carried out, but Fall River would have been brought within the bounds of one State, with no danger of its thickly-settled territory being again placed under a divided jurisdiction." In consequence of these representations, the Massachusetts Legislature refused to ratify the decision of the commissioners of 1848, and, by agreement of the two States, the question was referred to the United States Supreme Court.

In 1860 the Supreme Court appointed engineers, with instructions to measure and mark a described line which should be the true boundary between the two States, the decree to take effect in March, 1862. The full claim of neither State was granted, but such a boundary fixed as to give an undivided jurisdiction to densely-populated districts, without infringing on the rights of any. By this change of boundary, Massachusetts acquired a territory comprising about 11 square miles. Of this, about 9 square miles, with a population of nearly 3600 and a taxable property of some $2,000,000, were embraced within the limits of the city of Fall River.

The Great Fire, July 2, 1843.

A distinct point of departure in Fall River chronology is the devastating conflagration which in 1843 swept away in a few hours the accumulations of years of industrious enterprise. Few fires have wrought a more wholesale destruction than this. The community, which has builded a strong, robust city upon the ruins of the burned village, retains a very vivid memory of the scourge that levelled its best streets thirty-four years ago. Among these sad recollections there are, moreover, not wanting those that are pleasant, happiest of all being a cherished memory of the demonstrations of sympathy and material aid its desolation called out from all parts of the land, New Orleans and Savannah joining with New York and Boston in their contributions to the suffering people.

About three o'clock on the afternoon of Sunday, while the church-going part of the community were wending their way to the several houses of worship, an alarm of fire was heard. The crowd of citizens who hurried towards the locality of the danger most feared in manufacturing neighborhoods, discovered a small carpenter's shop on the north side of Borden Street, near the corner of Main, entirely enveloped in flames and the fiery element already threatening adjoining buildings. The early summer of 1843 was an unusually hot and dry period. The water in the stream was very low, and the flume, which was then undergoing repairs, was entirely empty. The time, moreover, was years anterior to the introduction of steamers, and the sole defence of Fall River against serious conflagrations consisted in a few small hand-engines, worked by volunteer firemen, and the improvised bucket brigade of house-owners.

Operating such poor agencies as best they could, and relying almost desperately upon their natural dependence, the half-depleted stream, for water, the citizens worked manfully in their fight against the terrible element. A strong, fresh wind from the south was blowing at the inception of the fire, and its fierce impulse hurled danger and ruin directly into the heart of the city. No rain having descended for weeks, the thickly populated quarter—largely constructed of wood, its roofs and cornices dried to the consistency of tinder by the prolonged summer heat—offered but the slightest resistance to the flying embers. At one moment more than a score of dwellings and stores were in flames, and but an instant's embrace of the raging element seemed sufficient to reduce the stateliest victim. For seven hours the devastation continued. Meanwhile, the sympathizing people of Bristol, ten miles distant, had hurried to the scene of disaster, the same gale that impelled the flames speeding their white-winged craft, with the fire-engine on board, through the ferry and up the bay. The scene was truly heart-rending—a thriving community absolutely in the grasp of a relentless enemy, with hardly a weapon of defence in its possession.

Strong men still living shudder at the remembrance of that sad Sabbath afternoon. Before the most hopeful vision, no hope seemed to rise. Happily, however, a merciful Providence intervened at last to save a portion of the town. Guided by His wise order who rules the powers of that nature which he created and governs, the wind suddenly changed its course, blew in an opposite direction from the district still untouched, and finally subsided.

The destruction had been very large, comparatively enormous. The area burned over covered twenty acres in the heart of the village, extending from Borden Street, on the south, to Franklin Street, on the north. All the stores in the place, except six or eight in the remote suburbs, were in ruins.

The occasion of the fire, as finally discovered, was the thoughtless mischief of a few Sabbath-breaking boys, who were amusing themselves with a small cannon, a burning wad from which inflamed a dry heap of wood-shavings that had accumulated under the floor of the carpenter's shop. Near the close of the conflagration, preparations were made to blow up with gunpowder several structures that stood as helpers to its progress, but the subsidence of the gale rendered such continued procedure unnecessary.

The following summary of buildings destroyed and trades temporarily dispossessed was published soon after the fire:

Number of families residing within the burnt district at the time of the fire	225
Persons belonging to those families	1,334
Persons in addition, employed or doing business in the burnt district, but living out, about	600
Number of buildings burned, not including the smaller ones	196
Of which there were used as dwelling-houses, and occupied by one or more families each	95
Hotels	2
Churches (Methodist and Christian Union)	3
Cotton factory (Old Bridge Mill)	1
Carriage factories	2
Banks	2
Cabinet warehouses	3
Marble factory	1
Tannery	1
Livery stables	4
Dry-goods establishments destroyed	17
Clothing " "	11
Grocery and provision establishments, including 3 or 4 crockery stores connected	24
Boot and shoe stores destroyed	6
Hat and cap " "	3
Book and periodical stores destroyed	3
Hardware " "	3
Milliners' shops destroyed	11

Mantua-makers' shops destroyed			5	School-house destroyed			1
Apothecaries'	"	"	6	School-rooms besides destroyed			3
Jewellers'	"	"	3	Athenæum	"		1
Harness-makers'	"	"	3	Custom-house	"		1
Stove and tinware	"	"	3	Post-office	"		1
Brass foundries destroyed			2	Auction-room	"		1
Blacksmiths' shops destroyed			3	Counting-rooms	"		7
Machine	"	"	2	Dentists' "	"		2
Carpenters'	"	"	8	Stage office	"		1
Reed-maker's shop	"		1	Printing offices	"		3
Shoe-makers' shops	"		7	Lawyers' "	"		5
Plane-maker's shop	"		1	Physicians' "	"		5
Roll-coverer's "	"		1	Barbers' shops	"		3
Turner's	"	"	1				
Painters' shops	"		8	Whole amount of loss on buildings			$264,470
Butchers' "	"		4	" " " other property			262,015
Soap-boiler's shop	"		1				$526,485
Cigar factory	"		1	Whole amount of insurance			175,475
Restaurants	"		7				
Bake-houses	"		2	Excess of loss			$351,010

POPULATION—1810-1875.

POPULATION OF FALL RIVER AT VARIOUS TIMES.

1810	1,296	1849	11,003	1858	12,815	1867	21,174		
1820	1,594	1850	11,170	1859	12,524	1868	23,023		
1830	4,159	1851	10,786	1860	13,240	1869	25,099		
1840	6,738	1852	11,605	1861	14,026	1870	27,191		
1844	9,054	1853	12,285	1862*	17,461	1871	28,291		
1845	10,290	1854	12,700	1863	15,495	1872	34,835		
1846	11,174	1855	12,630	1864	17,114	1873	38,464		
1847	11,646	1856	12,926	1865	17,525	1874	43,289		
1848	10,922	1857	12,395	1866	19,262	1875	45,160		

* The increase in population in 1862 was owing to the annexation of the town of Fall River, R. I., which contained a population of about 3,590.

VALUATION, ETC., 1854-1875.

VALUATION, TAX, ETC., FOR THE LAST TWENTY-TWO YEARS.

Year.	Valuation.	Tax.	Amount raised by Taxation.	No. Polls.	Year.	Valuation.	Tax.	Amount raised by Taxation.	No. Polls.
1854	$8,939,215	$5 80	$56,523 70	3,117	1865	$12,134,990	$16 50	$200,272 20	4,461
1855	9,768,420	5 60	59,425 15	3,148	1866	12,762,534	17 50	232,827 62	4,740
1856	9,888,070	6 20	66,078 26	3,181	1867	15,220,628	17 00	269,020 95	5,135
1857	10,041,610	7 40	83,161 61	3,241	1868	17,919,192	14 00	262,872 74	6,002
1858	9,923,495	7 20	77,929 35	3,208	1869	21,398,525	15 60	346,310 99	6,247
1859	10,700,250	7 00	79,583 25	3,121	1870	23,612,214	15 30	374,753 22	6,743
1860	11,522,650	7 40	90,124 61	3,238	1871	29,141,117	13 00	392,974 15	7,070
1861	11,261,065	8 60	102,162 04	3,544	1872	37,841,294	12 00	471,835 53	8,870
1862	12,497,720	11 00	146,045 30	4,288	1873	47,416,246	13 00	636,451 61	10,020
1863	12,696,105	11 50	154,218 76	4,105	1874	49,995,110	12 80	662,486 11	11,119
1864	11,057,645	18 00	207,731 61	4,304	1875	51,401,467	14 50	768,464 37	11,571

In 1840 the number of taxable polls was 1,603. The valuation of real estate was $1,678,603; of personal estate, $1,310,865; total, $2,989,468.

ONE HUNDREDTH ANNIVERSARY
OF
AMERICAN INDEPENDENCE,

July 4th, 1876.

OFFICIAL PROGRAMME.

GRAND
CENTENNIAL CELEBRATION
OF
AMERICAN INDEPENDENCE,

4th July, 1876,

AT

FALL RIVER, MASS.

4.30 A.M.

GRAND SALUTE of One Hundred Guns, on the Park. Raising of the National Flag.

6.30 A.M.

RINGING of ALL the BELLS of the City for half an hour.

9 A.M.

The several divisions of the military and civic procession will form as follows:

First Division on east side of Main Street, right resting on Bedford Street.

Second Division on north side of Pleasant Street, right resting on Main Street, with left of line extending along east side of Second Street.

Third Division on north side of Pleasant Street, right resting on Second Street.

Fourth Division (with the exception of the coal trade) on the north side of Bedford Street, right resting on Main Street. The coal trade to form on south side of Central Street, right resting on Main Street. And at 9.30 A.M., sharp, the procession will move in the following order:

Police Skirmishers.
Platoon of Police.

Marshal, Col. BRADFORD D. DAVOL.
Chief of Staff, Capt. S. L. BRALEY.

AIDS.

James T. Milne,   Wm. E. Dunham,
Nathan D. Chace, Charles C. Buffinton,
Clark Chase,   Earl P. Bowen,
Daniel E. Chace, Horatio N. Durfee,
Timothy T. O'Keefe, Alvan C. Seymour,
George H. Borden.

FIRST DIVISION.

Chief of Division,
Aids.   Major JOHN M. DEANE.   Aids.

Third Regiment Band.
Co. B, Third Regiment, M. V. M.
Friendly Union Lodge, I. O. O. F.
Court of Good Samaritans, 5910.
Caledonians.

SECOND DIVISION.

Aids. Chief of Division, Aids.
GEORGE O'BRIEN.

St. Mary's Band.
St. John's Catholic T. A. and M. R. Society.
Young Men's I. A. C. T. A. and B. Society.
St. Patrick T A. and M. R. Society.
Sacred Heart T. A. and B. Society.
St. Joseph's Society (Cadets), 60 muskets.
Ancient Order of Hibernians, Division No. 1.
Ancient Order of Hibernians, Division No. 2.
Knights of St. Patrick.

THIRD DIVISION.

FLORAL AND NATIONAL CARS.

Aids. Chief of Division, Aids.
R. K. REMINGTON.

1st Regiment U. S. Artillery Band.
No. 1.—FLORAL CAR.
No. 2.—GROTTO.
No. 3.—FLORAL CAR.
No. 4.—INDIAN SCENE.
No. 5.—1776.
No. 6.—DECLARATION OF INDEPENDENCE.
No. 7.—AMERICA.
No. 8.—ENGLAND.
No. 9.—IRELAND.
No. 10.—FRANCE.
No. 11.—1876.

FOURTH DIVISION.

TRADES.

Aids. Chief of Division, Aids.
JAMES P. HILLIARD.

American Linen Company.
Fiske & Munroe.
Covel & Sandford.
F. R. Water Works.
Davis & Fish.
Martin Wallace.
Cook & Grew.
Fraprie & Watters.

F. R. Laundry.
Kinsley's Express.
J. D. Flint & Co.
D. W. Baldwin.
Cobb, Bates & Yerxa.
F. R. Plumbing Co.
Dailey's Tea Store.
Edward Herbert.
F. R. Coal Co.
J. A. Bowen & Co.
M. T. Bennett, Jr., & Co.
Wm. Hawes & Co.

The Route of March will be as follows: North Main, Locust, Rock, Prospect, Highland Avenue, Winter, Cherry, Linden, Bank, Ford, Bedford, Quarry, Pleasant, Fourth, Morgan, and South Main Streets to the Park, from thence through South Main to the City Hall, where the procession will pass in review before His Honor the Mayor and the City Government and dismiss.

12 O'CLOCK M.

RINGING OF BELLS of the City for half an hour.

12.30 P.M.

TUB RACE on the Ponds for Prizes of $12, $8 and $5.

1 P.M.

GRAND YACHT RACE on the River, for Prizes amounting to $150.

2.30 P.M.

CALEDONIAN GAMES on the Park, fifteen in number, and Three Prizes for each game.
Music by the 1st Regiment U. S. Artillery Band.

LIST OF GAMES.

	$6	$4	$2
Throwing hammer,	$6	$4	$2
Standing high jump,	5	3	1
Sack race over 18-inch hurdles,	5	2	1
Putting stone,	6	3	2
Mile race,	8	6	3
Hitch and kick,	6	4	2
Highland fling,	6	3	2
Wheelbarrow race,	5	2	1
Pole vaulting,	8	4	2
Boys' race (under 12 years),	3	2	1
Hop, step, and jump,	6	3	2
Short race, twice around,	6	3	2
Tossing caber,	5	3	2
Three-legged race,	5	3	2
Quoits, on natural sod,	6	4	—

Twenty-five cents will be charged from all competitors for each game.

No person allowed within the ring but the committee, competitors, judges, pipers, and members of the press.

All persons wishing to compete will hand in their names to the committee at least one game ahead of the one they wish to compete for.

The judges to be appointed by the committee, and their decision to be final and indisputable.

The games to be conducted under the Rules of the N. A. U. C. A.

3 P.M.

PARADE OF BATTALION of ANTIQUES and HORRIBLES, which will be one of the finest events of the day.

Platoon of Police.
Aids.   Chief Marshal.   Aids.
Third Regiment Band.
Colonel and Chaplain in Carriages.
Cavalcade.
Staff.   GOVERNOR.   Staff.
Band of Tin.
Infantry.
St. Mary's Band.

Varieties of all kinds, both Ancient and Modern, representing every thing under the Sun and Moon, going from grave to gay, from civil life to City Hall; on the earth and under the sea.

In fact, comprising all that is laughable or serious on the earth or above it.

ROUTE OF PARADE.

From Torrent Hall to Park, where there will be a grand review; from Park to Morgan Street, Morgan to Fourth, Fourth to Pleasant, Pleasant to Main, and pass in review before His Honor the Mayor and City Government; Main to Franklin, Franklin to Winter, Winter to Prospect, Prospect to Rock, Rock to Franklin, Franklin to Main, Main to Torrent Hall, and dismiss.

6.30 P.M.

RINGING OF BELLS of City for thirty minutes.

7 P.M.

GRAND SALUTE of One Hundred Guns, on Highland Avenue.

7.30 P.M.

CONCERT ON THE PARK, from 7.30 to 9.30, by St. Mary's Band.

7.30 P.M.

CONCERT at CORNER of HIGHLAND AVENUE and PROSPECT STREET, 7.30 to 9.30.

During the evening the Balcony of the City Hall will be illuminated with gas jets, representing a shield, with the word "Liberty" over it, and the figures 1776 and 1876 on either side.

Fireworks of all kinds are prohibited on the route of the processions during their formation or march.

The citizens are requested to decorate their residences during the day and illuminate them at night; in fact, to unite as a people in making the day one we shall be glad to remember as the Centennial Anniversary of our Nation.

COMMITTEE.

Mayor JAS. F. DAVENPORT, *Chairman*,
Alderman HOLDER B. DURFEE,
Alderman BRADFORD D. DAVOL,
Alderman P. R. SULLIVAN,
Councilman WM. E. DUNHAM,
Councilman JOSEPH WATERS,
Councilman PHILIP H. REGAN,
Councilman C. V. S. REMINGTON, *Secretary*.

CORPORATE ANNALS

OF

FALL RIVER.

SKETCHES OF MAYORS

Hon. James Buffinton, First Mayor.

HON. JAMES BUFFINTON was born on "Chaloner Hill," in Troy,—now Fall River,—Mass., March 16th, 1817. His parents removed to Swanzey, near the village of that name, in his infancy, where the first years of his childhood were passed, and where he commenced attending school; but soon the interests of the family caused their return to his native village, which henceforward became his home. His earlier years were those of self-denial and constraint, yet all through his boyhood and youth his promptness in thought and independence in action were indicative of the coming man. His parents were members of the Society of Friends, his mother being an approved minister of that body of Christians for many years. She was careful in the training of her youngest born—the subject of this sketch—to inculcate in his mind the love of truth and virtue, to lay a foundation for the principles of honesty and uprightness, and to nurture him in a strict regard for the same.

He attended public and private schools a part of each twelvemonth, until he was some fifteen years of age, when he was sent for two or three terms to the Friends' boarding-school, in Providence, R. I., where he made good use of his privileges, and progressed satisfactorily in his studies. Here, as elsewhere, the activity of an irrepressible nature often led him to the front, and in sports and exercises of muscular power and skill he ever showed an ambition to lead. After leaving school, he commenced the study of medicine with the late Dr. Thomas Wilbur, pursuing his investigations in this science successfully to the period when he should have attended medical lectures, as a finishing step to make him a veritable M.D. Failing to obtain the necessary funds at the proper time satisfactorily to himself, he turned his attention to teaching, and spent two or three years as a preceptor in public and private schools at Westport, and afterwards in Dartmouth, at or near Padanaram, the southern extremity of the town. Here, from constant association with men interested in navigation, his thoughts were turned in this direction, and he finally shipped for a whaling voyage on board the ship South Carolina, about to sail from that port.

Making a successful voyage, he returned home and engaged in business as a druggist. Subsequently, abandoning this enterprise, he entered the dry-goods and millinery trade. About this time, also, he united in marriage with Miss Sarah Perkins.

These changes in his earlier life *may* seem to some evidences of a weak and vacillating mind, while in fact they were only caused by those circumstances which affect most young men dependent upon their own exertions.

During these years he possessed the full confidence of his fellow-townsmen, who often, by their suffrages, acknowledged his qualifications, electing him to positions of trust and usefulness. He was a prominent and efficient member of the Fire Department, and in 1851 was chosen selectman, being re-elected in 1852, and again in 1853.

On the adoption of a city charter, in 1854, he was elected mayor by a majority over all of 331, in an aggregate of 1261 votes. This was the year when the city was visited by Asiatic cholera, which raged as an epidemic, causing much distress and grief to many of our poorer families and to some of those in higher life. In this emergency he was often called upon for assistance, and in his official capacity met all calls wisely and well, promptly rendering services personally which others would not give for humanity's sake or for adequate reward. He visited the ill and destitute, and ministered to their immediate necessities with his own hands, removed the sick and dying to the hospital provided by the city for their comfort and care, and in several instances prepared the dead for decent burial. His course in these fearful weeks of suffering made him many firm personal friends, who never forgot his self-sacrifice and devotion when others, panic-stricken by the scourge, forsook and neglected them.

At the second city election, in 1855, he was re-elected mayor; but the same autumn, his executive abilities having become more generally known and appreciated, at a convention called to nominate a candidate for Representative in Congress, he was chosen by acclamation, and subsequently elected by a majority of several thousand. Thus was opened to him a wider field for those qualities of mind and heart which nature and culture had given him, and which secured for him a re-election again and again. He was in many respects a model Representative, faithful to duty, watchful over the interests of his own constituents, and eminently loyal to his country. His votes were invariably cast for the right, his voice outspoken for liberty, and his influence always in the interest of the welfare and prosperity of the nation at large. He was a consistent and persistent friend of the slave, losing no opportunity to swell the constantly increasing demand for universal freedom. When the rebellion was being inaugurated, his attention in the House was, if possible, increased, and no effort was lost to advance the nation's cause and preserve her life and usefulness. On his return home, early in the spring of 1861, he immediately set influences at work to raise a company of volunteers in person, joining the "boys in blue" in their drill, their marches through the street, and in all their preparations to become defenders of their country's life and integrity.

In 1864 Mr. Buffinton having declined a re-nomination for Congress, accepted an office in the Internal Revenue Department, tendered him by the United States Government during President Johnson's administration.

The duties of this office—General Treasury Agent—were satisfactorily performed for a year or two, when he was appointed Revenue Collector for the First District of Massachusetts, which office he held until after the death of Mr. Eliot, his successor in Congress, in June, 1870, when he was again elected, by those whom he had so faithfully served in previous years, as their representative in the national councils. He served two terms, and was re-elected for a third, when death intervened. Thus was spent the remainder of his useful life, the last few weeks in distress of body, yet to the last with the same alert mind, anxious to do his whole duty, prompt in his attendance upon each session of the House, and finally dying with the harness on. He remained in his seat, against the wishes of his friends, until the adjournment of Congress, when he came home to die in less than one hour after being welcomed by his beloved domestic circle, Sabbath morning, March 6th, 1874.

The news of his arrival home, and the sad and startling intelligence of his death, were rapidly spread from lip to ear throughout the city, and many of his devoted friends, political and others, hastened to offer their condolence and sympathy to his bereaved family.

His funeral obsequies were attended by a large concourse of relatives and friends, residents of this and many other towns in the State. Remarks were made by a number of the clergy of the city eulogistic of his manly and honorable course in life, and regretful, yet submissive to the decrees of divine Providence, for his comparatively sudden and unexpected removal from the scenes of earthly labor.

The procession bearing his body to its last resting-place, in Oak Grove Cemetery, passed through weeping hosts of his less-honored fellow-citizens, who remembered his care over and provision for them in their time of dire suffering and trial, and thus manifested their respect and regard for one who had proved himself unquestionably their friend in all the public positions of honor and of influence where, by their suffrages, they had delighted to assist in placing him.

Hon. Edward P. Buffinton, Second Mayor.

Under a government like ours, where arbitrary and conventional distinctions are unknown, and blood has but little or nothing to do with the advancement of men to positions of responsible trusts, and where all the avenues to preferment are open to honorable competition, it is in no wise surprising that so many from the humbler walks of life attain to places of coveted exaltation. Indeed the surprise would be greater were this not the case, for it is patent that, in human affairs, the great majority of persons of this class have come from humble life ; and it is this fact that gives greatest lustre to the spirit and genius of our institutions. With these few words do we preface the brief biographical sketch of one who in life endeared himself to all who knew him.

Edward Purington Buffinton, son of Aaron and Rebecca Buffinton, was born in Westport, Mass., November 16th, 1814. His parents coming to Fall River when he was but a lad, he was almost to the "manor born," and grew up personally interested in all that related to the prosperity of the growing town. Early in life he became satisfied that man was born to labor, and, acting upon the good sense and sound and comprehensive logic conveyed in the lines

> "He who by the plough would thrive,
> Must either hold, himself, or drive,"

applied himself diligently to business, proudly conscious that working for daily bread was as honorable as it was necessary to the development of manly youth and robust, healthy manhood. As a consequence, he was hardly in his teens before he was known as a hardworking, money-saving boy. His school advantages were quite limited ; but, like many other boys similarly situated, he tried to make up, as far as he could, his lack of school-hours, by devoting all his spare minutes to the acquisition of such knowledge as could be made practically available in after-life. His motto was, "Whatever I undertake to do, I will do it the best I know how ;" and his steady, undeviating fidelity to this line of action went very far towards making him the man he was. He was a great reader of the lighter kind of literature, and loved so well to read aloud that he would sit by the winter fireside at home and read for hours, to the comfort of his mother and the edification of the family. His reading, if it did not strengthen and sharpen his habits of thinking, at least gave him a good insight into the workings of the human organization, and developed, to their richest blossoming, those gentler attributes of our natures—love, kindness, affection—which constitute the charm of social intercourse, sweeten home-life, and make it so full of enjoyment.

Mr. Buffinton engaged in business for himself early in life as a market-man, following the occupation of his father. His market was on the corner of Main and Pocasset streets, until the erection of the town-hall and market-building in 1846, when he removed thither, and continued in the same pursuit until the close of his life, being one of the leading merchants in that department. Mr. Buffinton was "as honest as the days are long," regarding sham and pretence with a hatred as strong as was his love and respect for clean, downright, every-day honesty in everything and everywhere. Living and acting upon the grand old proverb that "worth makes the man," and realizing, in its fullest conception, the fact that every honest calling is honorable—be it preaching, pleading, or marketing,—he strove to dignify his business to the honorable rank of a profession by honoring it himself.

It is not surprising that one growing up with the growth of the town, interested in all that appertained to its prosperity, and actively participating in most of its earlier organizations, should become popular with all classes, secure the good-will of the people, and be complimented with honorable expressions of it. In 1852 Mr. Buffinton was elected to the Massachusetts House of Representatives, where he showed the same fidelity to his convictions that characterized him in all his business relations of life. Continuing to enjoy the confidence of the people, in 1854, when Fall River changed its form of government and became a city, he was honored with an election to the Board of Aldermen, and in November, 1855, was chosen by the city government to the mayoralty, to fill the vacancy occasioned by the resignation of Hon. James Buffinton, who had been elected to the national House of Representatives. The following year, 1856, he was elected to the same office by the people. The three succeeding years he devoted to his business and private affairs, during which he was free from the cares and responsibilities of official life, and happy in the change. In 1860, however, he was again elected to the mayoralty, and held the office for seven consecutive years—a period during which our country went through the most trying ordeal in its history.

From the inauguration of the rebellion to its close, Mr. Buffinton was at the head of the city government, and had an experience from which a man of weaker nerve and baser metal would have shrunk discouraged. But he bore up under the pressure laid upon him with a fortitude and firmness that astonished even his most ardent admirers. His labors were almost incessant day and night, in season and out of season, but he never for a moment faltered in the discharge of his duties, and his entire administration was distinguished for judiciousness, care, economy, and humanity. A patriot to the core, he did every thing that one in his position could do to help put down the rebellion and preserve our liberties. He stood the strain upon his patience with a moderation and resoluteness that reflect honor both upon his character as a magistrate and as a man, and, while doing all in his power toward the furtherance of the cause and struggle for freedom, was carefully considerate of those who went from our midst to fight its battles and win its victories, and humanely thoughtful of those they had left behind. With an eye to the economical administration of city affairs, he was uniformly careful in his dealings with those who thronged his office for aid, and if he ever erred in judgment, it was always on the side of humanity. Though a large man, his heart was the largest part of him, and the record of his administration during the years of our civil strife is one of noble heart-service. His love of approbation corresponded with his kindness of heart, and nothing grieved him more than to find that his best-directed efforts in any line of action failed to be properly appreciated. He was sensitive, as is every true man, to the touch even of ingratitude, and nothing wounded him deeper than the indifference of those to whom, some time in life, he had shown generous and timely favors. His sense of justice was remarkably keen, and rarely, if ever, was he at fault in judgment. His readiness to assist others became proverbial, and his generous nature often led him to do for his friends that which ended in serious pecuniary losses to himself. At home he was a devoted husband and a kind, indulgent father.

Not a great man, as the world estimates greatness, he was one who gained the highest respect of his fellow-citizens, and held it to the last.

His death occurred on the morning of October 2d, 1871, and with his burial was laid to rest all that was mortal of one whose life and service must, in the years to come, hold an important place, and constitute one of the brightest chapters in the history of our city.

Hon. Nathaniel B. Borden, Third Mayor.

Hon. Nathaniel B. Borden was born April 15th, 1801, and died April 10th, 1865. His birthplace was in a house which stood formerly on the south side of Pocasset Street, a short distance from Main Street. This house had a local celebrity from the fact that two British soldiers were shot and killed at its eastern doorway when the British made their attack upon the village during the Revolutionary War.

To a common country-school tuition he added a few months' attendance at the Plainfield Academy, Connecticut, but having soon abandoned the idea of acquiring a liberal education, he returned home, and, though scarcely twenty years of age, was elected clerk and treasurer of the Pocasset Company, then but just formed. He held this position till 1837, when he resigned on account of the press of public duties. He was a member of the Massachusetts Legislature in 1831, 1834, 1851, and 1864. He was a Representative in the Congress of the United States from

1837 to 1840 inclusive, and again in 1843-44. To his duties as a legislator he brought extensive practical knowledge, a cool, deliberative judgment, and a firm purpose to do what he believed to be right in itself, regardless of personal or party consequences, ever placing his convictions of public duty above real or supposed personal interests.

At the time of the agitation of Free Masonry and anti-Masonry he took decided grounds against secret institutions in a free country, and, it is said, opened his own house for anti-Masonic meetings when no other place could be obtained for the purpose.

He was among the early and prominent friends of the slave, and assisted many a fugitive, either directly or indirectly, on his road to freedom. At a time when it was fashionable to mob Abolitionists he opened the Washington School-House, then his private property, in which to form an anti-slavery society.

He was for many years in local public life as town clerk, selectman, highway surveyor, and a sort of general guardian to look after the interests and welfare of the community, thereby contributing largely towards securing the good order, credit, and prosperity of the town and city. He believed it to be a duty for every citizen to serve his country when called upon to occupy any official position for which he was qualified. Under the municipal organization he was an alderman for several years, holding that position at his death. In 1856 he was chosen mayor, and during the trying times of the winter of 1856-7, while the mills were stopped and hundreds were out of employment and destitute, he employed many of the idle laborers having no legal residence here, at a low rate, in necessary work about the city. He believed it to be a just and wise as well as a humane policy to provide for their wants temporarily, and secure to the city, at the same time, the benefits of their cheap labor. They were thus retained, at comparatively little additional expense to the city, where their useful services would again soon be required, and the objectionable course avoided of throwing them as a burden upon the State, with all the family disorder and social degradation consequent thereupon.

At various times he held the position of president of the Fall River Savings Bank, the Fall River Union Bank, and Fall River Railroad Company, performing the duties devolving upon him with efficiency and zeal.

He possessed naturally a happy, cheerful disposition, was a pleasant companion, and often manifested a versatile talent and great powers of endurance. With a moral integrity unimpeached and unimpeachable, a large heart, and generous sympathies, he passed through life shedding light upon and assisting, by kindly acts, his fellow-man wherever found, without regard to the color of his skin, the place of his birth, or the nature of his creed. Liberal in his religious faith and upright in his daily walk, he was to oppression an enemy, to the oppressed a friend. By his death the city lost a faithful public servant, and the poor their best benefactor.

Hon. Josiah C. Blaisdell, Fourth Mayor.

Hon. Josiah C. Blaisdell was born in Campton, New Hampshire, on the 22d of October, 1820. In his boyhood he attended the common district school, and later was a member of the Literary and Scientific Institution at Hancock, N. H. While yet a young man, he removed with his parents to Methuen, Mass., from whence, in 1843, he came to Fall River for the purpose of entering the law office of James Ford, Esq. Upon the completion of his studies, he engaged in the practice of his profession, and has continued its active duties to the present day, rising step by step, until he has gained a foremost position at the bar of his adopted town, and has become generally well known in this section of the State.

His first entrance into public life was in 1858, when he was elected a member of the Massachusetts House of Representatives. In 1864 he was appointed, by Governor John A. Andrew, a member of the Board of State Charities, completing an unexpired term of two years. In 1866 he was reappointed to the same office, by Governor Alexander H. Bullock, for a further term of seven years, but resigned after serving two years. He was chosen a member of the State Senate in 1865, and again of the House in 1866.

In 1858, by the suffrages of his fellow-citizens, he was nominated and elected mayor of the city, and in 1859 was complimented with a re-election to the same prominent and responsible office. His administration of public affairs was marked by a rigid attention to economy, and, if distinguished in no other respect, was, at least, peculiar in this, that it lived *within* its income. The years of his mayoralty coming just after the crisis and business depression of 1856-7, it was the demand and expectation of the citizens that the government should be conducted judiciously, faithfully, and economically; that no new enterprises should be entered upon unless imperatively demanded; that "acts and deeds of retrenchment" should be the watchword throughout the year; and in accordance with this well-known and positive expression of the people's wishes municipal affairs were administered.

Realizing that the head of the government exerted no inconsiderable influence upon his associates in office, Mr. Blaisdell clearly defined the scope of work demanded by the times, and, by careful and judicious suggestions, provided for such action only as would promote the interest and prosperity of the city. The two years of his administration were distinguished, therefore, by the preservation and continuance of existing public affairs rather than the inauguration of new and untried enterprises. Attention was chiefly devoted to the ordinary departments of municipal life; "to the public schools, those guide-boards to growth and intelligence; to the police, the conservators of peace and good order; to the fire department, that the means and facilities for extinguishing fires might be always ready; and especially to finances, that excessive taxation might not retard the growth of the city, nor parsimony belittle her position." Thus husbanding her resources, the city was placed in a position to enter upon that career of enterprise and expansion which has characterized her progress since the opening of the year 1860.

Since Mr. Blaisdell's terms in the mayoralty and as Representative and Senator, he has been brought by official life more or less continuously before the public, and in 1874, upon the organization of the "Second District Court of Bristol," in recognition of his qualifications as a lawyer and a man of sound and discreet judgment, he was appointed presiding judge. He has since that date filled the position ably and well, to the satisfaction of his brethren of the bar and the public at large.

Hon. George O. Fairbanks, Fifth Mayor.

George Otis Fairbanks, the oldest child—and only son—of a family of nine children, was born in Medway, Norfolk County, Mass., February 14th, 1815.

His parents lived upon a farm, and during the first ten years of his life he passed the time, as was customary in those days for farmers' sons, in light work about the homestead and in attending school, receiving all the advantages and privileges both of public and private tuition within convenient distance of his home. He left the public school when thirteen years old, but spent some portion of the following four years at a private school, or in study at the Medway Classical Institution.

Being then seventeen, he commenced teaching, and four of the next five years were spent —the autumn and winter months—at this employment in the neighboring towns of Upton and Canton. During these four years—the fifth being one of confinement by sickness—when not teaching or studying, he worked on his father's farm, or was engaged as clerk or assistant in manufacturing establishments within the limits of his native town. At the expiration of this period he commenced teaching as a permanent employment, and for some eight or nine years was thus engaged in the town of Dedham and in the city of Lowell, where he became a popular instructor, and won the esteem and confidence of the community.

Leaving Lowell, he went to the town of Newburyport, where he continued teaching two years more, and then, making one of those changes so common and characteristic of young men in New England communities, set about learning a trade. He commenced studying and practising to fit himself for the dental profession, and, after spending several months in preparation, chose Fall River as the place for his permanent location. He removed thither in December, 1845, and was for many years the leading member of his profession.

Doctor Fairbanks, on becoming a resident of the town, soon manifested a laudable interest in public affairs. This interest was recognized by his fellow-citizens, who elected him one of the General School Committee, three years after his entrance into the community, complimenting him with a re-election in 1849 and 1850.

In 1852 and '53 he was chosen a member of the Board of Selectmen; in 1861, elected to the Common Council, and, upon the organization of the board, chosen its president. In 1866 he was elected one of the General School Committee for the term of three years, and made chairman of the board, on its organization for business. In December, 1867, he was elected mayor of Fall River, and the following year re-elected to the same honorable and responsible office.

At the annual State election in 1869, Dr. Fairbanks was the choice of the city as one of its representatives in General Court, and, from the first, was an efficient and influential member of that body. He was re-elected to this office in 1870, '71, '72 and '73, and again in 1875.

At the second session of the Legislature, of which he was a member, he was appointed on the Committee on Railroads, and continued one of its number during his entire membership of the House, the last two years being second only on the list. His labors were arduous, but his efforts untiring, and fully appreciated by his associates on the committee. As he has risen step by step in usefulness and in influence in the community, so has his faithfulness to duty, and his promptness in its discharge, in each of these public positions won for him many warm friends among his fellow-citizens and in the State at large.

As a chief magistrate, his strong desire was to see the city give large attention to and take high rank in whatever would bring prosperity and happiness to the mass of the people. It was the aim of his successive administrations to look well after the more common and everyday wants of the people; to consider not only the important and more prominent features of city care and expenditure, as highways, police and fire departments, schools, the poor, etc., but to have in mind the moral and physical well-being of the citizens, their health, the sources of amusement, entertainment, and culture.

It was to this administration, and more particularly to his own personal interest and influence in the matter, that Fall River is indebted for the public parks in her northern and southern sections; for the magnificent roadway over the hills to the north, Highland Avenue; for the broadening and grading of Pocasset Street, that main thoroughfare from the shore to Main Street; for the first of the large and substantial as well as ornamental public buildings, the Morgan Street school-house; and—more than all, holding in view the greatest immediate benefit to the greatest number—that daily recurring blessing to the laboring poor of the community, the free public baths, the first of which was established as an experiment, after repeated and persistent efforts on the part of Mayor Fairbanks.

Hon. Samuel M. Brown, Sixth Mayor.

Hon. Samuel M. Brown is a native of Swanzey, in this State, and was born on the third day of February, 1825. The house in which he was born is still standing, a short distance directly north of Cole's Station, on the Fall River, Warren and Providence Division of the Old Colony Railroad, and is the same in which his paternal ancestors for three successive generations have lived and died. Here he spent his early years, enjoying the ordinary advantages and performing the various duties incident to farm-life.

In February, 1842, being then seventeen years of age, he came to Fall River, and obtained employment in the store of Caleb B. Snow, who was at that time engaged in the grocery business on Annawan Street.

In 1846, being out of health, he returned to Swanzey, where he remained until the early part of the following year, when he again came to Fall River, which has since been his residence. During these years he was engaged as clerk in the wholesale grocery business most of the time. In January, 1869, by the suffrages of his fellow-citizens, he was chosen to the important and responsible position of mayor, and so satisfactory was his administration of public affairs that once and again was he re-elected, serving four terms in all.

Since 1869, his time has been principally occupied with the duties of the public offices to which he has been called. He was elected to the Common Council in the fall of 1857, and held that office the three succeeding years, as also during the year 1864. He has served one year as clerk of the council, fourteen years as trustee of the Public Library, two years on the General School Committee, two years and an unexpired part of a third as treasurer and collector, and two years as assessor.

His administration as mayor fell within those years shortly following the war of the rebellion, noted as a period of unexampled business activity throughout the country. Fall River shared largely in the prevailing prosperity. The manufacturing business of the city was greatly increased, there was an addition of more than fifty per cent to the population, and the valuation of the city was more than doubled within those four years. A corresponding extension of the public works of the city was called for, and accordingly much was done within that period by the city government in the way of public improvements.

Several school buildings were erected, one engine-house was built, and the Fire Alarm Telegraph was established. Extensive improvements were also made in the streets and sewerage of the city. The water-works and the changes in the City Hall building were projected and work upon them considerably advanced within Mr. Brown's administration, but neither was completed until the following year. Many of the improvements named were recommended by the mayor, and nearly all received his approval.

The frequent elections of Mr. Brown to responsible positions, since his entrance upon public life, mark the high appreciation of the citizens of his integrity and worth, all his acts as a public officer having merited and received the cordial approbation of his constituents.

Hon. Robert T. Davis, Seventh Mayor.

Robert T. Davis, M.D., was born in County Down, North of Ireland, of parents and ancestry Presbyterian on the paternal, and Quaker, or Friend, on the maternal side, August 28th, 1823.

He came to America when three years old, his father having made a previous sojourn in this country, during which two daughters were born. His father, who was a linen manufacturer, went back to his native land in the interests of his business, but, returning soon to America, settled at Amesbury, Essex County, where the earlier years of our present subject were spent. Dr. Davis' academic education was received at the Friends' boarding-school, in Providence, R. I., and at the Amesbury Academy. He came to Fall River in his youth, and studied for the medical profession with Dr. Thomas Wilbur, on South Main Street, living in his family, and subsequently uniting himself more intimately with them by marriage with the eldest daughter. She died not long after, and some years later he was again united in marriage with a lady of Westchester County, New York, she also being a Friend. Dr. Davis pursued his professional studies for a period at the Tremont Street Medical School, Boston, but graduated from the Harvard Medical School, in 1847. He was Dispensary Physician a short time in Boston, going thence to Waterville, Me., where he spent three years, when he again returned to Fall River, and commenced practice as a physician and surgeon in 1850. With the exception of four years spent in New York City, Fall River has continued to be his place of residence and business. The doctor, soon after his permanent settlement in the city, became an active and prominent member of the Bristol County South Medical Society, and was elected president—at the time, probably the youngest man ever chosen to that position. For several years he likewise held the office of councillor in the association.

His more public life commenced about 1851. In that year a town meeting was holden in Town Hall, to see if the town would instruct its representatives in General Court to cast their votes for Hon. Charles Sumner as Senator in Congress, there being a prolonged contest in that body to fill this office. At this meeting Dr. Davis addressed his fellow-citizens in favor of thus instructing their public servants, and most eloquently and forcibly urged the importance of Massachusetts being represented in the Senate by men true and faithful to the interests of freedom.

In 1853 he was chosen a member of the State Constitutional Convention, and in 1859 and 1861 a State Senator. He was appointed, in his first term, chairman of the Committee on State Charitable Institutions, and was also a member of the Committee for the Revision of the Statutes, the latter committee sitting between the two sessions of the Legislature.

Dr. Davis soon proved himself to be a fluent, convincing, and pleasant public speaker, during his first term as Senator delivering a speech, which was published, in favor of the erection of the statue in honor of our commonwealth's great advocate of popular education, Hon. Horace Mann.

At a public meeting in Boston, on the day of the execution, in Virginia, of John Brown, he spoke in earnest condemnation of the spirit of the slave power, and predicted that this act would prove a fatal blow to the "peculiar institution."

In 1861, in the Senate, he was made chairman of the Committee on Education, also chairman of the Special Committee on the Abolition of Capital Punishment, whose report was written by him; the bill presented for this object, while adopted by the Senate, being lost in the lower House.

In relation to the change of boundary line dividing Massachusetts and Rhode Island, in 1861, a matter which caused great interest and much excitement in the community, he was very active and efficient in securing the line finally adopted and ratified by the Legislature of each State.

He was a member of the National Republican Convention which nominated Abraham Lincoln for President, in 1860, and also a member of that which nominated Gen. Rutherford B. Hayes as a candidate for the same office, in 1876.

He was appointed by Gov. John A. Andrew a member of the State Board of Charities, and is now, and has been since its organization, a member of the State Board of Health.

In 1873 Dr. Davis was elected mayor of Fall River, holding this position one year (but declining a re-election). On retiring from the mayoralty, he donated his entire net salary to the "Children's Home," a charitable institution of the city. In his inaugural, he recommended improvements involving large expenditures of money, but which seemed necessary in the changing circumstances of the city. These recommendations were mostly adopted and finally consummated by the city. His administration was one of unusual activity in all departments, great enterprises being made or projected during that year, and more labor performed than in the same period before or since. Some of these improvements were the erection of three spacious school-houses, three engine-houses and police-stations, the widening of Pleasant Street, from Sixth Street to the "Narrows" (a very important measure), the laying out and completing of other streets, etc. A plan of sewerage for the city was recommended and adopted by this government, and the "Betterment Law" was first put in operation. The City Hall was also completed in its remodelled form, and dedicated that year.

Dr. Davis is an earnest, public-spirited man, of good judgment, quick in perception, generally correct in his conclusions, prompt in his efforts to advance measures which he believes will prove for the good and welfare of the community at large, and broad in his views of the necessities of the hour.

The constant friend and advocate of general education, he was elected a member of the General School Committee first in 1851, and has always given his voice and his vote for the best interests of the scholars of our public schools. It was during his administration as mayor that the city government adopted the provisions of State law whereby all school text-books are furnished the scholars of the public schools free of expense to themselves—a plan which has worked well and satisfactorily to the entire community since its adoption. He is a gentleman of large mental culture and benevolent disposition, possessing a kind and sympathetic heart. Having made good use of the opportunities given him of self-improvement, he has wrought his own way in the world, and been successful in his professional practice as in other respects. Early in the revival of interest in manufacturing pursuits in the city, he became much interested, and manifested his confidence therein by making large investments in this kind of property as well as in real estate. He was elected president of one corporation and director in several others, and thus, in various ways, has come to be one of our best and most useful public men—one whom his fellow-men have delighted to honor, and one who has never disappointed their hopes or betrayed their trust and confidence.

Hon. James F. Davenport, Eighth Mayor.

The Hon. James F. Davenport was born at Belleville, New Jersey, March 4th, 1832. His father, a calico printer, died when he was but eighteen months old, leaving a widow with five young children. The family moved to Taunton, Mass., in 1839, and to Fall River in 1841. Mr. Davenport had but meagre educational advantages, attending the public schools in Fall River from 1841 to 1848, and then going to New Jersey to learn the trade of an engraver. He had a natural talent for mechanics, and, as a boy, found his happiest moments when at work upon or about machinery. In the process of learning the engraver's art, he worked in the print-works at Belleville and Paterson, N. J., and at Providence, R. I., but returned again to Fall River in 1853, where for the next twenty years he was employed in the American Print Works, filling, during the later years of this period, the position of superintendent of the engraving department. From this responsible private service he was called by his fellow-citizens in 1874 to become mayor of the city of Fall River. For the few years previous to this date, his close attention to the duties of his business had greatly impaired his health, and left him but a modicum of his wonted strength and vigor, entailing a physical weakness with which he has had to contend through most of the successive terms of his mayoralty.

Mr. Davenport at an early period manifested an active interest in public matters, always aiming to keep himself thoroughly informed on the questions of the day. His first official life was as a member of the Common Council of Fall River in 1862. In 1871 he was again elected a member of the council, and upon its organization was chosen president, but held the position only a few months, when he was transferred to the Board of Aldermen, to fill a vacancy occurring in his ward. He was re-elected an alderman in 1872 and 1873, and in 1874 received the Republican nomination for the office of mayor. To this honorable and responsible position he was elected by a large majority, and, by the action of his fellow-citizens, was continued in the same office during the years 1875, 1876, and 1877.

Mr. Davenport's administration as mayor developed executive talent of a high order. His term of service covers a period of four years, full of active labor, and calls for prompt, discreet, and decisive action. During these years he has ever striven to act up to the sentiments expressed in his first inaugural address, viz., "As public servants, let us openly and earnestly endeavor to perform honestly the duties incumbent upon us, deciding every measure that may be brought before us for our consideration upon its true merits, with no disposition to evade responsibility or ignore any reasonable demand made upon us by our fellow-citizens." His term of office coming just at the close of an unexampled period of prosperity and growth, when, within six or seven years, a population was added equal in number to that which it had taken more than half a century to reach, involved many great and necessary improvements and public works, and a correspondingly large expenditure of money. Many of these were authorized by previous governments, but the execution of them was left to Mr. Davenport's administration, and in providing the necessary funds and carrying out these important measures, fraught with the future well-being of the community for many years to come, the highest executive ability and most careful and considerate judgment were called into constant requisition. Thus, for example, a comprehensive system of sewerage having been adopted, upon an elaborate and scientific plan, suited to the wants of an expanding community, most of its main trunks and many of its connecting branches were constructed during the years 1873–77, involving an expense of over $250,000. Closely connected with sewerage was the system of public waterworks, costing nearly or quite a million and a half of dollars, the means for which, realized by the sale of bonds, were mainly negotiated for and funded under the special supervision of Mr. Davenport, as chairman of the Committee on Finance. The widening of South Main Street, from the Park to the Rhode Island line, something like a mile and a quarter; of Pleasant Street, from Sixth Street to the Narrows, perhaps a mile and a half; of North Main Street, from the Narragansett Mills to Steep Brook, about a mile; the erection of the Davis, Slade, and Davenport school-houses, and three engine-houses and police-stations, all authorized or begun by previous administrations and necessitating an outlay of over $400,000, were consummated within these years (1873–77). The City Hospital was also built, the Park graded and improved, and many other measures of public utility accomplished, an expenditure demanded by the urgent and imperative wants of a community which, within a few years, had increased twofold in wealth, population, and business, and had more than doubled the area over which its interests were spread.

To be at the head of a government supervising these vast interests has been no mere child's play, but has called for the highest wisdom and discretion of the chief executive, and in devoting his whole time and attention to the duties of his office, Mr. Davenport has fairly earned for himself the commendation and confidence of his fellow-citizens. Through his instrumentality the floating debt of the city, amounting to more than a million of dollars, was successfully funded at a long term of years and a low rate of interest, and the credit of the city so established that temporary loans to large amounts are easily secured, while the bonds of the city have passed into the hands of capitalists for permanent investments, the few that come upon the market being quickly disposed of at a good premium. Notwithstanding these very large expenditures, the government the past two years has been so economically administered, that it has lived within the appropriations, though smaller than usual, and the debt of the city has also been decreased.

The rapid expansion of the city involved many changes in the subordinate departments of municipal administration. The police force was reorganized, and its numbers increased, upon the completion and occupancy of the new police stations in the northern, southern, and eastern sections of the city. The *morale* of the force was brought to a higher standard, and greater efficiency secured in the discharge of their various and important, often delicate, duties. The introduction of water and the establishment of a large number of hydrants gave a new phase to the administration of the fire department, which led to its reorganization and distribution, and resulted in a more completely equipped department, and an improved *personnel* of the force. The appointment of the members of both of these forces devolves upon the mayor and aldermen, and in filling these positions Mayor Davenport has ever sought to increase the dignity and efficiency of each department, and to eliminate all elements that might impede the discipline, energy, and cohesion of either body of men.

Another outgrowth of the rapid extension of the city in all directions, and the consequent changes involved in the laying out of highways, and improving the facilities of communication between different sections, was the question of benefit and damage to abutters, the settlement of claims for land taken, the rights of owners, and the thousand and one questions which arise where municipal and private rights are involved. Time is always required to bring these various questions to a point, and it was the lot of Mr. Davenport's administration to receive from its predecessors a legacy of lawsuits and questions of land damages, the settlement of which he found at an early date to be one of the most perplexing of his duties. Happily constituted by nature, with a kind, conciliatory spirit, calm and undisturbed amid trying difficulties, and peculiarly apt and winning in his contact with men, Mr. Davenport was especially fitted to deal with all these cases, successfully adjusting most of the points in controversy without resort to the courts, and, in cases where litigation had already been begun, securing results far more favorable than the city could secure by negotiation with the opposing party. No small part of the time of the mayor has been required to examine the legal questions which have arisen, and, in the process of this schooling, Mayor Davenport has developed an exceptional aptitude for the comprehension and management of the intricate and perplexing problems of civic administration.

Mr. Davenport, upon his first election to the mayoralty, determined to devote his whole time to the duties of his office, and has continued to do so through the successive years of his administration. His services, as a result, have been eminently successful, and no mayor ever had the confidence of the community to a higher degree. Conservative and prudent in maturing measures, yet prompt and vigorous in action when occasion demands, Mr. Davenport has qualities that especially fit him for public life. In the several years of his mayoralty, during which the laboring population have become restless, and been prompted to covert, if not open, violence by irresponsible leaders, when the least symptom of wavering or uncertainty on the part of those in authority might have precipitated riot and bloodshed, the firmness and courage of the chief executive were put to the severest test, and so satisfactorily did Mr. Davenport meet the crisis, that his praises have been sounded on every side. Unassuming in demeanor, and slight in physical proportions, he nevertheless has shown that he possesses an unflinching spirit, equal to all emergencies. Most affable and amiable of men, he has always made hosts of friends among those with whom he has been brought in contact.

ACT OF INCORPORATION

OF THE

TOWN OF FALL RIVER,

BRISTOL COUNTY, MASSACHUSETTS.

1803.

COMMONWEALTH OF MASSACHUSETTS.

In the year of our Lord one thousand eight hundred and three, AN ACT to divide the town of Freetown, and to incorporate the southerly part thereof into a separate town by the name of Fall River.

BE it enacted, by the Senate and House of Representatives, in General Court assembled, and by the authority of the same, that the southerly part of Freetown, in the County of Bristol, as described within the following bounds, with the inhabitants thereon, be, and they are hereby incorporated into a separate town by the name of Fall River, viz.:

Beginning in Taunton Great River so called, and thence running south seventy degrees, east on the lines dividing the lands belonging to the heirs of Samuel Valentine, from the lands of the heirs of William Valentine, and so continuing the same course about eight hundred and sixty rods, till it intersects a line running from the town of Dartmouth, north twelve degrees east, by the easterly of the twentieth great lot owned by Thomas Borden and Richard Borden, thence on the line last mentioned to Dartmouth line. Thence by the lines of the town of Dartmouth and Westport to the State of Rhode Island, thence on the line of said State into said river, thence by the channel of said river to the bounds first mentioned. And the said town of Fall River is hereby vested with all the powers and privileges, rights and immunities, to which other towns are entitled by the constitution and laws of this commonwealth.

SECTION II. Be it further enacted, that the said town of Fall River shall pay all the arrears of taxes, which have been assessed upon them, together with their proportion of all debts owed by said town of Freetown prior to the date of this Act, and that all questions relative to property already existing, shall be adjusted and settled in the same manner as if this Act had not been made; and that all property rights and credits of said town of Freetown be received and enjoyed by the said town of Fall River, according to their proportion of the taxes of said Freetown, as assessed in the last tax-bills.

SECTION III. Be it further enacted, that the said town of Fall River shall take upon themselves, and support one half of all the poor now actually chargeable to said town of Freetown, and shall also bear, and pay one half of the expense of supporting such poor persons as may be sent back upon said town of Freetown from other towns, who removed from said town of Freetown prior to the passing this Act.

SECTION IV. Be it further enacted, that of all State and County taxes which shall be levied and required of said towns previous to a new valuation, the said town of Fall River shall pay four tenths.

SECTION V. And be it further enacted, that Charles Durfee, Esq., be and he is hereby authorized to issue his warrant, directed to some suitable inhabitant of the said town of Fall River, requiring him to notify and warn the inhabitants of the said town qualified by law to vote in town affairs, to meet at such time and place as shall be expressed in the said warrant, to choose all such officers as other towns within this commonwealth are required by law to choose, in the months of March or April annually, and the officers so chosen shall be qualified as other town officers are.

In the House of Representatives, February 24, 1803. This bill having had three several readings, passed to be enacted.

JOHN C. JONES, *Speaker*.

In Senate, February 25, 1803. This bill having had two several readings, passed to be enacted.

DAVID COBB, *President*.

February 26, 1803. By the Governor approved.

CALEB STRONG.

True copy attest.

JOHN AVERY, *Secretary*.

A true copy attest.

WALTER CHALONER, *Town Clerk*, for 1803.

CHANGE OF NAME.—"FALL RIVER" TO "TROY."

IN a warrant for the assembling of the legal voters of the town of Fall River, dated March 21st, 1804, a portion of article 5th reads—"Also to know the minds of the town respecting altering the name of the town, and if altered, by what name they would wish it called." At a meeting held May 8th, 1804, it was voted "that the present town of Fall River shall be called Troy." Tradition reports that this action was induced by a prominent citizen who had recently visited Troy, New York, and who became so enamored of its name, that, upon his return he induced his fellow-townsmen to give up the suggestive and appropriate name received from the red man, and assume that derived from the ancient and mythical Homeric city.

1804.

AN ACT *to change the name of the town of Fall River, in the County of Bristol.*

Be it enacted, by the Senate and House of Representatives in General Court assembled, and by authority of the same, that from and after the passing of this Act, the name of the said town of Fall River shall cease, and the said town shall hereafter be called and known by the name of Troy, any law to the contrary notwithstanding. And nothing in this act contained shall be construed to impair any rights of the said corporation; but the inhabitants of said town shall have, enjoy, and exercise all the powers, privileges and immunities as a corporation by the name of Troy, in as full and ample a manner as though the name of the said town had not been changed.

This Act passed June 18, 1804.

"TROY" TO "FALL RIVER."

AT a town meeting assembled March 18, 1833, it was voted "That it is expedient to have the name of the town of Troy altered to that of Fall River," and "that the selectmen be directed to petition the Legislature now in session, for an act to alter the name of the town of Troy to that of Fall River."

1834.

AN ACT *to change the name of Troy to Fall River.*

Be it enacted, by the Senate and House of Representatives, in General Court assembled, and by the authority of the same, that from and after the passage of this Act, the name of the town of Troy, in the County of Bristol, shall cease, and the said town shall hereafter be called and known by the name of Fall River, and by this name shall be entitled to all the rights and privileges, and subject to all the duties and obligations to which it would have been entitled and subject if the name had not been changed as aforesaid. February 12, 1834.

CLERKS OF TOWN AND CITY, 1803-1876.

Town Clerks of the Town of Fall River, 1803-1854.

1803,	Walter Chaloner,	1 year.
1804 to 1813 inclusive,	Benjamin Brightman,	10 years.
1814 to 1815 "	Wm. B. Canedy,	2 "
1816 from March to Nov. 2,	Nathaniel Luther, when at a town meeting was made the following record: "Nathaniel Luther, the Town Clerk, being absent, made choice of Joseph E. Read to act as Town Clerk the remainder of the year (at all town meetings and all other business pertaining to the Town Clerk's duty) in the absence of Mr. Luther."	
1816 from Nov. 2 to 1820 inclusive,	Joseph E. Read,	5½ years.
1821 to 1824 inclusive,	John C. Borden,	4 "
1825,	Nathaniel B. Borden,	1 year.
1826 to 1830 inclusive,	Benjamin Anthony,	5 years.
1831 to 1835 "	Stephen K. Crary,	5 "
1836 to 1845 "	Benjamin Earl,	10 "
1846 to 1847 "	George S. Baker,	2 "
1848 to 1852 "	Sam'l B. Hussey,	5 "
1853,	John R. Hodges,	1 year.

City Clerks, 1854-1876.

1854,	John R. Hodges,	1 year.
1855 to 1863 inclusive,	Alvin S. Ballard,	9 years.
1864 to 1876 "	Geo. A. Ballard,	13 "

TOWN OFFICERS, 1803-1854.

A.D.	Selectmen.	Treasurer.	School Committee.	Representative to General Court.	A.D.	Selectmen.	Treasurer.	School Committee.	Representative to General Court.
1803	Thomas Burden. Benjamin Durfee. Robert Miller.	Abraham Bowen.		Voted not to send.	1815	Benj. W. Brown. Sheffel Weaver. Bradford Durfee.	Joseph E. Read.		Joseph E. Read.
1804	Samuel Thurston. Benjamin Durfee. Robert Miller.	Abraham Bowen.		Abraham Bowen.	1816	Sheffel Weaver. Wm. Ashley. Wm. Read.	Joseph E. Read.		Hezekiah Wilson.
1805	Nathan Bowen. Pardon Daval. Elijah Blossom, Jr.	Abraham Bowen.		Jonath'n Brownell.	1817	Sheffel Weaver. Abraham Bowen. Wm. Ashley.	Joseph E. Read.		Hezekiah Wilson.
1806	Jona. Brownell. Abraham Bowen. Elijah Blossom, Jr.	Abraham Bowen.		Jonath'n Brownell.	1818	Benj. W. Brown. Charles Pitman. James G. Bowen.	Joseph E. Read.		Joseph E. Read.
1807	Jona. Brownell. Elijah Blossom. Stephen Leonard.	Wm. H. Canedy.		Abraham Bowen.	1819	Benj. W. Brown. Charles Pitman. James G. Bowen.	Joseph E. Read.		Joseph E. Read.
1808	Nathan Bowen. Henry Brighteman. David Wilson.	Charles Durfee.	Sheffel Weaver. Wm. B. Canedy. Wm. Read. Jr.	Abraham Bowen.	1820	Sheffel Weaver. Benj. W. Brown. Rich'd Burden, 2d.	James G. Bowen.		Voted not to send.
1809	David Wilson. Wm. Read, Jr. Chas. Durfee.	Charles Durfee.		Robert Miller.	1821	Robert Miller. Chas. Pitman. Enoch French.	James G. Bowen.		Abraham Bowen.
1810	David Wilson. Wm. Read, Jr. Charles Durfee.	Edward Shove.		Robert Miller.	1822	Robert Miller. Charles Pitman. Enoch French.	James G. Bowen.		Robert Miller.
1811	David Wilson. Wm. Read, Jr. Benj. Bennett, 2d.	Benjamin Brayton.		Robert Miller.	1823	Joseph E. Read. Benj. W. Brown. Edmund Chace.	James G. Bowen.		Wm. B. Canedy.
1812	Hezekiah Wilson. Wm. H. Canedy. Wm. Borden.	Edward Shove.	Edward Shove. Wm. B. Canedy. Edmund French.	Robert Miller.	1824	Enoch French. Hezekiah Wilson. William Read.	James Ford.		Wm. B. Canedy.
1813	Wm. B. Canedy. Wm. Borden. Isaac Winslow.	Joseph E. Read.		Robert Miller.	1825	Enoch French. Hezekiah Wilson. William Read.	James Ford.	Oliver Chace. Bradford Durfee. Robert Chappell.	James Ford.
1814	Wm. Borden. Benj. W. Brown. Sim. Hathaway.	Joseph E. Read.		Joseph E. Read.	1826	Enoch French. Hezekiah Wilson. William Read.	James Ford.	Jos. Hathaway. Jas. Ford. Jason H. Archer. Wm. R. Canedy. John Lindsey, Jr.	Voted not to send.

TOWN OFFICERS, 1803-1854.

A.D.	Selectmen.	Treasurer.	School Committee.	Representative to General Court.	A.D.	Selectmen.	Treasurer.	School Committee.	Representative to General Court
1827	Enoch French. Hezekiah Wilson. William Read.	James Ford.	Jos. Hathaway. Jas. Ford. Jason H. Archer. Wm. H. Canedy. John Lindsey, Jr.	Joseph Hathaway.	1835	John Eddy. Israel Anthony. Luther Winslow.	John S. Cotton.	O. Fowler. Asa Bronson. Simon Chough. Geo. W. Brigss. Nathan Durfee. Jas. Ford. Stephen K. Crary.	Micah H. Ruggles. Anthony Mason. Philip R. Bennett. Job B. Pierce. Elijah Pierce.
1828	Enoch French. Sheffel Weaver. William Read.	James Ford.	Rev. T. M. Smith. " Arth. A. Ross. E. T. Taylor. James Ford. John Eddy.	Enoch French.	1836	John Eddy. Israel Anthony. Luther Winslow.	John S. Cotton.	David Anthony. James Ford. Harvey Chace.	M. H. Ruggles. Anthony Mason. Caleb B. Vickery. William Ashley. Gilbert H. Durfee.
1829	Enoch French. Sheffel Weaver. William Read.	James Ford.	James Ford. Rev. T. M. Smith. " A. A. Ross. Hezekiah Battelle. John Eddy.	Joseph E. Read. Enoch French. Anthony Mason.	1837	John Eddy. Israel Anthony. Luther Winslow.	John S. Cotton.	James Ford. Joseph F. Lindsey. Benj. B. Sisson. George W. Brigss. Orin Fowler.	Micah H. Ruggles. Cyrus Alden. John Eddy. Constant H. Wyatt. Richard F. French. Philip S. Brown.
1830	Sheffel Weaver. John Eddy. William Read.	John S. Cotton.	Rev. T. M. Smith. Jason H. Archer. Arnold Buffum. Foster Hooper. Thomas Wilbur.	Fred'k Winslow. Anthony Mason. Joseph E. Read.	1838	John Eddy. Israel Anthony. Luther Winslow.	John S. Cotton.	Joseph F. Lindsey. James Ford. Benj. B. Sisson. Orin Fowler. Elijah Williams.	Fred'k Winslow. Benj. B. Sisson. Philip S. Brown. Hezekiah Boutelle.
1831	Samuel Chace. Robin'n Buffinton. William Ashley.	Pyam Jacob.	Foster Hooper. Rev. T. M. Smith. Thomas Wilbur. Rev. Brad. Almer. Leander P. Lovell.	Nath'l B. Borden. Foster Hooper. Fred'k Winslow.	1839	John Eddy. Israel Anthony. Russell Hathaway.	John S. Cotton.	Orin Fowler. Asa Bronson. James Ford. Elijah Williams. Joseph F. Lindsey.	Micah H. Ruggles. Iram Smith. Geo. Brightman, 2d John A. Harris.
1832	Samuel Chace. Leonard Garfield. William Ashley.	Pyam Jacob.	Thos. Wilbur. Rev. Orin Fowler. Harvey Chace. Rev. Brad. Miner. Dr. Nath. Durfee.	Simeon Borden. Azariah Shove. Anthony Mason. Barnabas Blossom.	1840	Nath'l B. Borden. Israel Anthony. William Read	John S. Cotton.	Orin Fowler. Asa Bronson. James Ford. Elkin Williams. Joseph F. Lindsey. Jon. S. Thompson. Geo. M. Randall.	John Eddy. Pierre Mason. Nathan Durfee. Enoch French.
1833	Samuel Chace. Matth. C. Durfee. Elijah Pierce.	Pyam Jacob.	Rev. Orin Fowler. Harvey Chace. Nathan Durfee. Thomas Wilbur. Harvey Harnden. James Ford.	Simeon Borden. Azariah Shove. Smith Winslow. Isaac Borden. Earl Chace.	1841	Matth. C. Durfee. Stephen K. Crary. Geo. Brightman,2d	Benjamin Earl.	Joseph F. Lindsey. Wm. H. A. Crary. Geo. M. Randall. John Westall.	Linden Cook. Nathan Durfee. Job B. French.
1834	Azariah Shove. Smith Winslow. Samuel Chace.	Jonathan Slade.	Rev. Asa Bronson. Harvey Chace. Harvey Harnden. Philip R. Bennett. Thomas Wilbur. Nathan Durfee.	Nath'l B. Borden. Micah H. Ruggles. Anthony Mason. Jervis Shove. William Winslow.	1842	Jervis Shove. Israel Anthony. Perez Mason.	Benjamin Earl.	Geo. M. Randall. Wm. H. A. Crary. John Westall.	Jonathan Slade. Wm. A. Waite. Wm. V. Read.
					1843	Jervis Shove. Israel Anthony. Perez Mason.	Benjamin Earl.	Geo. M. Randall. Wm. H. A. Crary. John Westall.	Jonathan Slade. King Dean. Wm. H. Ashley.

TOWN OFFICERS, 1803-1854.

A.D.	Selectmen.	Treasurer.	School Committee.	Representative to General Court.	A.D.	Selectmen.	Treasurer.	School Committee.	Representative to General Court.
1844	Thos. D. Chaloner, Israel Anthony, Perez Mason.	Benjamin Earl.	Henry Willard, Joseph F. Lindsey, Jonathan Slade, Louis Lapham, John Gregory.	Simeon Borden, Thos. D. Chaloner, Nathan Durfee.	1850	David Perkins, Thos. J. Pickering, Daniel Brown.	Sam'l B. Hussey.	Geo. O. Fairbanks, Sam'l Longfellow, Henry Willard, Eli Thurston, Thomas Wilbur, Jesse Eddy.	Iram Smith, Azariah Shove.
1845	Thos. D. Chaloner, Israel Anthony, Perez Mason.	Benjamin Earl.	Wm. H. A. Crary, David Perkins, Sam'l B. Hussey.	Simeon Borden, James B. Luther, Benj. F. White.	1851	Thos. J. Pickering, James Buffinton, Daniel Brown.	Sam'l B. Hussey.	Sam'l Longfellow, Jesse Eddy, Eli Thurston, Emery M. Porter, Azariah S. Tripp, Robert T. Davis, James M. Aldrich.	Nath'l R. Borden, Richard Borden, James B. Luther, Richard C. French.
1846	Israel Anthony, Leander Borden, James M. Morton.	George S. Baker.	Wm. H. A. Crary, Charles Aldrich, David Perkins.	Charles J. Holmes, Benj. W. Miller, Albert G. Eaton.	1852	James Buffinton, Geo. O. Fairbanks, Azariah Shove, Leander Borden, Chest'r W. Greene.	John R. Hodges.	Eli Thurston, James M. Aldrich, David A. Wallace, Azariah S. Tripp, Jerome Dwelly.	Nathan D. Dean, Iram Smith, Ed. P. Buffinton, South'd H. Miller.
1847	Azariah Shove, Israel Anthony, Benjamin Earl.	George S. Baker.	Wm. H. A. Crary, David Perkins, Charles Aldrich.	David Perkins, Benjamin Earl, Benj. W. Miller.	1853	James Buffinton, Ches'r W. Greene, Thos. T. Porter, Geo. O. Fairbanks, Azariah Shove.	John R. Hodges.	David A. Wallace, Eli Thurston, James M. Aldrich, Azariah S. Tripp, Jerome Dwelly, Job G. Lawton, Benj. H. Davis.	Three trials, and no choice.
1848	Benj. Wardwell, Israel Anthony, Benjamin Earl.	Sam'l B. Hussey.	Charles Aldrich, Geo. O. Fairbanks, B. W. Hathaway.	David Perkins, Hezekiah Battelle, Wm. R. Robeson.					
1849	Thos. J. Pickering, David Perkins, Benjamin Earl.	Sam'l B. Hussey.	Geo. O. Fairbanks, Henry Willard, Sam'l Longfellow.	Simeon Borden, Benj. Wardwell, James Ford, 2d.					

FALL RIVER A CITY, 1854.   243

Formation of a City Government.

PRELIMINARY ACTION.

At a town meeting, called by warrant, dated Jan. 25th, 1854, and holden Jan. 28th, inst.,

It was Voted, That a committee be raised to petition the Legislature in behalf of the citizens of Fall River for a City Charter, and also that the same committee draft the form of such a charter as they in their judgment may think the wants of the people may require, and report at an adjournment of this meeting.

Voted, That this committee consist of seven members.
Voted, To increase this committee by adding two.
Voted, To choose this committee by nomination at large.
Nominated and made choice of John Westall, Foster Hooper, Nathaniel B. Borden, Israel Buffinton, Thomas Wilbur, Robert C. Brown, Eliab Williams, Samuel L. Thaxter, and Louis Lapham.
Voted, That this committee have power to fill vacancies.
Voted, That the committee be instructed to report in print.
Voted, That the committee print and circulate fifteen hundred copies of their report of City Charter, and that said committee circulate their report one week previous to the time to which this meeting may adjourn.
Voted, To adjourn to three weeks from this day.

Pursuant to adjournment, the inhabitants met in the town hall, February 18th, 1854, James Buffinton, chairman, who called for report of said committee, which was read by Dr. Foster Hooper.
Voted, That the report be accepted.
Voted, That the selectmen be instructed to carry out the recommendations of the report.

At a subsequent town meeting, held by adjournment, after the adoption of several amendments in the draft for City Charter, it was voted to accept the report of the committee to draft a City Charter, as amended.
Voted, That the committee who made the draft of the City Charter be a committee to petition the Legislature to grant said City Charter.

At a town meeting legally convened, April 22d, 1854, in the town hall, to decide, Shall the act to establish the City of Fall River, passed by the General Court of this commonwealth, and approved by the Governor, April 12th, 1854, be accepted—yea or nay?
Voted, Yeas 529. Nays 247.

Fall River thus became the thirteenth city incorporated by the State of Massachusetts.

City of Fall River.

1854.

Pursuant to the provisions of the City Charter, a meeting was held in each of the six wards, May 6th, 1854, and a city government chosen, as follows:

For Mayor, James Buffinton.

Aldermen.

WARD.	WARD.	WARD.
1. James Henry,	3. Oliver H. Hathaway,	5. Edwin Shaw,
2. Edward P. Buffinton,	4. Alvin S. Ballard,	6. Julius P. Champney.

Common Council.

WARD		
1. Robert C. Brown,	Wm. Goodman,	Peter J. Dennise,
2. Henry Wilbur,	Obadiah Chace,	Henry Diman, Jr.
3. Oliver Grinnell,	Gardner Groves,	Howard B. Allen,
4. Chris. W. Tillinghast,	Nath'l Bonney,	Wm. M. Almy,
5. John Mason, Jr.,	David S. Brigham,	Thomas T. Potter,
6. Smith Winslow.	Sheffield Brightman.	Albert Winslow.

ORGANIZATION OF THE FIRST CITY GOVERNMENT.

May 15th, 1854.

At a session of the Mayor and Aldermen elect, May 15th, 1854, previous to the administering of the oath of office, the members of this Board, and Board of Common Council, made choice of Alvan S. Ballard, clerk pro tem.

Ordered, That a set of Rules and Orders presented by Alderman Shaw, be adopted by this Board temporarily.

Voted, That a committee of two, consisting of Aldermen Shaw and Henry, notify the Common Council that this Board is now ready to meet them in convention for such business as may legally come before the City Council.

In Board of Common Council, concurred.

Adjourned to City Hall, to meet in convention.

The officers present were then marshaled into the City Hall by Col. Wm. Sisson, accompanied by the selectmen, where a large number of the citizens were in attendance to witness the ceremonies, and to hear the inaugural address of Mayor Buffinton.

The meeting was called to order by Chester W. Greene, chairman of the Board of Selectmen, and the throne of grace was addressed by Rev. Benjamin J. Relyea.

The names of the city officers elect were called by the Clerk, and the oath of office administered by James Ford, Esq., Justice of the Peace.

Chester W. Greene then addressed the Mayor in behalf of the Board of Selectmen.

Mayor Buffinton then delivered his inaugural address.

After which the Boards of Aldermen and Common Councilmen separated, each going to their respective rooms.

MAYORS OF THE CITY OF FALL RIVER.

1854-1876.

Hon. James Buffinton,	. . .	1854, '55.
" Edward P. Buffinton,	{	1856, '60, '61, '62, '63, '64, '65, '66.
" Nathaniel B. Borden,	. . .	1857.
" Josiah C. Blaisdell, .	. . .	1858, '59.
Hon. George O. Fairbanks,	. . .	1867, '68.
" Samuel M. Brown,	1869,	'70, '71, '72.
" Robert T. Davis,	. . .	1873.
" James F. Davenport,	1874,	'75, '76, '77.

MEMBERS OF CONGRESS.

RESIDENTS OF FALL RIVER.

Hon. Nathaniel B. Borden,	XXVth Congress,	. . . .	1837-38
	XXVIth "	. . . .	1839-40
	XXVIIIth "	. . . .	1843-44
Rev. Orin Fowler, .	XXXIst Congress,	. . . .	1849-50
	XXXIId "	. . . .	1851-52
Hon. James Buffinton.*	. XXXIVth Congress,	. . . .	1855-56
	XXXVth "	. . . .	1859-60
	XXXVIth "	. . . .	1861-62
	XXXVIIth "	. . . .	1863-64
	XLIId "	. . . .	1871-72
	XLIIId "	. . . .	1873-74

* Elected to the XLIVth Congress, but died before the opening of the session.

STATE SENATORS AND REPRESENTATIVES.

STATE SENATORS.

RESIDENTS OF FALL RIVER.

Fall River was first honored in 1838, by the choice of one of her citizens to the position of State Senator of Massachusetts.* Since that date, she has often had a representative in this branch of the Great and General Court, viz.:

A.D. 1838, ... Hon. John Eddy.	A.D. 1857, . . . Hon. Jeremiah S. Young.
1840-1842, ... Dr. Foster Hooper.	1859-1861, ... Dr. Robert T. Davis.
1843, ... Dr. Phineas W. Leland.	1865, . . . Hon. Josiah C. Blaisdell.
1845-1847, . . . Hon. Nathaniel B. Borden.	1867-1868, . . . Hon. Samuel Angier Chace.
1848, ... Rev. Orin Fowler.	1869-1870, . . . Hon. John B. Hathaway.
1854, ... Col. Richard Borden.	1871-1874, . . . Hon. Charles P. Stickney.
1855-1856, ... Hon. Joseph E. Dawley.	1877, . . . Hon. Charles J. Holmes.

REPRESENTATIVES TO THE MASSACHUSETTS LEGISLATURE.

1854-1876.

1854,	Mark A. Slocum. Job G. Lawton.		1867,	Abraham G. Hart. John B. Hathaway.
1855,	Daniel Leonard. Asa P. French. Jona. E. Morrill. Benjamin H. Davis.		1868,	Abraham G. Hart. Weaver Osborn. Iram Smith.
1856,	Brayton Slade. Jona. E. Morrill. John S. Brayton. Job B. Ashley.		1869,	Abraham G. Hart. Weaver Osborn. Iram Smith.
1857,	Jona. E. Morrill. Vernon Cook. Brownell W. Woodman John E. Grouard.		1870,	Edward T. Marvell. George O. Fairbanks. Abraham G. Hart.
1858,	Josiah C. Blaisdell. Jona. E. Morrill.		1871,	Frederick A. Boomer. Weaver Osborn. George O. Fairbanks.
1859,	Stephen C. Wrightington. Thomas T. Potter.		1872,	Thomas F. Holder. George O. Fairbanks. George H. Eddy.
1860,	Lloyd S. Earle. Stephen C. Wrightington.		1873,	George O. Fairbanks. Charles J. Holmes. Weaver Osborn.
1861,	Lloyd S. Earle. Stephen C. Wrightington.		1874,	George O. Fairbanks. Daniel McGowan. John Davol, Jr.
1862,	Simeon Borden. Henry Pratt.		1875,	Southard H. Miller. Nicholas Hathaway. William Carroll.
1863,	Simeon Borden. Henry Pratt.		1876,	George O. Fairbanks. Weaver Osborn. Albion K. Slade.
1864,	Nathaniel B. Borden. Andrew D. Bullock.			
1865,	S. Angier Chace. Fred. A. Boomer.		1877,	Weaver Osborn. John B. Whitaker. Iram Smith. Franklin Gray. Pardon Macomber.
1866,	Josiah C. Blaisdell. John B. Hathaway.			

* While still a part of Freetown, Hon. Thomas Durfee, a citizen of Fall River, was chosen a Senator, from 1781 to 1788.

GOVERNMENT

OF THE

CITY OF FALL RIVER,

1877.

MAYOR.
HON. JAMES F. DAVENPORT.

ALDERMEN.

Ward 1. JOSEPH O. NEILL.
Ward 2. PATRICK J. LUNNEY.
Ward 3. QUINLAN LEARY.

Ward 4. JOHN A. MACFARLANE.
Ward 5. BRADFORD D. DAVOL.
Ward 6. HOLDER B. DURFEE.

CITY CLERK
GEO. A. BALLARD.

COMMON COUNCIL.
WILLIAM S. GREENE, *President.*

WARD 1.
WILLIAM WOLFENDALE,*
WILLIAM H. CHACE,
EDWARD P. BAGGETT.

WARD 2.
JAMES D. O'NEIL,
PATRICK J. MCCARTY,
MICHAEL L. IVERS.

WARD 3.
H. GORDON WEBSTER,
WILLIAM BURGESS,
JOHN A. CONNELLY.

WARD 4.
HENRY NORSWORTHY,
ANDREW MCDERMOTT,
DENNIS GARVEY.

WARD 5.
WILLIAM S. GREENE,
JOSEPH M. DARLING,
SIMEON B. CHASE.

WARD 6.
JOHN P. SLADE,
JAMES H. WILSON,
CHARLES L. RIPLEY.

AUGUSTUS B. LEONARD, *Clerk.*

* Resigned, March 5, 1877.

CITY GOVERNMENT OF FALL RIVER, 1877.

CITY OFFICERS.

City Clerk, GEORGE A. BALLARD.
Treasurer and Collector, JAMES C. BRADY.
Auditor, GEORGE W. BILLINGS.
Superintendent of Streets, DANFORTH HORTON.
Superintendent of Schools, WILLIAM CONNELL, JR.
City Marshal, ANDREW R. WRIGHT.
Chief Engineer Fire Department, WM. C. DAVOL, JR.
City Solicitor, MILTON REED.
City Physician, J. A. TOURTELOTTE.
Superintendent of Almshouse, JOSEPH BORDEN.
Superintendent of Oak Grove Cemetery, J. E. MORRILL.
Superintendent of North Cemetery, JAMES G. HYLAND.
Clerk of Common Council, A. B. LEONARD.
City Messenger, D. D. O'NEIL.
Warden Court House, EDWARD DRISCOLL.
Surveyor of Lumber, HERBERT A. SKINNER.
Sealer of Weights and Measures, D. D O'NEAL.
Inspector of Milk, ELISHA FULLER.
Measurer of Grain, ANDREW FERGUSON.

SCHOOL COMMITTEE.

Chairman,
JAMES M. ALDRICH.

Secretary,
WILLIAM CONNELL, JR.

JAMES M. ALDRICH,
JEROME DWELLY,
ANDREW J. JENNINGS,
CHARLES J. HOLMES,

WILLIAM H. BRIC,
WILLIAM W. ADAMS,
CHARLES E. MILLS,
IRAM SMITH,

THOMAS F. EDDY.

Supt. of Public Schools,
WILLIAM CONNELL, JR.

Truant Officers,
WILLIAM READ,   JOHN BRADY.

POLICE DEPARTMENT.

City Marshal,
ANDREW R. WRIGHT

Assistant Marshal,
ALBERT T. PIERCE.

Captain,
HENRY A. DEXTER.

Sergeants,

EMANUEL WILCOX,
CHARLES HINCKLEY,

WILLIAM B. LING,
JULIAN T. PEMBER,

JOHN DEARDON.

Clerk of Police Department,
STEPHEN B. GARDNER.

FIRE DEPARTMENT.

Chief Engineer,
WILLIAM C. DAVOL, JR.

Assistant Engineer,
ISAAC T. BROWNELL.

District Engineers,
District No. 1. ALVAN C. SEYMOUR, | District No. 2. BENJAMIN MOTT,
District No. 3. EDWARD T. MARVEL.

TRUSTEES OF PUBLIC LIBRARY.

MAYOR DAVENPORT,	SIMEON BORDEN,
HENRY LYON,	ROBERT T. DAVIS,
CHARLES J. HOLMES,	J. R. LEARY,

WALTER PAINE, 2D.

Librarian, WILLIAM R. BALLARD.

WATUPPA WATER BOARD.

PHILIP D. BORDEN, WILLIAM LINDSEY,
JOHN BUTLER.

Superintendent, WILLIAM ROTCH.
Registrar, C. H. CHURCHILL.

SINKING FUND COMMISSIONERS.

MAYOR DAVENPORT,	CHARLES P. STICKNEY,
GEORGE W. BILLINGS,	SIMEON BORDEN,
ALPHONSO S. COVEL,	WILLIAM S. GREENE.

ASSESSORS.

JEREMIAH KELLEY, SAMUEL M. BROWN,
JOHN H. ESTES.

INDEX.

	PAGE
Act of Incorporation of Fall River as a Town	237
Agents of Troy Co.	188
All Sorts, Newspaper	188
American Linen Co.	62, 113, 121
" Print Works	35, 37, 113
Annawan Manufactory	27, 113, 120
Anthony, David	11, 64, 76, 118, 122
" John B.	13
Appropriations for Union Defence	207, 208
Archetype, Newspaper	188
Area of Fall River	6
Argonaut, Sloop	10, 191
Argus, Newspaper	188
Arkwright's Inventions	73
Assessors, 1877	248
Assonet Neck	2
Bailey, Wheaton	17
Banks and Savings Institutions	168
Barnard Manufacturing Co.	113, 146
Bay State Print Works	41
Bay State Steamboat Line	50, 194
Bay State, Steamer	194
Beacon, Daily Paper	189
Bennett's Carding Factory	27
"Bing" of Cotton	100
Blair's Picking Machine	18
Blaisdell, Hon. J. C	229
"Bobbin"	103
Borden, John, of Portsmouth	2, 3
" John, Jr.	15
" Holder	24, 35, 191
" Jefferson	41, 50, 194
" Richard, a prisoner of the British troops	201
" Hon. N. B.	228
" Col. Richard	43, 47, 134, 191, 210
" Richard, Steamer	192
" Capt. Thomas	191
" Thomas J.	37, 113, 129, 135
"Border City," The	4, 143
Border City Mills	113, 143
Boston, Newport and New York Steamboat Co.	194
Boundaries, Change of State	4, 215
Bowers, John	11
Brayton, Capt. Benj.	192
"Breaker," Cotton	101
"Bridge Mill"	23, 26
Bristol, Steamer	195
Brown, Capt. William	194
Brown, Hon. S. M.	231

	PAGE
Buffinton, E. P.	208, 227
" James	209, 225
" D. & D.	23
Buildings, Public	153
Bulletin, Paper	189
Calico Prints	130, 135
" (First)	23
Canonicus, Steamer	192
"Carding"	101
Carding Machine	74
Cemeteries	157
Centennial Celebration, July 4th, 1876	220
Chace, Harvey	18
" & Luther	23
" Oliver, Sr.	15, 21, 23, 136
" Mills	113, 141
Change of Name, "Fall River" to "Troy"	238
" " "Troy" to "Fall River"	238
Church, Caleb	3
" Col. Benjamin	3
Churches	10, 154
City Government	153, 243, 246
" Hall Building	184
" Clerks of Fall River	239
" Officers, 1877	246
Citizens' Savings Bank	176
Climate	95
Clyde Line, The	196
Communication with other Places in 1813	10
"Cop"	107
Corporations, Organization of	113
Corporate Seal of Fall River	6
Cotton, First Culture in U. S.	71
" Annual Production (1825–1876)	72
" Cloth, Export	86
" Factories, First	78
" First Exportation	71
" First Manufacture	73, 77
" Machinery, Exportation forbidden	74
" " First Manufacture	75
" Gin	72
" Machinery (1830)	28
" Manufacture (1831)	83
" Mills, "New Era"	7, 65, 96
" Machinery, Inventions of	97
" "Grade"	99
" to Cloth, Time of	109
" Mills, Size of Standard	110
" Departments of	110

INDEX.

Cotton, Arrangement of.................. 110
" Manufacture (in 1812) Process, 9 ; (1876) 98
" Goods Price (1824).................. 20
" Atmospheric Effects.................. 95
" Storehouse.......................99, 111
" Picking............................ 18
" Mills (1810) 77, (1815) 78, (1850–'70) 84, (1874)............................ 85
" Manufacture in Europe.............. 94
" into Cloth, Process of.............. 98
Cotton's, John S., Store in 1825–'34.........186, 213
" Creel"............................... 107
Crescent Mills...........................113, 138

Daily Papers............................ 189
Daily News............................. 188
Davis, Hon. R. T........................ 232
Davenport, Hon. J. F................... 234
Davol Mills....................58, 65, 113, 127
" Stephen.......................... 56
" Wm. C......................46, 57, 127
"Departments" of a Mill................ 110
Dividends of Troy Company, 1820........ 20
"Doffer"............................... 102
"Drawing"........................... 103
Dressing Yarn in 1813................... 19
Drives................................. 159
Durfee, Major Bradford........26, 27, 43, 45, 127
" Bradford, Steamer................ 192
" Col. Jos....................8, 9, 198
" Charles........................ 10
" Mills...................... 114, 126
" Dr. Nathan...................... 53
Early Settlers........................... 4
Eddy, J. & J........................... 23
" Jesse............................ 32
Educational Interests................... 151
Eudora, Propeller...................... 191
"Evils" of Manufacturing Communities... 152

Fall River and its Industries............. 1
" First Settlement............... 2
" Incorporated...............4, 237
" Boundary Dispute............4, 215
" Motto of...................... 6
" Location of................... 6
" Natural Advantages of......6, 95, 190
" Water Power................. 7
" "New Mills".............7, 65, 96
" Spindles..................... 8
" In 1813...................... 10
" Manufactory.11,12, 16, 22,114, 118,166, 201
" Bleaching and Calendering Co..... 26
" Print Works............... 30, 114
" Iron Works............43, 63, 114
" Growth ("New Mill" era)......... 7

Fall River Resources (1858)............. 67
" Bleachery..................114, 147
" Manufacturers' Mutual Insurance Co. 114
" Merino Co..................... 114
" Railroad to Myrick's............ 50
" Railroad to New Bedford........114, 190
" Spool and Bobbin Co............ 114
" Steamboat Co................115, 196
" Warren and Providence R. R..... 115
" Monitor...................... 185
" In the Revolution.............. 198
" "The Border City"..........4, 143
" General View.................. 5
" Area......................... 6
" Hydraulic Power.............. 6
" Valuation (1813) 10 ; (1858)....... 67
" Recapitulation (1876)........... 68
" "Its Future"................... 97
" To other Cities................ 153
" National Bank................. 168
" Savings Bank.................. 170
" Five-cent Savings Bank......... 179
" and Warren and Providence R. R.. 196
" Sloop........................ 10
" In the Civil War............... 204
" "West End"................... 213
Fairbanks, Hon. G. O.................. 230
"Finisher" (Cotton)..................... 101
Fire Department....................... 160
" " Officers, 1877............. 248
" " The Great, 1843............ 217
First National Bank.................... 180
Five-cent Savings Bank................. 179
Flint Mills.........................115, 142
Flint and Steel, Newspaper.............. 188
"Flyer"............................... 103
Formation of City Government.......... 243
Freight Lines......................... 196
Freemen's Purchase.................... 2

Gazette, Newspaper.................... 188
Globe Mill..........................8–21
" Village....................... 8
Granite Mills...................65, 115, 123
" Product..................... 152
Great Fire, The.....................151, 217

Hancock, Steamer..................10, 191
Harbor of Fall River................152, 190
"Harness"............................ 108
Harris, Hawes & Co..........21, 26, 32, 46, 58
Haughwout, Rev. P. B................. 211
Healey's, Father, Smithy............... 214
Herald, Daily Paper................... 189
Hours of Labor....................... 28
Hydraulic Power...................... 6

INDEX. 251

	PAGE
Industries of State	94
" " Fall River	8, 67, 94
"Intermediate"	103
Inventions in Cotton Machinery	97
Irene and Betsey, Sloop	191
"Jack"	103
Journal, Paper	188
King Philip Mills	115, 136
" " Steamer	191
Labor Journal	188
Ladies' Work for the Union	212
"Laps" (Cotton)	101
L'Echo du Canada	188
Libraries	151, 153
Local Nomenclature	159
Location of Mills	70
"Loom"	108
Looms, First Built	17
Loom, Power	78
" Waltham	81
" Scotch	81
Machines, Cotton (1811) 9; (1830) 28 ; (1876)	98
Machinery, Inventions of Cotton	97
Manufacturers' Board of Trade	115
" Gas Co	115
Manufacturing, Process of	98
Markets for Yarn	18
Massasoit Mill	24, 35, 53, 115
" National Bank	175
Mayors, Sketches of	225
" of Fall River	244
Mechanic, Newspaper	188
Mechanics' Mills	65, 116, 128
Members of Congress	244
Merchants' Manufacturing Company	65, 116, 127
Metacomet Mill	57, 116, 130
" National Bank	177
" Steamer	192
Metropolis, "	194
Mill Buildings, Size of	56
" Groups	69
Mills, Fall River Standard	110
" Officers of	96
" Arrangements of	110
" "New Era"	7, 65, 96
"Mixing Room"	99
Monitor, Newspaper	185
Montaup Mills	116, 139
Moral Envoy, Newspaper	188
Mother's Brook	4
Mount Hope Bay	189
" Mill	116
"Mule"	58, 104
Murphy, Rev. F.	211

	PAGE
"Nankeen Mill"	22
Narragansett Mills	116, 136
" Steamship Co	194
National Union Bank	174
" Banks, Standing of	181
New Mills	7, 161
New York Line, The	50, 193
"New Pocasset"	23
Newport, Steamer	195
Newspapers	185
Nomenclature	159
North Cemetery	157
" Park	158
Number of Employés in Early Mills	17
Oak Grove Cemetery	157
Old Colony Railroad	50, 116, 190
" Steamer	195
" Steamboat Co	51, 116, 195
"Old Fall River Line"	195
Operatives in Mill	17
" Nationality	20, 28, 111
" Number in Mill	110
Organization of Corporations	113
" " a Mill	66
Orswell, John	17, 19
Osborn Mills	116, 140
Panic of 1837	53
Parks	158
Patriot, Paper	188
People's Press	188
"Pickers"	101
Picking Machine	18
Pocasset Purchase	3
" Manufacturing Co	23, 56, 117, 119
" National Bank	178
Police Department, 1877	247
Ponds, Flowage	17, 22, 25
Population Tables	219
Prices of Provisions, 1813	20
" " Cloth, 1813	20
Print Cloths, First Manufactured	28
" " Process of Manufacture	98
" " Standard (64 x 64)	99
Printing Machine, First	30
Providence Line, The	27, 49, 191
" Steamer	195
Public Buildings	153
" Library	153, 248
" Schools	151, 247
Quequechan	1
" Mill	23, 119
"Railway Head"	102
Railway Lines	153, 190

INDEX.

	PAGE
"Reed"	108
Remington, Hale	64, 122
Reminiscences of Colonel Joseph Durfee	198
Regiments to which Fall River contributed during the Civil War	207
Representatives to General Court	245
Revolutionary War	5, 200
Robeson, Andrew, Sr.	23, 29, 125
" Mills	65, 117, 125
Rodman, Sam'l	23
"Rolls"	103
"Roping"	19
"Roving"	104
R. Borden Manufacturing Company	117, 134
Ruggles, Micah H	62
Sagamore Mills	117, 144
Salaries of Agents and Treasurers, 1813	16, 76
Satinet Factory	23, 32
Savings Banks, Standing of	182
Schools	10, 151
School-Houses	
School Committee, 1877	247
Second National Bank	180
Settlement of State Boundaries	215
Sharp & Roberts Mule	58
Shipping	10, 152
Shove, Charles O	123, 145
" A. & J.	22, 23
" Mills	117, 145
"Shuttle"	108
Sinking-Fund Commissioners, 1877	248
Slade Mills	117, 133
Slade's Ferry	191
"Slasher"	107
Slater, Samuel	12, 75
"Sliver" (Cotton)	101
"Slubber"	103
South Park	158
Spark, Daily Paper	189
"Speeders"	19, 103
"Spindles"	105
Spindles, Cotton (1820—1876)	83
" in Fall River	8, 112
Spinning Frames	17, 74
Stafford Pond	147
" Mills	117, 131
" Foster H	131
"Standard" of Print Cloths	99
State Senators, Residents	245
Statistics of Mills, Spindles, etc.	77, 84, 94, 112
Stage Line	190
" Lines to Providence and New Bedford	191
Star, Daily Paper	189
Steamboat Lines	27, 49, 189
Steam Marine of Mount Hope Bay	189

	PAGE
Steam Ferry-boats	191, 196
Stone, First Quarried	13
"Sucker Brook"	147
Tariffs	29, 83
Taylor, Father	214
Tecumseh Mills	65, 117, 125
Thurston, Rev. Eli	211
Times	189
Town Clerks of Fall River	239
" Officers "	240
Transportation	10, 27, 95, 191
Troy C. & W. Manufactory	11, 14, 17, 20, 25, 117, 119, 199
Trustees of Public Library, 1877	248
"Tub-Wheel"	10
"Twist"	103
Union Mill Co	64, 118, 121
" Belt Co	118
" Savings Bank	181
United States Custom House and P. O.	182
Valuation in 1813	10
" Tables	219
Villages in Fall River	153
Village Recorder	188
Wages of Weavers (1818)	17
" " Cotton Pickers	18
" " Operatives, (1830) 28; (1876)	111
Wampanoag Mills	118, 135
Wampanoag, Paper	188
Wards, City	153
"Warp and Weft"	107
"Waste"	109
Water Frames	74
" Power, Height of Falls	7
" Works	160
Watuppa Lake	147, 161
" Mill	24
" Reservoir Co	26
" Water Board, 1877	248
Weaving First by Power	16, 79, 81
" Imperfect	19
"Web"	108
Weekly News	188
Weetamoe Mills	118, 133
"Weight" of Cloth	109
"West End" of Fall River	213
Wheeler, Dexter	12, 16, 118
"White Brook"	132
"White Mill"	22
Wilkinson Bros	12, 44, 76
Yarn, Dressing	19
"Yarn Beam"	107
"Yellow Mill"	22

www.ingramcontent.com/pod-product-compliance
Lightning Source LLC
Chambersburg PA
CBHW022107230426
43672CB00008B/1310